The Great Debates

The Great Debates

Kennedy vs. Nixon, 1960
A Reissue

Edited by **SIDNEY KRAUS**

INDIANA UNIVERSITY PRESS
BLOOMINGTON   LONDON

First paperback edition 1977

Copyright © 1962, 1977 by Indiana University Press

Published in Canada by Fitzhenry & Whiteside Limited, Don Mills, Ontario

Manufactured in the United States of America

ISBN 0-253-32630-3 cl   ISBN 0-253-32631-1 pa   LC62-7487

For the debaters

JOHN F. KENNEDY   RICHARD M. NIXON

. . . The network television debates between Mr. Nixon and myself have been a great service by the television industry to the American people. More than 60 million Americans have had an opportunity through each of these debates to hear extensive discussions of major issues.

While it might have been better to have had a somewhat freer give-and-take, and an opportunity for Mr. Nixon and myself to develop our thoughts more fully on some of the major and more complex problems, we did discuss a wide ranging number of matters. And we did it while facing one another . . . .

I place the highest value on television in any campaign, whether for the Presidency or for a county or city.

> —JOHN F. KENNEDY in the *Catholic Transcript,*
> Hartford, Connecticut, November 3, 1960

The variables that influence the outcome of an American presidential campaign are so many and so diverse that it is a rash man indeed who ventures to assign precise causes and effects. And with the addition of the 1960 campaign to our political history, we have still another factor to consider—the Great Debates. That these face-to-face confrontations viewed by tens of millions of voters were a radical innovation, that the electorate had a unique opportunity to take the measure of the candidates "under fire," that the television industry assumed new and far-reaching responsibilities in the public service, and that the specific form and format of the debates unquestionably influenced their impact—all this can be said with reasonable confidence. What we now need is a close and careful estimate of their precise effect on the election returns and, on this basis, a sober judgment of their worth and future status. This calls, in turn, for the most skillful of professional analysis. The present volume ought to contribute greatly to filling that need.

> RICHARD M. NIXON, letter to Sidney Kraus, May 15, 1961

Contents

PART III: TEXTS OF THE DEBATES

Illustrations

Charts

Tables

Editor's Note

I AM WRITING this preface to the paperback edition on the afternoon of the televised vice-presidential debate, the first in our political history. Tonight I will be part of the audience at the Alley Theatre in Houston, where Senator Robert J. Dole of Kansas, the Republican nominee, and Senator Walter F. Mondale, Democrat of Minnesota, will debate. At the kind invitation of the League of Women Voters, the sponsor, I have attended the debates between Gerald Ford and Jimmy Carter in Philadelphia and San Francisco, and next week I will be in the audience in Williamsburg for their final confrontation.

My purpose in attending is to gather material for a second volume of studies assessing the background and impact of presidential debates. Sixteen years have passed since the electorate viewed the series between Kennedy and Nixon; and now for the first time in the history of the United States an incumbent president is debating. I think it desirable that dialogues of this sort occur during every presidential campaign. However, serious questions exist about the televised formats of both the Kennedy-Nixon and the Ford-Carter face-to-face meetings. They were neither debates nor confrontations, but were more in the nature of televised news panels.

The assessment of the 1960 and 1976 series will provide a basis for exploring alternative formats for future televised joint appearances. It is hoped that with the reissue of this volume and the subsequent Indiana University Press publication on the Ford-Carter debates, the necessary information will be available for students, researchers, and those in policy-making groups to make recommendations for future presidential debates.

SIDNEY KRAUS

Houston, Texas
October 15, 1976

Preface

THE GREAT DEBATES of 1960, in which the two presidential candidates appeared together four times over all radio and television networks, dominating also the other news media, provided an unusual opportunity to assess the value of such a venture in political campaigning.

It is not the main purpose of this book to recommend that such debates be either continued or discontinued; but if intelligent future decisions are to be made, some sort of evaluation is necessary. It is equally important to provide future researchers and historians with an overview of this notable event in the history of communications. With these two tasks in mind, I have organized this compilation into sections relating to the *background* and *perspective* and to the *effects* of the debates. In doing so, I have used an interdisciplinary approach as a guide in the selection of articles.

I have had the valuable assistance of my friend and former teacher, Samuel L. Becker, Director of Television-Radio-Film at the State University of Iowa. He has given so much of his time to this project—suggesting contributors, reading their papers, offering valuable criticism, all this in addition to being a contributor—that he might indeed be named as a co-editor. While he shares in the virtues of the book, the responsibility for any of its failures is mine.

There are many people who, in one way or another, have helped to make this book a reality. First on this list are the contributors. In most instances they have written their contributions especially for this volume. Some of them have offered useful suggestions, many of which have been included. This is their book. I am particularly grateful to Elihu Katz and to Jacob J. Feldman, both of the University of Chicago, for their untiring interest in the book, especially with regard to the section on effects. I am also grateful to Paul F. Lazarsfeld, who read the entire manuscript and provided many helpful suggestions.

15

I am indebted to John W. Ashton, Vice President for Graduate Development and Dean of the Graduate School at Indiana University, who has supported this project with his advice and encouragement.

My appreciation goes to the faculty and staff of the Department of Radio and Television and the Radio and Television Service of Indiana University for occupying much of their time and space with the preparation of this book. In this connection, I should like to thank Professor Elmer G. Sulzer, Chairman of the Department and Director of the Service, for providing the necessary secretarial assistance when needed, and Professor Robert Petranoff, who not only encouraged this project with thoughtful comments, but gave willingly his precious office space for art work, manuscript revision, and many other tasks.

My thanks are also due to the staff of the Indiana University Press, who have been patient, considerate, and very helpful in the planning and preparation of this volume.

Finally, to Cecile, Kenny, Pammy, and Jody, whose activities for the past year were neglected by a busy husband and a "bye-bye" father, I offer my undivided attention.

SIDNEY KRAUS

Bloomington, Indiana
December 1, 1961

PART I

Background and Perspective

1

Introduction

HAROLD D. LASSWELL

THE MOST noteworthy event of the 1960 presidential campaign was undoubtedly the mutual confrontation of the candidates of the two major parties in four television programs. Should this innovation be continued, and if so, under what rules? In any case, is it likely to be continued? The present volume presents a body of analysis and data pertinent to this problem of public policy. We shall prepare the reader for the material to follow by commenting briefly upon three interrelated questions: (A) the definition of the proposed policy; (B) the overriding goals of the American commonwealth most deeply affected by the proposal; (C) information regarding the past, and estimates of the future most relevant to assessment of policy.

A. The first question concerns the definition of what is proposed for continuation. Even the title of the present publication—for reasons obvious to people who pass on titles—uses the conventional cliché of calling the programs "debates," and "great debates" at that. Fortunately, and wisely, the symposium has an article by Auer that challenges this usage. Auer denies that these confrontations were debates in any well-considered definition of the word. They lacked the element of direct mutual interrogation; and they had no clearly delimited focus of controversy.

Auer's challenge puts us in the middle of the difficult task of deciding what we are talking about. Is the question whether the candidates shall run two parallel press conferences on whatever topics are of interest to a few interrogators? Or is the proposal to agree upon a controversial topic to be discussed by the candidates, who are also free to examine one another?

Is the confrontation to be open to competitive manipulation for the benefit of the candidates, or is it to be run for the enlightenment of the electorate? In the latter case program control would be in the hands of the broadcasting authority, who might be a private commercial net, an informational and educational non-commercial net, or an agency of government with access to channels.

B. Rational evaluation requires that the proposal be considered in terms of the most pertinent postulates of the ideology of the American commonwealth. In the current symposium the interested citizen will find his attention directed to basic matters by several participants, notably by Seldes and Siepmann. If we were to make an explicit formulation of the goals and values most germane to the "debate about debate," the list would most certainly include the requirement that contending *candidates conduct themselves in a manner that enables the electorate to arrive at an informed estimate of their competence to lead the nation.*

Pertinent questions then arise: Is facility in debate an important skill for the top leaders of popular government? I give an unhesitating "yes" to this, joining with all who believe that a major obligation of statesmanship is to aid in clarifying public opinion regarding the ends and the instruments of policy. I subscribe to the view that the asking and answering of key questions in public is a procedure of importance to democratic discipline.

Does this mean that *oral* facility is essential? What about Jefferson's famous disinclination to speak? And what about the specific procedures to be employed in television? May not the cut and thrust of oral argument reward glib facility and penalize thoughtful and intensive consideration of public questions?

Having carried this discussion a certain distance, let us turn to another postulate. The *candidates are expected to serve the electorate* during a campaign not only by exhibiting forensic capability, but *by contributing to a process that helps to clarify probable consequences of the policy choices open to the nation.*

However: Does direct debate foster enlightenment? Or does it contribute to public confusion by encouraging competitive declarations of devotion to traditional ambiguities, and by tolerating the confident reiteration of half-truths and self-serving prophecies?

Undoubtedly another postulate is that *candidates are supposed to encourage voting by making the election issues appear to be of great significance.*

Again, however: Is it implied that voting is an end in itself to be encouraged by sensationalism and showmanship?

A non-American might assume that it is easy to state another postulate, namely, that *since candidates are party leaders, they are committed to the duty of persuading an effective majority that the positions taken in the platforms of their respective parties are sound, and the party is itself the best instrument of informed public action.*

Unhappily, the facts do not entirely square with this bit of political folklore. True, the candidates are named by parties. However, winning candidates working within the framework of the American political system are adroit leaders of group coalitions, and though loyal party groups are important, they are not necessarily the decisive members of victory coalitions. The strategy of a successful candidate is to retain the support of the solid nucleus of his party while reaching out to uncommitted and vacillating members of the electorate. Strategists perpetually estimate the net pay-off of gambits that may gain peripheral support (at the cost of nuclear strength) or that retain nuclear strength (at the cost of peripheral support).

The ideological and operating structure of the political system—a bipolar party system; a multipolar coalition of pressure groups; a system of electoral districts in which rural, small-town, and Southern white elements are overweighted—puts leaders under greatest stress when they must operate simultaneously at the focus of attention of one another and of (potentially) all elements in the electorate; and when the occasion is billed as a facing of policy issues.

Such confrontations are precisely what our presidents are especially adept at avoiding. Under our governmental conventions, no president engages in face-to-face debate with the titular head of the opposing political party. President Kennedy, for instance, does not ordinarily debate with Mr. Nixon or Mr. Eisenhower as head of the Republican Party. At most he engages in long-range sniping through press conferences.

Given the presently prevailing institutions of the American polity, we must not overlook the possibility that a true debate between presidential candidates would threaten the genius for ambiguity that is essential to the operation of our complex, semiresponsible, relatively democratic system of multigroup coalition. The implication is that the introduction of "genuine debate at the top" on TV calls for simultaneous changes elsewhere in the effective practices of American government.

I refer briefly to one other postulate relevant to political campaigning. An obvious goal is to *strengthen national unity* by the reaffirmation of national ideology, by reminding one and all of a shared tradition of struggle and victory, by providing a sense of identification with the whole to majorities who rediscover minorities, and to minorities who perceive that they are given respectful attention if not immediate acceptance.

If presidential campaigns contribute to the integrity of the commonwealth, it is evident that, at the same time, they are exceedingly dangerous. If they spread confusion about the power position of the nation in the world arena, if they widen the gap among component elements of the body politic, if they arouse expectations that are later frustrated, national campaigns are at once a symptom and a disintegrating factor in the process of discrediting the ideology of popular government in the United States and throughout the world.

C. We move abruptly to the main body of the book, which presents a number of research findings that can be interpreted to sustain or negate the idea of a genuine debate.

1. A summary is provided of the pre-1960 use of radio and television in presidential campaigns. Cursory as Becker and Lower's account must be, it none the less exhibits the halting steps by which the American commonwealth has been adapting itself to the remarkable potentialities of the new technology. In this connection, we note the unsettled problem of financing political communication on TV. The characteristic ambivalence of Americans toward money is reflected, on the one hand, by the brave new prescriptions of the Hatch Act, for example, and on the other by the connivance of persons concerned in obvious evasion of the Act for the purposes of financing party propaganda.

2. The bulk of the papers here search for the disclosure of factors in political communication that affect what happens. The aim is scientific in the sense that the task goes beyond the historical details of the Kennedy-Nixon programs to identify those interdependent factors which enable us to generalize beyond these incidents to recurring— and perhaps controllable—features of the political process itself. This implies, for instance, that it is not enough to demonstrate that Kennedy or Nixon won or lost support among members of the audience. The problem is to describe the situation in terms that can be transferred from one election to another; hence, to characterize the *predispositions* of audiences prior to exposure; the *content* of the media constituting

the exposure, and other significant features of the *environment*—such as partisan or non-partisan companions in a listening group; and the immediate and ultimate *responses*.

The problem is even broader, since the content of the program was itself an outcome of complex technical factors and especially of intricate calculations of advantage. Hence the task of dealing scientifically with the communication process calls for the description in transferrable categories of the physical facilities employed, and of all "controllers" (in addition to technicians) who made the decision to participate in the programs, or who affected the format or the messages in any way. As the present book makes abundantly, precisely, and vividly apparent, all sorts of participants interacted with one another at various cross-sections of the total process. Even a partial list includes the candidates and their advisors, network officials and their staffs, and government regulators of communication. The candidates' decision to participate was affected by expectations built up before their nomination; in fact, by the trend of opinion regarding TV and politics widely held by commentators, journalists, and other articulate elements in the body politic.

In summary, then, the papers provide partial answers to such questions as these:

Communicators. Who (described in terms of his role in the total process) expected to be better off (in terms of all his value objectives) by encouraging or by discouraging the programs? What were the values and goals involved and how specifically were they interpreted? What were the expectations of gain or loss, including estimates of risk? How did the role of "network official," to take one example, harmonize with the role of "pro-Kennedy" or "pro-Nixon" (i.e., what components of the "self-systems" of the participant were relevant to the appraisal)?

Situations. What were the significant situations in which the various communicators interacted? (E.g., under what circumstances were government officials formally and informally involved? What TV officials in what circumstances? What party officials in what circumstances?)

Assets. What assets were at the disposal of each participant who sought to block or to facilitate certain results? What liabilities did he contend against (e.g., Section 315 of the Federal Communications Act)?

Strategy. How did each participant seek his objectives (including the blocking of others) by managing the positive assets at his disposal and minimizing the negative ones? To what extent, if at all, were various forms of coercion used to supplement persuasion?

Outcome. How can the content of the programs be analyzed? (E.g., to bring out explicit issues; to exhibit the level of ambiguity; to note the probable "truth value" of the factual statements made about past events; to note the probability of estimates offered about the future; to locate policy problems not mentioned; to spot the frequency of possible anxiety reactions—speech errors, moistening of lips, perspiring, shifting eye movements, body jerks, etc.)

Effects. How much attention was paid by whom to what was presented? How were images of the candidates affected? How were opinions regarding policy questions and goals affected (etc.)?

The foregoing inventory is far from exhaustive but it indicates a context in which the pioneering papers published in this symposium can be read. The fact that such reports exist is an important indication of the growth of new institutions of self-observation in our society. Whatever limitations these specific investigations exhibit, they indicate that the nation is developing a network of specialists willing to focus contemporaneously upon developments of obvious significance to the commonwealth and to gather information by careful procedures pertinent to the appraisal of the events in question.

Nor is this all. Knowledge is cumulative and goes beyond a specific policy issue uppermost at the moment. To the extent that the dynamics of the political process have been disclosed, the results are transferrable to many other situations and to an infinite variety of policy questions as yet unthought of. Inquiry does not abolish debate; it sharpens the realism of the perspectives of all who discipline conviction by data. The present book is policy; it is history; it is science.

2

Broadcasting in Presidential
Campaigns

SAMUEL L. BECKER & ELMER W. LOWER

A NECESSARY condition for democratic elections is the free flow of
information and ideas to which the voter may expose himself. This
education of the voter is a prerequisite to intelligent decision-making.
As Woodrow Wilson put it, our choice is between government by control and government by discussion.[1] The national and international
issues which should affect the decision-making process have become
so complex, however, that it is impossible for the voter to go through
this process intelligently with only facts or the opposing views of contending parties to help him. There is an increasing need for independent agencies which help the voter to synthesize, analyze, and interpret
the data upon which he must base his decisions. These notes on the
history of broadcasting activities during political campaigns may help
to clarify the extent to which, and the ways in which, radio and television have played this role. We will attend primarily to presidential
campaigning and will focus upon the major developments during each
four-year period.

1924

Though radio was first used for a presidential election campaign in
1924, its political baptism had come eight years earlier when the Lee
De Forest experimental radio station at High Bridge, New York, carried the returns of the Wilson-Hughes presidential contest to about a
dozen people with receiving sets.[2] Not many more persons heard Wilson deliver the first presidential address to be broadcast, in 1919.[3]

25

The radio audience for the Harding-Cox election returns in 1920 was estimated between 500 and 1,000. This was the inaugural broadcast of the first licensed commercial station in the United States, KDKA in Pittsburgh.[4] Radio was injected into campaign politics first by Mayor John F. Hyland of New York City. From 1921 to 1925, Hyland's political propaganda on city-owned station WNYC was a familiar sound to New Yorkers. On September 5, 1925, New York State Supreme Court Justice Aaron J. Levy granted a temporary stay forbidding Hyland's use of the municipal station for political purposes.[5] Presidential politics was introduced to radio by Warren Harding in 1923 with a series of broadcasts on the stewardship of his administration.[6]

"Al-ah-bah-ma casts twenty-foah votes foah Askah double yew Underwood." Those words, drawled at the start of 103 successive ballots at the 1924 Democratic National Convention in New York's Madison Square Garden, became a household phrase largely because of radio. This was broadcasting's first major year of political coverage.

Radio had mushroomed rapidly during the past eight years. On the eve of the 1924 election there were over 500 stations in operation,[7] and an estimated 3,000,000 receiving sets.[8] Coolidge began his bid for the Republican presidential nomination five months before the convention with a series of radio broadcasts. The last of the series was broadcast just four days before the convention opened.[9] William G. McAdoo, who hoped to get the Democratic presidential nomination, also saw the possible influence of radio. Early in 1924 he applied to the Department of Commerce for a broadcasting license to permit him to install transmitting equipment in his home in Los Angeles powerful enough to reach all parts of the country. He planned to broadcast at varying hours of the day and night instead of taking long speaking tours, which he felt were unhealthy.[10]

Despite its rapid growth, radio was a novice in news and special events broadcasting in 1924 when it obtained permission from political party officials to broadcast the presidential nominating conventions. Graham McNamee, then an unknown tenor from St. Paul, Minnesota, was given the job of planning the coverage and supplying the commentary. He tells how WEAF went about setting up the broadcasts:[11]

No orders were given us by the office; indeed, there were no precedents or rules to guide us. . . . All we really knew was that people met and somehow got together on a candidate. How it came about we didn't know, nor just what the proceedings were we had to cover.

The Republicans met first in 1924. Their convention at Cleveland, Ohio, June 10 to 13, which nominated incumbent Calvin Coolidge, was a tame affair. This contrasted with the Democratic National Convention which opened June 24 in the old Madison Square Garden. The predicted fight between the "Klucks" (Ku Klux Klan and their sympathizers) and the "Turks" (anti-Klan forces) developed on schedule, first over whether the platform should condemn the Klan as an undesirable secret political society, then over the nomination. Neither Alfred E. Smith, (Wet, anti-Klan, Irish Catholic) nor William Gibbs McAdoo (Dry, Protestant, not a Klansman but strongly supported by the night riders) could come close to winning the required two-thirds of the ballots.[12] Day after day the balloting droned on until John W. Davis, J. P. Morgan's lawyer, was finally chosen. WEAF fed the entire 17-day marathon to a 20-station hook-up covering all of the United States east of the Continental Divide. WJZ fed the program to Schenectady on another hook-up.[13] Having burst out of its four walls for the first time since the founding of the nation, the Democratic convention had unintentionally presented the party at its worst.

With the 1924 conventions behind them, both parties considered how they might use radio most effectively. Broadcasters, too, were concerned with campaign broadcasts but in another way. Though the nominating conventions were broadcast as a public service,[14]

station managers were beginning to wail that somebody should pay the expenses of campaign broadcasts. . . . There seemed no logical reason why political parties, having campaign funds for other legitimate expenses, should not pay for radio time. Campaign managers were not slow to recognize this fact and to act accordingly.

Although there were no organized networks in 1924, both parties bought time on individual stations and occasionally arranged for informal station hook-ups. Davis and his running mate campaigned largely by train. Coolidge traveled little, relying on radio speeches from the capital. Political programs at this time showed little imagination. Except for an occasional incorporation of a speech into a musical program, the medium was used simply to transmit the traditional political speeches.[15] Radio expenses of the Republican National Committee totaled $120,000. The Democrats spent $40,000.[16] This was at a time when a one-hour coast-to-coast broadcast cost only $4,000.[17]

Many of the reactions to the radio broadcasts of the 1924 campaign are typified by that of the *New Republic*.[18]

Radio has found a way to dispense with the political middlemen. In a fashion it has restored the demos upon which republican government is founded. . . . No one will be able to capture the radio vote unless he faces the microphone squarely and speaks his mind, fully, candidly, and in extenso.

However, not all reactions to broadcasting's role in the campaign were favorable. The officials of Radio Corporation of America were accused of censoring speeches of political orators, which the president of RCA promptly denied.[19] In addition, inequities in the amount of radio time available to each party were pointed out.[20]

There were three reasons for this. First a majority of all broadcasting stations are owned and operated by the big industrial corporations; and their managers are likely to be conservative Republicans. Second, in the North and West, where the campaign was really fought, a majority of the "respectables," the men who usually receive—and accept—invitations to appear behind the microphone, are of the Coolidge faith; third, the Republicans, having a great deal more money to spend than their opponents, invested much of it in radio time.

Congressmen too were concerned about potentially unequal treatment of political candidates. Representative Emanuel Celler testified in the House on a bill to regulate broadcasting.[21]

I was asked to pay by the American Telephone and Telegraph Company $10 for every minute and I refused to pay it. I have no knowledge that candidates of the opposing party were asked to pay the same amount for the same use.

These criticisms of radio coverage of the 1924 campaign are closely related, and possibly have a causal relationship, to succeeding actions which shaped current political broadcasting. The two major criticisms, censorship and unequal time, became the foci of Section 18 of the Federal Radio Act of 1927.[22] Section 18 provided that the licensee had no power to censor material broadcast under the provisions of this section but, at the same time, he was not obligated to allow the use of his station by any candidate for public office. However, if one legally qualified candidate for public office was permitted the use of a broadcasting station, equal opportunities must be afforded all legally qualified candidates for that office. These provisions were the basis for a steady argument, which is still going on, between broadcasting stations, political candidates, and the government. Underlying many of these arguments over Section 18 (and later Section 315 of the Communications Act of 1934) was the fear that many broadcasters would avoid the problem by not carrying any political programs.

One other idea developed in 1924 which is interesting in the light of the 1960 campaign. An electronic debate between political candidates was suggested by William Harkness, Assistant Vice President of the American Telephone and Telegraph Company, at a Congressional hearing on the regulation of radio broadcasting in March, 1924, when he was questioned about the danger of one political party monopolizing the air waves.[23]

Our experience has been that on a controversial subject both sides should be presented preferably at the same time, more in the nature of a debate by the presentation of first the one side and then the other, and we have done this thing very much to the satisfaction of the public.

1928

The word "radio," mispronounced "raddio" with the "a" sounded as in "radish," took on unusual importance in the 1928 campaign. Changes in both the conventions and the succeeding campaigns were made upon the basis of what the parties and the broadcasters had learned, or thought they had learned, in the 1924 campaign. For example:[24]

In 1924, . . . a speaker's corral was sketched in chalk like a batter's box on the platform at Madison Square Garden mainly for the guidance of William Jennings Bryan. He could not be trained to direct his speech toward the microphone when he got excited. He dashed this way and that, hanging over the speaker's rail and gesticulating at his hearers, causing the radio to lose large portions of his address. Finally, the Commoner was lectured and then imprisoned in this white rectangle. He strove to stay within it, but in his anxiety to prevent any unpleasant reference to the Ku Klux Klan from getting into the platform, he broke out several times. Other speakers did the same. . . . To avoid further trouble of this kind, a narrow enclosure has been designed which keeps orators from leaping to the right or left and compels them to face the microphone at all times.

Not only movement was restricted at the nominating conventions. Oratory was also. In contrast to the more than 100 ballots in their

1924 convention, it took the Democrats only one ballot to nominate Al Smith in 1928.[25] The Republicans nominated Secretary of Commerce Herbert Hoover.

Neither candidate used radio to present the real issues confronting the nation, but the voter apparently did not care. He seemed more concerned with "Mrs. Al Smith's lack of social grace, her husband's lack of grammatical finesse. How he pronounced 'radio' engendered far more acrimonious debate than his animadversions on the evils of the power trust."[26] Bigots on both sides distorted the issue of Smith's Catholicism.[27]

The radio industry had grown rapidly in the four years between elections. There were approximately 8,000,000 radio receivers; at least 40,000,000 persons could be reached by radio.[28] Two networks had been organized. The first was the National Broadcasting Company, created by Radio Corporation of America on November 1, 1926. A few months later the United Independent Broadcasters, which was soon renamed the Columbia Broadcasting System, was formed. NBC had 49 wholly owned or affiliated stations; CBS listed 19 stations. The vast majority of the 677 stations were still independent.[29] Radio campaign costs kept pace with the rapid growth of the industry.[30] These soaring costs were obviously in the minds of the presidential candidates when they asked their audiences to remain silent during broadcasts.[31]

"Bear in mind that 'raddio' time costs money," were Governor Smith's opening words at one meeting. "You're eating up 'raddio' time," he cautioned another audience. In Boston he said, "Save your applause until the end of the speech. It doesn't cost anything then."

The political "commercial," believed by many to be a product of advertising agency influence on politics in the forties, appears to have been born in 1928. The Republicans organized a battalion of 6,000 so-called "Minute Men" to make very short talks on 161 radio stations with top audience coverage. The party supplied "canned" scripts to local speakers and planned the broadcasts so that the same speech was heard all over the country on one night.[32] In addition, the parties, for the first time, attempted to balance their political addresses "with high-class and appropriate entertainment features."[33]

The reaction to the political use of radio in 1928 was almost universally favorable. The *New York Times* editorialized[34] that:

If we have to sum up the political effect of the radio we may say that it is the greatest debunking influence that has come into American public life since the Declaration of Independence.

Republican John Calvin Brown, leader of the "Minute Man" organization, probably was expressing the thoughts of many politicians near the close of the 1928 campaign when he said that "today it [radio] is recognized by both parties as the most important and effective campaigning vehicle ever adopted."[35]

One historic broadcasting event went almost unnoticed in the excitement of the campaign. A strange, box-like contraption with a lens on the front was present when Governor Smith accepted the presidential nomination of the Democratic Party on the steps of the New York Capitol in Albany on August 22, 1928. This was the first "remote" television pickup on record. The signal was telecast over the General Electric station in Schenectady, fifteen miles away.[36]

Soon after the election, the interest of the nation was aroused by a proposal for another broadcasting innovation. North Dakota Senator Gerald Nye proposed that Congress erect a superpower station in Washington for, among other things, the use of all political parties in campaigns. He insisted that future political campaigns would be largely carried on by radio and that the station would assure national candidates of all parties the right to reach, without cost, the entire United States. He felt that commercial radio, because of its cost, tended to favor the political candidate with the most money.[37] It was found, however, that one station would not cover the country adequately, a network was too expensive, and the broadcast band was already overcrowded, so the project was abandoned. The idea that some means must be found to gain for candidates free access to the air waves is one that has been proposed periodically since that date.

1932

Radio and Roosevelt were made for each other. It was a radio speech, nominating the "Happy Warrior" at the 1924 convention, that launched Roosevelt on his comeback trail after he had been stricken with infantile paralysis in 1922.[38] Radio played a major role in all four of his presidential campaigns. And during his twelve years and one month in office he made the radio "fireside chat" an American institution, emulated on television, but not as effectively, by his successors.

In the 1932 campaign the most striking departure from the political methods of previous years was in the use of radio.[39] All of the addresses of both major candidates, Governor Roosevelt and President Hoover, were put on the air. Roosevelt's most sensational radio appearance climaxed the 1932 nominating convention when he shattered long-standing precedent, flying to Chicago to accept the nomination before the convention adjourned. Previously this ceremony had taken place a month after the convention. Radio had become such an important part of presidential campaigning that newspapers began to protest, using as a mouthpiece James G. Stahlman, president of the Southern Newspaper Publishers Association.[40]

Radio was one of the largest single items of expense for both parties in 1932. One source has estimated that a total of $5,000,000 was spent for radio time by the two parties in this campaign.[41]

The two networks had grown in the preceding four years and the number of radio sets in use had mounted from 8 to 18 million. Time costs were also higher.[42] The National Broadcasting Company had split into a Red network with 58 stations and a Blue network with 55 stations. CBS listed 91 affiliates. On August 11, 1932, Hoover launched his campaign with the largest political radio hook-up attempted up to that time, 160 stations.[43]

In spite of the ever increasing use of radio for political campaigning, the early hopes, or fears, that the air waves would completely replace the railways were becoming more realistic.[44]

Politicians have learned that it is not well to sit at home and conduct an armchair campaign. They must take to the road and take the microphone with them. . . . Travel works both ways. It affords the campaigner [a means] to give ideas and to receive them. . . . Furthermore, to see the people interested in him and to hear their cheers is likely to imbue him with an entirely different spirit than if he hid behind a parabolic microphone. The politician cherishes bands and cheers as much as a football team.

In the excitement of the Roosevelt landslide, which accompanied the unprecedented turnout at the polls, another hint of the future was scarcely commented upon at the time. Television was used for the first time in a political campaign by one of the parties. On October 11,

1932, the stage and screen division of the Democratic National Committee produced a program over W2XAB from the television studio of CBS at 485 Madison Avenue. The show, featuring entertainers rather than politicians, was seen only by a few newsmen and engineers.[45]

One of President Roosevelt's early acts was the appointment of an Interdepartmental Committee on Communications to study a possible national communications policy. After consideration of the report of this committee, Roosevelt, on February 26, 1934, recommended to Congress[46] that it

create a new agency to be known as the "Federal Communications Commission," such agency to be vested with the authority now lying in the Federal Radio Commission and with such authority over communications as now lies with the Interstate Commerce Commission—the services affected to be all those which rely on wires, cables, or radio as a medium of transmission.

An important issue in the Congressional debates over a new communications act was the regulation of political broadcasting. One much-debated version of the Senate bill extended the rules against censorship of broadcast political speeches to other speeches and discussions of public questions. It further specified that stations could not charge more than their regular commercial rates for political broadcasts.[47] Broadcasters had been fighting the no-censorship rule since the passage of the Radio Act of 1927 because of the confusing and varying interpretations concerning their liabilities under existing laws of libel.[48]

The precedent setting case in this area was the *Sorensen v. Wood* decision, 123 Neb. 348, 243 N.W. 82, 1932 (upheld by the U.S. Supreme Court), in which it was the court's opinion that *a broadcasting station is liable for defamatory statements broadcast over its facilities by a qualified political candidate, even though it has no power of censorship over material broadcast by such a candidate.*

In spite of these problems, the pleas of broadcasters, and efforts which were made in both houses of Congress to amend it, Section 18 of the Radio Act of 1927 was transferred intact to the Federal Communications Act of 1934. It became Section 315 in the new act.

1 9 3 6

The 1936 presidential campaign stands as a milestone in demonstrating radio's power to overcome unfavorable newspaper publicity.[49] No candidate since William Jennings Bryan in 1896 had to fight such a powerful array of newspapers as confronted Roosevelt. Late in the campaign, FDR staged an intensive month-long barnstorming trip around the country, making 23 formal speeches, many of them broadcast, and innumerable extemporaneous talks from the back platform of his special train. Of this effort James A. Farley, chairman of the Democratic National Committee and manager of the successful Roosevelt campaigns in 1932, 1936, and 1940, later wrote:[50]

Roosevelt's "one month" on the stump deserves to be recorded as the greatest piece of personal campaigning in American history. The radio . . . gave him an advantage over those early giants of the Republic who might have done the same under similar circumstances.

Farley was one of the great political managers of all time. While his opinion of radio is subjective, his long political campaign experience lends weight to his words.[51]

The influence of the radio in determining the outcome of the 1936 election can hardly be overestimated. Without that unrivalled medium for reaching millions of voters, the work of overcoming the false impression created by the tons of written propaganda put out by foes of the New Deal would have been many times greater than it was, and, to be candid, it might conceivably have been an impossible job.

It was in the 1936 presidential campaign that the influence of the advertising agency first became manifest. Casey reports some of these manifestations in the Republican campaign.[52]

Word went out that the medium no longer would be used simply to present the candidate but "to sell the idea of the campaign." . . . The rule was laid down that Landon's speeches must not exceed 30 minutes. "Make it brief and people will remember what you've said," was the dictum.

The ultimate in brevity was seen in an increased use of spot announcements in the presidential campaign.[53]

One even more questionable technique was utilized in the campaign.

On a broadcast over CBS, Senator Arthur Vandenburg carried on a pseudo-debate with the voice of President Roosevelt. Excerpts of recordings from Roosevelt speeches were edited together with responses by Vandenburg. The following example illustrates the result.

ROOSEVELT VOICE: Let it be from now on the task of our Party to break foolish traditions . . . and leave it to the Republican leadership . . . to break promises.
VANDENBURG: We'll discuss the "art" of broken promises a little later, Mr. Roosevelt. . . . Which of our traditions do you consider "foolish"? How about the traditions of free enterprise and free men?

It is to the credit of twenty-one of the sixty-six stations which scheduled the program that they cut it off. However, twenty-three carried it and "twenty-two performed an 'off again, on again, Finnigan' stunt."[54]

Heavy attention was given to the foreign language audience during the campaign. The parties directed 2,000 broadcasts over individual stations to Americans of foreign origin.[55]

Radio homes almost doubled between 1932 and 1936, from 18 to 33 million, and costs to the two major parties more than kept pace.[56]

1940

Two television firsts were seen in 1940. The video medium covered its first conventions[57] and coaxial cable was used for the first time in program service by NBC to bring the picture of the Republican National Convention at Philadelphia to New York for transmission.[58] An estimated 40,000 to 100,000 people in Philadelphia and New York thus had an opportunity to view some part of the proceedings in their living room, someone else's living room, or at the corner tavern.[59] Radio, however, was still the dominant electronic medium in the campaign. There were 814 radio stations on the air by the time of the campaign and 40 million radio sets.

Advertising agencies appeared to be playing an increasingly important role in the presidential campaigns, though apparently they were not yet openly employed by the political parties.[60] Blame for the now-familiar election-eve "spectacular," with its special mixture of political propaganda, entertainment, and testimonials, is laid at the door of the planners of the 1940 Democratic campaign.[61]

Radio expenditures for 1940 and subsequent years are difficult to obtain. The extension of the Hatch Act, passed on July 19, 1940, limited the annual expenditure of any political committee to $3,000,-000 and any individual's annual contribution to a national political campaign to $5,000.[62] The effect of this provision has been the creation of satellite committees such as the Independent Citizens Committee for Willkie and McNary. This means that in 1940, and all succeeding years, the publicized expenditures of the two major national committees represent gross underestimates of the total amount of money spent on the campaign of each presidential candidate.

1944

To many observers, the 1944 campaign represented virtually complete surrender of the political parties to Madison Avenue. Political columnist Arthur Krock reported:[63] "The Democratic National Committee . . . has enlisted the aid of Hollywood and its interesting five-minute and one-minute 'spots' are the result." The "1944 Republican Radio Report to Hon. Herbert Brownell, Jr.,"[64] includes as one of the major objectives of the Republican radio campaign:

Through one minute and chain break announcements, to set before the electorate, to pound home, drill in and instill by repetition, strong and irrefutable reasons to vote for Thomas E. Dewey, or against Franklin D. Roosevelt.

The 1944 campaign produced new evidence of the difficulties of obtaining accurate statistics on campaign expenditures for broadcasting. One Senate investigating committee compiled a list of several hundred committees which were active on either the Democratic or the Republican side in 1944, and these represented only a small proportion of the total. They ranged from the National Citizens Political Action Committee to the "Girls Who Save Their Nickels to Elect a Republican Club" in Chicago, which reported receipts of $44.76.[65] Before the passage of the Hatch Act, such independent party and non-party organizations were discouraged. They were now condoned, sometimes even inspired, by the party.[66]

The money spent for radio by the political parties, and the non-sponsored news and public affairs programs of the broadcasting industry, apparently had an effect. The National Opinion Research Center, questioning over 2,000 respondents just after the election, found that over 56 per cent of them thought they got their "most accurate news about the presidential campaign" from the radio. Less than 27 per cent cited newspapers; only slightly more than 6 per cent cited magazines.[67]

1948

Nineteen forty-eight was the year in which politicians and other "experts" were reminded that the outcome of an election is not necessarily determined before the campaign starts, that a candidate with the will to win and a determination to take his case to the people can overturn long odds. To bolster President Truman's "whistle-stop" campaign, the Democratic National Committee spent close to an all-time high on broadcasting. The Republican National Committee, perhaps a bit too cocksure, devoted less of its funds to radio.[68] Rival time-buyers jousted to obtain the best time for speeches during the evening hours. It was considered a coup when an agency could buy time just ahead of or just after one of the more popular shows such as the Lucky Strike Hit Parade.[69] In addition, the broadcasting industry contributed large amounts of time and money to present the candidates and the issues to the public.

There is some awareness of the increasing amounts which radio and television *networks* have spent on such coverage. There has been little recognition of the role played by local stations. That is, in part, due to the fact that evidence concerning this role is difficult to obtain on a large scale. Among the few attempts to do so are those of Cohen[70] and Weiser[71] following the 1948 campaign. They examined the coverage by local radio stations of the speeches made by Dewey and Truman during the western speaking tour which each candidate made during September and October, 1958. Truman delivered 115 speeches on his western swing. Of these, at least 50 were broadcast by local radio stations along the route. Most were broadcast by more than one station. Over 54 per cent of the broadcasts were carried as a public service, with no payment by backers of the Democratic Party. Similar results were found for Dewey's western swing. At least 34 of the 69 speeches he made were broadcast by 58 local radio stations along the route. Over 27 per cent of the stations broadcast Dewey's speeches on a sustaining basis.[72] Thus, even when candidates have gone in person to the people, the broadcasting media have accompanied them and helped substantially to increase the number of voters who could hear what they had to say.

Further substantiation of some of these data can be found in a study begun in 1951 which showed that over 20 per cent of radio stations and 24 per cent of television stations reported that they gave free time for "political broadcasts" during the campaigns.[73]

A large portion of the Democratic radio money in this campaign was spent on programs aimed at women and foreign-born Americans. Fifty thousand dollars of the radio budget went to a live disc jockey type program tailored for women and scheduled over the ABC Radio Network three times a week during the final four weeks of the campaign. It was slotted in prime soap opera time to catch the largest daytime women's audience. A sample of this program, proudly described by the Director of Public Relations of the Democratic Party during this period, is revealing.[74]

Noting the popularity of giveaway shows on radio, Drake [the announcer] announced the "Democratic Record" show would have a booby prize to give away too. The first award was made to Senator Kenneth Wherry for being an outstanding headache to housewives, based on his statement, "I'm the fellow that knocked out meat controls." The prize was a personally conducted tour with Senator Taft, through the nearest butcher shop.

Next on the program was a contest to identify the "hidden melody." It was "Why Was I Born?" . . . This title, said Galen Drake acidly, illustrated the question asked by many Americans during the Republican depression. Then he announced the guest star for the day, Mrs. India Edwards, who spoke for three minutes. First she said that Mrs. Truman and daughter, Margaret, were the kind of family "you'd like for next door neighbors." In a folksy manner she continued, "Goodness may be mocked at these days, but women like it in a leader."

Thus was the voter enlightened.

The use of broadcasting for appeals to foreign-born groups is exemplified by Tommy D'Alesandro's report on a trip to Italy. When he returned to the United States, the fiery Democratic Mayor of Baltimore reported emotionally that in southern Italy, women prayed in the streets for Truman as the savior of Italy. His remarks in Italian were recorded by the Democratic National Committee and distributed to every radio station which broadcast in the Italian language.[75]

It has been said that 1948 was to television what 1924 was to radio "when Coolidge, Davis, Dawes, Cox, Bryan and other orators picked up the microphone for the first time in a national campaign and marveled at its ability to reach the people."[76] However, as in 1924, because of limited coverage, the new medium was more important for its poten-

tial than for its current ability to perform. There were only 37 television stations on the air and 350,000 receivers operating at this time.[77]
Nineteen hundred forty-eight was radio's last great political stand
before its eclipse by the magic lantern.

The third development of the 1948 campaign which had important
implications for the future was the "great debate" in the Republican
primary which pitted Minnesota's ex-Governor Harold E. Stassen
against New York's Governor Thomas E. Dewey. The protracted negotiations for the Dewey-Stassen radio debate are somewhat reminiscent
of the long talks prior to the 1960 "Great Debates" between Kennedy
and Nixon. Stassen insisted that the people should have "a chance to
see, hear and participate in the debate. There will be applause, there
may be some heckling, but that's the American way." Dewey, however, held out for no audience participation.[78] By May 14, three days
before the proposed day of the debate, Stassen and Dewey were still in
disagreement about the form it should take. Finally, Stassen announced
"we will let Dewey write his own ticket and we will meet his terms—
reluctantly."[79] Though Stassen wanted to include other issues, one of
Dewey's terms was that the debate should be limited to the issue of
outlawing Communism.

The debate was held on May 17 in the Portland studios of Radio
Station KEX and transmitted over the ABC, NBC, and Mutual chains.
Dewey rehearsed at mid-afternoon a text which he had distributed to
the press but reserved the right to "change or alter" as he saw fit. The
absence of an advance speech by Stassen was explained by aides not
only on the ground that it was not ready but also that it would give
Dewey an opportunity to incorporate part of his rebuttal into his main
speech.[80]

The two candidates summarized in their 20-minute opening arguments all of the persuasive points they had been hammering in their
campaigns. Then, in 8½-minute rebuttal speeches, they tore at each
other's contentions. Stassen was the first speaker but Dewey had insisted on having the last rebuttal. The debate was set up entirely on
Dewey's terms.[81]

Who won? The Oregon primary victory went to Dewey by a vote
of 117,554 to 107,946. As to the debate itself, Who won? was the
question in 1948 as it was to be in 1960. The answers were subjective.
No public opinion polls were taken just before and after the Oregon
debate. Generally speaking, the press comments gave an unquestioned
edge to Dewey, though there was a noticeable lack of enthusiasm about

the quality of the debate. One of the state's leading papers, *The Oregonian,* said editorially that "if any votes were won by either debater, we fancy they were won by his debate conduct, rather than by what he said."[82] *The Oregon Journal,* more succinctly, called the exchange a "Debate of Tweedledum and Tweedledee."[83]

More to the point for the future were the Washington *Star's* comments:[84]

If judgment as to the winner of last night's debate remains a matter of personal and divided opinion, there should be no disagreement on the value of such debates. They are educational in character, they put the speakers on their mettle, they reveal weaknesses which are obscured in ordinary campaign speech-making. If there were more of them, we would have better campaigns, candidates better prepared to discuss the real issues of the day and an electorate composed of the American radio public, better able to judge both issues and candidates.

With the advent of television into the political picture, which promised to drive the already skyrocketing campaign costs into the stratosphere, repercussions in Congress were predictable. Though there had been earlier rumblings about radio stations charging more than their standard rates for political broadcasts, the issue began to erupt in 1949. One survey, done in conjunction with the 1948 campaign, had shown that 24 per cent of the radio stations admitted to having special rates for such broadcasts; some charged political candidates double what they charged for other types of broadcasts.[85] Senator J. Howard McGrath, chairman of the Democratic National Committee, introduced a bill in 1949 which restricted stations from charging more than their standard rates for political broadcasts. This bill did not get onto the Senate floor.[86] In 1952, however, Representative Walter Horan proposed an addition to Section 315 of the Communications Act of 1934 which was passed and signed by President Truman on July 16, 1952. This addition stated that "the charges made for the use of any broadcast station for any of the purposes set forth in this section shall not exceed the charges made for comparable use of the station for other purposes."[87]

1952

The year 1952 is of special importance in the history of broadcasting and politics. This was the first year in which the national political conventions and the succeeding presidential campaign were televised to a nationwide audience. There were 108 television stations on the air. The number of television receivers had risen from 420,000 to 18 million during the preceding four years.[88]

The continually increasing cost of broadcast campaigning is seen simply in the figure for Eisenhower's election eve program. This one broadcast cost $267,000.[89] Further cost increases for the political candidates were heralded in the winter of 1951-52 by an announcement from the networks and stations that they would henceforth sell time to candidates for the nominations prior to the national conventions. Previously, time during the primary campaigns had been made available free.[90]

Costs were rising not only for the political parties. The CBS, NBC, and ABC networks lost an estimated $2,500,000 on their radio and television coverage of the conventions and the election returns in 1952.[91] Probably the greatest tribute to the television coverage of the conventions was the demand from the magazine *Freeman* that radio and television be barred from all future conventions.[92]

Television, fixing its prying and disillusioning eye upon the antics and asininities of our shirtsleeved statesmen in Convention assembled, is likely to so disgust the plain citizen that he may continue to withhold his vote until zero is reached.

Television brought the viewer a sense of involvement in the conventions. As many of the delegates and the reporters covering the convention soon discovered, the television viewer could see more and know more of what was going on than the persons could who were on the floor of the convention hall.

In 1952, as in 1948, one of the major contributions of the television industry, and one of the developments which may have been most important to the future relationship of broadcasting and politics, started in the primary campaign. During the primaries, especially in New Hampshire, the television networks through news and public affairs programs provided evidence of their ability to inform the public on men and issues far better than had ever been done through the paid political broadcasts or other activities of the political parties.[93]

If a viewer watched a reasonable percentage of the nightly newsreel programs, the discussion forums and special primary presentations, the chances are that he saw a great deal more of the principal campaigners than the New Hampshire resident without TV. But, more pertinently, the home viewer *had a better understanding of the mechanics of the campaign as a whole.* [Italics ours]

Through the primary campaign and the nominating conventions of 1952, the broadcasting industry covered itself with glory. The record of the industry following the nominations is less brilliant. There was little reporting in depth, little attempt to provide the voter with a complete picture of the election campaign, as was done for the primary and the nominating conventions. There were some panel programs, interviews, and spot news but the real issues of the campaign were handled very gingerly, if at all.

The blame for this situation cannot be placed completely upon the broadcasting industry. Section 315 of the Communications Act, and its interpretation by the Federal Communications Commission, must assume part of the responsibility. In no previous campaign had the demands of minor party candidates and would-be candidates assumed such proportions. "Crackpots and other irresponsible people seeking public office are being given Open Sesame to the microphones and cameras on equal footing with bona fide candidates, by simply citing Section 315 to the FCC."[94] The problem is exemplified by the case of CBS versus William F. Schneider in early 1952. Schneider proclaimed himself a candidate for the Republican nomination and demanded time on CBS equal to that given certain other candidates. The network refused. Schneider then filed in the New Hampshire and the Oregon primaries and renewed his request, claiming to be a "legally qualified" candidate. When CBS again refused, saying that he had no chance for the Republican nomination and merely wanted publicity, Schneider appealed to the FCC. The Commission held that:

There appears to be no question but that the opportunities made available by CBS to other qualified candidates constitute a "use" of a broadcasting station within the meaning of Section 315. Mr. Schneider is a legally qualified candidate within Section 315 of the Communications Act.

CBS then gave Schneider two free network half-hours. Ironically, Schneider could not even get a ticket to attend the 1952 Republican convention.[95]

Some network officials and Congressmen were already interested in the possibility of broadcasting a debate between the 1952 presidential

"The Following Program Is Brought To You By Courtesy Of The F.C.C.!"

Greensboro, North Carolina Daily News, *Sunday, July 19, 1959*

candidates. However, the "equal-time" provisions of Section 315 made the idea impractical.[96]

The withdrawal of the broadcasting industry from a sharply penetrating coverage and analysis of the major part of the campaign which resulted from, or at least accompanied, these "equal-time" pressures from minor party candidates and would-be candidates meant that the political parties, through their paid broadcasts and commercials, determined in large part the kinds of information about the issues of the campaign to which the voter could be exposed. This was doubly unfortunate in 1952 because it appears to have been accompanied by increasing advertising agency influence. Signs of this influence can be seen in the remarks of Robert McConnell, member of the Republican National Finance Committee, in which he called for a vigorous all-out advertising campaign.[97] It can be seen even more clearly in the type of selective "spot" campaign which was used by the Republican Party, identical with many other advertising campaigns. This was probably the most important development in broadcasting strategy in this campaign. Not only were the commercials concentrated in regions of the country which were believed to be key areas for swinging the electoral college to Eisenhower, but the spots were placed either just before or just after the most popular programs.[98]

Six advertising agency executives created the commercials for this Republican campaign. Their "star" was General Eisenhower. (This was probably the first time that a presidential candidate appeared on such commercials.) Non-professional talent was used to deliver the filmed and recorded questions to Eisenhower. At a later date, "under Mr. Reeves' competent direction, General Eisenhower spent an afternoon making about a dozen different 20-second and 60-second spots." This is one of the products of this effort:[99]

VOICE: Eisenhower answers!
MAN IN THE STREET: Mr. Eisenhower, I need a new car but can't afford it at today's high prices.
EISENHOWER: Yes, a low-priced car today includes $624 in hidden taxes. Let's start saving the billions now wasted by Washington and get those taxes down.

Not all stations accepted these political "commercials." It was reported during the 1952 campaign that the Westinghouse Radio Stations had a policy for some time which prohibited the acceptance of political spot broadcasts. The president of Westinghouse, Joseph E. Baudino, reported that the policy was based on the fact that political issues cannot be discussed in one minute. At the same time, ABC, CBS, DuMont, and NBC indicated that they would accept such spots for their owned and operated stations.[100]

The Democratic party relied less upon a spot campaign, though not necessarily because of the ethics of such oversimplified appeals to the voter. They evidently felt that they had a different advertising problem to solve. The Republicans had an already popular figure. They needed only to clinch borderline or key areas. The Democrats needed to make Stevenson into a well-known, national figure. They also felt it was important to make a strong impact on minority and foreign language groups.[101]

Both parties bought the last five minutes of established entertainment programs in an attempt to catch more voters and, perhaps, to catch them in a more defenseless mood. This practice, however, caused some resentment from viewers.[102] Both parties also worked at getting speakers favorable to their presidential candidates on such radio and television programs as Town Meeting of the Air, Junior Press Conference, and the Kate Smith show. The Director of Public Relations of the National Citizens for Eisenhower-Nixon Committee estimated that the time secured in this way by the Republicans alone was worth $1,000,000.[103]

One of the best studies done on the impact of television in the 1952 campaign had these conclusions.[104]

The public went out of its way to watch the campaign on television. Only about 40 per cent of the homes in the U.S. have television sets, but some 53 per cent of the population saw TV programs on the campaign—a reflection of "television visiting." On the other hand, the campaign news and other material in newspapers, magazines and on the radio did not reach all of their respective audiences: more than 80 per cent of the population take daily newspapers and have radios and more than 60 per cent regularly read magazines, but in each case the number following the campaign in these media was smaller than the total audience. . . .

In the nation as a whole television, though available to only a minority of the people, led the other media in the number of persons who rated it most informative.

1956

The United States was almost 100 per cent saturated with radio receivers by 1956; the number of television sets in use had doubled in the four years since the last campaign. There was no major broadcasting innovation in the 1956 campaign; there was simply more of it and greater refinement of existing techniques.

The broadcasting networks tried to reduce costs of radio and television time for the political parties by reserving specific periods as long as a year in advance and by shortening 30- and 60-minute entertainment programs to make five-minute periods available. This eliminated, in many cases, the need for the parties to pay preemption costs.[105] Both parties utilized these five-minute periods for political speeches much as they had in 1952. The longer time periods were used for many of the questionable programs which appear to have become an accepted part of political campaigning. For example:[106]

On . . . a Citizens-for-Eisenhower-sponsored "Citizens Press Conference" on October 12, the President lent himself to a highly structured "spontaneous" televised press conference, based on the normal procedure of his weekly press conferences but without the possibility of surprise questions or press needling. . . . In this carefully plotted line-up was found a "discerning Democrat." . . . ("Will you tell the nation who is in charge, sir?") There was a TV money winner. . . . There was a member of the UAW. ("Some fellars feels that the Democratic party is on their side. I happen to know that you are on their side even more so. . . . And I wish, Mr. President, that you would explain and enlighten my buddies back home as to your stand on labor unions and the things that they are inclined to do.") There was a dairy farmer from New York. . . . There was a mother from Dallas. . . . There was a Negro pastor from Chicago.

Nor were the Democrats above this type of program, which attempted to make things appear to be somewhat other than what they really were.[107]

A nationwide Kefauver . . . show . . . featured Republican "corruption." The main purpose was to come as close to a "rogues gallery" technique as possible without using those very words for it—showing pictures of Republican officials from Adolphe Wenzell (Boston financier and former Bureau of the Budget consultant) to Sherman Adams in poses worthy of police files, and with commentary by Kefauver. These, he said, were faces of "friends Eisenhower would like to forget." They documented, he said, the charge that "more heads of Government agencies have been involved in corruption than . . . since the Republican Administration of Ulysses S. Grant."

Fortunately broadcast news coverage of the national campaign seemed to be both improving and increasing, though there was still a shortage of vigorous, penetrating, and independent analysis of the campaign issues and the positions of the major candidates on these issues. CBS estimated that roughly 20 per cent of its total television newscast time was devoted to some aspect of the presidential campaign. That this coverage reached a large proportion of the voters can be seen from the fact that the dinner hour newscast alone of this network was seen by approximately 35 million persons during any given week.[108] The data for the other radio and television networks are probably comparable. In addition, one must add to this the impact of local news broadcasts.

None of the newscasts or political programs achieved the coverage which television afforded the nominating conventions. Approximately 88 per cent of television homes saw at least one session in each of the two major conventions. This was 32,100,000 homes in the United States. One research organization estimated that the average home saw 25 per cent of the convention in 1956, compared to 20 per cent in 1952.[109] Thus, not only did the total television audience grow, but the average amount of time spent viewing the convention by each member of the audience also grew. The networks estimated their losses on convention coverage to be between $4,100,000 and $5,100,000. This included pre-emption charges as well as production costs not made up by revenue obtained from sponsors. Each of the networks was on the air with convention coverage for slightly over 56 hours.[110]

Problems with Section 315 were not absent from the 1956 campaign. One of the most publicized, and most difficult to judge, was the problem which arose when, shortly before the election, Britain, France, and Israel invaded Egypt. President Eisenhower discussed this Middle East crisis in a speech transmitted by all networks. Governor Stevenson immediately demanded equal time from the networks to express his views on the crisis. The networks asked the Federal Communications Commission for advice. The Commission, however, failed to give them an immediate ruling, noting that the problem was too complex. With the election practically upon them, the networks decided to play it safe and grant the time, though all had serious questions about their legal requirement to do so.[111] Earlier in the campaign, a somewhat different problem arose over the same provision of Section 315. President Eisenhower was scheduled to deliver a talk on behalf of the United Community Funds. The FCC advised CBS that if the network carried this talk it would be obligated to give free time to all qualified presidential candidates. CBS did not schedule the talk until it received a telegram from Adlai Stevenson urging it to do so and assuring the network that he would not ask for equal time, and until it sent for and received similar assurances from the candidates of thirteen other parties.

1960

Though 1959 was not an election year, it was an important year for the 1960 campaign and for the history of political broadcasting. Section 315 was both clarified and amended.

One of the problems which had been plaguing broadcasting since 1927 (first from Section 18 of the Federal Radio Act, then from Section 315 of the Communications Act of 1934) was the restriction against censorship of political broadcasts, without specifically limiting the broadcaster's liability for libelous statements so broadcast. After twenty-seven years of argument, in and out of court, the United States Supreme Court resolved the dilemma with a decision which held that the broadcaster could not be held liable for statements which he was enjoined from censoring.[112] This was a reversal of its decision a quarter of a century earlier when it upheld the *Sorenson v. Wood* decision of a lower court. (See p. 33 above.)

Probably more important for aiding adequate broadcast coverage of political campaigns was the amendment of Section 315 which was made in 1959. This amendment grew out of the argument over whether bona fide news broadcasts were exempt from the equal-time provision. This argument reached its climax with the Lar Daly case in 1959.[113] Daly was a perennial and unsuccessful candidate for office who liked to campaign in a red, white, and blue Uncle Sam suit. He called himself Lar "America First" Daly. In January, 1959, he entered his name in both the Democratic and the Republican primary for Mayor of Chicago. Daly kept track of the television newscasts in Chicago and found five in which either the Democratic or Republican candidate or both were shown welcoming the president of Argentina to Chicago, inaugurating the March of Dimes drive, filing their nominating petitions, etc. Daly wanted equal time and the local CBS station refused, claiming that Congress had not intended regular newscasts to be included under Section 315 and that to do so would constitute an abridgment of freedom of speech and of the press. The case was taken to the FCC, which, on February 19, ruled that newscasts were to be included in the equal time provisions of Section 315.

Spurred by the networks, especially CBS, a torrent of criticism was rained on this decision. From comments of the then chairman of the FCC, John Doerfer, it would appear that the FCC may have interpreted Section 315 in this strict fashion in order to bring the issue to a head and thus force Congressional action. Doerfer wanted the entire Section 315 repealed.[114] The Congress did not honor his wish. It did, however, amend Section 315 to exclude bona fide newscasts, news interviews, on-the-spot coverage of bona fide news events, and documentaries in which the appearance of a political candidate is incidental to the presentation of the subject covered.[115] This move, plus the special legislation passed by the Congress for the Kennedy-Nixon presidential campaign (which is described in other sections of this book), paved the way in 1960 for what proved to be the finest independent election coverage by the broadcasting industry in its forty-year history.

CONCLUSION

The story of the relationship between presidential campaigning and the broadcasting media which evolves when one examines its history to 1960, as we have done, is a story of skyrocketing costs for both the political parties and the broadcasting industry. It is a story of increasing attempts at "merchandising" candidates through programs and commercials paid for by proponents of each candidate. And it is a story of increasing ability and responsibility of the broadcasting industry to create "a picture of reality on which men can act"[116] by digging underneath the issues of the campaign and setting facts into relation with each other. In regard to this last, it should be noted that the industry has not consistently used its increasing ability to fulfill its growing responsibility. Hovering over all of these developments has been a continuing argument, involving the broadcasting industry, the political parties, the Congress, and the Federal Communications Commission, about the relative freedom and responsibilities of the industry in its coverage of political campaigns.

The rising costs of political campaigns can lead to many evils, not the least of which is the possibility of excluding some good potential candidates or the danger of a candidate coming into office with allegiances to a particular segment of the population which supported his campaign financially. We need only be reminded of the constant financial difficulties of Woodrow Wilson's pre-nomination campaign because his conversion to reform had cut him off from his original sources of funds.[117] It is probably superfluous to add that this problem has multiplied as the cost of campaigning has multiplied. The Hatch Act, which was designed to reduce this problem, has simply caused "decentralization, evasion, and concealment."[118] The result is that it is now virtually impossible to discover who is paying the political bills and, even more important, why.

The increasing use of advertising agencies by the political parties during election campaigns has been well documented. It should be pointed out this is not necessarily a bad practice. So long as the parties are buying broadcast time and producing programs to fill this time, the agency is almost a necessity. Buying broadcast time is an exceedingly complex business for which the political party cannot be expected to have adequately trained personnel. The same can be said for producing programs. The services of an advertising agency cost the party nothing since the agency fee comes out of the station or network time charges which the party would pay whether or not it used the agency. These facts indicate that it would be an error for a political party not to use the agency *for these legitimate purposes.* However, when the advertising agency plays a large role in the determination of issues to be stressed in the campaign, and the way they are to be stressed, one might raise serious questions.

It is obvious that the citizen needs information on which to base his voting decision. It should be equally obvious that not all information is of equal value in arriving at an intelligent decision. It would appear from the results of the present study that the voter has a greater chance of obtaining sound information and a balanced view of the issues from political programs which are presented by a broadcasting station or network as a sustaining program or under sponsorship of a nonpolitical agency (as has been the case for the convention broadcasts).

The dominant goal of broadcasts paid for by a political party is obviously the promotion of a candidate, not the enlightenment of the voter. This promotion takes its very worst form in the 30-second or one-minute commercial where political issues are so oversimplified or ignored that the voter is given no information or, worse, misleading information. With the paid political broadcasts of each party coming at different times, and the now well-established fact of "selective exposure" by the audience (that is, the tendency to view only the political candidate who reinforces one's biases), each candidate is largely speaking to a different audience. This allows each to ignore his opponent's points and to shape his presentation to make himself look good. On programs which are not sponsored by the parties or their advocates, the viewer or listener can be almost forced to expose himself to more than one side by the juxtaposition of these sides.

The broadcasting industry early laid the groundwork for this sort of independent campaign coverage by its insistence on editorial freedom in deciding how to cover the conventions.[119] We might note, for example, CBS's refusal to carry the promotion film which the Democratic party produced for its 1956 convention, and the argument which followed this decision. The point was clearly made that this is a public event for which the independent reporters with the interest of the viewer in mind, not the political parties involved, should retain editorial judgment. The same also should hold true for that part of the campaign between the nominating conventions and election day. When the stations and networks carry only paid political broadcasts and their news programs report only what the candidates have said and done, to a large extent they are relinquishing this editorial prerogative. The viewer is the loser.

There appears to be a tendency in recent years for the broadcasters to control a greater portion of their total election campaign coverage. The history of presidential campaigning on radio and television indicates that this is a good trend, which should be accelerated. Some of the most striking evidence for this conclusion are 1960's "Great Debates."

NOTES

1. John Wells Davidson, *A Crossroads of Freedom: The 1912 Campaign Speeches of Woodrow Wilson* (New Haven: Yale University Press, 1956), p. 454.

2. Alfred N. Goldsmith and Austin C. Lescarboura, *This Thing Called Broadcasting* (New York: Holt, 1930), pp. 195-205.

3. Samuel L. Becker, "Presidential Power: The Influence of Broadcasting," *Quarterly Journal of Speech*, XLVII (1961), 11.

4. Gleason L. Archer, *History of Radio to 1926* (New York: American Historical Society, 1938), pp. 201-04.

5. *New York Times*, Sept. 16, 1928, sec. 12, p. 4.

6. *Ibid.*, June 25, 1923, p. 2.

7. *Ibid.*, Oct. 19, 1924, sec. 9, p. 16.

8. *30 Years of Pioneering and Progress in Radio and Television* (New York: Radio Corporation of America, 1949), p. 16.

9. Archer, *History of Radio*, pp. 336-37.

10. *New York Times,* Feb. 20, 1924, p. 6, and Feb. 24, 1924, sec. 8, p. 15.

11. Graham McNamee, *You're On the Air* (New York: Harper, 1926), p. 71.

12. Karl Schriftgiesser, *This Was Normalcy* (Boston: Little, Brown, 1948), pp. 174-81.

13. Archer, *History of Radio*, p. 338, and *New York Times,* July 6, 1924, sec. 8, p. 13.

14. Archer, *History of Radio*, p. 345. Advertising had invaded radio in the summer of 1922 when WEAF began publicizing a real estate development in Queens. *Ibid.*, pp. 375-77.

15. Herbert R. Craig, "Distinctive Features of Radio-TV in the 1952 Presidential Campaign" (unpublished Master's thesis, State University of Iowa, 1954), p. 12.

16. Louise Overacker, *Presidential Campaign Funds* (Boston: Boston University Press, 1946), p. 98.

17. Craig, "Radio-TV in 1952."

18. *New Republic,* XL (Sept. 3, 1924), 9.

19. Archer, *History of Radio*, pp. 349-50.

20. *New Republic,* XL (Nov. 19, 1924), 284.

21. *Congressional Record,* 69 Cong., 1 sess., LXVIII, part 5, p. 5483, quoted in Robert Shepherd Morgan, "Section 315 of the Communications Act of 1934: An Overview of the Development of Political Broadcast Regulation" (unpublished Master's thesis, Boston University, 1960), p. 17.

22. Public Law No. 632, February 23, 1927, 69 Cong.

23. U. S. Congress, House Committee on the Merchant Marine and Fisheries, Hearings on H.R. 7357, *To Regulate Radio Communication,* 68 Cong., 1 sess., March 11, 12, 13, and 14, 1924, p. 83, quoted in Morgan, "Section 315," p. 10.

24. *New York Times,* Apr. 17, 1927, sec. 8, p. 18.

25. Roy V. Peel and Thomas C. Donnelly, *The 1928 Campaign* (New York: Roy V. Peel, 1931), p. 33.

26. Schriftgiesser, *This Was Normalcy*, p. 257.

27. Peter H. Odegard, *Religion and Politics* (New Brunswick, New Jersey: Rutgers University, 1960), pp. 47-49.

28. *Literary Digest,* IC (Dec. 1, 1928), 13.

29. Craig, "Radio-TV in 1952," p. 15.

30. *Ibid.*, p. 14, and *New York Times,* Oct. 28, 1928, sec. 10, p. 1.

31. Goldsmith and Lescarboura, *This Thing*, p. 204.

32. *New York Times,* Oct. 28, 1928, sec. 10, p. 1, and Nov. 4, 1928, sec. 10, p. 16.

33. *Ibid.*, Sept. 16, 1928, sec. 12, p. 4.

34. *Ibid.*, Oct. 28, 1928, sec. 10, p. 1.

35. *Ibid.*, Nov. 4, 1928, p. 16.

36. "GE in TV 25 Years," *Broadcasting-Telecasting,* XLI (Dec. 10, 1951), 94.

37. *New York Times,* May 12, 1929, sec. 10, p. 21, and Sept. 8, 1929, sec. 10, p. 17.

38. The "Happy Warrior" speech was hailed by press critics, who faulted Roosevelt only for using the phrase from a Wordsworth poem too far from the close. Judge Joseph M. Proskauer, one of Smith's closest advisors, suggested the phrase and had to persuade Roosevelt that it was not too poetic. Joseph M. Proskauer, *A Segment of My Times* (New York: Farrar, Straus, 1950), pp. 50-51.

39. Roy V. Peel and Thomas C. Donnelly, *The 1932 Campaign* (New York: Farrar and Rinehart, 1935), pp. 145-47.

40. *Ibid.,* pp. 116-17.

41. Jasper B. Shannon, *Money and Politics* (New York: Random House, 1959), p. 53.

42. Craig, "Radio-TV in 1952," p. 18.

43. *New York Times,* Aug. 12, 1932, p. 6.

44. Orrin E. Dunlap, Jr., "Stay-at-Home Idea Vanishes," *New York Times,* Sept. 25, 1932, sec. 8, p. 8.

45. *New York Times,* Oct. 12, 1932, p. 48.

46. S. Doc. 144, 73 Cong., 2 sess.

47. *Regulation of Broadcasting,* study for the Committee on Interstate and Foreign Commerce, House of Representatives, 85 Cong., 2 sess., on H. Res. 99 (1958), p. 29.

48. *Ibid.,* p. 45.

49. Samuel I. Rosenman, *Working With Roosevelt* (New York: Harper, 1952), p. 99.

50. James A. Farley, *Behind the Ballots* (New York: Harcourt, Brace, 1938), p. 316.

51. *Ibid.,* pp. 318-19.

52. Ralph D. Casey, "Republican Propaganda in the 1936 Campaign," *Public Opinion Quarterly,* I (April, 1937), 33.

53. *Ibid.,* p. 34.

54. Craig, "Radio-TV in 1952," p. 21.

55. Casey, "Republican Propaganda," p. 34.

56. Craig, "Radio-TV in 1952," pp. 19-20.

57. Charles A. H. Thomson, *Television and Presidential Politics* (Washington: The Brookings Institution, 1956), p. 3.

58. *Broadcasting-Telecasting,* XLI (Nov. 26, 1951), 130.

59. Thomson, *Television and Presidential Politics,* p. 3.

60. *Senate Report No. 47,* 77 Cong., 1 sess., Feb. 15, 1941, p .15.

61. Craig, "Radio-TV in 1952," p. 25.

62. *Public Law No. 753,* July 19, 1940, 76 Cong.

63. Arthur Krock, *New York Times,* Nov. 2, 1944, p. 18.

64. Robert F. Ray, "An Evaluation of the Public Speaking of Franklin D. Roosevelt and Thomas E. Dewey in the Presidential Campaign of 1944," (unpublished Ph.D. dissertation, State University of Iowa, 1947), p. 580.

65. Louise Overacker, "Presidential Campaign Funds, 1944," *American Political Science Review,* XXXIX (1945), 904-05.

66. *Ibid.,* p. 905.

67. *NORC Survey No. 230,* now on file at the Roper Public Opinion Research Center, Williams College.

68. Craig, "Radio-TV in 1952," p. 29.

69. Jack Redding, *Inside the Democratic Party* (Indianapolis: Bobbs-Merrill, 1958), pp. 241-42.

70. Herman Cohen, "A Survey of the Broadcasting by Local Radio Stations of the Speeches of President Harry Truman on the Western Swing of the 1948 Presidential Campaign" (unpublished Master's thesis, State University of Iowa, 1949).

71. John C. Weiser, "A Survey of the Broadcasts of the Local Speeches of Governor Thomas E. Dewey During the Western Campaign Swing—1948" (unpublished Master's thesis, State University of Iowa, 1949).

72. *Ibid.,* p. 50; Cohen, Broadcasting Speeches of Truman," pp. 78-80.

73. Richard M. Mall, "Some Aspects of Political Broadcast Policies of Radio and Television Stations in the United States" (unpublished Ph.D. dissertation, Ohio State University, 1952), p. 144.

74. Redding, "Inside the Democratic Party," pp. 239-40.

75. *Ibid.,* p. 221.

76. *Pioneering in Television* (a collection of David Sarnoff's statements; New York: Radio Corporation of America, 1948), p. 91.

77. Bruce Bliven, "Politics and TV," *Harpers Magazine,* CCV (Nov., 1952), 27.

78. *New York Times,* May 14, 1948, p. 19.

79. *The Evening Star* (Washington, D.C.), May 15, 1948, p. 2.

80. *New York Times,* May 18, 1948, p. 16.

81. *Ibid.,* pp. 1, 16.

82. *The Oregonian,* May 19, 1948, p. 10.

83. *The Oregon Journal,* May 19, 1948, p. 13.

84. *The Evening Star* (Washington, D.C.), May 18, 1948, p. 8.

85. *Broadcasting-Telecasting,* XXXIV (April 12, 1948), 25, and XXXVII (July 25, 1949), 34.

86. Morgan, "Section 315," pp. 129-30.

87. *Ibid.,* pp. 140-42.

88. Thomson, *Television and Presidential Politics,* pp. 4, 6, 7.

89. Malcolm O. Sillars, "An Analysis of Invention in the 1952 Presidential Campaign Addresses of Dwight D. Eisenhower and Adlai E. Stevenson" (unpublished Ph.D. dissertation, State University of Iowa, 1955), p. 130.

90. Thomson, *Television and Presidential Politics,* p. 26.

91. *Broadcasting-Telecasting,* XLIII (Nov. 10, 1952), 27.

92. Bliven, "Politics and TV," p. 30.

93. Jack Gould, "Video and Politics," *New York Times,* March 16, 1952, sec. 2, p. 11.

94. "Machine Against TV," *Broadcasting-Telecasting,* editorial, XLII (June 16, 1952), 56.

95. Morgan, "Section 315," pp. 144-45.

96. A suggestion for such a series of debates was made by Senator Blair

Moody on the CBS radio series, "People's Platform," on July 27, 1952. Both NBC and CBS officials showed immediate interest. See Mr. Sarnoff's paper below and letter from Dr. Stanton to Senator Moody on this subject dated August 6, 1952. A copy of the latter is in the files of CBS.

97. *Broadcasting-Telecasting,* XLIII (Sept. 15, 1952), 64.
98. Thomson, *Television and Presidential Politics,* p. 59.
99. Craig, "Radio-TV in 1952," pp. 77-78.
100. *Broadcasting-Telecasting,* XLIII (Oct. 6, 1952), 23.
101. Thomson, *Television and Presidential Politics,* p. 56.
102. Jack Gould, "Campaign on TV," *New York Times,* Oct. 28, 1956, sec. 2, p. 13.
103. Craig, "Radio-TV in 1952," p. 54.
104. Angus Campbell, Gerald Gurin, and Warren E. Miller, "Television and the Election," *Scientific American,* LCXXXVIII (May, 1953), 46-47.
105. *Broadcasting-Telecasting,* LI (Sept. 17, 1956), 42.
106. Charles A. H. Thomson and Frances M. Shattuck, *The 1956 Presidential Campaign* (Washington: The Brookings Institution, 1960), pp. 279-80.
107. *Ibid.,* p. 284.
108. John F. Day, Jr., "Radio and Television: Their Role and Influence in Elections," *Communications, 1960: Seeking a Balance Between Freedom and Responsibility* (Lexington: University of Kentucky, 1960), p. 19.
109. *Broadcasting-Telecasting,* LI (Sept. 24, 1956), 88.
110. *Ibid.,* LI (Sept. 3, 1956), 59.
111. *Ibid.,* LI (Nov. 5, 1956), 54.
112. *Farmers Educational and Cooperative Union of America v WDAY,* 79 S. Ct. 1302 (1959), quoted in Morgan, "Section 315," pp. 91-92. See also Jerry B. Martin, "Immunity of Broadcast Stations from Liability for Defamatory Statements by Candidates for Public Office," *Journal of Broadcasting,* IV (1960), 140-43.
113. Howard K. Smith, "Behind the News," CBS broadcast, July 26, 1959.
114. *Ibid.*
115. Morgan, "Section 315," pp. 254, 258.
116. Walter Lippmann, *Public Opinion* (New York: Macmillan, 1936), p. 358.
117. Shannon, *Money and Politics,* p. 40.
118. Overacker, *Presidential Campaign Funds,* 1946, p. 45.
119. Thomson, *Television and Presidential Politics,* p. 17.

3

An NBC View

ROBERT W. SARNOFF

THIS FALL television has achieved another major milestone—a development that creates a valuable precedent not only for this young medium but for our nation and its political life. For the first time, the two major candidates for the presidency of the United States are meeting face to face in a systematic effort to exchange views on the great issues of the day. They are meeting before a forum as large as the American electorate itself—an audience far larger than any presidential candidate has been able to reach before.

This "Great Debate" is an event that concerns all of us as citizens, and especially those of us with a stake in broadcasting. Therefore, I would like to explore it with you today, to examine how it came about, why it did not occur sooner, and what it augurs for the future in broadcasting as well as politics.

The famous Lincoln-Douglas debates in 1858 have been cited as a precedent for the current encounters. However, there are fundamental differences. The former took place not during a presidential campaign but when the two rivals were running for the office of United States senator from Illinois. There were seven Lincoln-Douglas debates in all, each in a different Congressional district. Each lasted three hours. The first speaker took an hour to make his case, yielded to his opponent for an hour and a half and then spoke for the remaining half hour, thus enjoying the advantage of having the last word as well as

This chapter is based on a speech delivered to the San Francisco Advertising Club, October 5, 1960.

56

the first. Since the debates were Lincoln's idea and held as the result of his challenge, Stephen Douglas seized the advantageous position in four of the seven encounters. In those days, candidates took a more casual view of the ground rules under which they met.

Lincoln and Douglas drew big crowds for the time and place—upwards of 15,000 in some places, though they attracted only 1,500 in the town of Jonesboro. Except for the newspapermen and party workers who followed them, no one heard more than one of the debates. Yet this hardly mattered since the debaters concentrated everywhere on the burning issue of slavery and, as a result, they kept repeating themselves. Thus the average person lucky enough to attend managed to hear only one debate lasting three hours—somewhat less than the time all Americans can spend listening to the arguments of Vice President Nixon and Senator Kennedy in their four joint sessions on the air.

It is a fascinating fact that, despite the distinguished example of Lincoln and Douglas more than a hundred years ago, there is no precedent in any presidential campaign for the kind of encounter that Senator Kennedy and Vice President Nixon undertook last week and will resume the day after tomorrow—on the anniversary, incidentally, of the Lincoln-Douglas debate at Galesburg.

Why has there been no such encounter between presidential candidates before? One reason undoubtedly lies in the attitude of candidates themselves—an unwillingness to risk the hazards of debate or a reluctance on the part of a better established candidate, such as a presidential incumbent, to help draw larger audiences for his opponent. But a more pertinent reason, I believe, is that until recently there has been no medium which, by its ability to bring both living images and words instantaneously to the whole nation, makes such encounters so logical and compelling. The existence of network television creates not only the opportunity but a strong incentive for face-to-face discussion by the presidential nominees before the whole nation.

This incentive made itself felt soon after television had become a national medium. I must confess that, as far as I can determine, the first proposal for televised debate between the presidential candidates did not come from a broadcaster. Yet, appropriately enough, it originated with a man whose career embraced journalism and politics. In July, 1952, the idea was put forward by Blair Moody, for many years the Washington correspondent of the Detroit News and at that time a United States senator from Michigan. It was an idea that quickly seized the imagination of broadcasters. Soon thereafter, NBC became the first network to try to adopt it. We wired both candidates, General Eisenhower and Governor Stevenson, that our television and radio facilities would be available for such debates.

This offer was declined. Yet it became increasingly clear that it would have been frustrated in any event. It would have run afoul of a legal stumbling block which deprived the American public of the full potential of broadcasting's unique power to inform.

The stumbling block was Section 315 of the Communications Act,* which, while having the avowed purpose of assuring fairness by broad-casters in presenting opposing candidates, ironically, has had the effect of discouraging the broadcaster from presenting any candidate.

The reason is simple. Until the present campaign, if a broadcaster wanted to offer an opportunity for discussion by the major-party candidates for president and vice president, the law said he had to offer equal time to every legally qualified candidate for those offices. In a modern presidential campaign, there are a dozen-odd presidential candidates, plus their running mates—and some of them are very odd indeed. To require hour upon hour to be devoted to the often quixotic antics of little-known candidates; to require this so that the public might listen for just one hour to the candidates in whom they are really interested, is clearly a price too heavy for the public, the broadcasters and common sense to bear.

During the prelude to the last two presidential campaigns, Dr. Frank Stanton of CBS and I, as well as other broadcasters, urged that the obstacle of Section 315 be set aside to give the public the full benefit of broadcasting's free exercise of its function as a medium of journalism. In 1956, for example, NBC, along with others, supported legislation that would have modified the effects of Section 315. I pledged that if it were adopted, NBC would offer appropriate opportunities on the air to the major candidates. Nevertheless, the legislation failed to pass.

Broadcasting's frustrating position under the so-called equal-time provision grew even worse before it was to grow better. In February, 1959, in the Lar Daly case, the Federal Communications Commission ruled that even if a candidate merely appeared in the course of regular news coverage, equal time had to be granted his opponents, under the law as then written. Such a requirement, if allowed to stand, would have rendered impossible effective broadcast coverage of the recent

---

* Cf. Becker and Lower, above, pp. 28, 33, 40, 42, 47-48.

conventions and the current campaign. It touched off a national outcry and brought the equal time provision under a new Congressional reappraisal for which broadcasters had campaigned so long.

But action from Congress came slowly and haltingly. Late last year, as a result of the Lar Daly ruling, limited progress was made with the passage of an amendment lifting the "equal time" requirement only in connection with candidates' appearances in news and regularly scheduled news interview programs. However, it failed to include debates, despite the urging of broadcasters. Early this year, in what many regarded as a cure worse than the ill, legislation was proposed which would have seized eight hours of television time from each network to turn over to each major presidential candidate, as a gift, to use as he desired. Happily, this legislation was abandoned, and just before Congress recessed in August, a joint resolution was passed suspending the "equal time" restriction for this campaign only—and only as it affects candidates for president and vice president.

At each of these stages, broadcasters were quick to seize the opportunity to bring their case to the public and to protect the position of broadcasting as a medium of the free press.

In April, on the basis of last year's amendment exempting news interview programs from the "equal time" requirement, NBC offered to present the major presidential nominees jointly in a series of eight hour-long editions of "Meet the Press." Under then existing law, this was the only feasible way of presenting the candidates on the air in a face-to-face exchange of views.

We at NBC are gratified that this offer and the good faith it reflected played some part in eliminating the proposed legislation that would have arbitrarily appropriated a substantial amount of television time and facilities from broadcasters. The House sponsor of this legislation, Congressman Stewart Udall of Arizona, graciously informed me that he was withdrawing his bill as superfluous upon learning of the NBC proposal to present the candidates together in a regular interview series. And the identical Senate bill was not submitted to a vote.

It was, instead, the joint resolution suspending the equal time requirement for this campaign, with respect to the presidential and vice presidential candidates, that finally made possible broadcasting's current "Great Debate." At the moment that the Republican Convention nominated Mr. Nixon for president, a week after Mr. Kennedy had won the Democratic nomination, we dispatched invitations by telegram to both candidates inviting them to take part in a special series

of programs as originally proposed on the NBC Television and Radio
Networks, to be called "The Great Debate." To the credit of both, they
were quick to accept.

I should like to nail some misconceptions about these unprecedented broadcasts. Because they are being presented at no cost to the
political parties, some observers have mislabeled them "free time" and
equated them with the programs that the abandoned legislation would
have compelled broadcasters to put on the air. Most emphatically, they
do not represent a donation of free time to the candidates. They are
rather an exercise of broadcast journalism in which the candidates have
agreed to appear within a framework calculated to stimulate a digni-
fied, genuinely informative airing of their views, and to test those views
against each other.

The implementation of this framework was left for the candidates
to develop through their own representatives in consultation with the
networks. It was the candidates' decision to engage in four of these
broadcasts; the networks had offered as many as eight.

Two formats have resulted from the collaboration between the candidates and the networks. Both entail the use of experienced newsmen
whose questions are intended to spotlight the issues and place the
candidates' positions in sharp focus. When this technique was announced, we heard some objections that it did not truly represent a
debate and that it would somehow short-change the public. Indeed, it
may not fulfill the traditional conception of a debate. Yet I believe it
is serving the public more effectively than the classic debating format
might have done: it is a disciplined, clear-cut method of pitting the
candidates' arguments against each other—which is, after all, the
quintessence of debate—while minimizing the formalities and flour-
ishes that debaters are prone to indulge in at the expense of the issues
themselves.

Another misconception that the arrangements for these programs
served to spread is of special interest to the advertising profession. It
is the antiquated notion that a so-called public service program is not
a public service if it is sponsored. By this odd reasoning, a broadcaster
cannot serve the public unless he loses money.

Actually, a broadcaster's entire program schedule is a service to the
public, and for that reason, I believe it is misleading to designate any
particular program category as public service. What is usually meant
by this designation, of course, is a program of an informational or
educational character. Only last summer an FCC policy statement re-

butted the old fallacy that an unsponsored program has special merit.

To maintain, as some people still do, that certain programs should not be sponsored is a disservice not only to broadcasting but to the viewing and listening public. Perhaps the most encouraging development in broadcasting in the last year or two is the dramatic upsurge in news and public affairs programming. It was recently estimated that, not counting special broadcasts arising from the election campaign, the United Nations, and unpredictable news developments, there will be twice as many network news and public affairs programs in prime evening time this season as last. Apart from the impetus of our times, and the initiative of broadcasters, this growth has been stimulated by a trend toward sponsorship of such programs by far-sighted advertisers in the front rank of American industry. This is a trend to be encouraged, not undermined by an archaic view which seeks to place certain programs off limits to advertisers.

That is why we at NBC saw no more objection to appropriate sponsorship of the Kennedy-Nixon broadcasts than to the sponsorship already found acceptable for the presidential inauguration or, indeed, the current sponsorship of various network programs in which the candidates themselves are appearing. However, after one network* publicly opposed any sponsorship of "The Great Debate," the question was foreclosed.

Perhaps some of those who resisted the possibility of sponsorship may retain traces of an ancient genteel distaste for advertising. May I remind you that advertising of any kind once had difficulty finding its way into the columns of the press. It took twenty-five years from the founding of England's first newspaper in 1622 for the first advertisement to appear; and it was almost twenty years later when the London *Gazette* decided to segregate its advertising in a special supplement, which it described as devoted to ads about books, medicines, and— here I quote—"other things not properly the business of a Paper of Intelligence."

We have come a long way since then. Advertising has earned a place as a vital constructive force in our society. Yet today advertising is under attack, perhaps as never before. To suggest that it is inadmissible in any undertaking of a medium that it supports is a form of surrender to that attack. At the same time, we cannot pretend for a moment that advertising is free of sins and shortcomings.

* CBS—ED.

Let us face the fact squarely that all of us who are engaged in advertising can do much to enhance its acceptability, as well as its effectiveness, by the taste and responsibility we exercise in carrying out our jobs. The profession can take some satisfaction in its recent efforts to raise advertising standards; we in broadcasting have also been striving to safeguard against excesses and impropriety and to encourage good taste. All of us must keep at it.

Along with this continuing test of responsibility, broadcasters today face a special challenge growing out of the chance we have been given to present the presidential and vice presidential candidates. The resolution suspending Section 315 in this campaign places us under special scrutiny by the FCC, which must pass judgment on how fairly and conscientiously we fulfill our opportunity. Congress will be watching closely as well; so will our colleagues of the print media and, most important, so will the American public.

What is at stake is nothing less than the freedom of expression that we believe the Constitution assures broadcasting as a medium of journalism. Broadcasters chafing under the restrictions of Section 315 have long warned that any curb on freedom of broadcasting is really a curb on freedom of the press. This bond between broadcasting and the press was never more vividly brought home than by two bills introduced in the House of Representatives a month or so ago. One bill would require newspapers to give equal space to all political candidates; the other would require every newspaper to file with the Postmaster General and publish a periodic report on how much space it has devoted to each political candidate and party. Even the possibility of such legislation must be appalling to every American who values freedom. Yet if these identical restrictions can be maintained against television and radio, their extension to other media is also frighteningly logical.

The limited suspension of Section 315 places on trial the responsibility with which our medium can use this new opportunity to fulfill its potential in the public interest. By that token, it is also a test of whether the "equal time" restriction should be permanently lifted; and whether broadcasting should be freed of this restriction not only in a presidential campaign but across the board.

We are in the process of fashioning a powerful new instrument of democracy. It is an instrument ideally suited to overcoming the barriers of bigness—the vastness of the country and our rapidly growing population—and giving all of us a sense of intimate political contact that a voter in Illinois could experience 102 years ago at a Lincoln-Douglas debate. It is an instrument no less suited to modern local self-government than to a national election campaign.

I am sure that by the time this campaign is over, broadcasting's record of performance will demonstrate its fairness and responsibility; and I earnestly hope that it will be freed to operate fully in all phases of the political process, whether in national, state, or local contests.

If and when the remaining barriers of Section 315 are removed, NBC will extend the technique of "The Great Debate" to the television and radio stations we own, for presenting the candidates and issues in political contests of particular interest in their areas. In the meantime, and as a token of our confidence in the service we can perform, we are undertaking pilot projects this month to test the political debate technique in broadcasting at the local level in San Francisco, Los Angeles, and New York.

In each of these cities, political contests are being conducted that would not impose the burdens of presenting a multitude of candidates under Section 315. In New York, our station WNBC and WNBC-TV will offer an opportunity for debate between John Lindsay, the Republican incumbent, and William Vanden Heuvel, the Democratic challenger, in what is usually the city's most closely watched and hotly contested Congressional District—the 17th or so-called "silk stocking" district of Manhattan.*

NBC's New York stations also plan a series of local debates of political issues between outstanding party spokesmen, who are not themselves candidates and therefore do not come under Section 315. In this series, entitled "The New York Debate," we hope to pit against each other such figures as Robert Kennedy and Leonard Hall, Governor Rockefeller and Governor Ribicoff, Averell Harriman and Thomas E. Dewey.**

Here in San Francisco on KNBC, as well as in Los Angeles on KRCA and KRCA-TV, we plan to experiment in a somewhat different direction. In seeking a compelling contest of sufficiently broad interest, we have found a highly controversial one—not between candidates but over a single issue. That is the fight over the statewide proposition to

* The debate, in accordance with the candidates' wishes, was held before an audience in a public hall and was broadcast live by WNBC and WNBC-TV on Saturday, October 22, 1960.

** Each was invited to debate as indicated, but no mutually agreeable dates could be established and none of the encounters took place.

supply water to southern California by building 1¾ billion dollars' worth of dams in the northern part of the state. We hope to enlist an outstanding spokesman for each side in a thoroughgoing airing of this highly important local issue.*

Arrangements are going forward to put these plans into effect while we move ahead with "The Great Debate" on a national scale. This is a momentous period for broadcasting and in the life of the nation. Even after only one of the broadcasts in "The Great Debate" series, it has been widely recognized that television and radio are bringing voters a new perspective in their critical task of selecting a president. As Jack Gould wrote in last Sunday's *New York Times,* "Overnight . . . there was born a new interest in the campaign that earlier had been productive of coast-to-coast somnolence."

By performing its job of journalism with skill and fairness, broadcasting is demonstrating its unique ability to bring politics home to the public. In doing so, it is more than meeting the test imposed by the temporary and limited suspension of Section 315. Its borrowed freedom should be made permanent—not as a benefit to broadcasting, but for the benefit of the public. When this is done, "The Great Debate" will become a lasting political institution that will reinforce the vigor of our country's democratic heritage in the challenging years ahead.

* Governor Brown agreed to appear in favor of the proposition, but although the News Departments of both stations sought for weeks they could find no opponent of sufficient stature to take the negative and it was necessary to abandon the plan.

4

A CBS View

FRANK STANTON

BEFORE I move on to my main topic today, I compliment all of you of the working press on the enormous amount of effective work that you put into the reporting of the past campaign. It was a long campaign and the most mobile and least relaxed in history, and you stuck with it without any prospect of respite. You worked hard and ably, and I salute you. Now I see that some of you are already going to work on the election of 1964, with the general conviction that it's not a moment too soon. There is something to be said for this unexampled diligence —something more than outright awe at both the mental verve and the physical endurance of the working press. Self-government is a continuous, a never-ending, never-recessing process. It is dependent upon continuous, never-ending, never-recessing reporting and analysis by the press.

I, for one, welcome the attention that journalists are already giving the 1964 elections. In our history we have erred far more on the side of casualness than of caution in the vital business of choosing leadership. We have depended far more on chance than on foresight not only in making our choices but also in determining the conditions under which the choice is made at all. We have tended too much to accept the inefficiencies characteristic of democracies as inevitable and permanent handicaps to be endured forever rather than as challenges to sensible and corrective action. If the spirited attention with which the press has been eyeing 1964 keeps up, we are not going to slouch off

This chapter is based on a speech to the journalism fraternity, Sigma Delta Chi, New York, December 3, 1960.

now, I am sure, to a passive return to outmoded techniques that the past campaign has forever branded as inadequate. Speculation about the fate of the losing party is always a classic topic for post-electoral columns. This year it has found some sturdy competition in discussions of the future of the broadcast debates.

This is an appropriate and important subject. As you know, the joint resolution (S.J. 207) making debates possible applied only to the 1960 election and only to the presidential and vice-presidential candidates. At midnight November seventh we automatically reverted to the equal time provision of Section 315 of the Communications Act, as revised, which, by requiring broadcasters to give equal time to all candidates of all parties including splinter groups and faddists, for all practical purposes outlaws broadcasts of face-to-face meetings. The question remains—and many of you have put it forcefully and well—whether we can afford to deprive ourselves of the use of any instrument we possess for broadening interest and understanding in our political campaigns. More particularly, can we afford to throw away something that worked well?

I do not think that we can. I want to take a look with you at some of the evidence that the debates were an unprecedented step forward in removing from elections the kind of blind voting behavior that is risky enough in democracies at all times but that could be disastrous in times of crisis.

There is one great commanding and overwhelming fact about the debates. It is this: For the first time in our history, partisans of *both* major political parties saw and heard *both* candidates and *both* sides of the issues. Moreover, these unprecedented broadcasts were seen by 101 million different Americans. The television audience for the average of the four debates stands at 71 million individuals—only a fraction of whom would watch either candidate individually.

You know better than I the strong emotional loyalties and the partisan attachments that all political campaigns bring out in the voters. There is nothing phenomenal in this. All human behavior is influenced by past associations, by pressures of conformity, by views and ways that, having once accepted, we are reluctant to abandon or even to hear challenged and questioned. So we are inclined to listen to those with whom we agree, to seek out evidences to support beliefs we already have, and to look for corroboratory arguments that strengthen choices we have already made. This tendency is not limited to political campaigns. Liberal publications are widely read by liberals, and conservative publications are most read by conservatives. We do not seek out challenges to positions with which we have become comfortable, however long it has been since we reexamined them.

In political action, this basic human quality is intensified. Much of the old-style campaigning of the torchlight parade era was based on a calculated effort to reinforce old emotional attitudes. It sought to discourage rather than to stimulate new awarenesses, fresh judgments, and a look at what the opposition had to say and at what the challenges and alternatives were. The political rally, for example, has always been intrinsically an occasion for the mass demonstration of approval of views already known and subscribed to by the party faithful. Its purpose was not to inform, or to create an atmosphere conducive to the appraisal of information, but to whip up attitudes capable of overcoming any temptation to judiciousness. Slogans, songs, the paraphernalia of attitudinal mobilizations were for years the indispensable props of political campaigns. You listened to your own candidate—and for social if not for personal reasons you wouldn't be caught dead listening to a speech by the opposition.

However much color this partisanship brought to the easy-going past, it is a hazardous anachronism in the grim seriousness of today's world. We can't afford it. We can't afford the blind, uncritical, automatic support of one man against another, whatever his insight, his judgment, or his qualities of leadership. We can't afford the emotional landslide that defies reason and negates the judiciousness that ought to be inherent in the grave act of choosing our leaders. I would hope very much—with some of you who have already commented on the lessons of this past campaign—that whatever else it did, it spelled the end of the time when the voters listened only to one side—the side to which they were already committed—and refused to hear the other side. This was the singular achievement of the debates as an aid to the democratic process: by their very nature they exposed the audience that tuned in to hear one man, the one it favored, to the views of the other man, the one it thought it opposed. Analyses of the vast audiences to the debates reveal that about half of them were Democrats, about one-third were Republicans, and virtually all of the remainder classified themselves as Independents.

Whatever the theory of advantages to Senator Kennedy as the lesser known of the two candidates before September 26, these figures dramatize an important compensating advantage for Vice President Nixon inasmuch as his party's strength was generally reported at approximately two-thirds that of his Democratic opponent. In other words, the better-known candidate coming from a party with substantially fewer members had to look to the majority party and the Independents for his support in order to win on November 8. In this way both candidates had something to gain from the debates.

From the candidates' point of view there is an enormous gain too— in a ratio of $3\frac{1}{2}$ to one—in sheer quantitative values favoring debates over the conventional political set speeches. Or putting it another way, the average paid political broadcast of the half-hour, night-time network variety attracted approximately 30 per cent of the audience of the average debate. The debate audiences, despite their vast size, were unusual also in the extent to which they stayed with the hour-long debates. A certain tune-out in long programs is customary in broadcasting, particularly when the content is serious and demands thoughtful attention. In the case of the debates, however, the record is extraordinary. The minute-by-minute audience tune-in to the four debates remained remarkably stable throughout the hour-long broadcasts with the average family tuning its set to the debates for 54 minutes of the hour.

There is one pair of statistics which provides a measure of public response to the debates as against the set speeches generally featuring an individual candidate. In the 1960 campaign the average half-hour paid political television network broadcast attracted approximately 30 per cent less audience than the program it replaced. The four debates, on the other hand, had audiences averaging 20 per cent larger than the entertainment programs they pre-empted.

Finally, when almost nine out of ten (89.8 per cent) television families tuned in the debates, when more than half of all television families (53.1 per cent) watched at least three of the debates, when one family out of four (26.6 per cent) tuned in all four debates, you have more than an indication of the tremendous public interest in these historic broadcasts.

All these figures dispute the speculation that either candidate did his own cause a disservice in face-to-face discussions with his opponent, because of "delivering" a greater audience than his opponent could get. The one demonstrable fact is that *both* got a much greater audience than either got alone and that each had an opportunity to speak to his opponent's followers that he would not otherwise have had at all.

Before we leave this question of audiences who saw and heard the debates, I ought to add that the nature of the audience was as important as its size. Not only did it represent similar proportions of members of the two major political parties and independents, but it cut across the whole fabric of the national population. In the subgroups we have analyzed—by age, sex, economic level, education, size of family, size of community, and geographic location—more than half of all television sets were tuned to the debates. There were no blacked out groups.

The wide and consistent attention paid by the public to the debates compared to that usually given to speeches will be readily understandable to you here. Straight exposition in any form is always the most difficult way to engage and hold the attention of anyone. Conflict, on the other hand, in ideas as in action, is intriguing and engrossing to great numbers of people. Drama has always got more attention than essays.

Early in this campaign, many observers were concerned by the comparative lack of public enthusiasm, underscored by public opinion polls, for either candidate. Yet on election day more voters went to the polls—by over 10 per cent—than ever before in our history: 68½ million compared to slightly over 62 million in 1956. Less than two-thirds of this increase can be attributed to a combination of the increased population of voting age and the addition of Alaska and Hawaii. It can be fairly concluded, then, that the debates so stimulated interest in the election and in the issues that more voters cast ballots for the presidency than ever before.

The debates not only brought an added voter participation; I submit they brought a more thoughtful participation. Ideally, the act of voting should be a judicious act, the dispassionate appraisal of contending approaches to the problems facing the nation. A thoughtless choice, representing a blind stampeding toward one man or another, is no choice at all. When it happens, the country is at the mercy of the accidental result of emotional forces. This is not to say that, as in most human actions, emotional attachments and attitudes were not at all involved in the past election. We know that they were. Nevertheless, as a whole, although this was one of the hardest fought campaigns in history—hard fought and tough—the failure of mass emotions to be the controlling factor in the election was conspicuous. And it was more than a coincidence. Certainly the debates could and did encourage the appraising element in the voting act.

It is impossible to overemphasize the importance of this in a democ-

racy where so much value is attached to the character of the man who
occupies the presidency. It was the character of Washington that set
the pattern of the executive branch, the character of Jackson that transformed our society politically, the character of Lincoln that saw the
nation through a bitter civil war. To measure a man's character is
a difficult thing. Amid the theatricalism and ballyhoo traditional in
political campaigns, it can be all but impossible. It cannot be done
satisfactorily by hearsay. And unfortunately you cannot, for purposes
of elections, wait for the verdict of history. To judge the character of
a man, you should catch him in the act of being alive, of responding
to a situation. This is the vision the Constitution-makers had in mind
when they devised the Electoral College as a means of making quality,
rather than quantity alone, the criterion of a choice. It was their clear
intention that the electors—far from being mere mathematical entities
—would choose the president not from among strangers, but from
among men known to them. This is essentially what the debates did for
all the American voters—they made the candidates known to the
people. The debates made it possible—as carefully prepared and unchallenged oratory could never do—for fundamental human qualities
to be revealed. It is true, of course, that not all the qualities of the
candidates can be revealed in such debates. It is *not* true that only
superficial, misleading, or irrelevant qualities can be revealed.

The format of the debates unquestionably had the limitations inevitable in any first breakthrough or major innovation. The interposition
of the panel was at the firm insistence of the candidates and represented a compromise with which the networks were not too happy.
The networks preferred the more traditional format in which each
candidate would question the other. But we were eager to get on with
the face-to-face broadcasts, even in the modified format, because we
believe that whatever the imperfections, they could be eliminated as
the debates evolved and it was important to take this first giant step
forward. Unquestionably in future years they will be improved. Nevertheless, the format was fundamentally the same question-and-answer
dialogue and commentary that, from Socrates' time, has been a favored
means of throwing light upon the characters and minds of men. The
charge that the debates were not only a failure but a menace, because
they did not constitute an all-revealing spotlight, is shortsighted and
shallow. The revelation of any man comes through flashes of light—
not through a single, glaring, carefully staged dissection. Any biog-
rapher or historian worth his salt has known this since the dawn of

letters. No good reporter or editor has ever forgotten it. The alternative posed by the debates on the one hand and the old campaign oratory on the other hand is simply the alternative between spontaneous, independent, unposed responses to vital problems and carefully constructed, committee-drafted, guardedly insulated declamations.

Both during the campaign and after the election, the objection arose that not only the head of government but anyone aspiring to be the head of government should be immune from questioning in public. This is the same view that for years precluded presidential press conferences and later, for many years after such conferences were instituted, forbade direct quotations from the president. In the pressure of events today, however, both the presidential press conference and direct quotes from it are generally considered as not only appropriate but necessary adjuncts to the democratic process.

I do not see how the essential point and values of the debates would be altered if one of the candidates were an incumbent president. Nor do I see any danger in a president's participating. The prime minister of England is regularly questioned by his opposition, the chief spokesman of which is usually his opponent for the office of prime minister, without any damage to the national interest. And when the British debates are thrown open, the questions are spontaneous. The opposition knows where dissent should stop. It is inconceivable to me that any man nominated by a major party in this country would not show as much sense of responsibility in debates with a president.

I can imagine circumstances, as readily as you can, when a president might be anxious to meet an aspirant to his office in debate. Six times in our history an incumbent president has been defeated. In cases where the president felt that a powerful case was being built by his opponent, or where the drift of the times and of events seemed to be against him, or where he felt that his own views were being inadequately reported or that the press was overwhelmingly against him, he might very well want to meet his opponent face to face.

But in the end this is irrelevant, for the problem centers not on the interests of the candidates but on the best interests of the voters. I cannot believe that, after the enormous contribution made by the debates in the last campaign, any responsible men and women in government will seek to resume outlawing them. It would certainly be incredible cynicism for any official to conclude that the people were entitled to see and hear candidates in face-to-face discussions only when it served the political interests of a candidate. The release of television and radio from the crippling restrictions of Section 315 of the Communications Act was an experiment this year to see if it would work—not to the advantage of one candidate over another—but to advance public interest in the campaign and to make the candidates and the issues better known.

If political action were solely a matter of logic, there would be an early and permanent revision of Section 315 of the Communications Act. If it were solely a matter of logic, the overwhelming success of the experiment this year would banish completely and forever the onerous equal time restrictions—for all elective offices. But I do not need to tell you that politics have never been overburdened with logic. Not one or two but a dozen political maneuvers are bound to crop up to prevent or to delay the necessary remedial legislation. It will be very easy for those who oppose this action to do so quietly and out of sight, hoping by delay to lose this potential for the public good. And— as in the case of Resolution 207, without which we should never have had the debates this year—all of us, print as well as electronic journalists, will have to keep this issue alive and before the people, until every such maneuver and delaying tactic is exposed and overcome.

I hope very much—and I have every confidence—that our senior partners will once again take the lead on this issue. If you do not, then the process by which we choose our leadership will take a giant step backwards, when we can least afford it. But if you do, if you bring to this effort the same insight, the same persistency and the same emphasis you brought to the battle for temporary relief, then once again American democracy will be forever in your debt.

5

Production Diary of the Debates

HERBERT A. SELTZ & RICHARD D. YOAKAM

THE FORUM for the 1960 presidential election was the living room of the American home. Because the debates were televised, few could avoid contact with them. Every word said on these programs was weighed by the editorial writers and pundits. Every motion made in front of the television camera was examined for meaning. Every eye-blink, every bead of perspiration, every exhibition of strength or weakness, sureness or doubt, was magnified as never before. Whether voting decisions were conditioned by what the voters saw has been the concern of others in this book. Our subject is the examination of the influences and pressures which ultimately shaped the four debates into what they were. Through study of the debates as TV programs, and through interviews with the production personnel, technical operators, network executives, political advisers, and observers, we have brought together this production diary of four television programs which became milestones in U. S. political history.[1]

If anyone thinks it was a simple matter to arrange a face-to-face meeting between presidential candidates, he is unaware of the complexities and impact of the mass media.[2] It was not just a matter of agreeing to dates and then showing up at the appointed TV studio on time. On the one hand, the American broadcasting industry was able to present such debates legally for the first time and was painfully conscious of the possible far-reaching consequences.[3] On the other hand, the candidates—both seasoned radio and television performers —and their advisers, both political and technical, realized the tremendous impact of the media with its "winner-take-all" implications.

Throughout the discussions of Section 315, it was clear that the networks were going to provide extensive free time for the candidates in the 1960 election, either under existing "equal time" provisions or under the desired suspension. Some of the proposals made by the networks included time for the candidates to appear on existing or specially designed public affairs programs. The major proposals by CBS, ABC, and NBC for the debate series in this campaign were first made by network officials in the spring of 1960.[4] The networks' formal proposals were made to both candidates immediately after Nixon's nomination in Chicago, July 27. That same evening NBC announced its "Great Debates" proposal. Apparently the NBC offer reached Kennedy first, and he accepted eagerly and without qualifications.[5] Nixon stated his acceptance through his press secretary, Herbert Klein, the same day, and confirmed it three days later. The other network proposals were also quickly accepted. Since both candidates favored the debates, it is not surprising that the House of Representatives approved Senate Joint Resolution 207 (suspending Section 315) on August 24, during its post-convention session.

THE FORMAT

The "Meet the Press" proposal, the debate idea, and Vice President Nixon's formal acceptance wire all played major roles in determining the formats for the programs which were planned during the next six weeks. The details were hammered out in twelve meetings between a committee of network news executives and the representatives named by the candidates. For the networks, the committee consisted of William McAndrew, Executive Vice President for News, NBC; Sig Mickelson, President, CBS News Inc.; John Daly, Vice President for News, ABC; and Joseph Keating, Vice President, MBS. Leonard Reinsch served as the chief adviser for Senator Kennedy, and William Wilson was his production adviser for radio and television; Fred C. Scribner Jr., Under Secretary of the Treasury, served as Nixon's chief representative, with Herbert Klein and Caroll P. Newton as advisers for radio-TV, and Edward (Ted) Rogers as technical adviser for radio and TV during the campaign.[6]

The first meeting took place at the Waldorf-Astoria Hotel in New York on August 9. It was agreed then that "debates were desirable," that they should be on all networks simultaneously, one hour in length, end by October 21, and be worked into the candidates' travel schedules

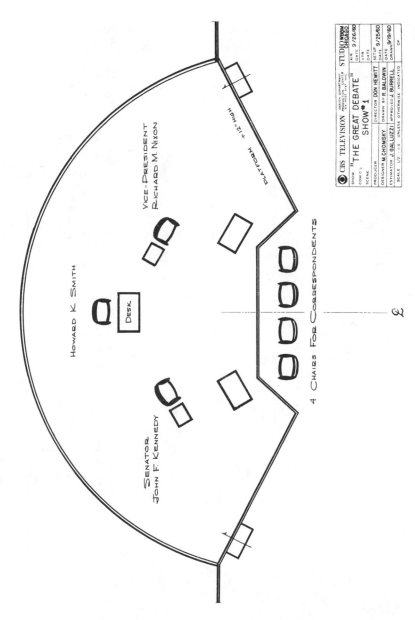

⬤ CBS TELEVISION   DESIGN DEPARTMENT
PRODUCTION CENTER
524 WEST 57 NYC

STUDIO WBBM CHICAGO

SHOW "THE GREAT DEBATE"	AIR DATE 9/26/60
COM'C'L	VTR DATE
SCENE SHOW #1	
PRODUCER	DIRECTOR DON HEWITT	SETUP 9/25/60
DESIGNER M.CHOMSKY	DRAWN BY R. BALDWIN	DATE
ESTIMATOR J. GALLUZZI	APPROVED J. BURRELL	DRAWN 9/19/60
SCALE 1/2" 1-0 UNLESS OTHERWISE INDICATED	OF

First debate floor plan: CBS's original concept for the setting for the debates was not materially changed by NBC or ABC when their turns came. The circular wall, candidates on a raised platform, a podium for each candidate, and a setting for the reporters so they would be facing the candidates.

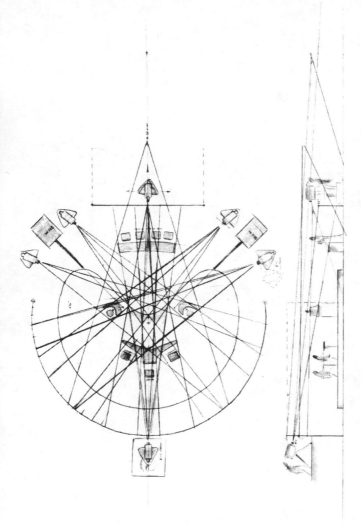

THE GREAT DEBATE · #2 · WASH. D.C. 10-7-60 (N.B.C.)

Second debate floor plan: Hjalmar Hermanson's original sketch of the floor plan, with camera angles, for the second debate. Lower portion is an elevation showing one candidate standing with the moderator and the other candidate seated with the press panel to the right. Camera on the left shoots the press panel through the porthole in the set wall. Camera on the right shoots the candidates over the heads of the press panel. The upper portion shows Hermanson's concern with providing a set which would give the director a wide variety of shots. Triangular shaped items are cameras, the winged desk is on the left, press chairs and table on the right, candidates' podia are the moon-shaped items in the center.

by mutual agreement.[7] The Democrats wanted a later closing date but agreed to October 21. Subsequent meetings between the candidates' representatives helped to determine the dates. And, according to network representatives, the candidates' teams also talked about the format.[8] Nixon, in his acceptance wire, gave the following general outline of what he wanted: "joint television appearances of the presidential candidates should be conducted as full and free exchange of views, without prepared texts or notes, and without interruptions . . . and with time for questioning by panels of accredited journalists."[9] The network committee also came up with proposals. All of these ideas were discussed at a meeting in the Mayflower Hotel in Washington on August 31, where the formats were established although, apparently, not agreed upon.

Formats for the first and fourth debates were quickly approved: opening statements, questions from the news panel, and closing statements. Kennedy drew the first position in the first debate, a turn of fate his advisers considered very important. Nixon, therefore, went first on the last debate. The candidates' representatives also gave the networks the dates and the cities agreed upon. The place of the second debate was later changed twice, and its date was moved up twenty-four hours.[10]

The format for the first and fourth meetings was the choice of the candidates' representatives. At the August 31 meeting the networks, led by Mickelson, proposed that the candidates engage in what is known as "Oregon Debate."[11] Under this form, debaters present opening statements, then are permitted to question each other directly. This suggestion was rejected by the candidates' representatives.[12] Neither the networks nor the candidates' teams were in favor of an outright debate, on the ground that it would not hold an audience. Furthermore, a major consideration for a good debate must be a relatively narrow, clear-cut issue, on which the debaters can take definite stands. However, the candidates' representatives were frank to admit no such clear-cut issue existed in the campaign. While the candidates disagreed on methods and approach, degree and application of policy on both foreign and domestic issues, their representatives and the networks feared that use of a debate format to present such "shades of grey" arguments would result in rapidly diminishing interest from the audience. In the immediate background were the West Virginia primary debates between Kennedy and Hubert Humphrey. Both men had been overly polite and the results had been disappointing. The debate format, in the view of at least one of the leading representatives, held hidden traps because accuracy of statements could not be checked immediately, and because one of the candidates, in the heat of an argument, could make an injudicious remark which would have immediate international repercussions.[13]

All of these considerations seemed to have prompted the candidates' representatives to insist upon the interposition of a panel of newsmen who would ask the questions. The representatives of both the candidates and the networks felt that such a format was well known to the American TV audience. To be fair, it must be pointed out that Nixon's telegram suggests a form closer to a straight debate than that used in the actual programs. The "Meet the Press" type of program, however, was specifically urged by Nixon's representatives during the negotiations. Kennedy's representatives said that they were not as interested in the format as in getting the Senator on the same TV program with the Vice President. They realized Kennedy's skill with the question and answer setup, and were really happier with it than with a straight debate format.[14]

Final format of the second and third debates was not established at the August 31 meeting. The candidates' representatives wanted the form that finally appeared on the air—question to candidate A, answer, comment by candidate B, question to candidate B, answer, comment by candidate A. The network representatives objected to this form, claiming it would be confusing to the audience and would not permit much follow-up or expansion of views. They continued to battle for the "Oregon Debate" system up to a few days before the second debate went on the air in Washington; but they never succeeded.

Concerning the subject areas of the first and fourth debates, it is not clear how the idea of having one program devoted solely to domestic issues and another solely to foreign policy evolved, but once the idea of having a news panel ask the questions was established, it must have become clear that some control over the direction of at least some of the programs would have to be exercised.

With the moderator-news panel format rather firmly entrenched, the question of who would serve in these roles also became an issue. The various factions wrestled with the idea of using a public figure as moderator. Along with other notables, the President of the American Bar Association was suggested. In the end, all sides agreed on a TV professional to be selected by the network responsible for a given debate.

The selection of the news panel was a more difficult problem. Since the networks were putting on the programs, they insisted that the panels for programs one and four be made up of network newsmen, but agreed to 50-50 representation between the electronic and print media on debates two and three. Not more than ten days before the first debate, however, Press Secretaries Pierre Salinger and Herbert Klein opened the question again with a protest—that the lack of newspaper reporters on the panels was discriminatory. But the networks stuck to their guns, and told Klein and Salinger to devise a method for picking the print media representatives on debates two and three. An elaborate lottery system was established by the press secretaries to provide for newspaper, wire service, and magazine representation as the argument concerning discrimination went on right up to the day of the first debate. There is evidence that Senator Kennedy was pushing most strongly for more newspaper representation; the Republicans do not seem to have been as much involved in this discussion. Immediately after the first debate, Klein, who was prompted by requests, suggested the possibility of representation on the panel of special interest groups such as the civil rights advocates. The networks rejected the suggestion on the ground that it would be impossible to satisfy all.

Shortly after the August 9 agreement that there would be debates, at least one network received inquiries from prospective sponsors as to whether the programs would be for sale. When the question was raised by House Interstate and Foreign Commerce Committee chairman Oren Harris, NBC publicly explained that it would consider sponsorship of the programs unless the candidates objected.[15] At the August 31 meeting, it was announced that there would be no sponsorship.

Each of the decisions and discussions we have outlined was reflected in the productions as they appeared on the air. The overriding attention to detail, the attempts on all sides to add a touch here and gain an advantage there was a prelude to what everyone—with 20-20 hindsight—now refers to as "four simple panel shows; but what a cast!"

Opening Night

First Debate
Date: September 26, 1960, 9:30 EST, CBS
Place: TV #1, WBBM-TV, Chicago, Illinois
Producer-Director: Don Hewitt, CBS, New York
Designers: Lou Dorfsman and M. Chomsky, CBS, New York
Lighting: Bob Barry, CBS, New York

Makeup: Frances Arvold, CBS, New York
Timer: Sig Mickelson, President, CBS News Inc.
Technical Supervisors: Robert Hammer and Robert Sammon for CBS; Al Pierce for WBBM-TV
Moderator: Howard K. Smith, CBS
Panel: Robert Fleming, ABC; Stuart Novins, CBS; Sander Vanocur, NBC; Charles Warren, MBS
Format: Domestic issues. Opening statements of eight minutes, questions and answers covering statements and domestic issues, closing statements of three minutes.

The task of being the first network ever to telecast and broadcast a live debate between two presidential candidates fell, by lot, to CBS. Chicago was picked as the site for the first debate in order to accommodate the candidates—particularly Kennedy's campaign schedule. The CBS-owned-and-operated station, WBBM-TV, had facilities which were ideal for the occasion. Furthermore, WBBM had the necessary room to accommodate the traveling press corps. WBBM-TV studio TV-1, which is 80 by 65 feet, includes a large fly area over one end of the studio, a modern light control board with complete dimming and patching facilities, and is in all respects a first-rate production facility.

On September 8, after drawing the assignment, CBS officials had a general production meeting. Agreement was reached on the matters of positioning the candidates and the news panel, and the general actions which would take place during the debate. In addition, they agreed that a special set would be built for the program. CBS President Frank Stanton took a close personal interest in the program and in particular, the set. Stanton is well known for his interests in design and the arts, and the set was designed for his personal approval.[16]

Lou Dorfsman was assigned the job of coordinating the set design, which CBS wanted as simple as possible to avoid distracting the viewers. Dorfsman said, "The set would be considered in sophisticated design circles as a fine set; even though it was not an exercise in outstanding TV set design, but an exercise in staying away from the two important elements—the candidates themselves."[17] The chairs for the candidates were personally selected by Dr. Stanton; they were Hans Wegner chairs borrowed from Stanton's executive office. The total effect attempted was one of "clean, uncluttered, modern design."

A week later, in Chicago, the final sketch of the set was shown to the candidates' representatives and it was approved. The background

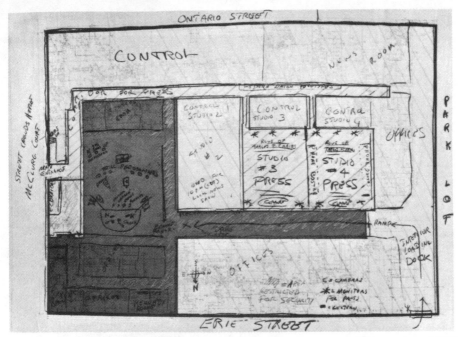

Photo courtesy of CBS

Debate traffic control: The first floor of WBBM-TV, Chicago, showing the traffic and security control for the first debate. The shaded area is the "red," or most secure, area, which includes the debate studio, the candidates' offices, and the entrance ramp along which the candidates' cars drove.

First minutes: View of the first debate, September 26, 1960. Senator Kennedy's image as he makes his opening remarks is seen on the control room monitor, lower right. Timekeeper Sig Mickelson is shown in center foreground, Vice President Nixon is seated right of center. The clock shows the debate has been on the air about two minutes. Men shown seated just below the candidates are members of the press panel.

Photo courtesy of CBS

Photo courtesy of CBS

During set and lighting adjustment: CBS President Frank Stanton, kneeling left, studies the lighting effects on the set wall as shown through a TV monitor. Kneeling right is Lou Dorfsman, CBS advertising and sales promotion creative director, who supervised set design. Standing are, left to right, Leonard Reinsch, Kennedy's chief TV adviser, and Don Hewitt, CBS debate producer-director.

Reporters cover the TV debate: A portion of the huge corps of reporters who covered the second debate at NBC Washington, October 7, 1960. TV monitors, through which the reporters viewed the debate, are set up against the outside wall of the debate studio.

Photo courtesy of NBC

chosen was a painted pattern of squares, given perspective by shading in a light grey color. This color was intended to equal No. 5—a middle tone—on the TV grey scale. The set had a curved back wall, 9 feet high by 39 feet long. The entire set—back wall, desks, chairs, podia— was placed on a platform eighteen inches high. In addition to the chairs for the candidates, there was a chair for the moderator, and lecterns which can best be described as austere music stands. The original design also included a large, moulded, spread-winged eagle symbol, which was to be mounted in the center of the back wall.[18]

The set was built in New York, set up in the CBS scene shop at the CBS Production Center, and viewed by various people, including the set designer. It was not seen by the producer-director or the lighting director, nor was it viewed on camera in New York. Such previews, as we will see, could have saved much time and trouble.

The set arrived in Chicago Saturday, September 24. Robert Link, WBBM-TV Production Manager, brought in a crew and the set was erected in TV #1 that day and evening. As Director Don Hewitt watched the setup, he immediately decided that the background tone was too light, and he ordered it repainted to bring it to the grey scale of #5 as originally prescribed. Hewitt, Dorfsman, and Stanton then became involved, along with the candidates' representatives, in a long series of discussions and changes in the dressing of the set which took almost two hundred man-hours to complete, and covered the next thirty-six hours in time.[19] Major aspects of this re-dressing included, in order: repainting the set to a darker tone at about 11 A.M. Sunday, September 25, relaying and restitching of the green carpeting which covered the candidates' platform, and building new furniture for the principals and the moderator.

The candidates' representatives asked that moderator Smith be seated behind a desk so that there would be more separation between the candidates and they requested that small tables with carafes be placed near the candidates' chairs. Since the addition of this furniture confused the original design concept, there was much resistance on the part of the CBS executives. Several people went looking for furniture in Chicago. The designer drew plans, and furniture was built in the WBBM shop. This home-made furniture was later rejected. The decorative eagle design for the back of the set was removed. Early in the setup period, Hewitt had pictures taken of the set from the various shooting angles he proposed to use. These pictures were processed Saturday evening, and Hewitt met Kennedy and Reinsch at the

Chicago airport Sunday morning to show them the pictures, spending about fifteen minutes discussing the production details with the candidate. He had no similar meeting with Nixon, although Hewitt had requested it.

The most complicated set change was not decided upon until about noon on the day of the debate, and was not completed until late afternoon. Dr. Stanton, when he viewed the set on camera after it had been repainted, still felt that the background was too "busy." A gauze scrim, long enough to cover the entire curved back wall of the set, was rented. Since the back wall was curved, the mounting of the scrim was no small task.[20]

Robert Barry, senior lighting director for CBS, was assigned to the lighting of the debates about two weeks in advance. He had seen a model and a sketch of the set in New York, but had not viewed it at the time of the trial setup in the shop. He arrived in Chicago, Friday, September 23, and "roughed in" his lighting while the set was being installed Sunday. But a detailed lighting job was held up because of the difficulties in redressing the set, and by a controversy between Hewitt and the candidates' representatives over the placement of the lecterns for the candidates. Hewitt wanted them closer together, and kept moving them to the accompaniment of protests from Rogers and Wilson.

Barry was in on the decision to darken the set. He, too, recognized that the lightness of the background would make it difficult for the television tube to differentiate between the flesh tones of the candidates' faces and the grey scale value of the set. TV #1 is equipped with a five-scene preset lighting control board with more than enough dimmers for each light to be connected to a separate dimmer. Barry said he approached the lighting job with the idea that it would be conventional. He put up key, fill, and back lights, and lit the background so that its light intensity could be controlled separately. Bruce Allan, one of Nixon's advisers, asked that Barry avoid "modeling" when lighting the Vice President; that he avoid sharply defined facial contours and shadows. This was done. By the time Barry had placed all of his lights, the set was covered with about 125 foot-candles of intensity. Nixon's advisers had requested the addition of two 500-watt spotlights shining up into the Vice President's eyes; one aimed at the level of his seated position, the other at the podium position. These were placed on the floor about twelve feet in front of the platform and were directed upward at about a 35-degree angle. Nixon's chief adviser, Ted Rogers, had prescribed these lights for Nixon wherever he went. From Rogers' point of view, there was nothing unusual about the addition of these two lights. Rogers, who told the authors that Nixon was an extremely difficult subject to light, said, "He's critical on television; there's an enormous contrast between his very pale, white translucent skin, and his jet black hair."[21]

Barry said the Nixon advisers pressed him for the addition of the floor lights during most of the day of the debate, and that they were added by 5 P.M., when the lighting job was finished. Barry was opposed to adding the lights because the height of the platform and the relatively low angle of the cameras would have forced the cameras to shoot upward and into Nixon's eyes anyway. However, he acceded to the request, and all parties said they were satisfied with the lights, set, and general production details at least two hours before air time.

About 7:30, one hour before air time, the candidates arrived at WBBM and were driven inside the building along a wide production corridor behind the studio. Nixon arrived first, Kennedy only a few minutes later, and each was greeted by the executives of all the networks. When Nixon went on camera for a pre-show check, his representatives were in the control room. They asked for certain lighting changes to reduce a shine on his temple and for the floor lights to be raised in intensity to increase his eye light. CBS personnel and the Kennedy advisers looked at Kennedy for about the same amount of time—three or four minutes—and made no changes.[22]

Although Frances Arvold, a CBS make-up expert who had been sent out from New York to make up the candidates, was on hand, both refused her services. Because of Nixon's heavy beard, Everett Hart, another of his advisers, applied a commercial product, Max Factor's "Lazy Shave," a pancake cosmetic, to Nixon's face. In the light of later reactions to Mr. Nixon's looks, it is interesting to note that Barry and Miss Arvold during the program discussed the fact that Nixon would have profited from professional make-up services, while the candidates' representatives were satisfied with his looks.[23] Kennedy had a rather heavy tan from open-car campaigning in California, and his advisers felt he needed no make-up at all. Rogers had recommended Nixon use a sunlamp as far back as August 15, but there is no indication that he took the advice.

There was little discussion of what the candidates would wear; both had originally chosen light to medium tone grey suits. Kennedy's advisers changed him into a dark blue suit after noting the light set background. Nixon wore the grey suit, as planned. At the last minute, the Kennedy people sent back to the hotel for a blue shirt, which he changed into after arriving at WBBM-TV.[24]

It is clear, both from what he said and the philosophy of his approach, that Don Hewitt thought of the first debate as a special event. He had had thirteen years of experience as a director with CBS, including an extensive special event role, much of it under extremely difficult conditions. It is interesting to note that Hewitt was named producer-director for the first debate, whereas the other networks split the job between two or more men. While this is not unusual it did put a heavy load on Hewitt. Hewitt said: "I realized that the most important function of my job as producer was not to be a producer, in other words, not to make a television program out of this. Just to make it possible for the people sitting at home to watch the significant event, probably the most significant event they had ever watched, and to fight the temptation to turn it into a show. I would have preferred an audience, that this debate take place in Madison Square Garden, and that we cover it as a special event, not as a television show."[25]

Hewitt even extended this audience feeling to the press panel. They were seated with their backs to the camera, "they were sort of the front row. The [home] audience was sitting back behind the cameras, and the reporters were sort of asking questions that the audience would have asked had they been there."[26] In the shots that he took, Hewitt was also trying to shorten the distance between the candidates and the home viewers—"I tried to have the cameras react more or less like Joe Average Citizen would have reacted if he had been able to sit there rather than have it fed to him on a coaxial cable."

Because the candidates were placed so far apart on the platform, Hewitt was unable to get a shot including both candidates other than the wide "cover" shot used at the beginning and the end. Later directors, using more cameras, solved this problem with set designs which gave more protection on the sides. A major factor in Hewitt's difficulty in getting "two-shots"* was a technical decision, that only fixed focal length lenses would be used on the studio cameras. Hewitt had requested "zoom lenses" for his main cameras. The CBS technicians, however, believed that the fixed focal length lenses would provide a "sharper" picture, and overruled Hewitt's request. So the main cameras were equipped with lenses of 17 and 15 inch and 135 and 90 milli-

* A one-shot shows one person; a two-shot shows two persons.

Photo courtesy of NBC

Kennedy becomes a lighting expert: During the pre-program lighting check on the second debate, Senator Kennedy objected to the number of lights on him, compared to the number on Vice President Nixon. Scratching his head on the extreme left is debate moderator Frank McGee.

Second debate action: Viewed over the heads of the press panel, Vice President Nixon waits for a question from the reporters. The camera taking the picture of the reporters is visible through the open porthole in the set wall (an innovation in the production of the second debate) just above and to the left of Nixon.

Photo courtesy of NBC

Photo courtesy of ABC

The two third debates: (above) The Lincoln-Cherney debate. Dan Lincoln, left, the stand-in for Vice President Nixon during the third debate pre-program lighting and camera checkout eyes Richard Cherney, Senator Kennedy's stand-in. The men are 3,000 miles apart, but here united on one TV screen. (below) The real debaters as they appeared on the air, Vice President Nixon in Los Angeles, and Senator Kennedy in New York. (photographed from TV screen)

Photo courtesy of ABC

meter focal lengths. The two center cameras used mostly the 90 mm. shot, the two main cameras on either side used the longer lenses for the close-ups of the candidates.[27]

Hewitt positioned his two main cameras at either end of the press panel, so that each candidate would be facing toward the other when they talked to the cameras. The other two cameras were placed behind the press panel, and took shots which included the reporters and the candidates. The lack of an easily obtainable "two-shot" forced Hewitt to take a "one-shot reaction shot."* This caused great concern to the candidates' representatives, and may have been at least partially responsible for the public reaction to Nixon's looks which developed after the first debate. The question of whether or not to use a reaction shot had been discussed extensively before the broadcast. Hewitt argued in this way: "I tried to put myself in the position of the viewer, and there were certain times when if the guy at home had been in the studio, I'm sure he would have looked over to see what Kennedy's reaction was to what Nixon was saying, and vice versa . . . I made no conscious effort to balance, I just called them as I saw them."[28]

Nixon's chief production adviser, Ted Rogers, had objected strenuously to any plans of using one-shot reaction shots. His objections were based on two things. First, his recognition that "Nixon's physical image on television was critical." Second, that one-shot reaction shots took the audience's attention away from what was being said.[29] It is apparent that Rogers and Hewitt argued a long time over the one-shot reaction shot. Hewitt finally took the question to Dr. Stanton and Mickelson for a decision. They supported Hewitt, and told him to shoot the show as he saw it. Kennedy's advisers favored reaction shots of any kind.

In effect, the argument continued even during the broadcast. Although the networks had agreed that each candidate could have two representatives in the control room during the broadcast, Hewitt had made clear that they would not be allowed to talk to him while the program was on the air. However, during the program Bill Wilson, in what Hewitt says was "a kidding manner," told Hewitt he owed Kennedy more reaction shots. As Hewitt described the conversation, he replied: "What do you mean, I've cut away from Kennedy more than I've cut away from Nixon . . . he [Wilson] said that's what I mean, we like

---

* A reaction shot shows one person's reaction when another person is speaking.

it when you cut away from Kennedy and show Nixon's reaction."
Wilson said, "Reaction shots are one of my loves; we were there to use
TV as a medium; I felt we ought to do it as well as possible."[30]

The Nixon camp had three more requests, two concerning shots and
one concerning the camera tally lights. Rogers had asked that Hewitt
avoid all left profile shots of the Vice President. As it happened, no
profile shots were used anyway. And, shortly before air time, Nixon
himself asked that Hewitt avoid taking a reaction shot while he was
wiping perspiration from his face. Although Hewitt assured Nixon he
would honor the request, one such action did appear on the program.
It came, on a wide shot, when Nixon wiped his face with his
handkerchief while waiting for a panelist to finish a question. Although
Hewitt had planned to have the tally lights turned off, he left them on
at the request of Nixon's advisers.

The timing of the program was given considerable attention. Robert
Hammer, of the CBS engineering department, had designed and built
special cueing devices. These were similar in size to a teleprompter,
and were mounted on top of the cameras. Using a system of colored
lights and numbers, these boxes warned the candidates when they had
one minute, thirty seconds, and no time left. The cue-boxes were controlled by CBS News President Sig Mickelson, who kept electric timers
on the candidates and saw to it that the warning lights were turned
on in proper sequence. In addition, a stage manager was located in
the studio with sets of cue-cards, which could have been used in case
the cue-boxes failed to work. The same cueing instruments were used
throughout the debates. Mickelson was in the studio, and there was
only one hitch in the plan. There was no way to tell moderator Smith
how much time was left, and Mickelson shouted it to him when Smith
asked for time, which may have been the only unplanned moment in
the entire four debates as far as the networks were concerned.

Howard K. Smith, the moderator, was to serve as program guide.
He had to set the scene for the audience including the reading of the
all-important "ground rules," to introduce and acknowledge the press
panel and to provide directions where necessary. He kept the order
of questioning straight—an order which was agreed upon, and he was
prepared to interrupt the proceedings to assure equal time to both
candidates. He went outside the simple task of announcing the order
twice: first, motioning to Senator Kennedy to stand and walk to his
rostrum for the first question from the panel; second, calling for the
amount of time left. Smith, Hewitt, and the panel had met earlier in

the day to affirm the order of questions, but, of course, not the content of the questions.[31]

Obviously, the head-on meeting of the two presidential candidates attracted attention. Hundreds of reporters for all media were present to watch and report on the program itself, what the candidates said, and to interpret, analyze, and record the event both as a political milestone and as a moment in history. Then too, the networks—because this was the first joint venture—had their highest executives on hand to greet the candidates; technicians were numerous both for the broadcast itself and for the communications necessities of the press. Caterers were brought in to serve the press, crew, and VIP's. And the candidates had their own entourage, including guests. WBBM originally planned to use its Studio 4 to accommodate the reporters, installing TV monitors, telephone and teletype circuits and instruments, running transcript facilities, and food service. So many reporters asked for accreditation (200 reporters had been expected, and 380 turned up), that another studio of the same size was opened and identical facilities provided.

It would not be a wild estimate to say that between 600 and 800 people were in the building when the program went on the air. CBS assigned specialists from its press information department to work with the Chicago police and the Secret Service in handling traffic and security problems. The WBBM building was divided up into six different zones; badges admitting people to the various zones on the basis of their needs were struck off. The hottest zone—the "red" area—was in the studio, the control room, and the office area assigned to the two candidates. Only those people who were directly connected with the broadcast were allowed in this area, i.e., the candidates and their advisers. Reporters and photographers covering the event were not allowed in the studio during the broadcast, with the exception of a small special press and still photo pool group. Three reporters, two for the wire services and one for the magazines, and five photographers were permitted in the studio during the broadcast, but were restricted to a specially marked area.[32] The rest of the press group viewed the program from the other studios over a battery of TV monitors. A large group of photographers were permitted in the studio prior to air time, to photograph the candidates on the set.

The VIP's, after greeting the candidates, went to the executive office suite and watched the program from there, except for NBC Board Chairman Robert Sarnoff and CBS Chairman William Paley, who stood in the back of the control room for part of the broadcast. They had no active part in the broadcast itself. Dr. Stanton also went into the control room for a time, and was observed taking pictures with his own miniature camera. There was nothing remarkable about the top executives being there; after all, it was "opening night," and a signally important one for the broadcasting industry.[33]

WBBM-TV technical personnel, supplemented by CBS technicians and supervisors from New York, handled the electronic problems with special care. Technically it was not a complicated program to produce. No special equipment was needed, and while a four-camera, two mike-boom program was a full effort for WBBM-TV, station personnel had presented many programs with more technical complications. Great care was taken in selecting the equipment used. The image orthicon tubes were specially chosen from stock. The candidates' voices were picked up from RCA "BK-5" microphones mounted on standard booms, and an identical microphone and boom were set up in the studio on standby. The panel of reporters and Smith wore "lavalier" microphones. In addition to the full crews assigned, many other technicians were present in case of an emergency. As a precautionary measure, AT&T had long-lines service personnel in the building.

During the day of the debate, the technicians had spent a lot of time "balancing" the four cameras so that all had the same picture quality. The lenses were stopped down to between f 11 and f 16, which is a slightly smaller lens setting than WBBM normally uses.[34] With all cameras balanced technically, video control operator Joe Grisanti thought the addition of the floor lights for Mr. Nixon tended to change the quality of pictures of the Vice President. Grisanti told the authors, "This was done at the expense of the grey scale; consequently, we had no blacks in the picture. We tried to compensate by dropping the black level, the average level of the picture down; so that we were in effect clipping part of the lower grey scale in trying to bring out some contrast in the picture." The Kennedy picture, therefore, by technical assessment, had a better grey scale, or in lay terms, more contrast.

It is interesting to note that because of, or despite, the extreme care taken about production details, they became front-page news after the first debate. Perhaps for the first time in television history professional information such as the make-up worn by a performer and the number of lights used on a television program were matters of public discussion. Much, if not all, of the general reaction in the press dealt with Nixon's appearance and the visual impact of the program. Reporters

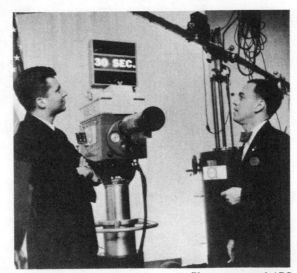

The production rivals: William Wilson, left, Kennedy's TV production adviser, and Ted Rogers, right, Nixon's TV man, in a conference before the fourth debate. Shown on top of the TV camera is one of the time-warning devices placed on all the cameras during all the debates.

Not all the pictures were on TV: A part of the photo corps which was allowed into the studio before the start of the third debate. Vice President Nixon, right, and Senator Kennedy posed for the pictures before the debates because only a few pool photographers were allowed in the studios during the broadcasts.

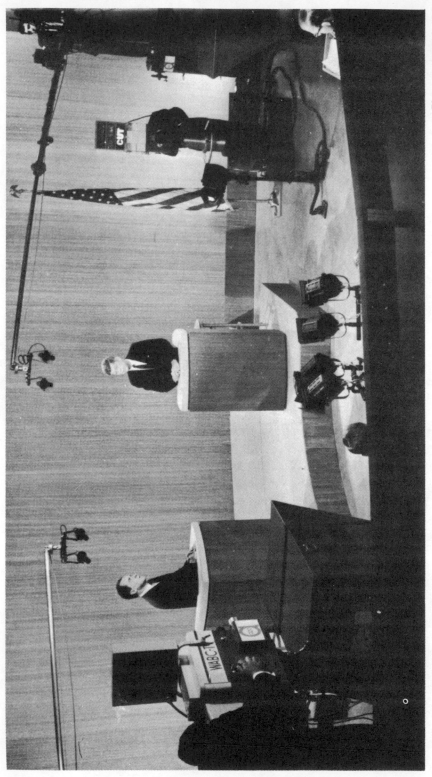

Photo courtesy of ABC

Closest together: During the fourth debate, the candidates were moved closer together on the platform. In the center the light fixtures are shown duplicated, an ABC safety precaution. The time-warning device on the camera to the right shows Vice President Nixon has run out of time.

continually mentioned that Nixon looked "tired, drawn and that he appeared to be ill." One Republican leader said Nixon must have been made up by people with Democratic leanings, and then the storm broke over CBS' head. The *Chicago Daily News* put reporter Richard Stoud onto the story of Nixon's appearance, and Stoud found John Hall, business agent of the Make-up Artists and Hair Stylists of America New York local willing to say the make-up job was very bad and could not have been the work of a professional make-up artist or union member. The Stoud story was headlined "Was Nixon Sabotaged by TV Make-up Artists?" and was widely reprinted. CBS received the brunt of the reaction, but its defense was undeniable: no CBS person had anything to do with Nixon's make-up—as the authors have already detailed—and subsequently, the *Daily News* clarified its story with quotes from press secretary Herb Klein that Nixon's make-up had been applied by one of his advisers.[35] For a day or two everyone was also a lighting expert, and Klein even blamed the TV cameras for Nixon's looks.

The fact is that Nixon was not feeling well the day of the first debate; he had appeared before a hostile union audience in Chicago that morning, and had been running a temperature most of the day. He had lost weight during his convalescence from a knee operation early in September, and had been campaigning hard. To quote Ted Rogers, "No TV camera, no make-up man can hide bone weariness, physical fatigue. He was actually sick, he had a fever. Because Nixon did not give viewers the expected performance . . . deliver . . . the predetermined mental picture of what they expected, they looked around to find out what was the matter . . . he was not the 'fighting commando' of the Republican cause. So for the first time, they were more conscious of his appearance than of what he was saying."[36]

Probably professional make-up services would have helped. Nixon's appearance was especially critical on reaction shots. He looked to many, including the authors, to be uncomfortable, unsure of himself. In reaction shots Nixon's eyes darted around, perspiration was clearly noticeable on his chin, and with the tight shots used by Hewitt these things were more obvious.

Kennedy's advisers had rested and briefed him during the day, and had avoided all public commitments with the exception of a brief appearance before the same union audience that Nixon had addressed earlier. Kennedy came through on the broadcast as a strong, self-assured personality. In the reaction shots Kennedy was seen looking at Nixon with an intense concentration, a look which gave the attitude, again to the authors, of command and comfort in the situation.

First Debate: Program Analysis

OPENING: Wide shot including moderator Howard K. Smith; Vice President Nixon seated right, Senator Kennedy left. Smith continuity establishes program, introduces Nixon and Kennedy on extreme close-up. At 00:20 Smith in the same opening wide shot reads rules, introduces Kennedy for opening statement; Kennedy rises and walks to rostrum; cut to close-up of Kennedy.

SHOTS: *Candidates:* Earliest shots are tight, barely including necktie knot; later shot selection includes chest or "top-button-of-the-coat" and one including lectern shelf and supporting stand.

Newsmen: Following opening statements reporters are introduced as they swivel their chairs around to acknowledge the camera; shot revealing candidates set in background. During questions shot is over the head and shoulders of the newsmen with the candidate listening in the background. The attention focused on the candidate.

Reactions: All reaction shots are one-shots of the candidate who is not speaking. There are 11 of Kennedy for a total of 118 seconds, and 9 of Nixon for a total of 85 seconds. First reaction shot at 07:02, during Kennedy's opening statement. The next at 10:35, during Nixon's opening statement, and there are two other reaction shots of Kennedy during Nixon's opening statement.

CLOSING: From one-shot of the last speaker, Kennedy, to one-shot of Smith, and on the cue: "Good night from Chicago," cut to wide shot over the panel, which pulls back to an even wider shot showing all four newsmen, the complete set and studio personnel and equipment. Over this shot, two graphics, containing identification of the three television networks, are superimposed.

COMMENT: Hewitt was free-wheeling in his approach and execution; reaction shots were numerous and paced with the content; additional candidate reactions were gained with shots of the candidates listening to the newsmen. Audio was without flaw.

HEAT, LIGHT, AND NERVES

Second Debate
Date: October 7, 1960, 7:30 EDST, NBC
Place: Studio A, WRC-TV, Washington, D. C.

Producer: Julian Goodman, Vice President, News, NBC, New York

Director: Frank Slingland, NBC, Washington

Designer: Hjalmar Hermanson, NBC, New York

Lighting: Leon Chromak, NBC, Washington

Makeup: Bob O'Bradovich, NBC, New York

Timers: Elmer Lower, News Director, NBC, Washington; Russ Tornabene, News Supervisor, NBC, Washington

Technical Supervisors: William H. Trevarthen, NBC, New York; John Rogers, NBC, Washington

Moderator: Frank McGee, NBC

Panel: Edward P. Morgan, ABC; Paul Nivin, CBS; Alvin Spivak, UPI; Hal Levy, *Newsday*

Format: News panel, unlimited to subject matter, no formal statements; 2½ minutes to answer questions; 1½ minutes for rebuttal comment by other candidate

If there was tension bred of newness and unfamiliarity during the first debate in Chicago, it is probable that there was even more tension before the second because of the sensitivity of the candidates to the effects of the first debate on the voters and politicians. NBC drew the responsibility for production of the second debate, and key NBC personnel had observed the production of the first debate. NBC was determined to iron out the wrinkles that developed at Chicago. In two memoranda from NBC President Robert E. Kintner to William Mc-Andrew, Executive Vice President, NBC News, the policy lines were carefully delineated. McAndrew was given complete authority for the production of the program, but he was instructed to yield to the candidates and their representatives on questions of lighting and make-up after first making the network's agreement or disagreement clear. Mc-Andrew was advised not to yield to any persuasion concerning changes in the set unless his producer and director agreed.

The question of a change in the site for the second debate arose shortly after Howard K. Smith signed off the first debate on September 26. After the first debate, Julian Goodman and Frank Slingland, who had been assigned the roles of producer and director respectively for the second debate, went from Chicago to Cleveland and met with John Rogers of the NBC technical staff, Rod Clurman, Goodman's administrative assistant, and Hjalmar Hermanson, NBC set designer, in order to form a survey team to study the production problems a Cleveland origination might pose. Also involved in the Cleveland survey were Leonard Reinsch, the Democrats' TV coordinator, William

Wilson, in charge of Kennedy's TV appearances, and Edward Rogers, the Republicans' TV man.

Both practical and political problems were involved in the Cleveland site. It was first planned that this debate would be in New York, but campaign schedules dictated a change. The Republicans felt that since they had accommodated the Democrats on the site of the first debate, and since it was easiest for the Vice President to meet Kennedy next in a Midwestern city, the Democrats should accommodate them by accepting the Cleveland site.[37] This was accomplished without much argument in the early stages of planning. But the overriding problems at Cleveland were those of space. The NBC affiliate, KYW-TV, has adequate facilities for its own productions, but the main studio where it was proposed that the debate take place was considered small by the survey team.[38] The major difficulty with the facilities was the lack of space to handle the nonparticipants—the press and VIP's who would come to cover the debate. We saw that in Chicago CBS had planned for 200 reporters and 380 attended. The survey team believed that setting up the facilities for at least as many as there were in Chicago would have been impossible at KYW. Since there were compelling reasons, however, for holding the debate in Cleveland, the survey team, with the cooperation of Cleveland civic authorities, tried to find a proper place. One network official called it, "the battle of the hors d'oeuvres . . . it was a question of who had the best hors d'oeuvres for the press. . . ."

Working steadily for the better part of two days, the teams examined hotel ballrooms, an industrial plant, and a university assembly hall. In many instances they found adequate space and comfort, or people willing to make changes by removing chandeliers from a ballroom, knocking out walls at the TV studio, adding sound baffling material, and adding air conditioning equipment; but a main objection was that the program would have to be a remote broadcast if it originated in the facilities offered by Cleveland. The fears of adding the problems inherent in a remote broadcast to the already serious production problems were very large and real at the time. The best facility was at one of the hotels, but its main ballroom fronted on a busy Cleveland thoroughfare and Slingland worried that the sound of a siren on some passing emergency vehicle might leak through the walls during the debate. For these reasons, the NBC group left Cleveland on Wednesday, September 28, with the recommendation that the debate be moved to the NBC studios in Washington.[39] Nixon apparently agreed to the

Photo courtesy of ABC

Home away from home: The inside and outside of one of the cottages ABC constructed for the candidates in their New York studio. Decoration and painting were carried out completely. The interior shows even the pictures on the wall were originals; the fact that the pictures were not identical was commented on by several reporters during a preview.

Photo courtesy of ABC

switch, but didn't or couldn't communicate with adviser Fred Scribner, who was campaigning. The NBC production team had to talk Scribner into moving, and finally he "reluctantly" agreed.[40] Kennedy's advisers agreed quickly.

Station WRC-TV in Washington, where the second debate was to be staged, is a spacious, modern installation, equipped for color in addition to black and white production. A large scenic storage area was particularly important here, because it could be cleared and used to house the reporters, as the adjoining studios were used at WBBM-TV in Chicago. The new facility also included a complete and modern set of executive offices, so that adequate accommodations for the candidates and their parties were easily arranged, close to the studio.

Hjalmar Hermanson had participated in the discussions about the set design in Cleveland, at first based on the probable origination from that city, and finished his planning by Friday, September 30. These discussions were influenced by the opinions of NBC personnel and the candidates' representatives, who felt that CBS had oversimplified the set for the first debate. The candidates' representatives in concert with Hermanson felt that the set should be "warmer" with more texture in the flats and furniture, that the furnishings should be more solid as contrasted with the spindly quality of the Chicago set, and that the candidates' legs should be masked by desks when they were seated and by some sort of rostrum when they stood. Producer Julian Goodman felt that the rostrums should be more substantial, so that the candidates could lean on them while talking; again a contrast from the Chicago set, in which the rostrums were little more than severely designed music stands. The approach was obviously different from that of the CBS designers, who had designed and executed a "modern" set; the NBC set, for veteran performers such as the candidates, was more in keeping with what they had used before, and was designed to be more "comfortable." NBC wanted a backdrop which would be a bit darker and less reflective than the CBS set; with this change they hoped to avoid the extensive background changes that had been necessary in Chicago. To achieve these goals Hermanson designed a center desk with canted wings and podia which were kidney-shaped to provide a side arm rest with a ledge in front; these were to be covered, as was the background, with a medium brown grass cloth.[41]

Hermanson and the others involved in the set design, and even the candidates' representatives, imagined that the second debate would be more like the NBC "Meet the Press" program than the first debate had been. The choice of Slingland as director seems to have been made on the basis of his four to five years' experience as director of "Meet the Press."[42] Most of the production details were carried out with this concept in mind. In fact, during the earliest discussions about the format, as we have seen, some of the candidates' representatives actually referred to the second debate as a "Meet the Press-type program."[43]

Therefore, the area for the reporters' panel was also handled differently. The background behind the candidates was composed of 29 grass-cloth covered panels 2½ by 10 feet set up in a semi-circle of slightly more than 180 degrees. The reporters were positioned behind a gently curved desk approximately 10 feet long. Behind the reporters Hermanson designed a low wall, 53 inches high, to provide a background for camera shots of the reporters when they asked questions. On the first debate there had been no full-face shots of the reporters except as they were introduced, and the NBC concept of a "Meet the Press" program called for seeing the reporters as they asked their questions. A porthole was built into the center of the large background behind the candidates, approximately eight feet up on the wall, so that a camera could be positioned to shoot directly into the press panel. The entire candidates' set was placed on a one-foot-high kidney-shaped riser which was covered with a rug. Because of the shortage of time, Hermanson did not make working drawings of the set or furniture, but did construct a model set of balsa wood and cardboard which he took to a meeting with the candidates' representatives, Wilson and Rogers, in Washington, Monday, October 2. It was indeed fortunate that they approved the set, since its construction in New York was almost completed. Most of this production meeting was involved with discussion of "shooting" angles, one of which the NBC people kept secret until shortly before air time the following Friday.[44]

Hermanson's set was trucked to the WRC studios Wednesday, October 4. That evening Hermanson personally supervised the setup. One additional variation he had included was to design the candidates' and moderator's desk so that it could be taken apart into three units, and provide a feeling of separation, if desired. The candidates' representatives looked at the set, viewed it on camera late Wednesday evening, and all agreed it had come off exactly as they had planned.[45] With the set in place and approved, Leon Chromak, an NBC technical director on the Washington staff, who had twelve years of experience with many of the political programs NBC originates from there, was brought in to light it.

The WRC-TV studio, despite its recent design, did not have dimmers included in its lighting control setup. Chromak, realizing the importance of the lighting, particularly the need for fine control of intensity, had six dimmers shipped in from New York. He took special precautions with his lighting plan. Contrary to the usual practice of suspending most lighting instruments from an overhead grid, Chromak mounted his key lights on floor stands so that he could make vertical and horizontal angle adjustments without the necessity of moving in ladders. On Thursday, Chromak "roughed in" his lights, set up spare instruments (using two assistants) beside the main light sources to protect against the failure of any one lamp, and set his over-all front light level at about 140 foot candles.[46]

Chromak said he lit for a modeling effect, with the key light a little to the left of center, fill light basically from the right, some low light coming into the eyes, and with set light and back light to finish it off. He said he had lit both Kennedy and Nixon many times before, and was familiar with their particular needs. He had, of course, talked with Slingland and accommodated all of the angles the director was going to use in shooting. By Thursday night, Chromak said, "I was 98 per cent ready, a little trim here and there, but even if I didn't trim I thought I was ready."[47]

But for the second time lighting changes started to become a part of the debate story. Wilson, Kennedy's TV adviser, saw the final light setup late Thursday evening, and told Goodman he wanted "blander lighting for Kennedy." Chromak and Goodman acceded to Wilson's request by adding scoop lights to fill in and give a more diffuse effect. Imero Fiorentino, formerly an ABC lighting director who had been hired as a lighting consultant for Nixon after the Chicago uproar, also viewed the light setup at about the same time and approved it. Although Wilson's request had added more lights to the Kennedy side of the set, Chromak told the authors he did not feel his light plan had been basically changed.

About 6:30 P.M. Friday, Kennedy arrived in the studio for the pre-show check, preceding Nixon by previous agreement. He was accompanied by Leonard Reinsch, his brother Robert, and Wilson. Shortly after Kennedy reached his place on the set, he walked over to the Nixon podium, then back again, and asked why there were more lights on his part of the set than on Nixon's. Robert Kennedy, standing in

Nixon's place, complained contrarily that there were more lights on Nixon's set. Both made several trips to the control room to view each other in the Kennedy portion of the set, carrying on a running discussion of the light with their advisers, demanding lighting changes replete with such comments as "did 'they' arrange our lights too?"[48] Chromak agreed to move one of the floor stand lights, and adjust the intensity of some of the other lights. Today he refers to it as a "psychological lighting change."[49] Whether it was a serious matter for the Senator, or whether he was just practicing "upmanship" as has been suggested by at least one of his advisers, will never be known, but again the candidate got what he wanted in what otherwise would have been a strictly routine lighting assignment.[50]

Kennedy forces, however, still were not satisfied with the conditions and raised a question about the temperature of the studio. No accurate record of the exact temperature of the studio was kept. Kennedy partisans say it was down to 64 degrees, and Kennedy himself commented, "I need a sweater."[51] In any case, the proper functionary was summoned, the studio thermostat raised, and everyone agrees that it warmed up during the program, whether from the words spoken, the TV lights, or the relief of the tension, no one will ever be sure. Nixon, in contrast to the first debate lighting squabble, agreed that Chromak's lighting was satisfactory for him, although his advisers recommended a slight raise in the intensity of the key light and back light, which was quickly done. The Kennedy party, with its nervous pacing, took about thirty minutes to get satisfaction; Nixon's few changes were accomplished in five minutes.

NBC, like CBS in Chicago, had brought in one of their top make-up men, Bob O'Bradovich, calling him down from a location job at Harpers Ferry, Virginia, to be on hand if needed. After the bitter argument over make-up in Chicago, Nixon had hired a professional, Stan Lawrence, to handle the job for the rest of the debates. Kennedy never used make-up; so O'Bradovich had nothing to do. Nixon wore a darker suit this time. Kennedy's was about the same shade as the one he wore in Chicago.

Frank Slingland, who had been an observer at Chicago, had the "Meet the Press" idea uppermost in his mind. Slingland ordered six cameras, dollies, booms, and other standard equipment. The only special consideration was having equipment which would lift the cameras high enough to shoot over the top of the low wall behind the reporters, and over the heads of the reporters themselves. The two main cameras

—those that would shoot the full-face shots of the candidates—were equipped with identical lens complements of 135 mm, 10 inch, 12 inch, and 17 inches. The camera located high and in back of the candidates was fitted with a six to one zoom lens.[52] The remaining three cameras had what would be considered a normal complement of lenses for a regular studio program. The longer lenses were dictated by the size of the set and Slingland's desire to take close-ups without having to move the cameras too close. A 35 mm lens was included in one of the camera complements, and it was used only twice for the wide opening and closing shots of the program.

Originally Slingland had planned to use the six to one zoom lenses on the main cameras. During one of the early production conferences the candidates' representatives raised a question about the sharpness of the zoom lenses. NBC's John Rogers said he felt that zoom lenses are a little "softer" than standard lenses, and so standard lenses of fixed focal length, similar to the complements used in Chicago, were agreed upon for the candidates.[53]

The innovation of Hermanson's design and Slingland's planning was the two-shot reaction shot. Slingland had told Goodman that he planned to use this shot, but had not shown it to anyone. He said: "This was something that Hjalmar and I had talked about and not looked at, because if we had looked at it, there would have been great discussion on both sides."[54] He rehearsed during the afternoon without using the shot, but about 5:45 P.M., one hour and forty-five minutes before the program went on the air, Slingland called up the combination reaction shots and showed them to Wilson and Rogers. When they were satisfied as to equal size and angle, both advisers approved use of these new shots. Again, unlike Chicago, where Hewitt used tight shots from very near the beginning of the program, Slingland saw his own early shot pattern as a series of pictures always moving closer to the candidates; but he refrained from using the special combination reaction shot until fifteen to twenty minutes into the program in order to add variety as the program developed. However, the Kennedy representatives in the control room, Reinsch and Wilson, began to ask for Slingland's combination reaction shot shortly after the program went on the air. As Slingland puts it, "I did feel breathing on the back of my neck, I think it was Reinsch."[55]

The Kennedy forces' first demand for more reaction shots—which they felt benefited Kennedy more than Nixon—was relayed to Slingland by the producer, Goodman, and Slingland turned it down. He said he was trying to let the content of the program motivate all his shots and didn't feel that the reaction shots were called for yet. But Reinsch and Wilson kept up their demands and their second request was granted.

The reaction shots led to another unusual action by Slingland. He kept a stop watch in his hand, and each time he took a reaction shot he timed its length on the air. He may have been under the impression, because of the discussion going on behind him, that the candidates' representatives were keeping track of the number and length of the shots. In the final analysis, Slingland's cutting point was dictated by the content, but he did take unusual care to provide "equal time." Otherwise, the timing on the program was controlled by Elmer Lower and Russ Tornabene from a post outside the studio, using the same cueing equipment as in Chicago.[56]

McGee, as moderator, explained the ground rules, introduced the news panel, and then provided transitions between questions and answers for the rest of the program. The order in which the reporters would ask questions had been agreed upon in advance. It was designed to provide for an equal number of questions for each candidate from each reporter, and to prevent any one reporter from questioning only one of the candidates. It was a simple 1, 2, 3, 4,—2, 3, 4, 1, etc., rotation, and McGee was in charge of seeing that it was carried out. There was no limitation on subject matter and the reporters gave no warning to the candidates in advance.

Again the responsibility and the desire to do the best possible job were felt by the technical people as well as by the NBC production staff. Six carefully chosen image orthicon tubes for the cameras were sent from New York, and the camera and tube combinations for all of the cameras at WRC-TV were tested until the best six were found. Care was also taken, while Slingland was matching his shots, to check the optical capabilities of the camera lenses, and in one instance a lens was changed. The eye level of each candidate was measured to within one-quarter of an inch and the cameras adjusted accordingly. The audio setup for the broadcast was carefully protected, with duplicate microphones for the candidates, and spare but "ready" microphones for the moderator and reporters in addition to those they used.

The program was fed to New York and from New York was fed to all radio and television networks. NBC used a special line to feed the program to New York, and backed this up with its regular round-robin lines.[57] With all the extra care, there was only one little hitch, and although it came at a heart-stopping time, it had no effect on the air program.

Ten minutes before air time, a circuit breaker, overloaded because two extra cameras were being used, broke contact, as it should. This cut off the power to two of the camera monitors in the control room. NBC technicians found the breaker, reset it, and then ran another line into the control room to provide more power. The program went on the air with technician John Platt holding a plug into a socket until the new line was installed minutes later. Slingland was prepared to view the two monitors "around" Platt, and went on the air shouting, "Move over, Johnny, we're going to take that camera now!"[58]

The production efforts of NBC to achieve a "warmer and more comfortable" set were recognized by the public. Although they did nothing radically different, the lighting and make-up men were credited with "doing a better job." But there were still comments about Nixon's "stiffness," especially on the reaction shots. When answering he seldom looked at the people who asked him questions, and on the two-shot reaction shots—seen in this debate for the first time—he was often caught staring into the studio rather than looking at Kennedy.

A rising tide of comment also developed from the format. Arthur Krock commented: "The panel form prevents the debate from realizing the incisiveness that occurs only when candidates ask questions of each other. . . ."[59]

The argument over lighting and air conditioning during the pre-show checkout was widely reported in newspapers and magazines. However, its total effect on the production, the authors feel, was nil. The emphasis was shifting from the production aspects of the program to the content of the candidates' messages.

Second Debate: Program Analysis

OPENING: On moderator Frank McGee in one-shot, including top of desk, at 00:30 pulls back to three-shot to include seated candidates at desk wings. Cut to long shot including backs of panel, rostrums, flags, and carafe tables, as McGee opening continuity continues. Cut to close-up of Nixon, then Kennedy, as they are introduced by name. Cut to McGee, who introduces panel as they are panned at table top level. Cut back to first newsman, Paul Nivin, for question to the Vice President.

SHOTS: *Candidates:* Shots start wide, including top of lectern, moving in to a mid-chest and then shoulder-level shot. In each sequence of question-answer-comment, shots are identical in size and angle.

Newsmen: Porthole in center of candidates' background permits head-on shots of the newsman. These are mostly a loose table-top shot, including name card of newsman.

Reactions: Both one-shot and two-shot reactions are taken. There are eight reactions of each, and in each case, the eight total exactly 1:42. There are five two-shots, and three one-shots in each case, the two-shots always with the speaker in the foreground. The first is of Nixon, a two-shot at 17:11. The first of Kennedy, also a two-shot, is taken at 18:24.

CLOSING: Cut from last speaker to a one-shot of McGee, which dissolves to a wide shot behind and above the panel. As this shot pulls back the lights on the panel area are turned off and the network identification graphics are superimposed across the lower portion of the screen.

COMMENT: Slingland's approach was systematic, with definite patterns in the shot sequences. He shot off the set, in the two-shot reactions, into a studio area which had been draped to cover this possibility. Later in the program he cut away from the newsmen to catch candidate reactions to the questions asked. Slingland's tightest shot was looser than Hewitt's. Audio was without flaw.

SEPARATE BUT EQUAL

Third Debate
Date: October 13, 1960, 7:30 EDST, ABC
Place: TV #1, ABC, New York (Kennedy); Studio A, Studio B, ABC, Los Angeles (Nixon and newsmen)
Producer: Donald Coe, ABC, New York
Directors: Marshall Diskin, Los Angeles, Controlling Director; Jack Sameth, New York
Designer: George Corrin, ABC, New York
Lighting: Everett Melosh, ABC, New York
Make-up: Rudy Horvatich, ABC, Los Angeles; Harry Burkhardt, ABC, New York
Timers: Donald Coe, Los Angeles, Controlling Timer; John Madigan, New York
Technical Supervisors: Robert Trashinger and Merle Woerster, ABC, New York
Production Manager: Fred Schumann, ABC, New York
Moderator: William Shadel, ABC
Panel: Roscoe Drummond, *New York Herald Tribune;* Frank McGee, NBC; Charles Von Fremd, CBS; Douglass Cater, *The Reporter*

Format: News panel unlimited to subject matter, no formal statements; 2½ minutes to answer, 1½ minutes to comment

Of all the debates, the third was truly the electronic debate. Because
of different campaign schedules, an agreement was reached that television should bring the candidates together electronically. They could
be on the same screen together even though they were three thousand
miles apart—Nixon being in Los Angeles, Kennedy in New York.
They merely had to go to ABC studios in each city, and with the aid
of an elaborate technical exercise, they met, in ABC's terms, "Face
to Face."[60]

Donald Coe, ABC director of special events and operations, drew
the producing assignment shortly after Labor Day. Since they were
responsible for the third debate ABC held some distinct advantages.
There was an obvious disadvantage when they were also responsible for the fourth debate, only eight days later.[61] ABC profited
greatly from observing the efforts of CBS and NBC; at least the jitters
of the premier production had worn off and the smoothing out that
took place during the second debate contributed to a calmer atmosphere. Coe was an observer at each of the two previous debates, and
set design plans were started even before the second debate in
Washington.

The studios for the third debate were at the ABC Production Center
in New York for Senator Kennedy, and at the Los Angeles ABC West
Coast Center for Vice President Nixon and the panel of reporters. In
both locations the studio facilities are excellent. ABC's New York
studio TV #1 is 75 by 90 feet, one of the largest and certainly one
of the best equipped television studios in the United States. It has an
extremely modern lighting system and a control room complete with
separate facilities for audio and video control and production. In Los
Angeles two studios were set up—one for Nixon and one for the
panel of reporters. Control of the program was in Los Angeles because
more of the production elements were there. Obviously ABC had to
arrange for twice as much equipment, crews, and production and technical personnel; as we will see, the concept for the third debate was
an exact duplication of facilities, even to the most minute detail.

Set designer George Corrin worked under a general directive to make
the candidates as comfortable as possible. This followed a line of
thought that permeated ABC planning: do everything possible to
prevent development of the kind of controversies between the candi-

dates' representatives and the production personnel which were so apparent earlier. The set for the third debate was a combination of warm-toned gold fabric and wood grained panels for the background, a large L-shaped standing desk for a podium—easily the most massive and substantial rostrum yet provided—and a floor-to-ceiling built-in bookcase unit to the side of the candidate.[62] Identical sets were constructed at New York and Los Angeles. Kennedy's set was, in a sense, the right half of the picture, and he faced in toward the center from the right. Nixon's set was the left half of the picture, and he faced in toward the center from the left—in both cases this was a conscious effort to maintain an east-west relationship between the candidates, their actual geographic orientation.

Set construction itself was not complicated, but an incredible amount of effort was expended to be sure that each set, studio, light unit, camera, microphone, and transmission element of the broadcast was absolutely identical. ABC bought the cloth for the background from the same mill run in an amount large enough to cover both sets. All of the paint used for both sets was mixed in New York. After the New York set had been painted, Fred Schumann, Director of Production Services for ABC, carried the same can of paint, by plane, to Los Angeles and delivered it personally to the west coast set painters.[63] At Los Angeles, the 80 by 90 foot studio was equipped with lighting instruments manufactured by the Mole Richardson company. The east coast studio had Kliegl Brothers instruments. Adhering to the equality dictum, the lighting director ordered the Mole Richardson instruments removed and Kliegl instruments, identical with those used in New York, installed in their place. An even more sophisticated refinement concerned the lamps used in the lighting instruments. The west coast bulbs, regardless of their wattage, were rated at a slightly higher Kelvin temperature than the bulbs used on the east coast. The lighting director ordered the bulbs in the east coast instruments removed and replaced with the higher Kelvin temperature units.[64]

The New York ABC Executive Offices would ordinarily have served as headquarters for the candidates, but since they are located some distance from the studio, the network decided to build a cottage in the studio for Senator Kennedy's use as a dressing room. This cottage contained a sitting room and office-dressing room, telephones, and a lavatory. In Los Angeles, Mr. Nixon used an office suite. The facilities on the west coast were more complex, because the panel of newsmen was there. Located in another studio building with the moderator, they were seated at a slightly curved desk-table, with a background of the same design and texture as that used behind the candidates. Facilities for handling the press corps which covered both ends of the debate were similar to those for the previous debates. Two hundred reporters were accommodated at New York, 160 in Los Angeles.[65] The air conditioning problem was easily solved this time. Nixon's representatives had his studio in Los Angeles cooled to between 58 and 60 degrees, a "refrigeration" that didn't bother Kennedy this time, because he wasn't there.

The real story of the third debate was in the technical problems involved in originating simultaneously from both coasts. While this procedure was not being done for the first time, the whole television industry was really on trial to prove the electronic face-to-face technique could be brought off without a hitch. ABC felt the pressure. They had worked with the AT&T long-lines experts far in advance on several highly technical but crucial problems.

The program was controlled from Los Angeles. The Kennedy half of the program was sent from New York to Los Angeles, mixed there with the Nixon half of the program, and the combined picture and sound of both candidates were sent back to New York, where they were fed to all networks. Electronic signals travel at a very rapid rate, but not so rapidly that this double transcontinental relay, complicated by the fact that half of the picture and sound traveled 3,000 miles further than the other, could have been made without a noticeable lag in sound. ABC employed "carrier signal" facilities to handle the problem. Without the special precautions taken, the Kennedy sound and picture might not have been synchronized. As it was Kennedy lagged 1/38th of a second behind Nixon—a time lapse so short that it was not noticeable to the untrained eye.[66]

A second problem was that all program participants had to be able to hear each other without wearing head-phones. Special circuits and loudspeakers were used, and great care was taken in adjusting the sound levels to avoid "feedback." Internal communication between the coasts was maintained by full period talk circuits, and every major production and technical position could talk to its counterpart on the opposite coast. Program audio and video lines, all duplicated, were under constant surveillance for the better part of three days to insure flawless performance.[67]

In all, twelve cameras were involved, three times as many as those used in Chicago, and twice as many as those in Washington. On the west coast Director Marshall Diskin had six cameras, three each in two studios, and a spare camera in each studio patched into a stand-by control room. The east coast used four cameras, patched into two control rooms, one of which was a standby. All cameras and image orthicon tubes were carefully checked. Each candidate's sound was taken from duplicate microphones, and fed through a battery powered console as well as the regular audio control board. Even if power had failed, the sound portion of the program would have continued without interruption.

Everett Melosh worked out his light plot with Imerio Fiorentino, Nixon's lighting consultant, and Wilson, Kennedy's TV adviser. He set up a complete duplication of each lighting instrument to avoid bulb failure. Each studio lighting plan was identical, down to the number, type, and size of instruments. Melosh placed his key lights to the right of center, shining downward at a 30-degree angle and his general fill and set lights on each side of the set. Every important instrument was on a separate dimmer. Each candidate had a floor-stand spotlight for his eyes. Again the light level was at about 125 foot candles.

The only change from Melosh's lighting setup was made twenty minutes before the broadcast when the candidates' representatives asked for a change in the background levels. The Kennedy forces wanted a darker background in New York, and the Nixon people a lighter one in Los Angeles; so slight changes in the set lighting were made. On the air, there were differences in the background tones. Melosh operated the light setup by watching the transcontinental monitor circuit and ordering changes over his private phone line.[68]

All these preparations were aimed at one thing: preventing any element of the broadcast from being affected by the 3,000-mile separation. ABC wanted to be certain that it did not have the Monday-morning quarterbacking that CBS had had. Starting the night before the broadcast, and continuing throughout most of the debate day, Marshall Diskin in Hollywood and Jack Sameth in New York matched the size of the shots, camera by camera, lens by lens, until they were identical in size and angle. With painstaking care they also matched the "split-screen" shot, so that the halves of the picture were identical. And there was a visual debate that was never seen—the "Lincoln-Cherney debate." Actor Dan Lincoln was hired to stand in for Senator Kennedy in New York because he has the same physical characteristics and coloring as Kennedy, and in Los Angeles, actor Richard Cherney took the role for Nixon for the same reasons. These two men stood in front of the cameras for hours at a time, talking and acting as if they were the real debaters.

The Diskin-Sameth plan for the actual direction of the program put Diskin in the driver's seat. He would put up a shot: for example, Nixon from the waist up. Sameth would then punch up on the preview circuit an identical shot of Kennedy. At the appropriate time Diskin would take his shot on the air. In this way, as shot followed shot, they were always in pairs.[69]

The hot question of reaction shots was raised again, but the technical conditions in this case saved Diskin many arguments. The reaction shots had to be one-shots because the candidates were not physically together. Diskin said the candidates' representatives talked to him about reaction shots during most of the day. Diskin said, "I tried to put them together the way I thought it would be most agreeable to both." But he took only one reaction shot of Kennedy late in the program. It was easier to shoot the newsmen this time; they were in the other studio with the moderator and it was a simple task to get head-on shots of them in the order previously decided.

In all, the checking, doubling up of equipment, and great care taken with the production and technical details paid off. For although the split-screen shot was used only once during the program, in a split second it brought the two candidates together and gave the American public one of the most memorable pictures of the campaign. Technically, the broadcast went off without any trouble.

There was little or no comment about the production after the third debate. Visually, Nixon came off the best thus far in the series, primarily, the authors feel, because only one reaction shot was used, and that was one of Kennedy. Whenever Nixon was on the air, he was speaking, which eliminated the one element of production with which he had had the most difficulty.

There was another internal uproar in this debate, which, while it had nothing to do with the production, did involve the whole area of the agreements between the candidates on the ground rules. Nixon and his group raised a public outcry over Kennedy's use of notes during the debate. Before the program went on the air, Kennedy took some papers out of his pocket and put them on his rostrum. The ABC director in New York, Jack Sameth, saw the papers, and asked his floor director to tell Kennedy to put them away because he thought they looked messy. The floor director spoke to Kennedy, who seemed to be confused, and so Sameth rescinded the order just before the program went on the air.[70] Nixon may have seen Kennedy with his notes over the monitor circuit before the program started. And he may have noticed that Kennedy looked down to read a quotation during the program. Kennedy had three documents with him: a photostat of an Eisenhower letter concerning United States treaty agreements in the Taiwan Strait; a photostat of a page from a book by General Matthew Ridgway; and a quotation from former Secretary of State Dulles.[71] Nixon was under the impression that there was a rule against the use of notes. In his acceptance telegram of July 28 Nixon said, "In general, it is my position that joint television appearances of the presidential candidates should be conducted as full and free exchange of views without prepared texts or notes, and without interruption. . . ."[72] There is no indication that Senator Kennedy accepted or acknowledged this as a rule, and Kennedy's aides continued to deny that there was any such rule.

Third Debate: Program Analysis

OPENING: On moderator Shadel at desk; cut to split-screen shot with candidates facing toward the center of the screen; shot includes top of lecterns. The words New York and Los Angeles are superimposed at the bottom of each frame. Cut to wide shot of panel, and to individual shots of newsmen. Shadel introduces first newsman, McGee, who addresses question to Senator Kennedy in New York.

SHOTS: *Candidates:* Four different shots are used, always in pairs: lectern level, middle-button-of-coat, handkerchief-pocket, and tie knot. In each sequence shots are always followed by identical shots, and the shot sequences become tighter as the program develops.

Newsmen: Two different shots, one close-up, the other at desk level. All are head-on.

Reactions: One reaction shot of Kennedy is taken at 47:05, and it lasts 20 seconds.

CLOSING: Cut from last speaker, Nixon, to one-shot of Shadel at desk, who explains there is not enough time for another complete sequence of questions. Shadel fills from 56:40 to 59:00 with material describing equal facilities afforded the candidates in the separate cities; cut to cover shot of newsmen with superimposition of network credits.

COMMENT: Diskin's approach was extremely conservative, but it was necessitated somewhat by the technical complexities of coast-to-coast switching. The split-screen shot functioned perfectly, but it was used only once and then not in the body of the debate. The L-shaped rostrum encouraged the candidates to lean on one elbow, which resulted in some shots in which their bodies were slightly angled. Audio was without flaw.

THE FINAL ROUND

Fourth Debate
Date: October 21, 1960, 10 p.m. EDST, ABC
Place: TV # 1, ABC, New York
Moderator: Quincy Howe, ABC
Panel: John Edwards, ABC; Walter Cronkite, CBS; Frank Singiser, MBS; John Chancellor, NBC
Format: Foreign policy, 8-minute opening statements, questions and answers, comment, closing statement

Note: Since ABC also produced the 3rd debate, the production personnel were virtually the same. Jack Sameth was a standby director.

The final round of the Great Debates moved into New York. The networks had drawn for the order of the first three debates on the basis that each would do one, and then they drew for the fourth to see who would do the odd one. ABC, which brought off the trying and difficult third broadcast, drew the assignment. Again ABC had as its main goal equal treatment for the candidates. The same studio which had housed Senator Kennedy on the eastern end of the third debate was set up for the fourth for both candidates.

The studio, as we have said, provided excellent production facilities, but now with two candidates, ABC cottage builders went back to work and constructed an identical dressing-room-cottage for Mr. Nixon. These were completely and uniformly furnished in every respect, but the floor plan was reversed so that the doorways to the cottages were as far apart as possible. After several plans, ranging from "vine-covered honeymoon" to "contemporary-simple," a modified colonial exterior was adopted. They were air-conditioned and each had two rooms, one of which included a lavatory but no toilet. A special rest-room for the candidates, just off the entryway to the studio, was constructed out of concrete block, and fixtures were installed in it. The cottages' exteriors were completely finished.

The set for the fourth debate was completely different from that used in the third. Designer George Corrin ordered a seamless, painted background in a wood-grained finish. He also designed new rostrums, which were similar to the L-shaped units used in the third debate.

Marshall Diskin all along had wanted the candidates to be closer together in the set, because it would be more natural, and would make it easier for him to obtain the two-shot reaction shot. Diskin and Corrin worked together on the design of the fourth set in order to achieve this. The rostrums were placed near the outside edges of a smaller platform. They were six feet apart and thus became the closest speaking positions of the debates. The news panel was placed behind four separate desks, on the floor opposite the candidates, with a low wall behind them similar to the setup for the second debate. The panel, however, was much closer to the candidates. The distance between them was only about twelve feet. The moderator, Quincy Howe, was seated in the middle of the panel.

The lighting again was routine and smilar to that of the third debate; by this time, the floor lights had become standard equipment. Monitors with clocks were provided for Nixon and Kennedy. The candidates used monitors on the third debate and now requested them. Each candidate could watch only his opponent; his own monitor was turned off when he spoke.

Diskin used seven cameras during the program, four on the candidates, two on the newsmen, and a spare.[73] The cameras were mounted variously on pedestals, Panoram dollies and a Houston crane. More shot variations were possible in this debate than in any of the others. Not only did Diskin have a set that gave him a great deal of flexibility, but he also had the candidates closer together, and the large number of cameras and mounts for variation. The candidates' cameras had standard lens complements; zoom lenses were used on the cameras which shot only the news panel. He used both one-shot and two-shot reaction shots, and by this time either the candidates' representatives had learned to live with them, or had given up the fight, because there is no evidence that anyone mentioned them during the time the show was on the air.

Relieved that the third debate was a success, ABC technicians set up the fourth debate giving the same attention to equipment used, duplicate channels and lines, and backstopping of the signal delivery to the telephone company.

Diskin used almost the same amount of rehearsal time for the fourth debate as he had for the third. He rehearsed with stand-ins for approximately eight hours, including some time on the day before the debate.

He worked with the news panel members in their places for an hour, and allotted twenty minutes for the candidates during the final pre-show check.

The attention to things small and large was universal. Because ABC realized that their building was old and not as attractive as some of the other debate sites, the order went out to clear and repaint the ramp area where the candidates would enter the studio. Special covers were made for equipment that could not be moved; part of the outside of the building was painted; coveralls and smocks were provided for the stage hands; and the crew members were instructed to wear suits. With a rambling facility such as ABC's Production Center, the security was a little more complicated than it had been elsewhere; so the measures started early. The morning of the day before the debate the buildings were carefully zoned off.[74]

After the program the public comment, and that of the political pundits and TV reviewers, was retrospective, and returned to the major theme that the format was still a limiting factor, and that the content was repetitive. One Washington columnist said: "The debates are probably over, and the Washington feeling is that it is none too soon. The candidates have been highly repetitive in their answers, and the feeling here is that it may not be in the national interest to get into strategic plans for dealing with Cuba, Quemoy and Matsu on a presentation of this kind. . . ."[75]

Fourth Debate: Program Analysis

OPENING: On a shot of moderator Quincy Howe from a side angle; cut to wide shot of candidates, full figure standing in the set; cut back to Howe, who introduces Nixon for opening statement. Panel introduced after Kennedy's opening statement in a series of two-shots, which pan to show each at table-top height.

SHOTS: *Candidates:* Shots are almost identical with those used in the third debate, and taken in a similar matched order within question sequences. Shots are tighter as the program progresses.

Newsmen: Zoom lenses permit a tightening of some shots as panel members ask questions. Shots are from slightly off center, particularly of the moderator, who is located in the center of the panel.

Reaction: Both two-shot and one-shot reactions. There are five shots of Kennedy for a total of 25 seconds, and four of Nixon for a total of 31 seconds. Kennedy has two two-shots and three one-shots, Nixon two of each. The two-shots are similar to those in Washington, with the speaker in the foreground, but the proximity of the candidates brings them to more nearly equal size on the screen.

CLOSING: From one-shot of the last speaker, Nixon, to two-shot of the candidates, full figure in the set; cut to Quincy Howe for closing wrap-up; cut to high overhead wide shot including set, panel, and candidates, for network identification superimposition.

COMMENT: Audio to Quincy Howe was cut as he cued Kennedy's response to a Nixon comment at 21:35, and the first word or two of Kennedy's answer was "up-cut." Direction again was straightforward, but candidates' mannerisms during the reaction shots were the most vigorous seen in any of the debates, and the candidates talked directly to each other numerous times. Just before the time for the closing statements Nixon was observed talking to Kennedy during a reaction shot, but since his microphone was closed, no sound was heard. Howe interrupted Nixon to announce it was time for the closing statements.

THE FIFTH DEBATE

The number of debates was settled early in the negotiations between the networks and the candidates. While it is apparent that the Democrats always wanted more debates than the Republicans, when it came to deciding whether there should be a fifth debate, the political considerations in the argument seem to have overwhelmed the two camps.[76]

The idea of a fifth debate was brought up publicly by Democratic Senators Pastore, Monroney, and Magnuson on October 8.[77] The trio had sponsored the legislation permitting temporary suspension of Section 315 of the Communications Act, which made the debates possible. Consequently, when they telegraphed the networks that they favored a fifth debate closer to election day, the Senators received immediate consideration. The networks implemented the idea immediately, and Senator Kennedy wired a blanket acceptance two days later, on October 11.[78] The Nixon reply the same day was not quite as all-inclusive, but he did accept the idea of more time. His proposal was to extend the fourth debate (which had not yet taken place) to two hours, with the second hour to be taken up with questions phoned in by the public.

The situation developed into a barrage of public statements in which the candidates accused each other of not wanting to go ahead with the fifth debate idea. Kennedy, in all his public pronouncements about the fifth debate, kept hammering away at the idea that the fourth debate was too far from election day. And he flatly accused Nixon of being afraid to meet him again after October 21. Nixon's television representative, Fred Scribner, continued to request an extension of the fourth debate to two hours. He proposed that telephone calls with questions from the public be handled by a moderator, and that each candidate have three minutes to answer. This is essentially what Nixon himself did in a nationwide TV marathon answering session from Detroit the day before the election.

On October 19 Scribner called for "immediate meetings" in order to discuss the extension of the fourth debate to two hours, and Kennedy replied that he was agreeable to an extension, but that it was "in no way a substitute for another joint appearance in the final days of the campaign."[79]

On the day of the fourth debate Kennedy wired Nixon again, urging a fifth debate, and perhaps more. He challenged Nixon to announce his acceptance of a fifth debate on the program that night. His wire said "In fact I believe that more than five debates would be helpful if the record were to be corrected properly."[80]

Nixon seems to have been worried about his tactical position in all this. There is evidence that on the day of the fourth debate the Nixon camp had decided not to become involved in a fifth debate if they felt Nixon was ahead in the campaign at the end of the fourth.[81]

The Nixon strategists did, however, hold open the possibility of a fifth debate, if Nixon came off second best in the fourth.[82] Nixon also proposed turning over the fourth debate to the vice presidential candidates, and held out the possibility of a fifth debate if Kennedy agreed to this.[83] In a 1,000-word telegram on October 23, Nixon renewed the idea of putting the vice presidential candidates on for at least part of a fifth debate, and suggested that the whole time period be devoted to the question of Cuba, and what to do about Castro—an issue which had been touched on briefly during the fourth debate. Nixon's long wire devoted much more space to his views on Castro and Kennedy's point of view on the same subject than it did to arrangements for the fifth debate. Kennedy's reply, on the same day, was similar, since it was primarily an attack on Nixon's point of view, although it was shorter. But Kennedy rejected the idea of limiting the subject matter of the fifth debate to one item.[84]

By October 25 the idea of a fifth debate seems to have been given serious consideration by both sides. Scribner and Reinsch met in Washington to discuss it once more, and the network committee—McAndrew, Mickelson, Daly, and Keating—met in New York to work out a format. They wired Scribner and Reinsch, suggesting a return to the original network proposal—one more try for a real "Oregon Debate." The wire read: "We urge that you consider reverting to the original format; a face to face appearance without a panel, but with a moderator to preside and to provide for a fair division of time."[85] The network representatives also suggested another modification of this plan—that the candidates present statements on subjects previously stipulated and that they reserve some time for direct questions. Reinsch and Scribner reached no decision on the 25th and met again on the 26th. On the 28th the network committee met again, and must have been convinced that there really would be a fifth debate. John Daly withdrew ABC from the production of the fifth debate, since ABC had already presented two, and CBS drew the assignment with the probability that it would originate in Washington on October 31.

The next twenty-four hours must have been the wildest in the entire debate series as far as the network committee was concerned. Mickelson's personal memoranda on the debates include a complete record of the activities.[86] While the network committee was meeting in Mickelson's office in New York, Reinsch and Scribner were meeting in Washington. Faulty communications resulted because all sides were firing off telegrams to each other, and releasing the texts of the telegrams to the press before they were received at the other end.

Scribner and Reinsch compromised on a format. First, they decided that the two vice presidential candidates, Lyndon Johnson and Henry Cabot Lodge, would each make a ten-minute statement at the beginning of the program. The presidential candidates would then work with a panel of newsmen as they had in the second and third debates, with the exception that the answers and comments would continue for five minutes. An additional two minutes would then be given the first speaker for "surrebuttal." Since twelve and one-half minutes were necessary for each complete sequence, time for only three questions would remain after the vice presidential candidates finished. Reinsch was less in favor of using the vice presidential candidates than Scribner, but a call from Scribner later in the afternoon indicated that he and Reinsch had agreed they would appear on the program.[87]

Somewhere along the way, the Republicans suggested that cameras be set up in New York's Central Park, so that the candidates could answered questions from anyone who wandered by—a truly soap-box approach.[88] The networks pointed out that such a plan might attract a mob of 100,000 persons or more, and that it was impractical from the points of view of security, production, and engineering.

Reinsch and Scribner both asked that the network committee come down to Washington the following day, October 29, for a meeting to work out production details. Mickelson agreed that he and McAndrew would go to Washington for the meeting, and it was scheduled for 11 A.M. at the CBS Washington headquarters. Reinsch promised to call back to confirm the meeting, and it looked as if a fifth debate would materialize.

However, early in the afternoon of the 28th, Reinsch sent a wire under Kennedy's name which Scribner took as a personal affront. Scribner felt that the wording of the wire accused him of bad faith, and tried to make it look as though the Republicans were resisting the fifth debate. Furthermore, he pointed out later, Reinsch released the text of the wire close to the time he and Scribner were meeting to discuss the final details of the fifth debate.[89]

Reinsch did not call back, but sent word to Mickelson late that evening that some sort of hitch had developed.[90] Mickelson could not tell from Reinsch's message whether there would be a fifth debate; he and McAndrew went to Washington the following morning. Mickelson made contact with both camps. He found Scribner very upset about Reinsch's wire. Scribner read Mickelson the text of his reply to Reinsch, in which he said that until Kennedy apologized for charging bad faith and withdrew what Scribner believed was an ultimatum, there could be no more negotiations, and there it ended.

CONCLUSIONS

Despite arguments over four debates or five, studio temperature, lighting and make-up, color of the background or design of a chair, the programs as seen by the millions came off in the way they had been planned. The competent network people did their jobs even though they were subjected to the most elaborate and often unnecessary pressures, some of which they brought upon themselves. According to standards of the industry, the debates were well produced public affairs programs. On the living room side of the TV set, the programs appeared as straightforward presentations of the candidates. The viewer saw little or nothing of the pressure-packed atmosphere which surrounded and shaped the production elements of the programs. In the studios these influences and pressures at many times also shaped the decisions of everyone involved.

Format: From a production point of view the formats facilitated a simple air show. However, they sharply limited the length of time the candidates had to answer questions, and put a premium on the candidates' ability to appear to answer a question in a short period of time. The formats did achieve equality of exposure for the candidates. The candidates and their representatives dictated the formats to the networks. The networks, though they tried to have a different format, were more concerned with assuring that the broadcasts of the debates would take place.

Staging: The scenery and lighting introduced no innovations, because the networks obviously were trying to prevent the staging from distracting the viewer. The networks were right in this approach, and while there were many influences at work trying to modify and control the staging, no one suggested radical departure from the existing scenery and lighting.

Directing: The directing was the implementation of the format. It was simple in approach, and carried out with skillful restraint. While the directing was basically objective, the reaction shots were admittedly subjective. The reaction shots gave power to the director to reveal the candidates in a more candid way than the vast majority of the audience could otherwise have seen them.

Technical: The technical elements were subservient to the production. The great care taken was a symptom of the networks' concern that the debate programs should take place without any failure which could be attributed to them.

Make-up: If the candidates chose to use make-up, they should have used professional help. Even so, the do-it-yourself make-up applied to Vice President Nixon in the first debate did not affect his appearance as much as his physical condition did.

Candidates' representatives: The traditional broadcast industry relationship between the "product representative" and the program producer was maintained. Nixon and Kennedy were the products to be sold. Scribner, Reinsch, Wilson, and Rogers were the "account executives" who constantly scrutinized the production elements and attempted to influence them in a manner that would favor their man. The basic policy agreements between the candidates and the networks permitted this partisan activity.

In the usual sense of the word the networks did not *produce* the programs—they had no choice concerning the talent, and did not choose the time, place, date, or script (format). They provided the very best facilities and personnel for the programs, and while they accommodated both sides, they were scrupulously fair. The networks came out second best on the formats for the programs, but this, to them, was not as important as having the programs on the air.

It is to the everlasting credit of the television networks that the debate programs were presented in the 1960 campaign, but the evidence is overwhelming that they relinquished essential control of the programs to do so. In only a few instances did the networks assert their independence of action.

If this investigation can be used as a guide for future debates, it is clear that one of the major decisions which must be made concerns the division of responsibility between the networks and the political parties. The one thing that both have in common is a duty to the voters. If the content and form of the programs are to be dictated by such external considerations as the industry's strategic position vis-à-vis government regulation, or the candidates' views of how best to present themselves, then ultimately the public is the loser. If, on the other hand, they use the experience gained to develop equitable ground rules formulated with the intent of informing the public in the best possible manner, then many of the production and policy difficulties will disappear. Certainly our sympathies are with the networks in their endeavor to have the debates on the air, and with the candidates for their courage in participating, but many of the pressures inherent in such a new venture must be removed so that the content is shaped only by concern for the best interests of the public.

NOTES

1. The authors shared equally in both the research and the writing of this study, which was supported by a grant from the Indiana University Faculty Research Division. Much of the material was obtained through personal interviews, recorded in New York, Washington, and Chicago between March 1 and May 1, 1961. The authors wish to recognize the help of the corporate vice presidents of the three TV networks, the candidates' representatives, Leonard

Reinsch and Fred C. Scribner, and many of the program principals, who threw open their personal files and helped with the record in a most candid and understanding way.

2. For a full account of the differences between the 1960 arrangements and those for the Lincoln-Douglas debates of 1858 see *New York Times,* Sept. 26, 1960, p. 25.

3. See articles by Becker and Lower, Sarnoff, and Stanton, above.

4. The offer by NBC for eight weekly hour-long broadcasts of "Meet the Press" was made by NBC president Robert Sarnoff on April 21, 1960 in a speech before the Academy of Television Arts and Sciences in New York. The offer by CBS of eight hours of prime evening time between Labor Day and Election was made by Dr. Frank Stanton in testimony before the Subcommittee on Communications of the Senate Interstate and Foreign Commerce Committee on May 17, 1960. He proposed a variety of program types. ABC president Oliver Treyz, in testimony before the same committee, proposed that each network set aside eight hours of its regular programming, picking the most-listened-to time periods, and pre-empting the regular programs for special programs by the candidates. Sarnoff used the term "The Great Debates" in a wire to House Speaker Sam Rayburn in urging House passage of the Senate resolution.

5. Kennedy's advisers told the authors they felt it was very important to be the first to accept, and thus "challenge" Nixon to the debates. The decision was quickly reached during a luncheon at Hyannisport, Mass., July 28.

6. Not all of these people attended every meeting; the composition of the meetings varied depending on what was to be discussed and other considerations such as travel schedules.

7. Leonard Reinsch told the authors that the most difficult part of the negotiations was arranging schedules.

8. McAndrew told the authors that both sides had been working on formats between the August 9 and August 31 meetings, and that he felt the candidates had virtually agreed on what they wanted before the August 31 meeting.

9. Text of the telegram from Nixon to the networks is in the networks' files; the ellipsis indicated is that of the authors.

10. Interview with McAndrew, New York, Apr. 6, 1961, also "Ground Rules," memo adopted at August 31 meeting.

11. For a fuller explanation, see "The Oregon Plan of Debating," *Quarterly Journal of Speech,* XII (April 1926), pp. 176-80.

12. McAndrew, Mickelson files. Stanton testimony before the Senate Interstate and Foreign Commerce Committee, Jan. 31, 1961, and interview with Reinsch, Washington, Apr. 4, 1961.

13. Letter from Fred C. Scribner, Apr. 9, 1961.

14. Interview with Reinsch.

15. Text of wire from Sarnoff to Representative Harris.

16. Interviews with Lou Dorfsman, CBS Creative Director for Advertising and Sales Promotion, and Don Hewitt, CBS Producer-Director, Apr. 5, 1961.

17. See note 16.

18. CBS floor plan provided by Dorfsman; interview with Bob Link, WBBM-TV Production Manager, Mar. 10, 1961.

19. WBBM-TV production services records.

20. There was considerable disagreement among the principals involved in these developments as to sequence of events. However, it must be said that much of this can be attributed to their reluctance to place this responsibility on the highest executive level. Dr. Stanton closely supervised the entire operation.

21. Interview with Rogers, Apr. 6, 1961.

22. Interview with Barry, Apr. 5, 1961.

23. Interviews with Barry and Miss Arvold, Apr. 5, 1961.

24. Interview with Leonard Reinsch, Washington, Apr. 4, 1961.

25. Interview with Hewitt.

26. See note 25.

27. Interview, Al Pierce, WBBM-TV technical supervisor, Chicago, Mar. 10, 1961.

28. Interview with Hewitt.

29. Interview with Rogers.

30. Interview with Wilson, Apr. 7, 1961.

31. Sig Mickelson, personal files memorandum, Sept. 15, 1961.

32. Interview with Virgil Mitchell, WBBM-TV Press Information, Chicago, Mar. 10, 1961.

33. Interviews with Hewitt and Link.

34. Interview with Pierce.

35. *Chicago Daily News,* Sept. 29, p. 1, Sept. 30, p. 4.

36. Interview with Rogers.

37. Interview with William McAndrew, NBC, New York, Apr. 6, 1961.

38. Interview with Frank Slingland, NBC, Washington, Apr. 3, 1961.

39. See note 38. Also interview with Julian Goodman and Hjalmar Hermanson, NBC, New York, Apr. 6, 1961.

40. Interview with McAndrew.

41. Interview with Hermanson.

42. Interview with Slingland.

43. McAndrew's hand-written notes of meetings between the network committee and the candidates' representatives, read to the authors, Apr. 6, 1961.

44. Interview with Slingland. Also interview with Elmer Lower, NBC, Washington, Apr. 3, 1961.

45. Interviews with Slingland and Hermanson.

46. Interview, Leon Chromak, NBC, Washington, Apr. 3, 1961.

47. See note 46.

48. *Life* magazine, Oct. 17, 1960.

49. Interview with Chromak.

50. Wilson said he had suggested to Salinger that some political hay might have been made out of the fact that Nixon had more television advisers than Kennedy. Wilson feels Salinger communicated this to the Senator, who chose the Washington occasion to bring the matter out into the open.

51. *Life* magazine, Oct. 17, 1960.

52. Hermanson's personal sketches, NBC set floor plan, shown to the authors.

53. Interview with Slingland.

54. See note 53.

55. See note 53.

56. Interview with Russ Tornabene, NBC, Washington, Apr. 3, 1961.

57. Interview with William H. Trevarthen, Vice President of Technical Operations, NBC, New York, Apr. 6, 1961.

58. Interview with Slingland. Also interview with Keith Price, technical director, NBC, Washington.

59. *New York Times,* Oct. 9, 1960, p. E-11.

60. ABC in all of its inter-office communications, press releases, and other public references to the third and fourth programs referred to them as "face-to-face" or "joint appearance," avoiding the term "debate."

61. Interview with Donald Coe, ABC, New York, Apr. 7, 1961.

62. Interview with George Corrin, New York, Apr. 7, 1961.

63. Interview with Fred Schumann, ABC, New York, Apr. 7, 1961.

64. See note 63. Kelvin refers to the color temperature—degree of "whiteness"—of a light source.

65. Letter from Ell Henry, Director, TV Network Press Information, ABC, Los Angeles, Apr. 21, 1961.

66. Interviews with Merle Woerster, ABC, New York, Apr. 7, 1961.

67. Interview with Ralph Drucker, Technical Director, ABC, New York, Apr. 7, 1961.

68. Interview with Everett Melosh, ABC, New York, Apr. 7, 1961.

69. Interviews with Marshall Diskin and Jack Sameth, ABC, New York, Apr. 7, 1961.

70. Interview with Sameth.

71. AP dispatch, date line New York, Oct. 13, 1960.

72. Text of Nixon wire to Robert Sarnoff, NBC president, July 28, 1960.

73. In this production, Sameth manned a spare control room as the ultimate precautionary measure.

74. Records provided by Michael Foster, Vice President, Press Information, ABC, New York, Apr. 7, 1961.

75. James Reston, *New York Times,* Oct. 22, 1960, p. 9.

76. In his letter to the authors dated June 9, 1961, Scribner stated that he felt strongly that the series was to consist of only four debates and that it was a violation of the rules for either side to challenge the other to a fifth debate.

77. AP dispatch, date line New York, Oct. 11, contains the sense of the wire to the networks.

78. Text of telegram in Mickelson's personal files.

79. Exchange of wires between Kennedy and Scribner, Oct. 19, 1960.

80. Text of Kennedy wire to Nixon, Oct. 21, 1960, CBS files.

81. Mickelson files.

82. See note 81.

83. See note 81.

84. CBS files. Texts of exchange of telegrams between Nixon and Kennedy, Oct. 23, 1960.

85. Text of wire to Scribner and Reinsch from McAndrew, etc., Oct. 25, 1960, CBS files.

86. Mickelson memorandum dated October 31, 1960.

87. See note 86.

88. McAndrew hand-written notes read to authors, Apr. 6, 1961.

89. Text of telegrams exchanged between Scribner and Reinsch, Oct. 29, 1960, CBS files.

90. See note 86.

6

Notes from Backstage

DOUGLASS CATER

COVERING the televised Great Debates on the spot was an eerie experience. We gathered in dim, cavernous halls, barred by armed guards from access to the scene of activity. We watched the show on monitors, silent for the most part, occasionally giving way to wry mirth. At the end of each debate, a pool reporter came out and dictated to us a meticulously detailed account of what he had seen and heard. ("Senator Kennedy took two deep breaths just before the program started. Vice President Nixon——" "Hey, you're going too fast! What was that again?" "I said Nixon appeared to wet his lips and then at twelve minutes after the hour he wiped his face the first time. He wiped it four times in all.")

When I served on the panel of interrogators in the third debate, I was somewhat baffled by the glimpse of reality I got. It was a strange mixture of planned method and unplanned content. The networks spared no expense or effort to perfect a split-screen arrangement allowing two candidates, who were a whole continent apart on that particular day, to appear to stand side by side. Each of us was given careful explanations of how the production was to be handled. A whole army of technicians worked to remove distortion in presenting the picture to what proved to be an audience of sixty million-odd citizens. Mr. Nixon's studio had been made frigid to eliminate undue perspiration.

Nobody showed much concern with what the program was to be about. The panel consisted of two men from the networks and two

Adapted from *The Reporter*, November 10, 1960; reprinted with the permission of the author.

journalists chosen by lot. The only qualification was to have accompanied each candidate at some time during the campaign. We prepared ourselves in isolation from one another. Only during the final anxious moments in the make-up room—where we submitted to the same pancake and lip-rouge adornment as Mr. Nixon—did we decide to reveal in confidence to fellow panel members what our opening questions would be. In the words of the announcer, it was unrehearsed.

For me at least, it was a frustrating assignment. Beforehand I had entertained Walter Mitty dreams of posing a question so trenchant and so to the heart of the matter that no candidate could attempt circumlocution. But trenchancy, I found, was not easily come by. The format of the Great Debate was neither fish nor fowl, not permitting the relentless interrogation of the "Meet the Press" type of quiz show or the clash of ideas that can occur in a genuine debate. The candidates had quickly mastered its special form of gamesmanship. No matter how narrow or broad the question, we could watch by the timing device the way each of them extracted his last second of allotted image projection in making his response. The panel's role was hardly more than to designate categories—animal, vegetable, or mineral—on which the two might or might not discourse.

During the legislative deliberations in 1960 over the temporary suspension of the equal time provisions of the Communications Act, the overriding concern was how television could be used to bring the campaign more directly to the people. Certain members, including Senator Mike Monroney (D., Oklahoma), thought that Congress should commandeer a number of prime viewing hours from the networks for whatever use the candidates wished to make of them. Network officials resisted, claiming that the First Amendment in effect guarantees them the right to fix such matters as format and scheduling. But they promised generous cooperation with the candidates if left to their own devices. One hour weekly, it was generally thought, could be tried without risk, as one broadcaster put it, of "overexposure, oversaturation, and redundancy."

Only Adlai Stevenson, who by now had acquired enthusiasm for the idea, attempted to paint a more detailed picture of the debates. He favored a ninety-minute program each week in which the candidates could deal, one at a time, with such issues as "disengagement or containment, farm policy, disarmament . . . ."

It was probably inevitable that this venture should get caught up in the strategies of networks and candidates alike. NBC Board Chairman Robert W. Sarnoff got the jump on his competitors the night of Nixon's nomination by offering eight hours of prime evening time for what he was first to dub "the Great Debate." Kennedy, as the challenger and the lesser known of the two candidates, promptly accepted without qualm or qualification. Four days later Nixon wired his agreement, stipulating a "full and free exchange of views without prepared texts or notes and without interruption."

In the course of three-power conferences at the Waldorf, there was a great deal of bluff and maneuver. Kennedy's men pressed for at least five debates; Nixon's wanted no more than three. (Fred Scribner, Jr., a Nixon aide, thought two would be plenty.) The Kennedy group, so strapped for funds that they had to cut back on paid TV commitments and anticipating a flurry of election-eve volleys by the Vice President, tried to get the series stretched out as long as possible. Nixon negotiators were adamant about an October 21 cutoff date. The matter of using notes was not raised again until Nixon accused Kennedy of cribbing in the third debate.

But on one important matter there was agreement. Both sides wanted the debates to be based on questions asked by reporters. A Nixon aide explained to me shortly before the first debate that this would serve to increase viewer interest. He feared that the candidates would be "too polite" if they interrogated each other. A Kennedy aide said very much the same thing: since nobody likes the prosecuting-attorney type on television, it was better to turn this thankless task over to others.

One thing was quite clear: as they approached this brave new frontier of television, the two candidates were far more concerned about their images than their arguments.

Both candidates proved themselves remarkably adaptable to the new art form. They were marvels at extemporization, wasting none of the precious media time in reflective pauses, never having to grasp for the elusive word, able in the peculiar alternation of reply and rebuttal to switch topics smoothly and without a hitch. Each could discuss anything within the allotted two and a half minutes for reply and one and a half for rebuttal.

To anyone who spent much time on tour with the two men, this was no great surprise. The dialogue was largely a paste-up job containing bits and snippets from campaign rhetoric already used many times. As the series wore on, the protagonists were like two weary wrestlers who kept trying to get the same holds. What became clear was how limited the vocabulary of the debate really was and how vague were the candidates' ideas about what to do. Kennedy, we learned over and over, wants to get America moving again. Nixon argues that it is moving, and, in an unfortunate phrase, "We can't stand pat."

Nobody around the candidates seemed to think that clarity of argument was the objective. For the sidelines observer trying to judge this new contest without benefit of rules or score card, it raised more questions than it answered.

Kennedy's trainers pointed out that he won an important victory simply by closing the maturity gap separating him from a rival four years his elder. He proved himself able to stand up to the man who stood up to Khrushchev. It was an accomplishment, they claimed, that no other means of communication could have effected so well and so quickly.

It may be so. But one kept wondering about those silent millions who sat before their television sets. Did they come any closer to a knowledge of their candidates? Not even a trained political observer could keep up with the crossfire of fact and counterfact, of the rapid references to Rockefeller Reports, Lehman amendments, prestige analyses, G.N.P., and a potpourri of other so-called facts. Or was the knack of merely seeming well informed what counted with the viewer? If so, Mr. Nixon did all right despite an amazing capacity to twist facts to suit his convenience. ("Now, as a result of our taking the strong stand that we did [on Indo-China], the civil war there was ended and today, at least in the south of Indo-China, the Communists have moved out and we do have a strong free bastion there.") Eventually, it seemed as if Kennedy gave up the Herculean effort to sweep up his opponent's fictions.

Who was judged more sincere? What may have been a major test was Nixon's soliloquy on Harry Truman's language and little children. It provoked loud guffaws among the press corps at the studio. But maybe other good Americans were deeply stirred by this pious man who promised, if elected, not to utter strong words in the White House. (He did, however, utter a few in the studio directly after the program, when he accused Kennedy of violating his no-notes proviso; afterward he told reporters that his spontaneous expressions were off the record.)

Last but not least, was the viewer really edified by the frantic clash on foreign policy? Neither of the men showed any regard for the fact that some things are better left unsaid if one of them expects to conduct that foreign policy next January. It was like a bastardized version of Art Linkletter's "People Are Funny" in which the contestant had to tell how he would deal with Castro in 150 seconds flat.

In closing what he thought was the last of the series, moderator Quincy Howe remarked, "As members of a new political generation, Vice President Nixon and Senator Kennedy have used new means of communication to pioneer a new type of political debate. . . . Perhaps they have established a new tradition." Howe may or may not be right in his prediction. But before this particular tradition becomes firmly rooted in American politics, it needs the kind of examination it never got before it started. The next time around, one of these pioneers will almost certainly be talking as our president.

7

Were They "Great"?

CHARLES A. SIEPMANN

QUESTIONABLE assertions of fact and a heavy smoke screen of irrelevant and at times inaccurate statistics have already combined with patent special pleading to obscure the truth (whatever it is) about "The Great Debates." The term itself, its currency and its already wide acceptance, suggest how susceptible we are to verbal ballyhoo. For, come to think of it, the debates were in no recognizable sense "great." If admittedly unprecedented, they were hardly "epoch-making," as they are sometimes described. It is by no means certain that, as some people assert, they contributed to the making of more intelligent decisions by the voters. Nor has it been established that the debates were responsible for the record turn-out of voters at the polls. Finally, it has been confidently asserted that, with the permanent suspension of Section 315, such debates will become a great and lasting political institution that will strengthen American democracy. But will they? Only as we clear our eyes of the verbal smog that has accumulated around the debates can we hope to see what actually happened, in what ways it was significant, and to what vital issues it related.

There are some hard facts to record, and some shaky ones. It is a hard fact that two out of sixteen presidential candidates were on four occasions given free television time to confront one another in debate and face questions from a group of broadcasting journalists. It is hard fact that the cost to the networks was high. CBS alone claims to have been $633,000 out of pocket. The viewing audience was vast, though here the precise figures (even in round millions) get pretty shaky. Dr. Stanton, speaking at a Sigma Delta Chi luncheon, gave it as 101 million separate viewers. By the time he came before a Senate subcommittee, his figure had jumped to 115 million, while the president of

NBC, testifying the same day, upped it to 120 million. But what are a mere 19 million viewers when it comes to ratings? Just state a figure, these days, and you establish a fact.

Who listened and for how long? Some statisticians tell us (without establishing how they know it) that half were Democrats, one-third Republicans, and one-sixth uncommitted. The so-called "average family" tuned in to the debates for precisely 53 minutes of the hour, while more than half of TV families saw three of the debates and over a quarter saw four. And how did they react? Mr. Schwerin has one story to tell here and Mr. Gallup another. Both agree that Kennedy outpointed Nixon, though by percentages widely at variance between the pollsters. Mr. Roper tells us that 57 per cent of the people say the debates influenced their vote, while 4 million (a figure later revised to 3,400,000) ascribed their vote to the debates alone.

The rest is for the most part pure speculation. Mr. Kennedy, perhaps rightly, feels that "it was TV more than anything that turned the tide." Of speculative interest is the fact that the absentee ballots, cast by Americans overseas, were so overwhelmingly pro-Nixon. Could it be that, long exposed to Mr. Nixon's "public image" as vice president and scarcely having heard of Kennedy, and not having seen him on TV, they voted for a man at least familiar to them? The influence on voting of the TV debates seems strongly suggested here. But while this, like much else about the debates and the election, is interesting, how much of it bears on the one essential question—the pros and cons of these debates as related to the democratic process?

In most democracies voters in a national election are called on to make one decision only, namely, to vote for the party of their choice. But in a presidential year in the United States the peculiarities of our Constitution force a twofold task upon the voter. He has to vote for the party of his choice, and he has to elect a president—both. Closely related as these choices are, they are nonetheless to be differentiated. For, disastrously as it may affect the subsequent smooth conduct of government, it is yet possible and may be reasonable (as it is far from unprecedented) for a man to split his vote between president and party. Let us consider the pros and cons of the "Great Debates" as related to these two separate choices.

THE PARTY CHOICE

Choice between parties, if it is to be responsible, involves knowledge of events and issues and just appraisal of the policies proposed to deal with them by the contending parties. Obviously such fair appraisal is impossible if you are not prepared to listen to both sides of the question. Yet the sorry fact is that large numbers of us make up our minds on party choice before the election campaign begins, as we remain largely unaffected by it to its close. Such an attitude is unintelligent but it is human and widely prevalent.

The outstanding importance of the debates, in this reference, is the fact that millions of voters tuned in, and apparently stayed with the debaters to the end, thus exposing themselves (in innumerable instances, probably, for the first time) to both the candidates and their conflicting points of view. There is, of course, no guarantee that all heard (in the sense of taking in) both views expressed. Indeed, research suggests that many people, even when tuned in to a debate, actually "take in" only the viewpoint to which they are predisposed. But if we are concerned to advance the democratic process, the principle of "double exposure" is sound, and any means of achieving it is to be commended—if other important considerations are not jeopardized. Were there any such in the debates? I suggest that there were several.

Worth repeating and underscoring is the proper rationale for the voter's decision as he chooses between parties. The essential choice here is not, normally, between persons (exceptional situations will occur) but between party principles and policies. Hence, in the degree to which the appeal of personality intrudes on or prevails over rational judgment of principle or policy, the vote-getting process is degraded. We listen, of necessity, to men, but it is to their matter (as they speak for their party) that, if we seek to be rational, we should pay attention.

There is little doubt in my mind that the television medium puts a high premium on facets of "personality" (they may be crude, as they may be subtle) that are impertinent to choice of party precisely as they divert our interest from the matter of his discourse to the man. Note, also, that the diversion of our interest is not merely to personality but to the distinctive and adventitious attributes of *TV personality*. (That TV has distinctive impact, involving differential psychological response, is strongly suggested by the finding that, while both audiences heard the same words, radio listeners to the debates judged the contestants to have scored evenly, while TV viewers judged Kennedy to have won hands down.)

Nixon and Kennedy, in their different ways, were both "telegenic." It is not certain that future candidates will be so. And the more marked the disparity between them on this score, the more surely will the dice be loaded in favor of the one who, whether by chance or (worse still) by conscious artifice, is best adapted to the peculiar requirements of effective TV communication. Electioneering, on one side, is admittedly a popularity contest, but only the mere politician will see this as its prime objective. It has another, more essential side to it. It is, or should be, an educative process. "Democracy," said Jefferson, "will not long survive without frequent return to funda-mentals," and it is to these that self-respecting politicians will address themselves, as it is to such men that self-respecting citizens will listen. If the democratic process means anything at all, it is the voice of the statesman, not of the TV star, that we need to hear.

But the cult of personality is commercial television's stock in trade, its natural tendency. True, to the credit of TV and of the candidates, the recent debates were soberly conducted. There is no assurance, however, that they will or can be so conducted in the future. TV, essentially, is (or rather has become) show business. And in show business it is what sells that counts, and what sells is popularity. Despite resounding phrases about service rendered to the public, the true center of his professional preoccupation peeps through in Dr. Stanton's revealing statement that "Straight exposition in any form is always the most difficult way to engage and hold the attention of anyone. Conflict, in ideas as in action, is intriguing and engrossing to great numbers of people. Drama has always got more attention than essays." Listen, also, to the President of NBC. Debate, he says, gives "a far better insight into a candidate and a more meaningful gauge of his fitness than his recitation of a *carefully prepared speech.*" Whip it up, boys, and never mind the quiet voice of reasoned and considered thought. The big audience is all. These are dangerous thoughts as they affect our estimate of qualities we look for in our statesmen. For if the TV debates had (and may in future have) anything like the power to influence the voter that is claimed for them, the very nomination of candidates to run for office is likely to be influenced by such essen-tially irrelevant considerations as their skill as debaters and as TV personalities. We may end up in the situation faced by Coriolanus as he risked election by scorning to expose his war wounds to the populace.

In the light of these considerations it is, surely, with dismay that one reverts to Mr. Roper's alleged claim that 3,400,000 voters deter-mined their party choice on the basis of the debates alone. We have no means of knowing on what basis, but for the debates, these voters would have made up their minds; but the true interests of democracy as distinguished from the sovereignty of ignorance and irresponsibility are surely not advanced as we facilitate choice on such flimsy and questionable grounds for party choice as the debates provided.

All of which prompts discussion of the specific character and format of the debates we heard in 1960. It would seem to me unreasonable and unfair to dismiss the idea of such TV debates, *per se,* by criticism centered on weaknesses in these particular debates—at any rate until we are satisfied that these are inherent weaknesses. I suggest that many of them could be easily corrected. My own criticisms would focus on the following points. The contestants discussed more issues than could be treated in the time at their disposal, while avoiding others altogether (e.g., civil rights) which were of central importance. There was consequently little argument in depth and little explanation of issues in detail. Much of the time they were, as Dr. Johnson put it, "arguing for victory," seeking to score points rather than to clear them up, picking holes in one another rather than in the ideas that each of them championed. The period, moreover, allowed for "rebuttal" was so short as to preclude intelligent criticism. The cross-questioning by correspondents seemed, to me at least, an egregious error. It stole precious time, was an open invitation to mere snap replies, and extended yet further the already diffused area of debate. It also gave to mere reporters the power, by the leading questions that they put, to shape in some measure the salient election issues. I doubt if this kind of emasculated press conference serves any useful purpose in such a situation, but if it does, we need men of considerably greater stature for the job than those chosen on this occasion.

But eliminate these and like defects, and what, *as related to party choice,* is the net gain or loss? Even under optimum conditions, however you define them, you still have the debate format and the adventitious odds inherent in TV communication. There are ample opportunities to get party platforms across without the "great debates"—opportunities on the road, in face-to-face confrontation with the voters, opportunities on radio and television for selective treatment in depth of single issues. Thus, as related to party choice, the debates seem in no way essential and in some ways dangerous. For their one great merit, that of "double exposure," would seem to be offset by distortions of the democratic process that seem to me inherent in use of the television medium as we have it. There is, for example, only one way to secure the desired extensive treatment of important issues. For as it is unlikely that viewers' interest in any one debate can be sustained beyond one hour, there is nothing for it but to increase their number.

Diminishing returns of interest are then likely to set in—and even if they don't, you thereby only aggravate the danger that the man, rather than the matter, becomes the focus of attention. The cult of personality is thus advanced, and of TV personality at that.

THE CHOICE OF A PRESIDENT

What, next, of the debates as related to our choice of a president? What other factors now enter into the equation? Those attributes of the man that bear on his role, not only as leader and spokesman of a party, but as the nation's Chief Executive and Commander-in-Chief of its armed forces, as the man on whose statesmanlike qualities and powers of wise and resolute decision the very survival of the nation may depend. Questions at once more fateful and personal are here raised than those of principle and policy alone. Every dimension of character, of personality, and of intellectual and moral stature is involved. Close personal scrutiny is here the essence of decision for us.

It is true that, for those who seek it, there are many other opportunities to gather impressions of the candidates. We may read what others write about them. We may see and hear them on their campaign tours or, for that matter, on television—on paid time. But always we see them on ground of their own choosing, discussing such issues at such times as they deem advantageous. And always we see them separately. There is, I would say, virtue in seeing them, on occasion, on ground not entirely of their choice, indeed under exacting conditions, as they are thrown on their own resources and stripped of the pomp and circumstance, to say nothing of the hoopla, of the staged rally in the bedecked auditorium.

It remains likewise true that (just as with reference to the party platform) debating skill, as such, has little to do with a man's essential qualifications for the presidency, and that even more irrelevant are those physical, psychological, and histrionic gifts of which TV personality is compounded. Our judgment may, indeed, be warped, our attitudes affected, by such irrelevancies as the mere matter of appearance, even of sex appeal, of ease of manner, of quick-witted repartee. But it is, perhaps, no mere debating point to claim that, in this matter of choosing a president, even if we thus err in judgment, it is at least error in a pertinent context—for it is a man, now, and all the facets of his personality (the above irrelevancies among them), and not his principles and policies alone, that we are estimating.

It is in this context of choice, too, that the principle of "double exposure" assumes peculiar importance. For to choose a president only because he is spokesman and leader of our party is to undermine the Constitution (as it provides for the separation of powers), to misread his role, and to demean his office. For the president of the United States is neither a figurehead (like the British monarch), nor a mere party leader (like the prime minister of Britain, who holds office only as long as his party holds power.) He holds office for a fixed period and must execute that office irrespective of the fortunes of his party in the Congress. Thus a weak president, though heading a strong party, constitutes a double liability—to his party's ultimate fortunes and to the nation's immediate needs.

Our choice of the president thus transcends our party interests and embraces our responsibilities as citizens. We may vote for our party from force of habit or from prejudice and be called to account only for our sloth or our stupidity. But to choose our president without knowledge of the candidate is a near treasonable act of folly. That so many do so is merely the sad measure of the unfinished business of democracy. The TV debates achieved something of vital importance as, by their apparent power to attract a vast audience, they forced on some, and facilitated for others, the appraisal of both candidates.

Thus, although they are touted for specious and disingenuous reasons, and may be dangerous on one side and on another inessential, I would plead for their continuance. The ground rules, obviously, need changing. I would limit the debates to three, evenly disposed from start to finish of the campaign period, with each debate confined to some one topic of supreme importance, with some ten minutes allowed for mutual rebuttal, and with journalists barred from the studio. Life being by its very nature dangerous, I would risk the attendant dangers earlier described, trusting to the self-interest of the networks to preserve the dignity of the occasion without which the debates could rapidly degenerate to the level of gladiatorial displays. But my plea would be dependent on satisfactory solution of a problem that remains to be considered.

SECTION 315

Whether TV debates between the presidential candidates should continue or not forms part of a larger question. For the debates we saw were made possible only by temporary suspension of the equal-time provisions of Section 315 of the Communications Act.* The FCC's ruling in the Schneider case opened up floodgates of disaster for the networks. Any crackpot or political adventurer could now, by filing in the primaries, get as much air time, for free, as bona fide candidates—once a network decided to cover the primaries at all. Faced by this nightmare liability, the networks have, seemingly, only two alternatives—either to refuse the free use of their facilities to every candidate, or to sell them at the going rate, trusting that only parties with ample campaign funds will come forward as buyers. Neither course seems calculated to advance the democratic process..

Apply the principle of Section 315 to incumbent and aspiring senators and congressmen, to say nothing of state and municipal office-seekers, and the complications increase by geometrical progression. Confine it to presidential candidates alone, and the poor broadcaster still finds himself confronting the nightmare of minor party candidates. Small wonder, then, that broadcasters have long chafed under the restrictive "all or none" provisions of Section 315. But it is unfortunate that they have recently exploited the popular success of the "great debates" to try to persuade Congress to revoke it. Without revoking it, they rightly claim, you cannot have the debates. But it is questionable logic to say that it should *therefore* be revoked. For more may be (and in fact is) at stake here than continuance of the debates. Section 315 may have merits on other counts that are not worth forfeiting. Before these have been weighed, its revocation in the interests of preserving the debates alone is foolhardy—unless the debates (as I have earlier attempted to disprove) are essential to the democratic process.

Section 315 is concerned with fair play in party politics. But it applies a crude and unworkable rule of thumb to secure it. What is wrong, surely, is the assumption that *all* parties have an *equal* right to be heard on the air. This seems to me a false and even foolish kind of egalitarianism, as unsound in theory as it is unworkable in practice. For the fact, surely, is that political ideas do not all have equal weight. Their weight, rather, if we think realistically, is a function of their capacity to get accepted in the market place of thought.

This is not to argue that only opinions that are already widely accepted should be expressed over the air. Quite the contrary. One of the grave defects of broadcasting for years past has been its meager provision of

* Cf. Becker and Lower, above, pp. 28, 33, 40, 42, 47-48.

ideas of any kind, and more especially of unpopular or unorthodox opinion. But we are concerned here, not with our need for variant exposure to ideas (which is part of the ongoing educative responsibility of broadcasting) but with the practical exigencies of a political campaign of limited duration, and of broadcasting facilities likewise limited in the time available. In such a time-bound situation it seems sheer sentimentality to allow concern for such political minorities as those represented by the fourteen candidates to blind us to the fact that ours, at present, is a two-party system and that, in an election year, clarification of the conflicting policies of the major parties is the paramount consideration. If total exclusion from the air of all these minorities is necessary, the price does not seem too high. Their death knell will not thereby be rung, for to claim that publicity, these days, is the condition of party survival is to pay the hucksters too generous a compliment. The growth of a party, like its birth, stems from the incentive to common action of people's associated needs. As people sense such needs, they will organize to see them satisfied.

But total exclusion of lesser parties for all time is not contemplated. I suggest only that, under a revised Section 315, the condition of a party's claim to air time be evidence of some significant degree of popular support. We need a "floor," some minimum figure of registered party membership (say 5 million—the precise figure is here immaterial) before any such claim is honored, and even then, perhaps, only on a basis of representation proportional to the membership of other parties.

For the fourteen minor parties in last year's presidential campaign the time for such recognition is, obviously, not here yet. But for one or more of them it may well come. There is nothing sacrosanct about our two-party system (for all that the spawning of multiple parties, as under the Weimar republic, tends to defeat the ends of a smooth-working governmental system), and the day may well come when a third party may command the support of a considerable body of voters. And on that day the debates will be doomed, for even a three-ring circus would be cumbrous to arrange, as it would remove the "drama" that gave to the 1960 debates their peculiar attractiveness.

Anyhow, we should not, by hasty action, foreclose on future eventualities that we cannot now foresee by abolishing a provision of the law whose intent is sound, however unworkable its present execution. As long as our two major parties remain substantially unchallenged by any rival parties, the case for a limited number of debates between their presidential candidates can stand. Such debates are by no means indispensable, they involve certain risks to the operation of the democratic process on a rational basis, but they have advantages that, on balance, warrant our support of them. But we should not tolerate their use as the big stick with which to beat down Section 315 in its entirety.

I have introduced the seemingly extraneous matter of Section 315 into this discussion because this is precisely what the broadcasters are trying to do. "I urge you to put a permanent end to the equal time provision of section 315 . . . on the basis of the demonstrated responsibility and good faith of American broadcasters in the 1960 campaign . . . and the successful introduction of the 'Great Debate' as a valuable instrument of the democratic electoral process." Thus the president of NBC before a Senate subcommittee. And Dr. Stanton, before the same committee, echoes his plea. "It is clear and unmistakable where the public interest lies: the public itself made that judgment when the debates went on the air. And the public is the only touchstone for the solution of the persistent problem of section 315. . . . I hope most earnestly that the Congress will promptly, completely and permanently free broadcasting from restraints that, however noble in purpose, were abortive in operation and have now proven unnecessary in fact."

I dispute the proof and question the fact. This goes too fast and too far. Section 315 and the debates are related matters, but they are also distinct. While our two major parties remain substantially unchallenged by others, let the debates (for all their merely marginal advantage) remain exempt from the provisions of Section 315. But let us concurrently pursue the ends, "noble in purpose" as Dr. Stanton properly conceded them to be, that Section 315 seeks to protect. The equities involved here are too complex to elaborate further in an essay primarily concerned with the debates. But that they exist and are important is something we should not overlook. To foreclose on further discussion of how best to protect them, merely to secure continuance of the debates, is at once to confuse issues and to risk throwing the baby out with the bath water.

8

The Counterfeit Debates

J. JEFFERY AUER

WOODROW WILSON once told an AFL convention that "It is always dangerous for a man to have the floor by himself." G. B. Shaw declared that "The way to get at the merits of a case is not to listen to the fool who imagines himself impartial, but to get it argued with reckless bias for and against." These epigrammatic observations characterize the philosophy of the traditional public debate in English-speaking nations. The purpose of this brief comment is to provide an historical background to the Nixon-Kennedy debates, examining them within the context of the debate tradition, and judging them as contributions to it.

The public debate is one of the great traditions in American life. It provides for a forensic confrontation by those holding divergent views, an orderly and comprehensive review of the arguments for and against a specific proposal before minds are made up and votes are cast. As Reuben Davis observed of political debating a hundred years ago, "constant practice had made our public speakers so skillful in debate that every question was made clear even to men otherwise uneducated."[1] Debate also provides a fair method for a minority to challenge an established majority. Indeed, Americans pay the salaries of minority members in state and national legislatures so that they will oppose in debate the majority views on controversial issues.

In short, debate has historically been regarded as an essential tool of a democratic society where the majority rules in a milieu of free speech. This concept is illustrated in a review of debate as an educational method, as a legislative process, and as a judicial procedure.

As an educational method debate was first employed more than

142

2,400 years ago by one Protagoras of Abdera; his pupils argued both sides of questions similar to those agitating their elders.[2] In the schools of the Middle Ages debating appeared in assigned student disputations, "Some for a show dispute and for exercising themselves . . . others for truth."[3] Records as early as 1531 refer to joint disputations by students at Oxford and at Cambridge,[4] and this teaching device was adopted in the American colonial colleges as admirably suited to train young men for the ministry and for leadership in government. While instruction in dialectic was commonly included in the collegiate course of study, the practice of debate most often centered in the literary societies. From these society activities developed intramural and then intercollegiate debating, the latter probably dating from 1883 and a first forensic contest between Knox College and the Rockford Female Seminary.[5] The college literary society of the eighteenth and nineteenth centuries is now virtually extinct, but extensive programs of debate on current public questions continue in high schools and colleges. They provide, as President John F. Kennedy observed, "a most valuable training whether for politics, the law, business, or for service on community committees such as the PTA and the League of Women Voters. . . . The give and take of debating, the testing of ideas, is essential to democracy."[6]

As a legislative process debate is basic to democratic parliamentary action. In some pseudo-democracies, of course, there is a pretense of consulting the people by giving them a chance to vote "Yes" under circumstances that make it unlikely that they will vote "No." But when the people, or their elected representatives, have a real voice in the affairs of government, final decisions follow parliamentary debate. This has been true in American government since the first colonial legislatures, and the history of Congress could well be written in a sequence of chapters focusing upon significant debates over the bank question, the slavery issue, imperialism, the tariff, the League of Nations, the neutrality controversy before World War II, and involving such stalwarts as Benton, Beveridge, Calhoun, Clay, Corwin, LaFollette, Lodge, Taft, Vandenburg, and Webster. It is here in the debate of the legislative process, believes Walter Lippmann, that freedom of speech is best conceived, "by having in mind the picture of a place like the American Congress, an assembly where opposing views are presented, where ideas are not merely uttered but debated, or the British Parliament where men who are free to speak are also compelled to answer."[7]

As a judicial procedure debate has been the instrument of equity for both plaintiff and defendant in a system of justice where witnesses testify and are cross-examined, where each party is represented by a lawyer, debating the same issues before the same judge and for the decision of one jury. That this is the only way to resolve issues of guilt or innocence we believe so strongly that if a defendant is too poor to employ an attorney, the government assigns counsel to see that his legal rights are protected and that his defense is heard. Each generation in the history of jurisprudence has its roster of distinguished legal debaters, from Cicero to Grotius, and down to Morris Ernst and Thurgood Marshall.

While it has been in the classroom, the legislative chamber, and the courtroom that debate has been most systematically employed, perhaps the most significant elements of the debate tradition in America have been the forensic clashes in debating societies and in public debates on political, social, and religious questions. In the first century of American democracy, the debating society provided an important forum for shaping informed opinion. In 1824 Thomas Jefferson encouraged the organizer of the Debating Society of Hingham: "The object of the society is laudable, and in a republican nation, whose citizens are to be led by reason and persuasion, and not by force, the art of reasoning becomes of first importance."[8] And in 1852 Dr. Daniel Drake, the distinguished physician-historian of the Ohio Valley, asserted that "I can recollect no association for intellectual improvement, except this primitive, old-fashioned organization, which I really think has done much good in the world."[9]

One of the chief contributions of these early societies was the training it offered future statesmen, sharpening their thinking by compelling them to defend their views in debate. Abraham Lincoln regularly walked seven miles from New Salem to take part in the debates of a small village society; Henry Clay joined first the Richmond Rhetorical Society, and then a similar group on the Kentucky frontier; and Tom Corwin, in Lebanon, Ohio, spoke frequently in the debates at the Mechanics' Institute.[10] Society debates were truly practical schools for politics in the period of "the rise of the common man," when, as Judge Hall reported, "Everything is done in this country in popular assemblies . . . all questions are debated in popular speeches, and decided by popular vote."[11]

Even the clerics helped form the great American tradition of debate. In 1829 Alexander Campbell defended Christianity against the agnosticism of Robert Owen in a Cincinnati debate that lasted eight days; and in 1843 Campbell debated the "New Light" theology with Reverend N. L. Rice, at Danville, Kentucky, with Henry Clay as the moderator, daily for sixteen days![12]

In short, whether the critical question of the day concerned slavery, imperialism, the gold standard, socialism, public power, or evolution, public debate was in order, and involved such distinguished protagonists as "Parson" Brownlow, Abraham Lincoln, Stephen A. Douglas, William Jennings Bryan, Robert Ingersoll, Scott Nearing, Clarence Darrow, Norman Thomas, and George W. Norris.

It was inevitable that the electronic age should strengthen and perpetuate the debate tradition via the broadcast media. On a national network basis the first regular debates were probably those on Theodore Granik's American Forum of the Air. Two speakers, commonly drawn from Congress, confronted each other with sharply divergent views on a public question. Granik introduced them, asked a provocative question and then, in effect, sat back to see what would happen. What happened was a direct clash, sometimes sharpened by further questions from the moderator, with each speaker taking about half the program time.

Heard by as many as five million listeners weekly at the height of its popularity, America's Town Meeting of the Air, moderated by George V. Denny, Jr., was first fashioned in 1935 from the same tradition. "If we persist," said Denny, "in the practice of Republicans reading only Republican newspapers, listening only to Republican speeches on the radio, attending only Republican political rallies, and mixing socially only with those of congenial views, and if Democrats . . . follow suit, we are sowing the seeds of the destruction of our democracy. . . ."[13] To reverse this tendency by compelling listeners to hear both sides, Denny adapted the pattern of debate, with two or four opposed speakers dividing a forty-minute period, and then responding to studio audience questions for the rest of the hour. For the audiences at home, Hadley Cantril found in a study of Town Meeting mail, the program had an impact: 34 per cent changed their opinion as a result of the broadcast, 28 per cent always and 50 per cent usually followed the broadcast with further discussion, and 11 per cent always and 24 per cent usually followed the broadcast with their own readings on the subject debated.[14] Among new programs launched in 1960, Face the Nation, moderated by Howard K. Smith, continued the tradition.

Aside from regularly scheduled programs, the national networks have contributed to public enlightenment on current issues through special debate series, such as that between T. V. Smith and Robert Taft in 1939,[15] or single clashes such as that between Thomas E. Dewey and Harold Stassen in the Oregon presidential primary in 1948.[16] Although these broadcast debates have always been condensed to fit the presumed patience of the public—and the industry pattern of thirty- or sixty-minute shows—they have otherwise generally adhered to the debate tradition, with equal time for speakers of comparable prominence and skill, time enough for coherent argument on a single critical question, and some possibility of direct questioning and refutation. Howard K. Smith, indeed, has referred on the air to the program he moderates as an "Oregon style debate," a pattern familiar to all intercollegiate contestants as an alternation of constructive speech, cross-examination, and rebuttal.

With all of this accumulated experience it might have been assumed that the ultimate in a union between the broadcast media and the debate tradition would have been "The Great Debates" between Nixon and Kennedy in the 1960 campaign. Certainly this is what was in the mind of Adlai Stevenson, teachers of speech, and others who supported the proposal for such contests even before the presidential candidates were named.[17] In his recent and significant study of the problems of creating an informed electorate, it was again the traditional pattern of public debate that Stanley Kelley found ideal as a format for campaign speaking.[18]

Before looking directly at the Nixon-Kennedy "debates," however, let us isolate the specific elements of debate as it has developed in the American tradition. There are five, commonly agreed upon by writers on debate.[19] *A debate is (1) a confrontation, (2) in equal and adequate time, (3) of matched contestants, (4) on a stated proposition, (5) to gain an audience decision.* Each of these elements is essential if we are to have true debate. Insistence upon their recognition is more than mere pedantry, for each one has contributed to the vitality of the debate tradition. For example:

(1) One man alone, unrefuted, is but a verbal shadow-boxer. (2) Even two men, without a timekeeper, have only a harangue. (3) There is no equity for unequal opponents, even with equal time; the law clerk does not oppose the veteran pleader. (4) As there is no collision when two trains pass in opposite directions on parallel tracks, so the best matched men may talk safely past each other if they have no common focus. And (5) even men on opposite sides of the same issue

must try to win the listeners, not just to outwit each other. Omission of any of these elements makes a "debate" not a debate, and certainly not in the sense of the Lincoln-Douglas contests in the tradition of which we were assured Nixon and Kennedy stood.

Where did the Nixon-Kennedy debates stand? Where, that is, in terms of the accepted criteria of debate as we have known it in the American tradition?

(1) *Confrontation.* In the physical sense the candidates did confront each other: they could see each other in person or on their television monitors, but they did not talk to each other, much less debate. Instead they were fitted into a new format, like a double public press conference for simultaneous interviewing, and subjected to a "let's put him on the pan" procedure, first developed in the Lawrence Spivak broadcasts, and now standard in the "meet the press" type of shows. The nearest thing to actual confrontation came when the candidates braced themselves for the next probe of their reporter-interrogators. In the great American tradition of debate, however, it will be recalled that it was Lincoln who put the questions to Douglas at Freeport, not an itinerant journalist.

(2) *Equal and adequate time.* Equal time, yes; adequate time, no. The nature of this complaint is no mere carping that today's politicians are growing soft, compared with Lincoln and Douglas, who divided three full hours for each of their seven debates.[20] Instead the complaint is that few of the questions posed to Nixon and Kennedy could conceivably be answered in three minutes, nor could even such brief responses adequately be refuted in one minute. Not only was this unreasonable; it was also dangerous. It created the illusion that public questions of great moment can be dealt with in 180 seconds. This is a dangerous fiction in a time when the future of the free world may depend upon the decisions of the American president.

(3) *Matched contestants.* Though it was Nixon who risked the most in the broadcasts, on other counts the candidates were closely enough matched for a real debate, had they been willing to hold one.

(4) *A stated proposition.* On this count the problem of the "debates" was not singular, but plural. Instead of a critical and comprehensive analysis of a single and significant issue, the listeners were exposed to a catechism as far-ranging as Allen Ludden's questions on the GE College Bowl. In fact, the interrogations suffered by comparison even with the unlamented quiz shows: contestants in those orgies of obscurantism were at least permitted to stick to one category. But

the contestants, Nixon and Kennedy, fencing with their quizmasters, were compelled to contrive facile answers to queries on an encyclopedic range of topics, with none of the rhetorical elements of unity and coherence to bind them together. These limitations were especially apparent, of course, in the middle two broadcasts; the first and the fourth presumably had some central focus.

(5) *To gain a decision.* Judged on this criteria the "debates" were least adequate. In the debate tradition the emphasis has been upon the issues, even when, as in the Scopes trial, such dramatic personalities as Bryan and Darrow were in opposition. But Nixon and Kennedy might each have fairly quoted Lincoln's words at Gettysburg: "The world will little note, nor long remember, what we say here. . . ." Indeed, there was no deathless prose from either candidate, and least of all from Nixon. In rhetorical terms it may be generalized that their invention was shallow, their organization was adapted only to the faceless middlemen who asked the questions, and their style was unexciting. The emphasis, considering the format of the broadcasts, was inevitably upon instant reactions, not upon developed arguments. The result was sometimes to create an illusion of agreement when in fact there was none (for which Mr. Nixon's Republican friends criticized him after the first meeting),[21] and sometimes to magnify the extent of disagreement. In neither case did the answers contribute much to the enlightenment of listeners, or provide them a rationale for thoughtful decisions on the issues. The broadcasts emphasized personalities rather than issues, and this may have been intentional. But debates in the American tradition have been clashes of ideas, assumptions, evidence, and arguments, not "images."

It is unhappily necessary to conclude that "The Great Debates" were not debates in the American tradition, and the rhetorical critic sighs for what they might have been. In candor, however, he must concede that there are some values even in pseudo-debates. Here are a few:

(1) Even in their seven debates in the Illinois campaign of 1858 Lincoln and Douglas were heard by no more than 75,000 people.[22] More than 85,000,000 persons, on the other hand, heard at least one of the encounters between Nixon and Kennedy.[23] This electronic extension of political speaking is an obvious virtue.

(2) Despite the charge that the "debates" projected each candidate's "image" more than his ideas, 1960 was a campaign between two personalities, and the television listener 2,000 miles from the studio had a better close-up on his screen than did the man in the front row at Peoria in 1858.

(3) Nineteen hundred sixty was a year of great and sometimes bitter political tension and the Nixon-Kennedy broadcasts, whatever their weaknesses, did provide a much-needed example of good-tempered discussion on controversial matters. The candidates demonstrated the fact that it is possible to disagree without being disagreeable.

(4) Even short and incomplete answers to their questioners did permit Nixon and Kennedy to stir up some thinking on campaign issues by listeners. For its contribution to this good end, any device must be prized.

(5) Perhaps (and this is a critic's wistful hope), the obvious inadequacies of the 1960 "debates" may lead to more realistic debating in future campaigns. Should this be true, future critics will no doubt praise the "courage" of the two men who took the first step in 1960.

Despite these virtues of the Nixon-Kennedy broadcasts, when viewed in the long perspective of the tradition of American public debating they must be appraised as counterfeit debates.

NOTES

1. Reuben Davis, *Recollections of Mississippi and Mississippians* (Boston, 1889), p. 195.

2. Bromley Smith, "The Father of Debate: Protagoras of Abdera," *Quarterly Journal of Speech,* 4 (1918), 196-215.

3. William Fitz-Stephen, ca. 1190, in Foster Watson, *The English Grammar Schools to 1660* (London, 1938), p. 92.

4. Thomas Fuller, *History of the University of Cambridge* (London, 1840). p. 64.

5. Henry Lee Ewbank and J. Jeffery Auer, *Discussion and Debate* (New York, rev. ed. 1951), p. 383.

6. Kennedy to Clarence K. Streit, Aug. 22, 1960, in John Holladay, "Nixon, Kennedy, 55 Statesmen Advise Student Debaters," *Freedom & Union,* 15 (Oct. 1960), 5.

7. Walter Lippmann, "The Indispensable Opposition," *Atlantic Monthly,* 164 (Aug. 1939), 188-89.

8. Jefferson to David Harding, Apr. 20, 1824, in Adrienne Koch and William Peden, eds., *The Life and Selected Writings of Thomas Jefferson* (New York, 1944), p. 713.

9. Drake's speech to Cincinnati Medical Library Association, January 1852, in Edward D. Mansfield, *Memoirs of the Life and Services of Daniel Drake* (Cincinnati, 1855), p. 73.

10. James Q. Howard, *The Life of Abraham Lincoln* (Cincinnati, 1860), p. 18; Calvin Colton, *The Life and Times of Henry Clay* (New York, 1846, 2 v.), I, 25, 78-79; Lebanon *Western Star,* Jan. 4, 1866.

11. James Hall, "On Western Character," *Western Monthly Magazine,* 1 (1833), 52-53.

12. W. H. Venable, *Beginnings of Literary Culture in the Ohio Valley* (New York, 1891), pp. 221-22.

13. Harry A. Overstreet and Bonaro W. Overstreet, *Town Meeting Comes to Town* (New York, 1938), p. 19.

14. Henry Lee Ewbank and J. Jeffery Auer, *Discussion and Debate* (New York, 1941), p. 36.

15. Transcripts in Robert Taft and T. V. Smith, *Foundations of Democracy* (Chicago, 1939).

16. See Robert F. Ray, "Thomas Dewey: The Great Oregon Debate of 1948," in Loren Reid, ed., *American Public Address: Studies in Honor of Albert Craig Baird* (Columbia, Mo., 1961), pp. 245-67.

17. Adlai Stevenson, "Plan for A Great Debate," *This Week,* Mar. 6, 1960, pp. 14-15; Austin J. Freeley, "The Presidential Debate and the Speech Profession," *Quarterly Journal of Speech,* 47 (1961), 60-64. It is interesting to note that as early as Apr. 8, 1960, John F. Kennedy wrote to Annabel D. Hagood that "I would be delighted to participate in national TV debates with the Republican candidate should I win the Democratic nomination. I think such a debate would be both educational and fruitful for the American people." See Freeley, p. 62.

18. Stanley Kelley, Jr., *Political Campaigning: Problems in Creating an Informed Electorate* (Washington, D.C., 1960), pp. 18-22, 67-69, 149-50, 152-53, 155.

19. See A. Craig Baird, *Argumentation, Discussion, and Debate* (New York, 1950); Waldo W. Braden and Earnest Brandenburg, *Oral Decision-Making* (New York, 1955); Arthur N. Kruger, *Modern Debate: Its Logic and Strategy* (New York, 1960); David Potter, ed., *Argumentation and Debate: Principles and Practice* (New York, 1954).

20. See Paul M. Angle, ed., *Created Equal? The Complete Lincoln-Douglas Debates of 1858* (Chicago, 1958).

21. See editorials in *Buffalo Evening News, Chicago Tribune,* Indianapolis *News,* Sept. 27-29, 1960; David Lawrence, in Louisville *Courier-Journal,* Sept. 29, 1960; telegrams to Nixon, in *Chicago Tribune,* Oct. 9, 1960; Arthur Krock, in *New York Times,* Oct. 9, 1960. An AP dispatch, *New York Times,* Oct. 8, 1960, quoted Nixon: "Some people thought I was a little too easy on Senator Kennedy. . . . We're really going to give 'em hell from now on."

22. Forrest L. Whan, "Stephen A. Douglas," in William Norwood Brigance, ed., *A History and Criticism of American Public Address* (New York, 1943, 2 v.), II, 792.

23. Gallup Poll, Nov. 3, 1960, in Louisville *Courier-Journal,* Nov. 4, 1960.

9

Personalities vs. Issues

SAMUEL LUBELL

ON THE MORNING after the first TV debate I was interviewing in Free-born County, in southern Minnesota. Near Bancroft one young farmer was fixing his plough when I drove into his farmyard. Asked whether he had heard the debate, he nodded and volunteered, "Before I tuned in I was afraid neither man was fit to be president. But they both handled themselves well. The country will be secure with either man."

The reaction of this farmer points to one definitely constructive contribution of the TV debates—they made both candidates and the election result more acceptable to the electorate.

Before the debates many voters whom I talked with were critical of both John F. Kennedy and Richard M. Nixon. Often voters interviewed would complain, "Neither is a big enough man" or "Johnson or Lodge are better than the men they are running with." Democrats and Republicans declared, "I'd vote for either vice president if he were on the top of the ticket." Once the debates got started this talk of voting for vice president rather than president died off. Strong Democrats conceded, "Nixon gave intelligent answers. If he wins it won't be a catastrophe." Life-long Republicans remarked, "Kennedy might turn out to be a great leader even though I don't like his philosophy."

If the TV debates had not been held, the razor-thin election outcome would probably have left much more rancor and ill feeling in the country. Certainly Kennedy's TV performance removed much of the sting from the resentment of many voters who were troubled at the prospect of a Catholic in the White House. There was also general satisfaction that both candidates had had a fair chance to present themselves to the nation.

151

This fact, that the debates made it easier for the electorate to accept the election results, can be chalked up as a distinct public service, and an important plus in favor of repeating these debates in future elections. But if the debates are to become a permanent campaign institution we face another less pleasant prospect—that they will strengthen the trend toward actor-presidents and, in the process, sap away some of our traditional political stability.

All sorts of revolutionary implications have been read into the TV debates; probably this has been overdone. To me, the main challenge posed by the debates is stirred by two changes in our established political ways.

First, the debates tend to lessen somewhat the importance of issues and party and to elevate the significance of personality, particularly on its theatrical side.

Second, the debates threaten to upset one of our more deeply-rooted political habits—the habit of not listening to the candidates.

Normally, American voters pay only small attention to what Wendell Willkie once dismissed as just "campaign oratory." And when people do listen to campaign speeches, usually it is to someone they already agree with. This practice may annoy those political activists who believe the Republic will be saved by getting Boy Scouts to shame people into voting even when they don't know what they are voting about. Still, the public's relative indifference to campaigning contributes considerably to political stability. The proportion of voters who shift their party support from one election to the next is kept down. The balancing of Democratic and Republican strength is held more even.

In the 1960 campaign, though, through the TV debates a surprisingly large part of the electorate actually tried to follow the arguments of both candidates, blow by blow. The net effects of this heightened campaign interest were not entirely heartening.

In my interviewing during the campaign I systematically asked each voter, "Did you listen to any of the TV debates?" and "What do you think of them?" The overwhelming majority responded in terms of how the candidates looked and handled themselves rather than in terms of the issues that were argued about. Many voters explained that they tried to make sense of the arguments of the candidates "but the more we listened the more confused we got." In Greensboro, N. C., one housewife voiced a typical lament when she protested "you need a diagram to follow what they're talking about."

The debates, in short, touched off a crude sort of contest in the voter's mind between issues and personality. Many voters, finding themselves unable to cope with the issues discussed in the Kennedy-Nixon exchange, settled back and judged the debates as a personality contest.

Some of this popular confusion can be attributed to the format in which the debates were cast. In Akron, a plumber's wife watched one debate while washing diapers. She complained, "They never really answer the questions the reporters ask. Both men just wander around in their talk." Again in Queens, a salesman protested, "They don't answer each other directly. Each says the other is wrong. But they don't give us any proof of what they say."

However, much more than format is involved. Comprehension of complex issues is never easily achieved through any media, let alone through an exchange of verbal punches. The essential difficulty, let me stress, is not a lack of intelligence on the part of the public. Much of the electorate, to repeat a point made earlier, is not accustomed to following campaign arguments in detail. When people try to do so they find that they do not have at hand the mental frame of reference that is needed to organize the disconnected "facts" or arguments that get flung about in a debate.

In Jacksonville, Florida, when I asked one housewife whom she intended to vote for she hesitated and replied, "Well now, let me see, who did I listen to last." A fair number of voters I talked with shared this tennis-ball experience of shifting back and forth between the candidates.

Significantly, the issues which registered most strongly through the debates were those which listeners could translate into their own personal and even selfish calculations. Medical care for the aged was a good example. Before the TV debates began relatively few voters talked much about this issue. After the presidential nominating conventions, Congress had passed a law enabling the states to provide medical care for elderly people who could prove their need. But four different bills were debated in Congress and relatively few persons knew what the law provided. As they listened to the first TV debate, many voters awoke to the realization that Kennedy's proposal would make medical care available to all elderly people under social security, while under Nixon's plan such care would be limited to the needy aged.

The sharpening of this choice caused voter shifts. In Minneapolis, a retired electrical worker had told me in 1958, "I won't vote for a Catholic President." When I reinterviewed him in 1960 he was going for Kennedy. "Nixon's medical bill," he explained, "would make me sell my house and become a welfare case before I could be eligible. If the medical plan is under Social Security, I'd come in it." Again in Lakewood, California, a woman in her sixties said, "We were Republicans but are switching to get this socialized medicine. My husband has heart trouble. We can use someone to pay our bills. We're not thinking of war or peace—just of what will help us." As a third example, in East Meadow, Long Island, a 35-year-old policeman explained, "My father-in-law lives with us. We have to pay his Blue Shield and Blue Cross. Under Kennedy's plan social security would pay for it."

In contrast, federal aid to schools remained a jumble to most voters, despite the TV debates. On this issue the chief difference developed by the candidates was whether states should be able to use federal funds to increase teachers' salaries directly, as Kennedy urged, or whether giving states money for school construction would release funds to raise teachers' salaries, as Nixon argued. Even school teachers interviewed after the debates were not clear which plan would benefit them most. In fact, quite a number of voters attributed to Kennedy the views Nixon voiced and vice versa.

Another common source of annoyance to many voters was the use of statistics in the debates. Kennedy, in particular, impressed voters with how "he just rattles off those figures." But even Kennedy supporters were troubled as to how accurate the figures might be. Scores of voters echoed much the same complaint: "One fellow throws out a figure. Then the other fellow contradicts that with some other figures. How does one know who is right or who is lying?" It would have helped public understanding considerably if after each debate the newspapers had stated what was right or wrong about the statistics advanced by each candidate.

If the debates become permanent and hold their audience—an important if—far-reaching changes will be needed in newspaper and TV commentary. These changes should be directed toward lessening the confusion in which key issues are left in the public mind.

Still, whatever journalistic changes are tried, we must expect that future TV debates will continue to put the prime emphasis on the personality of the candidates rather than on party and issues. Given the nature of TV, the contest between personality and issues is bound to remain an uneven one—as uneven perhaps as matching the crowd appeal of a chorus girl against a she-intellectual with horn-rimmed glasses.

Perhaps I should hasten to add that I am not against chorus girls—in their place—or against personality in political candidates. A strong case can be made that it is more important to get a measure of the personal qualities of the man who will be president than to know how he stands on particular issues.

The real 64-million-vote question is what is it that comes through the TV screen—the real man or the actor? On this question the voters themselves are divided. My interviews across the country indicate that most people think that TV does give one penetrating and intimate insights into the candidate. "You hear each man directly," was one typical comment. "There's nothing between you and what he says." Another commonly voiced remark ran, "You can see which man gets rattled easily." But other voters shared the feeling of an auto worker in Detroit who said, "It's all phony. This has become an actor's election."

What I have seen of political campaigning inclines me toward the view of the Detroit auto worker. The TV debates place a high value on a candidate's skill as an actor and, if continued, would make American politics more theatrical in nature. Of course, the TV debates did not start this trend. Dwight D. Eisenhower had his Robert Montgomery helping with TV appearances long before Section 315 was suspended.

Some observers are troubled at the effect this theatrical emphasis has on the voters. Henry Steele Commager has argued that some of our better presidents might have been defeated had they been forced to expose themselves on TV against a more glamorous but less able opponent. Much concern has also been voiced that TV debates could hinge the presidency on some small mischance like a blooper remark, an awkward mannerism, or the effects of poor lighting or pallid make-up. Many Republicans, of course, feel that Nixon was defeated for just that reason, because "his knee must have been hurting him" or "he doesn't screen well." However, the closeness of the 1960 vote—and this is something I will come back to later—does not indicate that the TV debates swept the electorate off balance.

I am not particularly troubled at the effect TV debates may have on the public, but I am concerned about their effect on the candidates, about the pressures exerted by the debates to project some contrived "image" across the screen into the national living room.

This new "image worship" is one of the more corrupting influences in American political life today. For one thing, the effects of image-making are not limited to campaigns alone. Some years ago presidential campaigns could be shrugged off as temporary aberrations that were indulged in for a few fevered months, after which the candidates and parties settled back to more sensible ways.

But politics in the United States has been changing to where campaigning never really ends. Both the Democrats and Republicans have reorganized their party machinery so it will function day in and day out, year in and year out. And the business of image-making is also becoming a continuous operation.

One result is that it has become virtually impossible to tell the man from the actor in the White House. This was true when Dwight D. Eisenhower was president. It remains true under Kennedy. Then image-worship breeds a treacherous philosophy of leadership and government. The president tends to fall victim to the delusion that his role is to serve as a kind of screen personality—a "father" figure or an "action" figure—with whom "the public" can identify itself vicariously. Proportionately less emphasis is given to the undramatic task of organizing the thinking through of the harsh choices our nation faces.

Some degree of stagecraft is essential to all politics and government. This I recognize fully. But there are limits beyond which it becomes perilous for a democracy to personalize its problems and conflicts. To cite one illustration, we follow a meeting of Kennedy and Khrushchev as if it were a global prize-fight. In doing so our conflict with Soviet Russia tends to become a spectator sport. Our attention is diverted from the fact that the real test of survival is the ability of the American people, as a people, to mobilize the resources and power needed to stabilize scattered parts of the world. To succeed in this effort we— each of us—have to get off our comfortable spectator seats and involve ourselves personally in this struggle.

Perhaps I am more alarmed than is justified. Still I do not think our national needs were furthered by the image-making that took place in Eisenhower's administration and I do not think these needs are being met by the image-making of the Kennedy administration.

There is, of course, a school of thought which holds that the black magic of government will be found in techniques of manipulating the masses. This belief is strongly held not only on Madison Avenue but in many of our better universities. Everything I have learned about public opinion challenges this notion that persuasion can serve as a substitute for thinking. The crucial need in Washington is to think through what needs to be done and to explain it to the public in patient detail. Our difficulties over the years have arisen less from inaction than from a low quality of government thinking, from the failure to work out an integrated cold war strategy, in which our domestic and foreign aims are synchronized under a carefully considered system of priorities.

The arts of persuasion become valuable after the thinking has been done. We shall not find a substitute for thinking in actor-presidents, in the dazzle of political "style," or in the intellectual escapism of eloquent speech-writing.

To return to the contest between personality and issues, it should be stressed that this conflict extends far beyond the TV debates. Many other forces are giving personality a rising importance in American politics. In fact, TV's influence may not be as weighty as the tendency for Democrats and Republicans to adopt identical positions on so many issues. The absence of sharp party differences encourages voters to look to "the man not the party." This trend is strengthened all the more by the fact that to many voters, particularly those under forty, the symbolism attached to both parties is largely obsolete, being a hang-over of the conflicts of the Roosevelt era.

It is also important to bear in mind that the vote-changing power of TV exposure still seems a limited one—which brings us to what remains the big mystery of the 1960 debates. The evidence is over-whelming that Kennedy emerged as the "winner" in the sight of the vast majority of viewers. Why, then, if the impact of the TV debates was anywhere nearly as dramatic as is claimed, did not Kennedy win by a landslide?

My own voter interviews leave no doubt that the debates changed for the better the image of Kennedy that most voters held. Kennedy, it is true, started the campaign with one advantage which is often overlooked—people were curious about him. Even before the presidential conventions, I found as I went around the country that four to five times as many comments were volunteered by the voters about Kennedy as about Nixon. Often people would interrupt my interviewing to ask me questions about Kennedy. Hardly anyone ever asked me about Nixon. On the night the Republican convention ended, in an NBC broadcast from Chicago, I stressed that this popular curiosity would make Kennedy the headline star of the campaign, that Kennedy's audience was there waiting to look him over, while Nixon would find it difficult to gain attention for his views. Even if Nixon had not agreed to the TV debates the campaigning advantage would have been Kennedy's.

At the outset of the campaign the "images" of the two men held by most voters were not too favorable for Kennedy. During the early summer typical comments being voiced about Kennedy ran, "He's so good-looking I'm afraid to vote for him," or "He's so new and inexperienced you wonder what he would do." Nixon's strategy, of course, was framed around the idea that with war a constant threat the public would decide it was unwise to choose someone new and uncertain over "the man with experience." The first debate almost completely demolished this "experience against youth" argument.

The morning after, a farm implement dealer in Hayfield, Minnesota, told me, "I've been for Nixon but Kennedy was much the sharper man." A dental technician in Minneapolis said, "I heard so much about Kennedy being inexperienced that I was surprised how well he did in the debate."

As the debates continued the image of Kennedy that registered with the voters was of a "sharp" and "aggressive" man who "talks like he knows what he wants to do." Even Republican voters remarked, "He is surer of himself" or "He's straightforward and direct in his answers."

Kennedy was also helped by his distinctive accent. During the 1928 campaign, Al Smith irritated many voters with his East Side accent and mispronunciation of "rad-dio." Kennedy's accent pleased many voters, who laughed as they remarked, "It's nice to hear something different on TV" or "He sounds intelligent and educated."

"Conservative" and "mature" were the adjectives most frequently voiced by voters about Nixon. Stalwart GOP adherents contended, "What counts is not smooth talking but who has the sounder views," or "A man who answers questions so fast can't be thinking." Another feeling was "Nixon knows the value of a dollar, having worked hard all his life."

There is no question that Kennedy looked like the stronger personality to the electorate. In my interviewing I did not run into a single Kennedy voter who thought Nixon had "won" the debates. By contrast fair numbers of Nixon supporters thought "Kennedy gave better answers" or even that "Kennedy is the better man."

In Cleveland Heights a valve salesman declared, "I believe in the Republican philosophy but Kennedy has that wonderful self-assurance. He seems to know where he is going, even though he may be wrong." A 58-year-old inspector for the city of Jacksonville said, "I'm voting for one man but like the other. Kennedy is the stronger man but I'm a little afraid of taking a chance on him at this time."

The mystery remains: why, then, did Kennedy only squeak through?

First, many voters like the valve salesman in Cleveland Heights stuck with their party even though they felt Kennedy might be the better man.

Second, some aspects of the Kennedy image clearly cost him votes. His quickness in replying to questions thrown at him and the number of proposals he urged caused some voters to feel, "Kennedy is too aggressive. He may try to do too much." A salesman in Decatur, Illinois, thought, "Kennedy is more direct in his answers but I'm afraid he'll overspend."

Many voters, in other words, tended to project into the TV debates their own feelings about basic issues. More and more of this went on with each debate. The voters tended to make the candidates and their conflicting personality characteristics symbolic of *what the voters thought were the main issues*. For example, a Chicago bank clerk summed up how the two men looked to him by saying, "Kennedy plays the part of the bold idea man while Nixon pulls Kennedy down to earth by asking how much will it cost?" In Los Angeles toward the close of the campaign, a lawyer's wife explained, "My husband thinks we need a complete change in Washington. He's all for Kennedy. But I'm not sure too much of a change would be good." She then went on to pose a choice that troubled many voters: "I don't know whether to vote for the man who may do too little or the man who may try to do too much."

In short, the TV debates did not stand alone as a campaign influence. How people reacted to the debates merged with and was even shaped by all the other campaigning efforts, by party loyalties and feelings on varied issues.

This all-in-one effect is worth bearing in mind when one looks at the impressive statistics that have been collected to show how much of the electorate followed or was influenced by the debates. In all elections, long before the actual campaigning begins, most voters have their minds made up or are strongly predisposed toward one of the parties or candidates. These voters may tell an interviewer that the campaign influenced them but the campaign may have merely pushed them in the direction they favored. Take a factory inspector's wife I interviewed in Des Moines, Iowa. She and her husband had voted for Eisenhower in 1952 and 1956 but were switching to Kennedy. She was a Catholic. When the campaign started, she explained, "I was determined I wouldn't vote for Kennedy just because he was a Catholic. In fact," she went on, "I was for Nixon until these debates. Kennedy seemed so much more intelligent that I decided last week to shift."

This woman spoke with complete sincerity. As it happened though, I had interviewed her during the 1958 campaign. At that time, my notes showed that when asked "Who will you vote for in 1960?" she replied, "I'll go for Nixon against any Democrat but Kennedy. He's a Catholic and I want to see him elected."

Did the debates really shift her vote or did they provide her with the justification she was looking for to swing to Kennedy? And if there had been no TV debates would not some other campaign development have served the same purpose?

Some observers have credited the heavy voting turnout to the TV debates. The debates unquestionably stimulated campaign interest but my own interviewing indicates that religious prejudice was much more powerful in getting out the vote. Repeatedly I ran into persons who told me they hadn't voted for years but had registered because they either were opposed to or wanted a Catholic for president.

Another curious aspect of the 1960 election was the high proportion of voters who described themselves as "undecided" to the pollsters. Most of the "undecided" voters I interviewed were torn by the religious issue. But some termed themselves "undecided," even when their minds were settled, simply because they did not want to say that they had prejudged the candidates before listening to them.

Many of these voters waited until the fourth debate was over before declaring themselves openly. Some polls may show these voters as having swung in the last few weeks but their vote had been set for months.

One cannot isolate with precision the influence of the TV debates from all the other factors which shaped the vote. One can only advance a judgment as to their effect. My own judgment is that the debates did not bring any basic change in the voting pattern of the nation. In the end the vote pretty well matched the mood of the nation as it stood before the debates began.

Early in September I wrote a newspaper article in which I compared the election to "a football game without any touchdowns." Neither candidate, I explained, had been able to generate a decisive issue that was capable of sweeping the electorate. At most the issues being agitated by both candidates were gaining them only a few yards, a few votes here and there, but nothing decisive.

This judgment reflected the curious mood of half-way conflict that I found through the country. On foreign policy, for example, Kennedy was trying to get the electorate to repudiate the Eisenhower administration. This the public was not ready to do. But the voters weren't willing to give the Eisenhower policies a ringing endorsement either. On one hand voters would say "We're not at war" and this was a considerable Nixon asset. But deep concern was also voiced over the course of events since the U-2 incident, particularly over Castro in Cuba. Nixon's contention that the prestige of the United States was higher than ever collided with the oft-repeated feeling, "The Russians are kicking us around. We need a tougher foreign policy."

On economic issues, I found a noticeable shift to Kennedy in cities where unemployment was high. However, most of the people I interviewed said, "We're better off than ever" or "We're as well off as we have ever been."

But the main reason why the vote was dividing so closely was the religious issue. In every state some Stevenson voters would say, "We're Baptists and Democrats" or "We're Lutherans and Democrats," and then ask, "What should we do?" Offsetting such losses was the shift to Kennedy of Catholics who had voted Republican for at least the three previous presidential elections. So strong was this religious conflict that it cut down the force of all other issues. And it was this which kept the campaign action on the fifty-yard line. The feelings of Protestants and Catholics stood like two walls, one on each side, limiting the ground that could be gained with any issue. Farmers who were mad at Ezra Benson balked at "voting for the Pope." Many Catholics liked Nixon's long recorded stand against Communism and his part in jailing Alger Hiss. But Nixon could carry the foreign policy ball only so far and then would run into the feeling "There has never been a Catholic president. We want to lift that barrier."

The election returns confirm this judgment. If one examines how the vote fell across the country, state by state, county by county, precinct by precinct, it becomes clear that the religious issue structured the 1960 vote. At every voting level the change from 1956 corresponds more closely to the proportion of Catholics and Protestants in the population than to any other factor.

No issue raised by either candidate proved strong enough to break through the walls of religious feeling for a touchdown run. This was the fate of the TV debates, as well. They did stir a personality surge in Kennedy's favor but the sweep was blocked by anti-Catholic opposition and by divided feelings among the voters on Eisenhower's "peace" record and fears that Kennedy's ideas would raise taxes.

To sum up, if this analysis is valid it still leaves one tantalizing door unopened—that the TV debates might have produced a Kennedy landslide if it had not been for the anti-Catholic feeling. Surely some of the jump in Kennedy's popularity after his inauguration can be attributed to the feeling voiced by numerous voters during the campaign, "I've got nothing against Kennedy except that he's a Catholic."

Still when all the evidence is put together it does not seem to justify the contention that the TV debates brought about a revolution in our political ways. So far at least television appears to have had more effect on the candidates and their campaigning methods than on the voters.

Television is certainly changing the relative importance of party, issues, and personality. If strong emotional issues are absent, how the candidates project on the TV screen could be decisive. During the 1958 gubernatorial campaign in New York many of the voters I talked with switched to Nelson Rockefeller because Averell Harriman seemed "a tired old man over TV" while Rockefeller looked like "an eager beaver."

The shape of future campaigning will hinge on which of the three factors—party, issues, or personality—mounts into the ascendancy. Right now the leaders in both parties seem to believe that personality and image-making are the most powerful forces in swaying the electorate. It is my own belief that more votes can be changed by giving our parties a sharper meaning in terms of the issues of today. This sharpening of party differences is also needed if the American people are to face up to our national problems.

10

The Future of National Debates

GILBERT SELDES

THE ACCEPTED essential condition of a public debate is that the participants start on even terms. Nothing may be contrived to heighten the *natural* advantage in talent or intelligence of one or conceal the *natural* deficiencies of another. A debate between candidates for the presidency on these conditions can occur only once in eight years. In the intervening campaign one of the debaters is usually president of the United States.

My own impulse is to say that one of the debaters suffers from the disadvantage of being president. But the principle is the same if one takes the office as an advantage to the candidate. Once in every two elections the debaters are placed in the same framework but are not seen in the same perspective.

This principle applies to any kind of confrontation. A second may have more bearing on the specific kind of debate in which the candidates meet, the debate by television, for instance. It requires us to consider that while the qualities of mind and temperament which make a good debater are highly desirable, there may be other qualities which at certain times are equally, or even more, desirable in our chief executive.

It is my guess that if President Eisenhower had been eligible and nominated for a third term, the debates of 1960 would not have occurred. One cannot be sure of the reasons that would have been given since no one can say openly that a candidate's health does not permit him to do what his opponent does, nor is there an acceptable phrase to conceal other disqualifications for debate which do not imply disqualifications for office.

In 1956 no pressure to accept debate existed. In 1964 and thereafter the pressure will be intense. Consequently, the selection of a candidate may be decided by attributes desirable in a debater. We do not have to say that these are necessarily opposed to or cannot coexist with qualities most desirable in a president. We can say that of two men, virtually equal in statesmanship, the one who has proved readier in debate will be preferred. We can, with some confidence, shift the testing period back to the pre-convention period—and again we face the gross inequality once in each eight years—that the incumbent is not compelled to outrun others for the nomination.

My argument leads me to at least a tentative conclusion: that certain kinds of confrontation between candidates should not become fixed ("traditional") as part of the process of choosing the president. Before examining the possible confrontations closely, I am compelled to recognize—and in self-defense to say that I do recognize—a fact of American political life which is an unsanctioned part of the whole pre-convention process, namely: that the capacities of each candidate *as a campaigner* play a considered—and considerable—part in the final choice. Again there is a difference if the incumbent chooses to run because the party machinery and the psychological danger of repudiating the head of an administration while asking for the return of that administration to power combine to force the nomination even though everyone knows that someone else might be a better vote-getter. The avowed candidates within the president's party are not taken seriously; they may be working for the vice presidency if it is open or laying the ground for next time. The incumbent candidate, consequently, has no need to prove himself in pre-convention argument and actually misses an opportunity to show his mettle; he is virtually disqualified during the pre-convention period from open politicking.

When, however, both parties must put up new men, the primaries become a magnificent free-for-all and if the political mechanics could be worked out, the place for the great confrontations would be here. The difficulties are probably insurmountable, but if all candidates were to declare themselves in all states, and if all the states held their primaries the same day, the situation would have an almost mathematical elegance since none of the debaters would be, at the time, the chosen representative of his party, and, potentially, the next president.

In the above situation, the condition of equality would be met, each candidate having the same degree of freedom, each indicating, without the advantage of position, his degree of responsibility, each free (without the compelling necessities of office) to expose his irresponsibility. At such a moment, the most penetrating cross-questioning is not only permissible, it is desirable. To be sure, the meetings would be intramural; the decision between parties would still have to be made. But the total presentation of each man's temperament and the total rendering of his character and intellect could be properly accomplished. (Apart from the financial complexities involved, the method has the defect of virtually eliminating the non-campaigning dark horse.)

Changes in our present system of primaries may give us greater opportunities to know the eventual candidates, but they will not significantly alter the pressure on delegates to pick a good campaigner. If we accept this as a fact of our political situation, we can ask whether the introduction of face-to-face debates is anything more than a shift in technique. If the tradition of choosing a good campaigner or the best campaigner, out of all the postulants considered fit to become president, hasn't, on the whole, imposed intolerable burdens on the candidates or unbearable presidents on the country, why should we have reservations about a new and in many ways superbly useful device?

The reason stems from that imposed inequality which must occur in the alternate elections when a president is also a candidate. If the debates become an accepted form of campaigning, they will be expected; and it is conceivable that a president, feeling himself on sure ground, might insist on a debate whereas a president who felt that his office or some delicate situation (as in foreign affairs) made debate dangerous might not be able to avoid a challenge from his opponent.

The president, in that event, would be compelled to do what no president has ever had to do before: accept conditions imposed on him from the outside. Until now, both candidates have been able to choose their own ground—to make a grand tour, to appear, televised or not, in large halls, to submit to spontaneous (or fake-spontaneous) questions, to be initiated into Indian tribes and to kiss babies. Each has, in a sense, chosen his own audience. And, in consequence, each has been able to decide what to say and what to leave unsaid. Each has challenged the other in such terms as to allow for the exercise of choice and judgment. Unless the debates are greatly altered from the form in which they appeared in 1960, a thoughtful candidate might not feel free to ask a president certain questions, as a thoughtful president might feel compelled not to answer them. A demagogue in either position, especially a non-incumbent, might ask such questions that a refusal to answer or an evasion might prejudice the welfare of the state.

It isn't even necessary to impute low motives to such questions. An outsider, without the information which had reached the president, might in all candor ask a question. In the House of Commons it is accepted that a minister may insist on "having notice" and refuse an instant response. But such a reply, in a debate with another candidate for the presidency, would immediately draw attention to the delicacy of a situation—an incident might follow—and worse.

This is, perhaps, a proper place to bring into the open the reasons for some of the reservations implied above. One is that I do not believe we need the same kind of individual in the presidency at all times. A master of political economy might have been useful in many ways in 1932, but if he was also dour in temperament, without a certain lightness, he could not have done what Roosevelt did. I am, therefore, afraid of anything which would dictate the qualities of the candidates and particularly dubious of such requirements as the TV debates impose. And I cannot accept the proposition that those who are not good on the screen are exhibiting deficiencies in their essential character. Nothing was more marked in Governor Stevenson's campaigns than his obvious dislike of the apparatus of transmission—he was effective on television only if he stood before an audience; at home when he recorded for TV and in studio conversations, he was ill at ease and hurried and basically uncommunicative. I remember also the radio and newsreel appearances of Huey Long and remember also how frighteningly persuasive he was.

I shall, in outlining the safeguards which I think essential, indicate why I think the debates should be limited in number. One reason connected with my present argument is that if they become only one of several methods, and not the essential one, delegates will feel more free to choose candidates who have other qualifications.

Exposing myself to contempt, I confess to feeling that at times we might need in the White House a man who dislikes and cannot cope with the mass media. We might need a man whose total training (let us say in science) had removed him from all public arenas. We might need a man so analytical as to preclude action on the spur of the moment. We have needed Washington and two Adamses as well as Jefferson and two Roosevelts.

I turn now to the future. Can we invent conditions to eliminate the wrong questions and to make telltale evasions unnecessary? It is my strong conviction that the ground rules will have to be the same for all occasions, that we will not have one set for the campaigns in which a president is running and another when he is not. (I have been assured that I am wrong; the simple expedient offered was that the president would appoint a deputy to debate for him! This was offered by a respected elder statesman among journalists who had no connection, I must add, with the Eisenhower or the Kennedy administration.)

If we are to have the same rules, we can arrive at them, at the future structure of the debates, by asking what their function is. As we go through the list—excerpted from the triumphant announcements of television executives, from enthusiasts who believe that the television debates were the decisive factor in Kennedy's (almost invisible) majority, from the reported man-in-the-street comments—we find that only one element stands clear of reservations and doubts: people who wanted to hear the candidate of their choice were compelled to hear also his opponent. Pendant to this: it is quite possible that the undecided, who might not have troubled to observe either candidate, were drawn to both because of the publicity surrounding the event. If the campaigns are, as I believe them to be, part of our pluralistic educational system, this inescapable attention to "the other side" is of prime significance. This is what must be preserved in whatever rules are contrived.

It follows that whatever distracts the attention must be eliminated. The producing networks have been unduly criticized for trifles, most of which were natural errors in a first time out. The press was the great offender, coming to a low point by vaguely imputing to someone the idea of a conspiracy among make-up men to ruin Mr. Nixon's appearance (as a sort of counterweight, no doubt, to the discussion of Mrs. Kennedy's hairdo, which also seemed for a time to be the major issue of the campaign). The original error was that the production structure prevented the debate from taking place and substituted an awkward panel show. As the series progressed the candidates moved forward, the confrontation was more direct even if they were in different cities.

It is not too difficult to discover the lessons for the future. Assuming that the debates will occur, they can be planned and spaced and a gentleman's agreement, if possible during a campaign, must exist so that neither side can demand additional events. The subject or subjects of each debate must be agreed upon and, although this is a sensitive area, the speakers must be kept within the agreed bounds. Many people feel that the debaters should face one another *and no one else.* (There is no reason why they should not each face other questioners at other times.) The debates should be few in number so that the candidates would be forced to use other forms of campaigning on and off the air. Other rules will no doubt be developed. They should all be framed with one intention: to give the debates a unique character, to prevent them from being confused with programs.

Anyone critical of the debates as they occurred in 1960 and anyone suggesting that total freedom of questioning (with total compulsion to reply) may be undesirable is promptly accused of lacking faith in the American people or in the democratic process. I think it the part of common sense to admit that democracies are capable of making mistakes. I think it salutary to remember that when the debates were first discussed in 1960 one network specifically and one tacitly invited advertisers to participate. I do not suggest that the usual forms of sponsorship with the conventional commercial messages would have been used, but these networks were willing to associate advertisers and products in some way with the debates. It was only the forthright declaration by Dr. Frank Stanton, President of CBS, that his network would not accept advertisers that put an end to the project—which would, if carried out, have given a further "program" air to the proceedings.

I note this because the ground rules for the debates must be founded on realities. Those who make them must have clear concepts of what the debates are intended to accomplish and what their effect on the presidency may be. They must know that just as commercial broadcasting has created the audience for the debates, it has created certain expectancies in that audience, has taught the audience to recognize certain moves and attitudes as being desirable or unworthy. The tempo of television has, for instance, put a premium on speed and this is reflected in a superinduced admiration for the quickness rather than the quality of wit and has somehow equated the process of contemplation—the painstaking working out of a judgment, the careful consideration of what has been said before replying—with slow-wittedness, with the stooge for the popular comedian's brightness. We know very little yet of the effects "in depth" of television, but we know enough to say that in such an event as campaign debates it is the informational, and not the entertainment, side of the medium that must prevail and wherever the two tend to be assimilated harsh measures must, if necessary, be taken to identify the nature of what we are doing.

No ground rules will overcome the basic inequality of the campaigning situation in alternate elections. None I can think of will do more than diminish the tendency to nominate the good TV campaigner (who may conform to, or alter, the image of the TV "personality"). But since we are going to have them, let us understand that their structure and tone cannot be left to either showmen or political strategists to improvise. We must examine the capacities of television, find all the possible ways of using it, speculate on the consequences and in my opinion, if we must make guesses, let them fall on the side of too much, rather than too little, skepticism. It will do little harm to move cautiously into a new and at moments obscure terrain.

11

The Debates in the Light of Research:
A Survey of Surveys

ELIHU KATZ & JACOB J. FELDMAN

TO DATE we have been able to locate thirty-one independent studies of public response to the Kennedy-Nixon debates and there may well be more. It is almost certain that this is the largest number of studies of a single public event in the history of opinion and attitude research.

We want to express gratitude to all those who cooperated with us in locating studies of the debates, in making research results available, and in commenting upon our earlier draft. Without these ingredients, of course, the synthesis which this paper attempts to make would have been impossible.

The names of the individuals and organizations who permitted us to examine the results of their research, published and unpublished, appear in Table 1.

Particular thanks for preparing special tabulations and analyses or providing additional information and helpful criticism are due to the following: Joseph R. Goeke and Reuben Cohen (Opinion Research Corporation); John F. Kraft and Fran Farrell (John F. Kraft, Inc.); Paul K. Perry (The Gallup Organization); Arthur J. Laird (Canadian Broadcasting Corporation); Philip E. Converse (Survey Research Center, University of Michigan); Thomas E. Coffin (National Broadcasting Co.); Mervin D. Field and Robert Heyer (Field Research Co.); Sidney Goldish (Minneapolis *Star and Tribune*); Elmo Roper (Elmo Roper and Associates); Richard F. Carter (Institute for Communication Research, Stanford University); John V. Roberts (Schwerin Research Corporation); Percy H. Tannenbaum (Mass Communications Research Center, University of Wisconsin); Paul J. Deutschmann (Communications Research Center, Michigan State University); Kurt and Gladys Lang (Queens College); Wynn Bussman (A. C. Nielsen Co.); Alex S. Edelstein (School of Communications, University of Washington); Bradley S. Greenberg (Institute for Communication Research, Stanford University; Sidney Kraus (Indiana University).

The Social Science Research Committee of the University of Chicago provided a small grant-in-aid to defray incidental expenses. We are also grateful to Mr. Don Tonjes for expert typing and assistance.

Considering how little advance notice was given that the debates were to be held, the response of the social research fraternity is as interesting as the public response. We propose to examine both.

Our search began with the invitation to us, from the editor of this volume, to comment upon six of the studies which follow.[1] Five of the six were initiated by university groups—four of them in schools of journalism—and were based on small samples of respondents living in communities near by. The sixth was conducted on a very small budget, by a young market research organization in Chicago.

In attempting to compare and contrast these studies and, hopefully, to arrive at some general conclusions concerning the impact of the debates, it occurred to us that there were probably other studies of the debates that would be worth examining. At the very least, we thought, we would find relevant data in the national and regional polls and it seemed like a good idea to confront the small-scale, presumably more intensive, studies with the polls. And so we obtained the results of polls made by Gallup, by Roper (for the Columbia Broadcasting System), and by the various state polls (California, Iowa, Minnesota).

In addition, we knew of the continuing study of election behavior at the Survey Research Center of the University of Michigan and discovered, upon inquiry, that some questions on the debates had been included in their national post-election interview and that some part of the results had already been analyzed.

We learned, too, that each of the candidates had worked closely with a survey research organization. Claude Robinson of Opinion Research Corporation had studied the entire campaign very closely for Richard M. Nixon and, in addition, ORC's Public Opinion Index for Industry conducted supplementary research for its regular business clients. Louis Harris and Associates—in what was surely the closest relationship ever established between a presidential candidate and survey research—worked for John F. Kennedy. ORC agreed to give us access to their data; Harris did not.[2] We also learned that a group (acting as individuals and on a voluntary basis) associated with Social Research, Inc., interested the Kennedy organization in the desirability of obtaining depth interviews on reactions to the debates but the results of this study were collated informally, presented orally, and, at least to date, have not been formally analyzed. Market Psychology, Inc. of New Brunswick, New Jersey, also contributed the results of a small study to the Kennedy campaign.

As we proceeded from agency to agency, we learned of even more work. Albert I. Sindlinger and Co., the market research firm which asks people not only what they are thinking but what they have been talking about recently, conducted an elaborate study of the campaign and paid particular attention to the role of the debates. Similarly, the marketing and opinion research firm of John F. Kraft collected extensive and interesting data. Both of these groups conducted national surveys, as did the market research firm of R. H. Bruskin and Associates. We discovered that the Schwerin Research Corporation, which maintains a special studio-laboratory for observing audience reactions to television programs and advertising under controlled conditions, asked its test audiences about the debates. Then, in the course of reading the Gallup Poll, we found that the Gallup organization had actually gathered an audience in Hopewell, New Jersey, especially to record their minute-by-minute push-button responses to the first debate.

We remembered, too, that the regular TV-radio rating services, which supply the networks with data about their audiences, would have reported on the debates and, with the help of the research department of the National Broadcasting Company, and, later, of one of the agencies concerned (20),* we gained access to these. It was with considerably more surprise that we learned that the Research Division of the Canadian Broadcasting Corporation had investigated the reaction of Canadian audiences and these data, of course, promised to provide a new and non-partisan perspective.

And, finally, informal circulation of a first draft of this manuscript unearthed still more studies, most of which were carried out on campuses of colleges and universities.

THE VARIETY OF RESEARCHES AND RESEARCHERS

There are a number of ways in which this proliferation of studies can be meaningfully classified. Table 1 (see page 000) attempts this in terms of various aspects of research design and in terms of a catalogue of primary substantive concerns. Thus several studies are based on non-representative, small samples of students (e.g., 16, 24), while others employ representative national samples of 2,000 or more (14, 21, 22, 25, 27). Most studies were conducted by means of personal interviews; but some were conducted by phone (4, 6, 7, 25), by self-administered questionnaire (e.g., 17, 23), or by various combinations

* Numbers in parentheses refer to studies in Table 1.

TABLE 11—1. THE STUDIES

No.	Name	Locale	Size of Sample	Timing[a]	Characteristics of Sample	Data Collection Procedures[b]	Principal Concerns[c]
1[d]	Arbitron	National	1,400	Coincident	Random sample of listed phone nos. and probability sample of metered homes	PH; metered devices to record tuning behavior	Audience
2	R. H. Bruskin	National	2,500	V_2	Modified sample area	I	
3	California Poll	State of Calif.	Varied from 619 to 1,270 (A_2)	P_2 (twice) A_2 D_2	Modified area sample representing entire adult population (P_2); registered voters (A_2 and thereafter)	I	Audience Images Who won Favorability Issues Evaluation of performance
4	Canadian Broadcasting Corporation	7 major Canadian cities	4,800	D_2	Individuals in systematic sample of English-speaking telephone households	PH	Audience Images Good idea? Evaluation of performance

5	Richard F. Carter, Inst. for Communic. Res., Stanford	4 cities near Stanford, Calif.	Approx. 100	A_1-A_2-D_2	Sample deliberately designed to contain ½ Republicans and ½ Democrats—probably well above average in SES	I	Audience Images Who won Issues Good idea? Recognition of content
6	Creative Research Associates	Chicago	996[e]	B_1-B_2 C_1-C_2 D_1-D_2	Modified area sample of individuals old enough to vote	PH	Audience Images Favorability

a. P_1 = previous election (same respondents).
P_2 = early in 1960 campaign.
A_1, B_1, C_1, D_1 = just before 1st, 2nd, 3rd, 4th debate.
A_2, B_2, C_2, D_2 = just after 1st, 2nd, 3rd, 4th debate.
V_1 = before election day.
V_2 = after election.

b. I = personal interview.
PH = phone.
SA = self-administered.

c. Principal concerns are limited to those aspects of each study that deal directly with the debates.

d. Several of these studies are cited in the text only rarely or not at all. This is because, at the time of writing, they had not yet been formally analyzed (19, 26); or because they were not in a form that was immediately amenable to our purposes (1); or because we discovered them too late (8, 12, 13, 30); or because they were not made available to us (10).

e. About one-third of total interviewed before and after each debate.

f. In both Kraft and ORC a sub-sample of the original sample was re-interviewed on each of the successive waves.

TABLE 11—1. THE STUDIES, *continued*

No.	Name	Locale	Size of Sample	Timing[a]	Characteristics of Sample	Data Collection Procedures[b]	Principal Concerns[c]
7	Paul J. Deutschmann, Communic. Res. Ctr., Mich. State Univ.	Lansing and E. Lansing, Mich.	159	P_1-A_1-A_2	Those individuals from a '58 general public panel who could still be located and were willing to be interviewed again (40% of original panel). All had listed phones and were registered voters. Sample above average in interest in politics.	I PH	Audience Change of intention
8[d]	Alex Edelstein, School of Communic., Univ. of Washington	Seattle, Wash. (campus)	407	V_1	Students (about 50% under age)	SA	Audience Images Favorability Role of debates in decision
9A	Gallup Poll	National	Varied from about 1,500 to 8,000	P_2 A_1 A_2 D_2	Modified area sample of individuals old enough to vote	I	Audience Who won

No.	Organization	Location	N	A (coincident)	Televote sample	Program analyzer	What liked
9B	Gallup Poll	Hopewell, N. J.	60 in televote sample, 65 interview only		Televote sample composed of undecided or wavering voters		What liked
10d	Louis Harris and Associates						Who won
11	Iowa Poll	State of Iowa		P_2 B_2 V_1	Modified area sample of adults		
12d	Noel W. Keys and Alan Whiteleather, Univ. of N. C.	Chapel Hill, N. C. (campus)	28	V_1 (kinescope of 3rd debate)	Students	SA; program analyzer	Images What liked
13d	Frederick Koenig and Carol Thometz, So. Methodist Univ.	Dallas, Texas (campus)	223	A_1-A_2-B_2	Students	SA	Images Change of intention
14	John F. Kraft Inc.	National	2,200f interviews at P_2; about 300 at A_2, 300 at B_2, 500 at C_2, 1,000 at D_2	P_3—B_2—D_2 with A_2, C_2	Modified area sample	I PH	Audience Who won Issues Change of intention

The Debates in the Light of Research

TABLE 11—1. THE STUDIES, *continued*

No.	Name	Locale	Size of Sample	Timing[a]	Characteristics of Sample	Data Collection Procedures[b]	Principal Concerns[c]
15	Sidney Kraus and Raymond G. Smith, Indiana Univ.	Indianapolis	142	A_1-A_2-D_1-D_2-V_2	Restricted to registered voters in families with TV sets and generally to families with listed phones. Approx. 16% completion rate among eligible individuals in original random sample.	I	Audience Images Issues Change of intention Actual vote
16	Gladys E. Lang and Kurt Lang, Queens College	New York City (and college campus)	95	A_1-A_2-D_2	24 self-administered questionnaires by college seniors, 71 interviews with respondents selected by student interviewers. Well over ½ sample aged under 35, 13 individuals under voting age. Sample above average in socio-economic status.	I SA	Audience Images Change of intention
17	Market Psychology, Inc.	New Brunswick, N.J.	231	D_2		SA	Evaluation of (Kennedy) performance

18	Minnesota Poll	State of Minnesota	1,000	C_2 D_2 A_1	Modified area sample of adults	I	Audience Who won Favorability
19[d]	Roger E. Nebergall and Muzafer Sherif, Univ. of Okla.	Campuses in Okla., Kansas, Wash., and elsewhere	Over 1,500	V_1	Purposive sample of politically active students and others	SA	Who won Favorability
20	A. C. Nielsen Co.	National	1,100	A, B, C, D (coincident)	Probability sample (fixed panel)	SA (diary); metered device to record tuning behavior	Audience
21	Opinion Research Corp.	National	2,672[f]	A_2 B_2 P_2—C_2 D_2 V_2	Probability sample of the general public—4 callbacks	I	Audience Who won Change of intention Actual vote
22	Elmo Roper & Associates	National	Approx. 3,000	P_2 D_2	Modified area sample	I	Audience Images Who won Issues Role of debates in decision

TABLE 11—1. THE STUDIES, *continued*

No.	Name	Locale	Size of Sample	Timing[a]	Characteristics of Sample	Data Collection Procedures[b]	Principal Concerns[c]
23	Schwerin Research Corp.	New York City	About 250-300 after each debate	A_2 B_2 C_2 D_2	Quota-controlled audience assembled to preview new TV shows	SA	Audience Who won Favorability Good idea?
24	Hans Sebald, Ohio State Univ.	Columbus, Ohio (campus)	152	V_1	Students of sociology	SA	Recall of content
25	Sindlinger & Co.	National	Approx. 3,000 at each point in time	A_1 A_2 B_2 C_2 D_2	National cross-section of individuals with listed phone numbers	PH	Audience Who won Issues Good idea?
26[d]	Individuals associated with Social Research, Inc.	6-10 cities (different for each debate)	70-120 each time	A_2 B_2 C_2 D_2	Randomly selected individuals with listed phone numbers interviewed by pro-Kennedy volunteers	PH	Images Who won Evaluation of performance

27	Survey Research Center, Univ. of Mich.	National	1,803	P_1-P_2-V_2	Probability sample of the general public; long-term panel was supplemented by new sample to compensate for panel mortality and for new voters	I	Audience Favorability Actual vote
28	Percy H. Tannenbaum, Bradley S. Greenberg and Fred R. Silverman Mass Communic. Res. Ctr., Univ. of Wisc.	Madison, Wisc. (campus)	187	A_1-A_2-D_2	Predominantly females residing in married student housing developments at the Univ. of Wisc.	I SA	Audience Images
29	Texas Poll	State of Texas	520	B_2		I	Audience Evaluation of performance
30	Malachi C. Topping and Lawrence W. Lichty, Ohio State Univ.	Columbus, Ohio (campus)	114	D_1-D_2	Sample of married students and wives in student housing development	SA	Audience Images
31	David Wallace, Bureau of Applied Social Research, Columbia Univ.	Westport, Conn.	Approx. 500	P_2 V_2	Sample of lists of registered voters		Who won

of these methods (14, 16, 28). Two studies (9B, 12) employed a "program analyzer" for recording and cumulating individual reactions of like and dislike during the actual broadcast of the first debate.

By the same token, some studies were conducted at only one point in time, others are based on the responses of matched samples of respondents at various points in time, while still others are based on repeated interviews with the same sample of respondents. To make this clear, we have labeled the four debates A, B, C, D, and have given the designation A_1 to information collected immediately (within a week or so) before the first debate, A_2 to information obtained immediately after the first debate, and so on. The designation P_2 refers to the early part of the 1960 campaign—any time up to the period immediately preceding the debate. P_1 refers to information obtained before the 1960 campaign began. V_1 is the period after the fourth debate and before the election; V_2 refers to the days immediately after the election. Thus Deutschmann (7), for example, returned just before the first debate (A_1) and immediately after it (A_2) to a sample of respondents he had interviewed in a previous election (P_1). The use of this "panel" technique is indicated by the use of dashes (P_1-A_1-V_2) in Column 5 of Table 1. Other uses of the "panel" method are illustrated in the studies (5, 16, 28) that interviewed before and after the first debate and then, once more, following the last debate (A_1-A_2-D_2), or in the rather more complex designs of the Opinion Research Corporation (21) or of John F. Kraft (14), in which large samples were interviewed before the first debate, and sub-samples of the original sample were re-interviewed after each successive debate. In the Kraft study, the entire sample was interviewed again after the final debate, while ORC obtained the record of actual voting by returning after the election (V_2).

The studies range in focus from an exclusive interest in the size of the audience (1, 20), to a concern with the influence of the debates on voting intentions (6, 7, 16, 21). A number of studies were interested in perceptions of "who won" (e.g., 7, 11, 14, 22, 23, 31) and in various more specific evaluations of the performance of the two debaters (3, 4, 17). A number of studies focused on the related topic of changes in the "images" of the candidates as a result of the debates (e.g., 5, 6, 15, 22, 28). The public's perception of the issues and the substance of what was debated was also examined (5, 14, 15, 22, 25), but far less intensively. Several studies attempted to determine whether the debates themselves were considered a good idea (4, 5, 25). We shall attempt to summarize all of this in what follows.

This record of what actually was done calls back to mind a question that was raised at the outset: What explains the extraordinary number of studies? Given the short notice, and the elaborate resources required to carry out a survey, how are we to understand the overwhelming response of this large variety of research organizations?

The answer, in part, may become clearer from a closer look at the organizations themselves. Essentially, there seem to be two helpful dimensions in terms of which these organizations can be classified. One is whether the organization looks for its primary sources of support, its "audience," and its "profit," to the academic world or the business world. Although commercial and academic research organizations are often staffed by people with the same background, and although there are several forums which provide for interchange between them, there are some obvious differences which must be taken into account in explaining a decision to undertake a study.

The second dimension that seems relevant is whether or not the organization is a veteran in the study of election campaigns. The veterans, of course, could provide for the debates very easily in the normal course of their business; they really didn't need much warning. But what about the others?

The four types of organization which emerge from interrelating these two dimensions present the following picture:

The *commercial veterans,* it is clear, were all ready for the debates. The announcement that the debates were to be held called merely for revision of some questions and, probably, some revision in the timing of the interviewing periods. The motivation for organizations of this kind (3, 9, 11, 18, 21, 22, 25, 29, etc.) is keeping the public abreast of public opinion and, incidentally, calling attention to themselves, to their marketing and opinion services and to the accuracy of their results. Support for these studies typically comes from the newspapers and newspaper chains which carry their releases and, occasionally, from private clients such as a candidate for office on the national or state level (e.g., 21).

There are not many *academic veterans* but the best known of these is surely the Survey Research Center (27). Like the commercial veterans, these were already "in the field," so to speak, when news of the debates arrived. Support for this work typically comes from foundation grants and results are reported in academic books and journals. There is, in addition, a more explicit concern with testing hypotheses rather than simply presenting facts.

The non-veterans, of course, are harder to explain. If the academic veterans' primary interest is in the field of election and opinion research, the *academic non-veterans* appear to have been drawn primarily from communication research. Rather than being interested in elections *per se,* they seem to have been attracted by the opportunity to assess the impact on the process of decision-making of a new form of communication—indeed, one that may become an institution in democratic politics. Thus almost all of the studies in this group (5, 7, 8, 12, 13, 15, 16, 19, 24, 28) were carried out by professors in centers of research in journalism and communication and, in the case of Kurt and Gladys Lang (16), by a team which has become famous for what has been called "fire-house research" in the field of communication. It is this quality of rousing a few volunteers, assessing the extent of the fire and devising a strategy for coping with it that characterizes these studies. As a rule, there was no established routine on which to fall back, no staff already in the field and, of course, no elaborate financing. The emphasis, instead, is on the more microscopic examination of the processes involved. (When there are other, more comprehensive studies in the field this, of course, can be the only acceptable rationale.) The locale for these studies is necessarily confined to one or several communities in the immediate environs of the university (see Table 1) or sometimes to the student body itself (8, 12, 13, 24), and the results are reported in journals and in books such as this.

Some of the *commercial non-veterans,* too, share a special interest in communication research. This is blatantly obvious in the case of the rating services (1, 20) and, indeed, these should not be treated as special "studies" at all since they are merely by-products of a non-stop operation. The Canadian Broadcasting Corporation (4), though not altogether a commercial organization, or the Schwerin Research Corporation (23), provide better examples. Each has a continuing interest in communication research which explains their interest in the debates. Somewhat different, however, is the motivation of the several market research organizations which are not veterans of election studies. In one case (2), questions about the debates were hitch-hiked onto other studies then in the field. In another case (6), a special study of the debates was hurriedly designed and fielded—but not until after the first debate had come and gone. A third case—the major study in this category—seems best explained in terms of the determination to become a veteran. This is the case of John F. Kraft, Inc. (14), which, like the veterans, had already resolved to study the elections and, when the debates were announced, decided to modify the research design to take the debates into account. Two studies (17, 26) were designed to make contributions to the Kennedy campaign.

This group of studies, then, combines elements of some of the other groups. As with the commercial veterans, there was a staff and a sample available, but as with the academic non-veterans, there was no readily available routine of election study. Again, as with the commercial veterans, some studies (6, 14) were reported in newspaper columns (presumably in return for a certain amount of financial support) and some (2, 23) were reported in house organs.

Altogether, then, it took a special combination of resources and interests to move into the field so quickly. There was no time to apply to a foundation, and very little time to find a client (and difficult to think of a likely one). The commercial organizations had staff on hand; the academic organizations had students. The veterans were already in the field; the non-veterans were attracted by the research opportunity. Many had an immediate audience in mind; typically, these were newspaper readers. Those who had neither money or clients were motivated by the quest for knowledge or, perhaps, by bets with their friends as to "who won." In any case, our guess is that these studies range in cost from $5 to $100,000 and while the veterans spent more money than the non-veterans, and the commercial organizations more than the academic, the correlations are by no means perfect.

THE AUDIENCE

In examining the findings of these studies, we shall be concerned with both their similarities and their differences. Similarities of research results will give some assurance of their reliability. Differences will cause us to question the accuracy of one or another study, to point out aspects of research design that might explain discrepancies, and, if worst comes to worst, to cast doubt on survey research.

The place to begin, of course, is with the audience. Who heard the debates? Who was available to be influenced? (See Table 2.)

Most of the studies have an answer to this question, at least in terms

TABLE 11—2. PER CENT OF ADULTS VIEWING (OR LISTENING TO) DEBATES[a]

Study No.	Name and Locale	First Debate	Second Debate	Third Debate	Fourth Debate	One or More	All 4	Remarks
3	California Poll (state)	65						Registered voters
4	Canadian Broadcasting				54 (weighted)			% of TV households
5	Carter (local)	81	76	67	61			
6	Creative Research Associates (local)		71	64	64			
7	Deutschmann (local)	75						44% stayed tuned throughout
9A	Gallup (natl.)	60				80		Registered voters
14	Kraft (natl.)[b]	65	66	65		87		
18	Minnesota					88		
20	Nielsen[c] (natl.)	66	62	64	60	90		% of TV households viewing 6 minutes or more

								Remarks
								1st debate viewing only; others viewing plus listening
21	Opinion Research Corp. (natl.)	66	49	51	49			
22	Roper (natl.)				56	83	30	Viewing only ("seen on television")
23	Schwerin (local)	65	47	47	59			
25	Sindlinger (natl.)	66	69	58	61			12 yrs. or older; approx. 45% stayed tuned throughout each debate
27	Survey Research Center (natl.)					79		
28	Tannenbaum (local)	87						

a. Viewing plus listening unless otherwise noted (see Remarks). Approximately 10% of total are listeners rather than viewers.
b. Figures for debates 2 and 3 on the assumption that those (about ⅓) who could not be contacted watched or did not watch in same proportions as those who were contacted.
c. An estimate of proportion of total population viewing may be obtained by using the Nielsen estimate of total individual viewers. Percentaging these on a base of 129 million (population of 12 years and over) gives figures of 60%, 62%, 64%, 54% for the four debates respectively.

of the over-all total of viewers and listeners. The national studies are virtually unanimous in placing the figure for the first debate at 60 to 65 per cent of the total adult population (9A, 14, 20, 21, 25). Some of the local studies show higher figures (5, 7, 28) because they tend to include respondents with higher education and greater political interest. Altogether, some 70 of the 107 million U. S. adults—and perhaps another 10 to 15 million younger people—watched or listened to the first debate.

Compared with the first debate, the figures for the various studies are less consistent concerning the subsequent debates. Furthermore, it is difficult to know how to account for the effect of the different days of the week (Monday, Friday, Thursday, Friday) and the different hours of the day (9:30, 7:30, 7:30, 10:00 Eastern Time). The Nielsen ratings (20) show a decline in per cent of TV homes tuned in[3] (measured by coincident metered readings) but, interestingly, a larger total audience (measured by diary records) for the second and third debates (80 and 82 million individuals) than for the first (77 million) or the last (70 million). This is almost certainly due to the fact that the second and third debates were on the air early enough in the evening to have included more children and, possibly, more adults with early bedtimes. In any event, a conservative estimate would be that at least 55 per cent of the total adult population watched or listened to each of the debates and, altogether, that upwards of 80 per cent of the population saw or heard at least one of the debates (9a, 14, 20, 22, 27). The average debate viewer was in the audience for some 2½ hours—that is, for three of the debates.

Surely this is one of the great political assemblages of all time. Still, there are some other facts which ought to be noted for the sake of a balanced perspective. First, it should be borne in mind that the proportion of adults who turn on their sets on an average weekday evening—according to a study made in July, 1960 (25)—is in the neighborhood of 70 per cent and, from another study, that about 45 per cent of adults are at their sets during an average evening hour.[4] In other words, a very large proportion of the debate audience was immediately accessible; little effort had to be exerted to rally them. Moreover, there is little doubt that the relative absence of alternative program choices inflated the debate audiences. Among the Canadian cities studied, for example, audiences ranged between 50 and 60 per cent for the fourth debate, except in Calgary—the only city among those surveyed offering an alternative program—where the figure dropped to 35 per cent (4). Again, two studies (7, 25) suggest that the attention-span of the audiences is an important factor to reckon with. There is reason to believe that as much as one-third of the audience for each of the debates watched less than the entire program (25). The fact that the Nielsen (20) figures for TV homes reached by the first debate does not decline similarly (68.5 per cent for the first half hour, 64.2 per cent for the second half hour) may mean only that the set remained on even though family members drifted away, or that the tune-outs only slightly exceeded the tune-ins.

Nevertheless, it is evident that the audiences for the debates were exceedingly large. A comparison of Monday, September 26—the evening of the first debate—with the previous Monday evening reveals a higher proportion of sets in use throughout the evening and a *rise* in the size of the audience when the debate began at 9:30 P.M. (65.9 to 68.5 per cent of TV homes) in contrast to the previous week's *decline* (59.5 to 55.0 per cent). As Stanley Kelley, Jr., infers from his examination of these figures, it seems clear that people stayed home (and stayed up) to watch the debate.[5] Analyzing other Nielsen reports to assess the meaning of the figures, Kelley points out that whereas the first debate entered 66.4 per cent of homes with television, the most popular evening show around the time of the first debate attracted some 39 per cent of television homes, while huge audiences for the Sunday game of the 1960 World Series and the most popular half hour of the three-network broadcast of the Democratic convention reached about half the TV homes. On the other hand, according to Nielsen, 92 per cent of TV homes tuned in one or both political conventions (for an average of 15½ hours of viewing) and a like proportion were at their sets to view the election returns (for an average of 2½ hours.)[6] Both of these events slightly eclipsed the debates audience, though the latter, of course, was much more concentrated in time.

Concerning the composition of the audience, several studies found almost equally high proportions of both Nixon and Kennedy supporters attending (9, 18).[7] While there was a correlation between educational level and viewing, over 50 per cent of those with a grade school education or less were there (9), although the first debate was much more successful in this respect than subsequent debates (21). And several studies show (7, 25) that those who did not actually see the programs read about them or heard about them. Sindlinger (25) reports that

67 per cent of all newspaper readers (which consists of virtually the entire adult population) read about the first debate within twenty-four hours and about half talked about each of the debates within the same time period (7, 25). Naturally, most of these were people who also heard or saw the programs but some also learned about them—and, certainly, many understood them better—by virtue of exposure to these supplementary sources of information. We have the impression that not more than 10 per cent of the population failed to learn about the debates within twenty-four hours.

But listening to the debates, as we have said, did vary according to education (7, 9, 18), ranging for the first debate from three-fourths of the college-educated to just over half of those with grammar school or less. It varied with occupation (80 per cent of business and professionals; two-thirds of clerical and sales; half of manual workers and farmers). People in the East and West (and perhaps in the Midwest) listened more than those in the South (9, 25). Most interesting of all, it varied with religious affiliation. Three studies (7, 9, 18) find disproportionately more Catholics in the audience, despite the fact of the generally higher educational and occupational status of the Protestants. Indeed, those Protestants who mentioned religion as the "most important issue of the campaign" were much less likely to be viewers (7).

Research on voting behavior has all but dispelled the myth of the "independent voter"—the ideal citizen who does not make up his mind until election eve, when he retires to the quiet of his study to weigh the opposing arguments of the two parties. The truth is that people who make up their minds late in the campaign are likely to have very little interest in the election.[8] This is reflected in the debate audience, too. Viewing of the debates was related to strength of commitment to candidate or party. "Independent voters" were far less likely to hear the debates (7, 9, 21, 27). It is also worth reiterating that by a wide margin, the first debate drew in larger proportions of the less informed segments of the public than any succeeding debate.

Only two studies (5, 25) report on the context in which the listening or viewing took place. Carter (5) found that viewing was done in the company of family members (usually just the spouse) and, occasionally, of friends and neighbors. Only one-fifth of the respondents listened alone. There is evidence (14, 20, 25) that, over the period of the debates, people were increasingly in their own homes. Radio listeners (some 10 to 20 per cent) were much less likely to be at home; indeed, about one-half listened in their cars (25).

INTEREST IN THE DEBATES

A Gallup Poll (9A) taken before the first debates found 55 per cent of a national sample of adults looking forward to the debates with "a lot" of interest. Sindlinger (25) found that 90 per cent of the population aged 12 and over knew of the debates in advance. Furthermore, compared with both the 1952 and the 1956 campaign, more people were interested in the campaign (9, 25) and more were open to influence than had said so in '52 or '56. For example, more people said they "thought a lot" about the campaign in 1960 (9), and there was some tendency to make up one's mind later in the 1960 campaign than in '48, '52, and '56 (76 per cent knew whom they would support at the time of the 1956 conventions as compared with 60 per cent at the time of the 1960 conventions [27]).

No less important was the over-all increase in the use of television as a medium for the presidential campaign (8, 27). In 1952, 31 per cent of a national sample credited TV with bringing them "most information" about the campaign; 49 per cent of the same respondents said so in 1956, and 60 per cent in 1960 (27).[9]

The TV debates, then, were introduced into a campaign which was attracting unusually high interest and were presented via a medium which had emerged as the predominant source of campaign information.[10]

Did people find the debates interesting? Did they think the debates were a good idea? The evidence that the overwhelming answer is "yes" is abundant, though much of it can only be inferred rather than established directly. Only three studies asked directly. Sindlinger (25) asked after each debate, "Do you think these face-to-face meetings between Nixon and Kennedy are a good idea, bad idea, or just what do you think?" The California Poll (3) asked, "Do you feel that this kind of debate between Presidential candidates is a good way or a poor way to get the issues across to the American public?" The Canadian Broadcasting Corporation (4) asked, "Are you glad you had the chance of seeing the debate [fourth debate] on TV, or would you rather have seen something else instead?" In both the United States and Canada, more than two-thirds (in California 83 per cent) of those who saw the debates responded positively (3, 4, 25). Indeed, the positive response increased from debate to debate. Women were consistently more positive than men and the largest proportion who thought it was a bad idea, interestingly, favored Nixon (25).

It may well be that the explanation for the greater approval given each successive debate is a product of self-selection and the resultant increase in sophistication and political involvement of the audience. At any rate, this is the suggestion implicit in the Canadian findings, which establish that the *smaller* the audience, and the more *selective* the audience, the more it will be likely to approve. Thus Calgary and Vancouver attracted proportionately fewer listeners than the Eastern cities (and Calgary, as has already been stated, had an alternative program available) but these two Western cities had the highest vote of appreciation for the program (4). Incidentally, 60 to 70 per cent of English-speaking Canadians in the seven cities surveyed felt that the debate format should be employed in Canadian politics.

More indirect indices of interests are reflected in the extent to which the debates were discussed or read about by those who listened. Deutschmann (7) found that 77 per cent of those who saw the debates sought additional information about them. Only four or five news events have had comparable audiences in the past few years (25). About half the population discussed the debates within twenty-four hours and, although this is less than the number who discussed such things as Khrushchev's visits in 1959 and 1960, or Eisenhower's stroke, or the Russian and U. S. conquests of space, or even the Little Rock episode, it is an important high point in political discussion (7, 25).

Inquiring more specifically into what people liked and disliked about the debates, Carter (5) found that the clash of personalities was what seemed to be most attractive. Thus, the later debates were liked better because they were considered more "direct, lively, emotional, peppy, spirited."[11] Similarly, in the analysis of the high points in the reactions (recorded by machine) of viewers assembled especially to watch the first debate, the Gallup Poll's Hopewell study (9B) found that generalized "inspirational" material (Kennedy: "If we fail, then fredeom fails;" Nixon: "A record is never something to stand on, it's something to build on") or effective counterattack (Nixon: "It is very difficult to blame the four Republicans for the eight Democrats not getting something through that particular committee") far outscored the facts and statistics of gross national product, etc.[12] There is no doubt that the immediate response, at any rate, was to the drama of the combat and to the rhetoric. Fifty-four per cent of the Schwerin respondents (23) considered the first debate "a considerable improvement" when asked to compare it "with other political speeches on

TV." When asked to compared it "with other political programs of the panel or interview type," 37 per cent said "considerable improvement" and 40 per cent "some improvement."

Just as the audience responded to the rhetoric more than to the statistics, so they responded to the personalities more than to the issues. And many were quite aware of that fact. Asked which were better portrayed, issues or candidates, 19 per cent of Carter's respondents (5) said the candidates; only 7 per cent said the issues; 50 per cent said both. There is little doubt, from this study and others (4, 16), that the audience was busy analyzing the character of the contestants— their "presentations of self." Indeed, several of the academic studies focused exclusively on "images" rather than "issues" as the proper subject for investigation.

There was a minority which did not like the debates. Most of these, as has already been pointed out, did so because they felt that their man had been bettered. Indeed, in anticipation of the first debate, there is some evidence that Kennedy supporters were preparing to discount the outcome of the debate on the ground that competitive performance in the debate is irrelevant to the office of the presidency (16).

Alone among the studies, Carter (5) asked how the debates might be improved. Surprisingly, some 70 per cent were able to volunteer suggestions (and even considering that Carter's sample was a politically involved one, this seems like an extraordinary response). Of those who responded, 20 per cent thought the debates should be longer; almost that many urged the elimination of the interviewer panel; a smaller number suggested that each debate be limited to only one topic; and there was a large variety of other suggestions.

WHO WON?

In contrast to the paucity of specific questions concerning the format of the debates, it is surely revealing that so many of the studies asked, unabashedly, "Who won?"—or words to that effect.

Again, the studies are very consistent concerning the results (see Table 3). The first debate was clearly won by Kennedy. That is, a plurality of respondents in every one of the thirteen applicable studies reported this result. The second debate was very close. The third debate was won by Nixon. And the final debate, again, was very close. (Only the Schwerin study [23] disagrees that the second and fourth

TABLE 11—3. WHO WON?
(*per cent of all viewers*[a])

STUDY	QUESTION	FIRST DEBATE		SECOND DEBATE		THIRD DEBATE		FOURTH DEBATE		ALL DEBATES	
		RMN	JFK	RMN	JFK	RMN	JFK	RMN	JFK	RMN	JFK
3 California Poll	"Made better impression"	24	35								
5 Carter	"Who benefited"									11	49
7 Deutschmann	"Won votes"	7	26								
9 Gallup Poll	"Better job"	23	43							30	42
11 Iowa Poll	"Gained most"	23[b]	35[b]							21	32
14 Kraft		31	40	42	41	39	34			30	42
18 Minnesota Poll	"Gained the most"									17	51
21 Opinion Research Corp.	"Best job stating his case"	25	39	31	36	46	28	39	35		

22	Roper	"Best job"							31	36	21	37
23	Schwerin	"Outscored"	23	39	28	44	42	39	27	52		
25	Sindlinger	"Who won"	24	26	31	28	40	23	35	36		
29	Texas Poll	"Best job"	26[b]	46[b]								
31	Wallace	"Better impression"									23	54

a. The difference between sum of totals and 100 represents "no choice."
b. Question was asked following second debate and referred to first two debates.

debates were inconclusive. In both cases, the New Yorkers in the Schwerin laboratories declare Kennedy the winner by large margins.) Over-all, when the question was asked about the debates as a whole (5, 9, 11, 14, 18, 22, 31) Kennedy was far ahead.

Table 4 provides some insight into the major basis upon which people decide who won. Examining results for the first debate only, several things are evident from the table: (a) With the exception of two local studies (7, 31), individuals with a party affiliation or with a specific voting intention declare their own candidate the winner more often than they choose the opposition candidate. (b) More Republicans and Nixon supporters choose Kennedy as the winner than Democrats and Kennedy supporters choose Nixon; this is true of every one of the studies. (c) More of the former than the latter insist that they cannot decide who won. In other words, there is a marked tendency to choose one's own candidate as the winner, though among the relatively small number who concede to the opposition (5 to 10 per cent in the state and national polls), there is a greater proportion of Republicans and Nixon supporters. Republicans, too, are more likely than Democrats and Kennedy supporters to say that they have no choices. (d) Finally, note that the Undecided—those who had not yet made up their minds between the candidates—choose Kennedy more often than Nixon, though most of them report no choice.

Most of the other factors which differentiate between those who thought that Kennedy won and those who thought that Nixon won (education, occupation, age, religion, etc.) are confounded with voting intention and, therefore, we shall not report them. Only sex (happily) tends to be relatively free of statistical contamination. As it turns out, Nixon's debate performance seems to have impressed proportionately more women than men (14, 18, 25).

Roper (22) asked those who named one or the other candidate as having won the final debate, "In what ways would you say that (Kennedy, Nixon) was better?" and the answers were cross-tabulated by voting intention. Three categories of reasons characterize the loyal partisans as compared with those who conceded defeat: they said that the winner was better, first of all, because they *agreed with his views;* secondly, because he was *better informed;* and, finally, because he was more *sincere,* honest, truthful, etc. Those who decided for Kennedy were much more likely than those who decided for Nixon to emphasize that their choice was *specific,* gave facts, answered questions directly rather than evasively. Comparing only the two (very small)

TABLE 11—4. "WHO WON" FIRST DEBATE: PERCENTAGE DISTRIBUTION OF
CHOICE OF WINNER ACCORDING TO VOTING INTENTION OR
PARTY AFFILIATION[a]

(each row equals 100%)

	STUDY	QUESTION	INTENTION OR AFFILIATION	WINNER		
				Nixon	Kennedy	No Choice[b]
3	California Poll	"Made better impression"	Republican	39	17	44
			Democratic	11	51	38
7	Deutschmann	"Won votes"	Republican	10	27	63
			Democratic	4	30	66
			Independent	4	19	67
9A	Gallup	"Better job"	Pro-Nixon	45	17	38
			Pro-Kennedy	3	71	26
			Undecided	12	26	62
11	Iowa Poll[c]	"Gained most"	Pro-Nixon	39	16	45
			Pro-Kennedy	3	62	35
			Undecided	8	30	62
14	Kraft[c]		Pro-Nixon	59	17	24
			Pro-Kennedy	7	65	28
			Undecided	25	31	44
21	Opinion Research Corp.	"Best job stating his case"	Pro-Nixon	52	8	40
			Pro-Kennedy	2	73	25
			Undecided	4	22	74
23	Schwerin	"Outscored"	Pro-Nixon	47	6	47
			Pro-Kennedy	4	79	17
			Undecided	7	39	54
31	Wallace	"Better Impression"	Republican	28	46	26
			Democratic	2	87	11
			Independent	26	48	26

a. Information on voting intention and party affiliation was obtained during the same interview as evaluation of the debates. It is conceivable, therefore, that some people aligned their party affiliation or voting intention according to their evaluation of who won the debate. Although several studies have pre-debate information available, only the Kraft study actually employs voting intentions obtained in an earlier interview.
b. No Choice and/or Don't Know.
c. Question was asked following second debate and referred to first two debates.

groups of conceders, it appears that Nixon supporters who conceded that Kennedy had won did so primarily on personality grounds: they liked his personality, they said. And they concurred in his partisans' admiration for his specificity.[13] Kennedy supporters who conceded that Nixon had won the debate were unique in attributing the victory to his having kept his opponent on the defensive, and they were much more likely than Nixon's own partisans to feel that he had displayed greater confidence in presenting his position.

Although there are various ways in which the many categories of response classified by Roper might be combined and recombined, it seems that a candidate's general informedness and his style of presentation of facts and arguments were more important criteria for judgment than either what he said or his personality as a whole. In other words, if these attributes are separable at all, the Roper data seem to argue that style of presentation was more important than either the content of the presentation (issues) or the personality of the debater (image).[14] This is in contrast to those who have speculated that the audience was interested only in the personalities of the candidates.

The Canadian study (4) feels that *both* personality and style of presentation were important frames of reference and agrees that the subject matter of the debate—the issues—was rarely mentioned as a factor which "counted in favor of" or "counted against" each candidate. Thus, "the questions we asked here were carefully worded so as to allow respondents to talk either about what the candidates said or about the two men themselves and how they performed. . . . The fact that so little comment was directed at the subject matter of the debate or at any of the arguments involved, and so much more at the candidates themselves and the general quality of their respective performances as debaters, would seem to confirm what some commentators have already suggested. This is that a television debate of this kind, which focuses attention so sharply on the contestants themselves, leaves a mass audience with (as we have seen) some very distinct impressions of the capabilities of the two men as debaters and as persons, but (as our results suggest) with very little idea of what the debate was all about." (4)

LEARNING FROM THE DEBATES: THE ISSUES

That does not mean that people learned nothing from the debates about the issues. Indeed, Carter (5) gave a 16-item information test to his respondents based on statements made by the candidates in the first debate and found not only that at least some of what was said was remembered but, even more, that there was no evidence that a process of "selective recall" was operating. That is to say, Democratic viewers were no more likely to recognize statements made by Kennedy than statements made by Nixon and the same thing holds true for Republican viewers. This is an extraordinary finding, suggesting that the debates not only overcame the well-established tendency toward selective exposure (which insulates one from opposition arguments) but also—at least as far as information is concerned—the tendency to perceive and recall selectively.

A related study by Sebald (24) also finds respondents—sociology students at Ohio State, in this case—equally able to identify correctly statements made by either candidate (regardless of their own preferences). Sebald's concern, however, was rather different from Carter's (5). Respondents were presented with a set of statements made by the two candidates and were asked, first, to agree or disagree with each statement and, second, to name its author. While the over-all attribution of statements to the two candidates was equally correct, statements with which a respondent disagreed were most often attributed to the opposition candidate—even when actually made by the respondent's own candidate—while statements with which the respondent agreed were much more accurately attributed to the candidate who made them. This implies that it may be more painful to disagree with one's own candidate than to agree with some statement of the opposition. In still another aspect of the same study, respondents were asked to recall spontaneously statements made by the candidates. Here, the students tended to recall those of their own candidate's statements with which they personally agreed and statements of the opposition candidate with which they disagreed.[15] It is not clear, however, whether the students' opinions on the issues preceded or followed exposure to the candidates.

Of course, there is plenty of other evidence to illustrate the workings of selective perception in audience reaction to the debates. The distribution of votes on "who won" according to voting intention or political affiliation (Table 4) provides an obvious example; and there are many others. An especially pertinent example is reported by Kraft (14), who finds that those who say that the most important thing discussed in the (second) debate was foreign policy were much more likely to be pro-Nixon than pro-Kennedy, whereas those who say that some domestic matter was the most important topic discussed tended to be for Kennedy.

The evidence (21, 25) suggests that foreign affairs was the paramount issue during the entire campaign and, according to Sindlinger (25), it increased in importance following the second, third, and fourth debates. Since Nixon was generally conceded to be the more expert and experienced in foreign affairs—he was far ahead of Kennedy in perceived ability at "handling the Russians" and "keeping the peace" (9A, 21, 22)—the focus on foreign affairs was clearly to Nixon's advantage. In the debates themselves, the Quemoy-Matsu issue seemed to work for Nixon. Roper (22) asked specifically, "How do you feel about this—that Nixon scored against Kennedy in these discussions about the offshore islands of Quemoy and Matsu . . . or that Kennedy scored against Nixon or that neither one of them handled this issue well?" While partisans said that their own candidate had outscored the other, the Nixon supporters were surer of this than were the Kennedy supporters. Similarly, in Carter's study (5), California Republicans were much surer than Democrats that their man got "the best of the argument" over issues such as "peace," "Cuba," "U-2 flights," and "disarmament."[16] Public perception of Kennedy's ability in foreign affairs did increase as a result of the debates (3, 18, 22) but, even so, Nixon might well have won, if perceived ability at handling foreign affairs had influenced more votes.

There seeems to be little doubt that the debates made some issues more salient, as all campaigns do. Quemoy and Matsu (from which Nixon profited), U. S. prestige (which benefited Kennedy [5]), and domestic issues such as unemployment, old-age medical insurance, aid to education, and farm policy (all of which benefited Kennedy [5, 21]) were the major ones. But the Kraus-Smith study (15), which investigated the extent of actual changes in opinion on the issues as a result of the debates, found no change at all, while the Carter study (5) found high proportions insisting, on most issues, that neither candidate had gotten "the best of the argument."

Still, it is worth bearing in mind that people seemed to remember some of the content of the debates. Moreover, when asked, 27 per cent of the respondents in one study (5) assert that the debates helped them learn something about the issues, and this is not far from the percentage that say they learned something about the candidates (35 per cent) or that the debates generally increased the level of their information and interest in the campaign (17 per cent).

As far as issues are concerned, then, the debates seem to have (a) made some issues salient rather than others (the issues made salient, of course, may or may not have been the most "important" ones); (b) caused some people to learn where the candidates stand (including the stand of the opposition candidate); (c) effected very few changes of opinion on the issues; and (d) focused more on presentation and personality than on issues.

LEARNING FROM THE DEBATES: THE CANDIDATES

Sixty-one per cent of the Kennedy voters said they learned "a great deal . . . . about the candidates and what they stand for" from the TV debates (21). Only about half as many said they learned "a great deal" from other TV appearances of the candidates, from news in the newspapers, from columnists or editorials. The Nixon voters are more grudging about the debates—since their outcome is so clearly associated with the victorious Kennedy. Still, 35 per cent of the Nixon voters say they learned a "great deal"—as large a percentage as for any other source of information.

We have already seen that viewers learned something about the issues, though perhaps not very much. But there is considerably more reason to believe that they learned something about the candidates themselves. They discovered how well each candidate could perform in a debate and they formed images of each candidate's character and abilities.

Many will argue that this is unfortunate learning in the sense that whether a candidate is perceived as sincere, or tough, or quick on his feet is, first of all, probably not an important qualification for the office of president and, secondly, probably misperceived anyway. (Some would say similar things about the issues as they were presented in the debates.) But is it altogether unfortunate? Is it irrational to assume that the observation of two men interacting (albeit with many restrictions) under extreme pressure may be somewhat diagnostic of performance in a high-pressure job? Is the candidates' manner of handling rhetoric or statistics really so remote from the American voter's task of evaluating the qualifications of the man, as much as of the party, for the presidency? It is certainly much more rational than judging an automobile by its body or a book by its cover, but— as some sympathetic soul has pointed out—even these actions may not be as demented as they seem. People are not so foolish as to equate an automobile with the design of its body but, when mechanical sophistication is lacking, they use the body, and whatever other clues are available to them, as indices of the quality of the car.

Whatever the case, there is evidence from several studies (3, 5, 16, 28) that Kennedy fared far better than Nixon as far as positive images are concerned. Of course, Kennedy had the "advantage" of being all but unknown. Nixon had to maintain his image; Kennedy had to attain his—and the latter (or so it seems after the event) is the easier thing to do.

The most elaborate of the several image studies is that of Tannenbaum (28), in which respondents are asked to choose the attributes of their Ideal President in terms of a set of scales such as weak-strong, agitated-calm, old-young, and the like, and then—before and after the first debate and, once more, following the last debate—they were asked to rate the two candidates in terms of the same scales. The first debate moved the ratings of Kennedy, on all twelve scales, in the direction of the Ideal President, the most important shift being on "experienced-inexperienced." Changes in the before and after ratings of Nixon seemed random and inconsistent by comparison. Both men moved away from Ideal by the end of the debates but Nixon moved away more decisively than did Kennedy. Tannenbaum concludes that "Kennedy did not necessarily win the debates, but Nixon lost them. . . ."

Both Tannenbaum (28) and Carter (5) find that Kennedy's performance in the first debate impressed Democrats and Republicans alike as far as positive images are concerned. Over the entire period of the debates, the Carter findings (5) indicate that the Democrats boosted Kennedy higher and higher while the Republicans' appreciation of Kennedy increased almost as much. Nixon barely maintained his original position. Two studies of university students (12, 13) identified a decline in the favorability of the Nixon image among pro-Kennedy people as the major change and one of the studies (13) found a corresponding improvement in the image of Kennedy among pro-Nixonites.

Not so in Chicago, however. Creative Research Associates (6) found that Nixon's image improved even more than Kennedy's in the second, third, and fourth debates and that Nixon lost ground not so much in the debates but outside them ("between" them).

But this is the only exception and, in any case, CRA (6) does not discuss the first debate, which, apparently, made most of the difference. The first debate seems to have served, primarily, to rally the doubting

Democrats. A respondent in the Langs' study (16) is quoted as saying that, as a result of the first debate, he "switched from being an anti-Nixon Democrat to a pro-Kennedy Democrat." According to the Langs, many Democrats expected Kennedy to do less well and, in anticipation, were prepared to discount the connection between performance in the debates and qualification for the role of president. Kennedy's victory not only strengthened confidence in him among partisans and potential partisans but, by making the performance criterion universally legitimate, made the institution of the debates more important than they otherwise might have been and the defeat of Nixon all the more serious (16).[17]

These changes in the image of Kennedy surely account for the increase in the over-all favorability toward Kennedy over the period of the debates. Five studies inquire specifically into the generalized attitudes of voters toward the two candidates, and the results are summarized in Table 5. Just as in the evaluation of "who won," it is evident from the table that (a) the Democrats reported that their opinion of Kennedy had improved more often than Republicans reported an improvement in their general opinion of Nixon; (b) Republicans became more favorable to Kennedy than Democrats to Nixon; (c) indeed, two of the studies (3, 23) suggest that the Democrats became much more unfavorable to Nixon following the first debate than the Republicans did to Kennedy; (d) Independents (23, 27) moved more toward Kennedy than Nixon. Important as these figures are, however, it is no less important to note that close to half of the respondents in each of these studies reported no change at all.

IMPACT OF THE DEBATES ON VOTING DECISIONS

But did this affect any votes? That is a hard question to answer.

Ideally, to test for the impact of a given debate on voting intentions it would be necessary (a) to have before and after measures of the voting intentions of the same group of respondents; (b) to compare viewers and non-viewers. And, in order to assess the impact on actual voting, it would be necessary (c) to establish that a change in voting intention resulting from exposure to the debate had persisted until Election Day.

But this is very elusive information. Most studies are not based on panels of the same respondents (trend studies, of course, reveal only changes in the total distributions and conceal internal changes) Fur-

TABLE 11—5. IMPACT OF DEBATES ON FAVORABILITY TOWARD CANDIDATES ACCORDING TO POLITICAL PREDISPOSITIONS (VIEWERS ONLY)

Note: Read this table as follows: Considering the California Poll, for example, 33% of Republican viewers became more favorable to Nixon, 8% less favorable, and (not shown in the table) 59% remained unchanged. Among Democratic viewers, 15% became more favorable toward Nixon, 33% less favorable, and (not shown in the table) 52% remained unchanged.

STUDY	QUESTION		% MORE FAVORABLE			% LESS FAVORABLE		
			Rep	Dem	Ind	Rep	Dem	Ind
3 California Poll (First Debate)	"Did seeing the debate make you more favorable or less favorable toward Nixon? Toward Kennedy?"	Toward Nixon	33	15		8	33	
		Toward Kennedy	25	54		19	4	
5 Carter (after four debates)	"Did your feelings about either candidate change in any way as a result of the television debates? In what way?"	Toward Nixon	25	14		17	29	
		Toward Kennedy	19	39		32	16	
18 Minnesota Poll (after three debates)	"Has your opinion of Kennedy (Nixon) changed in any way as a result of the debates? In what way?"	Toward Nixon	29	13	20	2	12	8
		Toward Kennedy	6	23	19	17	2	11

23	Schwerin[a] (first debate)	"Having seen this debate, what is your attitude toward Vice-President Nixon? Toward Senator Kennedy?"	Toward Nixon	57	13	16	2	31	11
			Toward Kennedy	25	72	36	14	6	2
27	Survey Research Center[b] (after four debates)	"Was your feeling about (Kennedy) (Nixon) any different after you watched those programs?"	Toward Nixon (against Kennedy)	40	11	17			
			Toward Kennedy (against Nixon)	19	56	40			
			Neither	41	33	43			

a. In the Schwerin study, political predisposition was indexed by preference for candidates rather than for party.
b. Whereas the other studies percentaged changes in favorability separately for each candidate, the SRC study combined pro-Kennedy and anti-Nixon changes and pro-Nixon and anti-Kennedy changes and percentaged these over the total viewers of each party.

thermore, even a panel study cannot focus so narrowly on the debates as to be sure that it was a debate rather than some other campaign event which best explains changes in voting intention. Then, too, it is almost impossible to compare viewers and non-viewers since these were somewhat different kinds of people to begin with and, what's more, non-viewers got the word so quickly. For example, Deutschmann (7) finds a certain amount of change presumably as a result of the first debate but no difference between viewers and non-viewers.

Bearing all these limitations in mind, let us look at the evidence.

First of all, it seems safe to say that the debates—especially the first one—resulted primarily in a strengthening of commitment to one's own party and candidate. This was much more the case for Democrats than Republicans but the former had much greater room for improvement. Thus, according to ORC (21), the 63 per cent of Republicans who were "strongly committed" to Nixon in August dropped upon re-interview following the first debate to 59 per cent, whereas the percentage of Democrats "strongly committed" to Kennedy increased from 39 to 46. Similarly, the Langs (16) found that most of the changes following the first debate were those of undecided Democratic party sympathizers whose votes had "crystallized" as a result of the debates.

Secondly, trend data on changes in strength of commitment from debate to debate follow the pattern of evaluation of "who won." Consider Table 6, based, again, on the ORC study (21). In the two

Table 11—6.   CHANGE IN COMMITMENT FROM DEBATE TO DEBATE[a]

		% CHANGE IN "STRONG COMMITMENT" TO OWN PARTY'S CANDIDATE	
DEBATE	WINNER	Republicans	Democrats
First	Kennedy	−4	+7
Second	Tie	+9	+8
Third	Nixon	+7	−1
Fourth	Tie	−4	+2
	Net Change	+8	+16

a. Adapted from ORC study (21). Note that successive interviews are with different sub-samples of original August sample of respondents, nationwide, and thus the changes reported are essentially "trend" data rather than "panel" data.

debates with a clear-cut winner (first and third) there is an increase in strength of commitment to the winner and a decrease in commitment to the loser. Between the first and second debates (the second being a tie) both candidates gained strength equally. The fourth debate (also a tie) fits the pattern somewhat less well, though the net gain for Kennedy results from Nixon's loss of Republican strength-of-commitment rather than an increase in commitment among Democrats.

Finally, still drawing on the same study, Table 7 compares the pre- and post-debate positions (on a nine-point scale) of viewers and non-viewers.[18] The first thing to note in the table is that viewers of the debates, if anything, changed *less* than non-viewers. This is not as surprising as it sounds considering the fact that the non-viewers were far less interested in the election and far less committed to a candidate than the viewers. Previous election studies have shown that these are the people who are most open to influence, who are least likely to vote, and whose responses, in any case, are of dubious reliability. The second important point to note in the table is that among those who did change their voting intentions, by and large, neither candidate gained; this is true for both viewers and non-viewers of the final three debates. *Only in the first debate* is there evidence that viewing made a difference for one of the candidates. The net gain for Kennedy among viewers of the first debate is 8 per cent, compared with the usual negligible difference (2 per cent) among the non-viewers.[19]

As previously noted, Deutschmann's (7) report is rather similar. He found no difference in the extent of change among viewers and non-viewers of the first debate. He also found that 25 per cent of his panel made a change (on a seven-point scale) before and after the first debate, of whom 11 per cent crossed over from one candidate to the other. Kennedy profited slightly more than Nixon from the net result of these moves. Again, the Creative Research study (6) found that non-viewers changed at least as much as viewers of the second, third, and fourth debates. There is a whisper of a suggestion that there was more movement from undecided to a specific voting intention among the viewers than among the non-viewers.[20]

From these studies (7, 16, 21) it appears a reasonable inference that the debates did have some effect or, more exactly, that at least the first debate accelerated Democratic support for Kennedy among viewers.

To put these findings in a somewhat different perspective, however, it is instructive to consider the long-term trend within which the above-

TABLE 11—7. CHANGES IN COMMITMENT OF VIEWERS AND NON-VIEWERS[a]

	FIRST DEBATE		SECOND DEBATE		THIRD DEBATE		FOURTH DEBATE	
	Viewers	Non-Viewers	Viewers	Non-Viewers	Viewers	Non-Viewers	Viewers	Non-Viewers
	%	%	%	%	%	%	%	%
Unchanged	58	52	65	66	73	69	70	67
Change to Kennedy	25	25	17	17	14	15	16	16
Change to Nixon	17	23	18	17	13	16	14	17
Net gain for Kennedy	+8	+2	−1	0	+1	−1	+2	−1

a. Based on special tabulations by ORC (21) of before-and-after interviews with the *same* individuals. Before and after the first debate, for example, 58% of the viewers indicated precisely the same commitment (on a 9-point scale), while 25% made a change in Kennedy's favor (e.g., from "leaning" to "strongly committed") and 17% changed in favor of Nixon.

mentioned changes were going on. Consider Table 8, in which the trend results of the Gallup Poll (9A) are reported for the entire campaign. The results reported on September 25 were obtained immediately before the first debate and the interviewing for the report of October 12 was conducted immediately after the first debate, during the period September 27-October 4. Here, too, it appears that Kennedy scored a net gain in the debates, advancing three percentage points while Nixon lost one. But consider the long-term trend, which suggests that Kennedy was gradually advancing anyway!

TABLE 11—8. THE GALLUP POLL (9A)[a]

(each row equals 100%)

Release date	Kennedy Johnson	Nixon Lodge	Undecided
August 17	44	50	6
August 31	47	47	6
September 14	48	47	5
September 25[b]	46	47	7
October 12[c]	49	46	5
October 26	48	48	4
November 4 (adjusted for probable voters)	51	45	4
November 7	49	48	3
Actual vote	50.1	49.9	

a. "If the election were held today, which ticket would you vote for—Nixon and Lodge or Kennedy and Johnson?" Results reported above include those registered and intending to vote who were more or less certain of their choice. Note further adjustment of November 4.
b. Before first debate.
c. After first debate.

Did the debates really affect the final outcome? Apart from strengthening Democratic convictions about their candidate, it is very difficult to say conclusively.

But if you *ask* people whether the debates influenced their voting decision, they say yes. As Table 9 reveals, a sizable proportion of the voting population feels that the debates helped them decide. This is more true for Democrats than for Republicans, as has already been pointed out.[21] But consider the 6 per cent in the national Roper study

TABLE 11—9. PERCEIVED ROLE OF DEBATES IN DECISION-MAKING PROCESS ACCORDING TO VOTING INTENTION[a]

	Study	Question	Answer	Pro-Nixon %	Pro-Kennedy %	Unde-cided %	Total %
11	Iowa Poll[b] (after two debates)	"Do you feel that these television debates between Nixon and Kennedy have helped YOU DECIDE which candidate you will vote for or haven't the debates made any difference?"	Yes, helped decide	28	42	34	34
			No, no difference	70	57	64	64
			Don't know	2	1	2	2
				100	100	100	100
22	Roper (after four debates)	"Different people have said the debates did different things for them. Some say the debates made them *decide* who they'll vote for; some say they made them *more sure* their choice was right; some say they left them *less sure*, and others say the debates had practically no effect on them one way or the other. Which is *most* true for you?"	Made them decide	3	9	1	6
			Made them more sure	39	49	4	41
			Made them less sure	5	3	24	5
			No effect	49	35	52	43
			Don't know	4	4	19	5
				100	100	100	100

a. Per cent of pro-Nixon, pro-Kennedy, Undecided, and all respondents.
b. The Iowa Poll also reports on results of a similar question asked after all four debates were over: helped, 29%; no difference, 63%; don't know, 8%. No breakdown is given according to voting intention. Note the decline in the proportion claiming that they were helped in their decisions.

(22) who say that the debates "made them decide" or the 39 per cent in the Bruskin study (2) who mention the debates in answer to a very different question concerning "the one most important thing" that led to Kennedy's victory.[22] Even these people, almost certainly, were reinforced by the debates in their prior inclinations rather than converted. On the other hand, who is to say that the doubts and reservations which existed among Democrats regarding Kennedy might not have been dispelled at all if it had not been for the debates?

SOME IMPLICATIONS FOR FURTHER RESEARCH

So much by way of summarizing and integrating the results of social research on the Kennedy-Nixon debates. In conclusion, we want to venture some additional thoughts on the conduct of both the research and the debates. Under the heading of research, we want to respond to a variety of procedures, findings, and interpretations that, explicitly or implicitly, bear on theoretical and methodological issues current in social science. Under the heading of the debates, we want to draw some implications from these studies for policy governing possible future public encounters between presidential candidates.

Most of these studies, it must be borne in mind, were designed almost accidentally as a by-product of continuing reports on campaign developments. All were designed in a hurry. The remarks that follow, therefore, are not meant primarily as negative criticism, but rather as guide lines for future research. Indeed, for anybody who might want to take the trouble, it is worth mentioning that many of the studies reported here have storehouses of unanalyzed data, the analysis of which would contribute substantially to illuminating those questions which have had to be left unanswered. What follows, in effect, is a series of suggestions which, we hope, may contribute to doing even better next time:

1. *The Panel Method and Voting Intentions:* Although a number of studies employed the panel method of repeated interviewing, little use was actually made of panel-type analysis. In other words, the responses obtained from an individual at one point in time were seldom cross-classified against the responses he gave at an earlier time. Instead, the data are presented as if they were obtained from different people at each point in time.

The loss of information which results from this procedure is best illustrated, perhaps, by the fact that, according to the Gallup Poll

(9A), the net increase in the pro-Kennedy vote was only 5 per cent while the pro-Nixon votes fluctuated only a few percentage points during the course of the entire campaign. At the same time, we know from several of the panel studies (7, 14, 21, 27) that during the course of the campaign as many as 20 to 25 per cent of the electorate changed in some way: from decided to undecided (or the reverse) in strength of commitment to a candidate; or, to a smaller extent, from one candidate to the other. Similarly, the gross change connected with any one of the debates must have been far larger than the net change.

2. *The Panel Method and Images:* The panel method is applicable not only to voting intentions but, perhaps even more, to the study of images, which figures so prominently in a number of the reports. The image studies, however, tend to present only over-all "profiles" before and after exposure. While the group of respondents is the same on both occasions—therefore decreasing the sampling error as compared to what it would be if two separate groups were interviewed—the real potential of the panel design is rarely realized. For example, just as in the case of voting intentions, one can ask whether the absence of net change between the two time periods means that no individuals were changing or, perhaps, that a large number of people changed but in a mutually compensating manner. By the same token, where change does occur on a number of different image dimensions (e.g., hot-cold, active-passive, etc.), it seems important to find out whether a few people have made changes on many scales while most have remained unchanged or whether a large number of people have changed on only a few scales each. If the former, not many votes could be affected; if the latter, many votes might be involved. Then, too, one would want to know whether an individual whose image of a candidate becomes more favorable on one scale also tends, rather indiscriminately, to move in a more favorable direction on the other scales or whether there are certain psychological "associations" which lead to greater unfavorability on some scales as a consequence of improved favorability on others. Isn't it possible—to invent an example—that a perceived favorable change on a "smart-stupid" dimension might be accompanied by a negative change on a "modest-conceited" dimension, and so on? Again, we would want to know whether an individual who moved Kennedy toward the "experienced" pole was induced thereby to move Nixon in the other direction. And so on.

3. *The Consonance of Images and Intentions:* Indeed, one of the real possibilities of a panel analysis of images would be an assessment

of the extent to which changes in the image of one candidate can occur apart from changes in the image of the other and, in general, whether images can change independently of voting intentions. This opens onto the whole area of analysis of cognitive balance which is so much in the forefront of current social-psychological research.[23] The generic problem is: how can people keep on smoking and believe, at the same time, that cigarettes are a probable cause of lung cancer? Of course, it is a lot easier for somebody who continues firm in his commitment to Nixon to admit that Kennedy has some of the qualities which he feels are appropriate to an Ideal President (28) than it is for somebody who is strongly committed to smoking to admit that cigarettes cause cancer. Still, research on the relationship between images and commitments in election campaigns offers a real opportunity to explore the various patterns of coping with such "contradictions." For example, we know from Sebald (24) that it is apparently more comfortable to *agree* with the opposition candidate than to *disagree* with one's own. Can images be changed radically without any corresponding change in voting intentions? How do people isolate one from the other, if they do?

4. *Other Aspects of Cognitive Balance:* One way to reduce the dissonance, of course, is to avoid perceiving the contradictory evidence —to miss the point, or deny the validity, of the anti-smoking propaganda. The data on "who won" (Table 3) provide a good illustration of the much-studied mechanism of perceiving selectively so as to avoid upsetting prior commitments and loyalties to self and to others. The fact that the Democrats rather than the Republicans claimed to have learned "a great deal" from the debates (21), or that the Protestant Democrats tended to avoid the debates (7), or that Nixon supporters hardly mention foreign policy as a factor in the Kennedy victory (21) are further illustrations of the ways in which individuals manage their perceptions and cognitions and memories so as to hold things together in as neat and consistent a package as they can. Equally interesting in this connection is the anticipatory discounting of the debates on the part of fearful Democrats as reported by the Langs (16). Most intriguing of all is the Carter (5) finding that, at least for the first debate, retention was *not* selective on the basis of party affiliation or predisposition.

5. *Images and Role Expectations:* Returning to image research, it is evident that this is one of the most interesting aspects of these studies. And much more can be done on political images, it seems to us, in

addition to panel analysis. For example, wouldn't it be interesting to know what kinds of performances stimulate what kinds of images in what kinds of people? The fact that proportionately more women than men responded positively to Nixon's debate performance (14, 18, 25) provides a good illustration: were the women "seeing" the same things as their husbands but reacting to them differently or were they "seeing" different things? One might ask many questions of this sort: why didn't Nixon's first-debate performance universally suggest contemplativeness and profundity the way it did for some people (16) rather than suggesting uneasiness and slow-wittedness? And wouldn't it have been interesting to know not only the attributes that different kinds of people want to see in an Ideal President (28) but also the relationship between these attributes and those which they value in other roles? More, wouldn't it be interesting to know whether the attributes of the Ideal President for a given type of individual more closely match the attributes ascribed to, say, a performer rather than a father or a foreman rather than a friend, etc.? Referring again to the male-female difference noted above, one might speculate that women want a president who is more like a father than a lover.[24]

6. *The "Uses" of Mass Communications:* This brings to mind a current concern in communication research with the "uses" to which people put the media. Very little attention is given in these studies to the ways in which the debates as a form, as distinct from the personalities of the candidates, were perceived. After all, TV is a medium of entertainment; it is far less often thought of or employed as a medium of serious information. How did the debates fit into this context—or was their effect so powerful that they were able to change the image of TV itself? Did people who thought that the candidates had been tipped off in advance (and there seem to have been such) think of wrestling matches? Or quiz shows? Was this entertainment or education or politics or what?

And how did people actually "use" the debates in their daily lives? We know that they talked about them; we know that they read about them (25). But what aspects of the debates did they find discussable? And with whom did they talk? Their spouses? Their children? The men at the office or the shop? These are really important matters, it seems to us. We wonder, for example, whether people still think that their child might become president of the United States and whether the debates offered any clues as to how to achieve this. And how did people who watched with their children explain what was going on?

Similarly, we wonder whether there was any amount of identification with the candidates (as there is with contestants on quiz programs): "How would I answer that question if I were running for president?" Did people bet on the outcome of the debates in an office pool? Who were the people who spent the next day explaining to others what had really gone on? Which people would rather have seen the debates than their favorite programs (or vice versa) and why?

7. *The Two-Step Flow of Communications:* A current hypothesis suggests that individual decisions are influenced less often by direct exposure to the mass media than to the opinions of other people. The theory holds that the individuals who are influential for others are more likely to be exposed to relevant mass media than are the people whom they influence.[25]

Several studies (7, 21) address themselves to this hypothesis, claiming in the present instance that (a) when the media are so pervasive there is little room for interpersonal transmission; (b) when voting intentions changed—predominantly among those with low interest and low "initiative"—they probably changed in direct response to the media rather than as a result of interpersonal influence.[26] Indeed, Deutschmann (7) suggests that talking to others *reduced* the likelihood of change as a result of exposure to the debates.

These ideas pose interesting questions for the theory. Without going deeply into the matter, one cannot omit notice that viewing of the debates was a group (at least a household) affair (5) and, furthermore, that talking to somebody of *opposite* political persuasion did, apparently, change voting intention (7). Most people talked to others who agreed with them, of course, and such talk is at least as likely to be strongly reinforcing as talking with a member of the opposition is likely to be an influence toward change.[27]

8. *Microscopic vs. Macroscopic Research:* The present review affords an opportunity to compare the results of the intensive small-scale study with those of the large high-powered survey organization. The former are said to excel in theoretically relevant concerns even though their sampling and other methodological refinements must necessarily be inadequate; the latter are said to be technically proficient but lacking in imagination.

Judging from the present instance, we cannot completely agree. It is true that most of the small-scale studies draw certain theoretical implications from their findings and that many of the large studies are rather more descriptive. But the best of the large-scale studies compete, in imagination and theoretical interest, with the best of the small-scale studies. Far from piously calling for merging the best of both worlds, it seems far more important to urge that the traditional division of labor be taken even more seriously. The smaller studies might well be more daring conceptually.

9. *Isolation:* The fact that so few of the researchers knew of each other's activities is a curiously interesting phenomenon. There is some merit in such "independent" findings of course. In general, however, there does seem to be some need for more interchange, in order to standardize where appropriate and diversify where appropriate.

SOME POLITICAL AND POLICY IMPLICATIONS

Turning from considerations of method and theory as they bear on social psychology and communications behavior in general, we want to close with several thoughts about the more specific political implications of the debates with an eye to the formulation of policy governing possible future debates. Of course, these ideas, too, have more general theoretical and methodological considerations so they cannot really be separated from what has been said so far.

10. *The First Debate:* The drawing power of the first debate, particularly its ability to attract almost equal proportions of both parties and large proportions of even the least educated groups, may be a unique occurrence. Later debates showed a decline both in numbers and representativeness—though the audience was still phenomenal. Debates in future years, if they are institutionalized, may have considerably less appeal.

It is interesting to note that, in the present instance, the "primacy" effect was more powerful than the "recency" effect. Though Nixon had the better of the last two debates by common consent, appraisal of the debates as a whole consistently finds Kennedy the victor.[28]

11. *The Issues:* There is no doubt that the debates were more effective in presenting the candidates than the issues. If anybody is interested in communicating the issues, it might be well to take account of some of the suggestions made by the viewers and reported above (see page 27). The idea of limiting a given debate to a single issue is one such idea. (5).

12. *Social Functions of the Debates:* The role of the debates (and of the campaign generally) in focusing public attention on the national drama, for all its intended divisiveness, is probably a highly integrative

force in American life. In this connection, one of the extraordinary aspects of the debates was, to everyone's surprise, that voters learned something about the candidate they opposed (even though they very rarely gave him their vote). For one thing, they remembered what he said (5); for another, they learned that he was human, that he could become nervous, tired, etc. (16). And, over the course of the campaign, there is evidence (14) of a decline in the percentage who report "dislike of other candidate" as an explanation of their own choice (though, it should be noted, this may simply be a product of learning better answers to the question as time went by). It seems that the debates might make for a greater acceptance of the winning candidate— even if one voted against him: one knew more about him, one felt that he was more human and more accessible.[29] But these are just guesses, and the pity is that in their concentration on the combat, the studies failed to get so much of either the context or the latent consequences of the institution of the debates.

13. *The "Mistake" of the Debates:* The word "debate" is probably the major mistake of the debates. It is probably more responsible for what went wrong with the debates, from a variety of points of view, than anything else. The decision to call the encounters between the candidates "debates"—especially since they were not really debates at all—surely contributed to the trivializing of the issues, to creating differences where none existed, to the exaggerated and formalistic concern with "who won," to some of the ritualistic rules that were adopted, and, to a certain extent, perhaps even to a discounting of the possible significance of the candidates' encounters for voting decisions in the election campaign. It appears, in other words, that the structure implicit in the concept of a "debate" influenced the format of the programs, the behavior of the candidates, and the reactions of the audience —as well as the design of research.

NOTES

1. Chapters 13-18. Chapter 12, which does not deal with audience reaction to the debates, is not included in the present survey.

2. Information about Harris' role in the campaign appears in Theodore H. White, *The Making of the President 1960* (New York: Atheneum, 1961), and

in (unpublished) papers delivered by Harris at the 1960 and 1961 meetings of the American Association for Public Opinion Research.

3. Since the debates were carried by the three major networks, there was little choice open to the viewer if his set was on at all. About 88 per cent of sets in use during the hours of the debate were tuned to the debates (20).

4. *Report on Audience Composition,* Television Bureau of Advertising, 1959. Note that this study is somewhat dated and, moreover, that seasonal fluctuations are tremendous. According to the A. C. Nielson Co. report, *Television '61,* the average evening audience for January-February (when 55 per cent of TV homes tune in their sets for an average of about 6 hours per day) is 64 per cent greater than the July-August audience.

5. For an interesting account of the campaign as a whole, and the debates in the perspective of the campaign, see Stanley Kelley, Jr., "The 1960 Presidential Election," in K. Hinderaker, ed., *American Government Annual, 1961-62* (New York: Holt, Rinehart and Winston, 1961).

6. From *Television '61.*

7. Opinion Research Corporation (21) finds somewhat higher proportions of Nixon supporters in the audience for Debates 3 and 4. Interestingly, as we shall show below, these were the debates in which Nixon is thought to have done better. But the more likely explanation is that Nixon supporters, on the whole, were somewhat better educated and therefore more likely to continue in the audience.

8. See Bernard Berelson, Paul F. Lazarsfeld, and William N. McPhee, *Voting* (Chicago: University of Chicago Press, 1954).

9. Almost all of the decline came from radio; newspapers continued to be credited by about one-quarter of the population as the source that brings "most information."

10. The crediting of TV with so much importance as a source of information concerning the campaign probably reflects the importance of TV as a medium of up-to-the-minute news. In most other areas of ideas and advice, people tend to choose magazines over TV. As we shall argue below, TV is primarily perceived as a medium of entertainment. For data on this general area, see "A Study of the Magazine Market," Part II, conducted for the Magazine Publishers Association by the Market Research Corporation of America.

11. Kennedy voters liked the first two debates better than Nixon voters and the opposite was true for the last two. The obvious explanation for this is below.

12. The machine graphically records "like" and "dislike" on a moving tape. Given the conceptual limitations of the machine, it is no surprise that the more stirring parts of the exchange scored most positively. It should be pointed out, however, that the facts and figures scored high on "dislike." The Schwerin organization conducted a similar "program analyzer" study during the Korean War, recording audience reactions to a speech by President Truman. "Liking" responses rose during appeals to patriotism, Americans' strength, etc., and dropped with references to sacrifice, higher taxes, etc. Another "program analyzer" study of a film of one of the debates, carried out at the University of North Carolina by Noel Keys and Alan K. Whiteleather (12), focused on party differences in the extent of approval or disapproval of the statements of

each candidate. They found that Democratic students (N = 13) allocated approval (of Kennedy) and disapproval (of Nixon) less extremely than the Republicans (N = 14), though the mean differences were small.

13. Still, pro-Kennedy people and those who leaned toward Nixon (but not those "for" or "strongly for" Nixon) apparently would have liked Kennedy to be even more specific. Asked by Market Psychology, Inc. (17) to complete the sentence, "I would like Kennedy a little more if he would only . . . ," large proportions of these groups (in New Brunskick, N. J.) said, "If he would only be more specific," especially about details of his foreign policy. Sizable proportions of the same groups said he should be "less rash, less double-talking, more mature, time his phrases, speak more slowly and more clearly, speak right to us, not end so abruptly, show the sense of the Presidency as an awful trust rather than merely a political goal, etc."

14. The Kraus-Smith paper (15) finds the "images" attributed to each candidate closer to the "images" of some issues than of others. E.g., it is suggested that the "profile" of the Democratic image of Kennedy matches the "profile" of Catholicism, federal aid to education, and the U.N.

15. This line of analysis is developed in Berelson, Lazarsfeld, and McPhee, *Voting*, chap. 10.

16. Citations to Carter (5) in this and the following paragraph are based on material omitted from Carter's chapter in this book.

17. An analysis of the Tannenbaum data (28) subsequent to the one reported in the present volume tends to confirm the notion that the first debate was especially influential for Democrats and Independents. Of particular interest here is the marked improvement in the eyes of Democrats and Independents in Kennedy's position relative to Nixon's with respect to such traits as "experience" and "strength." While Kennedy's image as a "TV performer" showed particular improvement with respect to these traits, there was also improvement in the corresponding components of his "presidential" image. The results are reported in Bradley S. Greenberg, "The Political Candidate Versus the Television Performer," a paper read at the annual meeting of the Pacific Chapter, American Association for Public Opinion Research, Los Angeles, January, 1962.

18. These data are based on before and after comparisons of the *same* respondents. There are four sets of comparisons, one for each debate. Any movement on the scale (e.g., from "leaners" toward Kennedy to "strongly committed" to Kennedy) is classified as a change—in this case, of course, a pro-Kennedy change.

19. The absence of a clear-cut net gain for Nixon among viewers of the third debate conflicts with Table 6. It is difficult to reconcile these two sets of data.

20. The ORC (21) and Deutschmann (7) data just presented were analyzed as "panel" data, comparing the response each individual gave before the debate with his post-debate response. Creative Research Associates (6) also interviewed the same respondents before and after each debate but presented only the overall marginal distributions at each point in time and therefore could measure only the "net change."

21. A study of University of Washington students by Edelstein (8) finds

5 to 6 per cent who consider the debates the "most important" factor in their decisions and some 35 per cent who feel that the debates were at least "fairly important." There is little, if any, support here, however, for the finding of other studies that the debates were considered more important by Democrats than by Republicans.

22. ORC (21) asked a question only slightly different from Bruskin's (2) but with very different results. The questions "What do you think were the most important issues or factors in deciding who won the election?" Only 8 per cent mentioned the debates, while 18 per cent mentioned religion, 12 per cent mentioned labor vote, 10 per cent mentioned personality, and, in addition, a large number of specific issues were named. A phenomenon similar to the difference between the Roper (22) and Bruskin (2) results noted in the text has been often observed in survey research. In studies of medical care, for instance, very few people ever attribute their *own* failure to have an illness attended by a physician to a fear of the diagnosis, while a large proportion of the same people ascribe this motive to "most people."

23. See, for example, Leon Festinger, *A Theory of Cognitive Dissonance* (Evanston, Ill.: Row, Peterson and Co., 1957); the Summer 1960 issue of the *Public Opinion Quarterly;* Fritz Heider, *The Psychology of Interpersonal Relations* (New York: John Wiley and Sons, 1958), chap. 7.

24. The Tannenbaum study (28), whose respondents were primarily women, finds Kennedy much closer to the "virility" pole than Nixon. Nixon was more "experienced," "older," more "conservative," etc. We do not know from this study whether the women who rated Kennedy higher on "virility" were more or less likely to vote for him.

25. For the original statement of this hypothesis in connection with voting, see Paul F. Lazarsfeld, Bernard Berelson, and Hazel Gaudet, *The People's Choice* (New York: Columbia University Press, 1948), chap. XVI. Subsequent work is reviewed in Elihu Katz, "The Two-Step Flow of Communication: An Up-to-date Report on an Hypothesis," *Public Opinion Quarterly* (Spring 1957), 21:61-78.

26. See Joseph R. Goeke, "Two-Step Flow of Communication: The Theory Re-Examined," a paper presented at the sixteenth annual conference on public opinion research of the American Association for Public Opinion Research, 1961, and based on the Opinion Research Corporation study (21).

27. The Edelstein study (8) finds that a positive relationship exists between the number of debates viewed and the tendency to talk about them with like-minded people. This implies that people with higher interest in something are more likely to talk with people who share their views.

28. An alternative explanation would be that none of the succeeding debates (even the third—on foreign policy—which Nixon won decisively) produced a difference of the magnitude of the first debate. On "primacy" and "recency," see Carl I. Hovland et al., *The Order of Presentation in Persuasion* (New Haven: Yale University Press, 1957).

29. In "Religion and Politics: The 1960 Elections," a paper delivered at the 1961 meetings of the American Sociological Association in St. Louis and based on the SRC study (27), Philip E. Converse suggests that the debates served to

combat easy stereotyping of the candidates. He refers particularly to the concern of Protestant Democrats over Kennedy's Catholicism. "The mass media," says Converse, "—and the television debates in particular—filled in more fully an image of Kennedy. They did not modify cleavages by convincing Protestants that Catholicism *per se* was not black. But they did serve up a host of other items of information about this man. He was not only a Catholic, but was as well (in the public eye, from interview material) quick-witted, energetic, and poised. These are traits valued across religious lines, and act at the same time to call into question some of the more garish anti-Catholic stereotypes. While in the grand scheme of things such perceptions may seem superficial, they are real to the actors, and the fact that such perceptions compete with some success against the initial cognition of the candidate's group membership gives some sense, in turn, of the superficiality of the latter as a cue for many people. Bit by bit, as religiously innocuous information filled in, the Protestant Democrat could come to accept Kennedy primarily as a Democrat, his unfortunate religion nothwithstanding. Vote intentions angled away from group lines toward party lines."

12

Pre-Debate Campaign Interest
and Media Use

REUBEN MEHLING, SIDNEY KRAUS & RICHARD D. YOAKAM

EVEN BEFORE the Great Debates there was a high degree of interest in the presidential campaign of 1960. Furthermore, this pre-debate interest in the campaign was apparently related to various patterns in the use of media and preference for certain media, as well as to the audience's political and religious affiliations.

These findings are suggested by a survey of 140 Indianapolis citizens just before the first debate. The study was an attempt to provide information about the "general media climate" immediately before the Kennedy-Nixon television debates.[1]

AMOUNT OF MEDIA USE

How much time did the average respondent spend watching television and reading newspapers before the Great Debates? Ninety per cent spent an hour or more a day viewing television, but the distribution of viewing time was fairly even—the proportion watching TV four hours or more a day was almost as large as the proportion watching two hours a day and not much smaller than the proportion watching an hour or less a day. Table 1 indicates the amounts of time different respondents spent in television viewing.

For newspapers, on the other hand, it is interesting to note that whereas 90 per cent spent 30 minutes or more a day reading newspapers, less than one-sixth spent more than an hour. Table 2 shows the amounts of time different respondents spent reading newspapers.[2]

It is also worth noting here that, of the 140 respondents, more than

TABLE 12—1. TELEVISION VIEWING

Television Viewing in an Average Day	Number of Persons	Per Cent of Total
More than 4 hours	23	16.4
3½ hours	15	10.7
3 hours	9	6.4
2½ hours	20	14.3
2 hours	24	17.2
1½ hours	20	14.3
1 hours	14	10.0
Less than 1 hour	15	10.7
Total	140	100.0

TABLE 12—2. NEWSPAPER READING

Newspaper Reading in an Average Day	Number of Persons	Per Cent of Total
More than 2 hours	1	.7
2 hours	7	5.0
1½ hours	14	10.0
1 hour	36	25.7
45 minutes	25	17.9
30 minutes	43	30.7
15 minutes	14	10.0
Total	140	100.0

half (54 per cent) reported that they read a weekly news magazine.

One might ask whether respondents who spent more than the average amount of time watching television spent less time reading newspapers. Actually, the opposite is true. In nearly three-fourths of the cases where a respondent was above the average (group median) in time he spent viewing, he was also above the average in time he spent reading—and vice versa. Furthermore, in two-thirds of these cases the respondent spent about the same amount of time with both media, as measured by his similar ratings on the time categories for television viewing and newspaper reading.[3]

MEDIA PREFERENCE PATTERNS

In order to obtain a measure of program and news preferences, each respondent was handed lists of items based on television program and newspaper content and was asked to rank them in order of importance to him personally; that is, to indicate the sort of program or article he would be most likely to watch or to look for. Considering only the respondent's two top choices, Table 3 shows the per cent naming each of the types of TV programs on the list.

TABLE 12—3. PROGRAM PREFERENCE

Type of TV Program	Number of 1st & 2nd Rankings	Per Cent of Total
News..........................	59	21.1
Adventure series...............	46	16.4
Dramatic plays.................	41	14.6
News analysis.................	38	13.6
Sports events..................	34	12.2
Musicals......................	21	7.5
No responses..................	41	14.6
Total........................	280	100.0

Similarly for newspapers, the per cent of respondents naming a subject as either first or second choice led to the ranking of the subjects listed as indicated in Table 4.

TABLE 12—4. NEWSPAPER CONTENT PREFERENCES

Type of Newspaper Subject	Number of 1st & 2nd Rankings	Per Cent of Total
National news.................	85	30.4
World news...................	70	25.0
News of Indianapolis...........	38	13.6
Sport news....................	20	7.1
Editorials....................	15	5.4
Comics.......................	12	4.3
Women's news................	6	2.1
Politics......................	6	2.1
News of people you know in town	3	1.0
Crime news...................	1	.4
Political columnists...........	1	.4
No responses..................	23	8.2
Total........................	280	100.0

Here again, since former studies have indicated that the uses of several media are related, one should be interested in what interrelationships, if any, exist between television and newspaper preferences.[4] Inspection of each person's answers shows that those respondents who gave first or second rank to national or world news when their newspaper preferences were recorded were in almost all instances the same respondents who gave highest ranks to similar categories in television preferences. Of the 36 respondents who ranked TV news programs as "most important" to themselves, for example, all but three gave a "first" rating to news content in newspapers. Furthermore, when considering only those who ranked TV news analysis programs as their number one choice, every one ranked national or world news as his first choice in the newspaper.

Thus, more than 93 per cent of those giving a first-place vote to news content did so for both media. This high positive correlation also holds true for second-place choices.

Only eight respondents ranked newspaper editorials as their number one choice in newspaper reading. Five of the eight said they also read a weekly news magazine, and three said they did not. It is interesting to note that the five who said they read news magazines also said that to them the news programs were the most important programs on television; whereas, of the three who didn't read news magazines, none ranked TV news as most important.

CORRELATION OF CAMPAIGN INTEREST AND MEDIA USE

The foregoing would indicate that there is a substantial group of "high media users" in terms of national and world news in both media. One may well ask here, "Do these high media users tend to be the same persons who report a high interest in the political campaign?"

The answer is a qualified "Yes."

The distribution of responses to the question regarding how closely respondents had been following the campaign is shown in Table 5.

Of the 74 per cent reporting that they were following the campaign "quite a bit" or "very closely," all but 3 per cent fell into the "high media user" group which gave a first or second rank to news content both on television and in newspapers. However, when only the first choices for news content on TV and in newspapers are compared separately with respondents' campaign interest, one discovers that it is

TABLE 12—5. CAMPAIGN INTEREST

Following the Campaign	Number of Persons	Per Cent of Total
Very closely..................	32	22.9
Quite a bit...................	72	51.4
A little bit...................	35	25.0
Not at all....................	1	.7
Total.......................	140	100.0

television viewing which contributes most strongly to this high correlation.

All but two, or 95 per cent, of the 44 persons rating TV news or news analysis programs as most important to themselves said they followed the campaign quite a bit or very closely; whereas only 65 per cent of the 96 respondents who rated programs other than news as most important spent this much time following the campaign. Conversely, only 5 per cent of those rating TV news first and 35 per cent of those not rating it first said they spent little or no time following the campaign.[5]

In contrast, a similar analysis of the relationship between first-place rankings of national and world news in daily newspapers and high interest in the campaign indicated that there was merely a small and insignificant positive correlation between the two. However, the eight respondents who considered newspaper editorials the most important item in the daily paper all said they were following the presidential campaign closely.

When one cross-tabulates respondents' replies to whether or not they read a weekly news magazine with how closely they were following the campaign, a significant positive correlation is obtained. Whereas 64 per cent of the magazine readers said they were following the campaign quite a bit or very closely, only 36 per cent of the non-readers replied in this fashion. Conversely, 75 per cent of the non-readers stated they were following the campaign just "a little bit or not at all," while only 25 per cent of the readers made such a reply.[6]

The fact that readership of news magazines is a fairly good predictor of interest in the campaign in this instance is all the more interesting in view of the lack of significant correlation between campaign interest and either the time spent reading the daily paper or the sorts of things the reader considers most important in his paper.

RELATION OF POLITICAL PARTY AND RELIGIOUS
AFFILIATION TO MEDIA USE

In the 1960 presidential campaign the two candidates differed not only in politics, but also in religion. Because the interaction between politics and religion was a vital issue in the campaign, we attempted to relate the respondents' political party and religious affiliation with their media use. By dividing respondents into high and low media users according to whether they were above or below the sample median in time spent with either television or newspapers, cross-tabulations were possible with their party and religious affiliations.

In making such cross-tabulations on the basis of daily newspaper reading, no significant differences were obtained. For similar cross-tabulations on the basis of TV usage, however, a number of significant differences were noted. Table 6 represents the actual number (rather than the percentage) of respondents broken down according to their TV usage, political party, and religious affiliation. Of the various cross-tabulations one can make from these data, significant differences were obtained between the TV usage of Democrats and Republicans as a whole and also for Protestants and Catholics when considered within each political party separately. However, there was no significant difference between religions per se, that is, when all Protestants were compared with all Catholics of either party.

It is interesting to note that, where significant differences were obtained, they were largely due to the complete separation of the Cath-

TABLE 12—6. MEDIA USE, POLITICS, AND RELIGION[a]

Politics and Religion	Number of High TV Users	Number of Low TV Users
Democratic		
Number of Protestants.........	18	13
Number of Catholics..........	8	0
Republican		
Number of Protestants.........	42	41
Number of Catholics..........	0	8
Total.....................	68	62

a. Ten respondents failed to provide the necessary information, hence the total of 130 rather than the sample total of 140.

olic respondents when cross-tabulated on the basis of both TV viewing time and political party. Thus all of the eight Democratic Catholics were high TV users, and all of the eight Republican Catholics were low TV users.[7] Attendance to the "news" aspects of newspapers and television contributed largely to respondents' use patterns; and during the pre-debate period a large part of the news in both media dealt with the presidential campaign. One could, therefore, hypothesize that strong cross-pressures may have played a part in these results. For example, the Republican Catholic may have had conscious or subconscious desires as a Republican to favor Nixon and as a Catholic to favor Kennedy. According to one theory, the existence of such a conflict situation is psychologically uncomfortable, and it will motivate the person to try to reduce the dissonance (inconsistency) by actively avoiding situations and information which would likely increase the dissonance.[8] At the same time he will tend to seek out information which supports his beliefs.

Since news about Kennedy's activities would be consistent with the Democratic Catholic's beliefs, he might tend to be a high TV user during the campaign. The Republican Catholic, however, would need make some compromise in his political and religious beliefs, and might find news about either candidate an uncomfortable reminder of this fact. The result might well be that he would tend to spend less time with TV during the early days of the campaign.[9]

SUMMARY

In summary, this local sample would indicate that during a political campaign the respondents' exposure to various media is interrelated with their interest in the campaign. The degree to which these two factors are correlated differs frcm medium to medium. Television viewing, in both time and subject matter, appears to be a better predictor of campaign interest than is time spent reading the daily paper or the newspaper items read—with the exception of editorials. Reading of weekly news magazines also is positively related to high interest in the campaign.

Another finding, supporting previous investigations of psychological dissonance, relates to the effect of political and religious cross-pressures on TV viewing: Catholic Republicans were all below average in viewing time, in contrast to Catholic Democrats, who were all above average.

Judging from the overwhelming audience "attending" to the debates, it is probable that the debates brought the findings of this study into even sharper focus.

Notes

1. The same sample constituted the panel from which Sidney Kraus and Raymond G. Smith obtained the data for their study of political issues and the TV debates, which is reported in Chapter 16. For a complete description of sampling method and sample characteristics see page —.

2. These figures on media use are similar to those obtained from a series of studies at Indiana University by the Bureau of Media Research, under the directorship of one of the authors. See, for example, Reuben Mehling, "Television's Value to the American Family Member," *Journal of Broadcasting* (Fall, 1960), 4:307-13.

3. Previous investigators some time ago discovered that people highly exposed to one medium of communication also tend to be highly exposed to other media. See Paul F. Lazarsfeld, Bernard Berelson, and Hazel Gaudet, "Radio and the Printed Page as Factors in Political Opinion and Voting," from *The People's Choice* (New York: Columbia University Press, 1948), pp. 120-36.

4. Paul F. Lazarsfeld, "Audience Research," in Bernard Berelson and Morris Janowitz (eds.), *Reader in Public Opinion and Communication* (Glencoe, Illinois: The Free Press, 1950), pp. 337-46.

5. Put into a two-by-two contingency table, this relationship offers a tetrachoric correlation coefficient of .52, significant by chi square test at the .001 level.

6. This results in a tetrachoric correlation coefficient of .55, significant beyond the .001 level.

7. A chi square test, using Yates' correction for continuity, indicates that the difference is significant beyond the .001 level; however, this value must be accepted with some reservations in the light of the rather small theoretical cell values.

8. Leon Festinger, *A Theory of Cognitive Dissonance* (New York: Row, Peterson, 1957), p. 3.

9. One investigator, in a study of Catholic members in a Communist-influenced labor union, found indications that the greater the cross-pressures, the greater the decrease in interest in the issue and the tendency to avoid the conflict situation by withdrawing attention. See Martin Kriesberg, "Cross Pressures and Attitudes, A Study of the Influence of Conflicting Propaganda on Opinions Regarding American-Soviet Relations," *Public Opinion Quarterly* (Spring, 1949), 13:5-16.

13

Viewing, Conversation, and Voting Intentions

PAUL J. DEUTSCHMANN

IN THE COURSE of modern political campaigns, a wide variety of messages is delivered by mass media to the American public. These range from individual speeches of candidates transmitted by radio or television, reports of them in newspapers, political advertisements in a variety of media, to reports on the front page of the newspaper about the day's activities in the two principal camps. This study approached the first of the "great debates" as a special case of the general class of media messages just described.

Whenever such an event occurs, a natural "field experiment" takes place. Individuals are either exposed to the message or not exposed to it; either it modifies their attitudes or it does not. The problem of each field experiment, of course, is that there are many extraneous, uncontrolled variables. At the same time, we are not helpless in the face of these. For example: (1) We can reduce the time span from mass message event to measurement of potential effect, thereby minimizing the opportunity for other variables to creep in, and maximizing recall of the events we seek to examine. (We did this by making telephone interviews 24 to 36 hours after the debate.) (2) We can obtain measurements in advance of a key variable in any change of attitude—the

This study was made possible by a grant from Scripps-Howard Research, a division of the E. W. Scripps Company. The author would like to acknowledge the aid of Drs. Lee Barrow, Malcolm MacLean, Jr., and Erwin Bettinghaus of the Communications Research Center, and of Dr. Frank Pinner, director, Bureau of Social and Political Research, Michigan State University, who participated in the design and execution of the study.

"predisposition" of the individual toward the object or objects of the message. (We did this by establishing party preference two days before the debate.) (3) We can follow the teachings of Katz and Lazarsfeld and discover after the event the degree to which our subjects were involved in various aspects of the two-stage flow of communication and influence, which augments, distorts, and sometimes cancels the effects of any mass message.[1] (We did this by determining the amount and variety of media exposure and the nature of face-to-face conversation on the debate.)

If we follow these procedures, we have these possible yields: (A) Some indications of the frequency of various patterns of political predisposition, mass media exposure, and face-to-face communication. (B) Through indices of changes in such an expression of political opinion as "voting intention" on a "before-after" basis, some indication of effects which may or may not be related to the communication patterns. (C) Some notion of the manner in which these patterns interact.

THE SAMPLE

For such purposes, the sample of individuals utilized should guarantee the presence of the various patterns of communication and of predisposition outlined above. Each pattern provides us with a "field experimental" condition, analogous to the condition we might create in the laboratory. If, beyond this, our respondents are representative, we may make some inferences about the frequencies of the patterns in the population group studied—in this case Lansing and East Lansing, Michigan.

Our sample was made up of individuals drawn on an every "nth" basis from the list of telephone households in the Lansing-East Lansing area. About 94 per cent of households have phones. The community has a combined population of approximately 140,000, including 110,000 in the industrial capital city of Lansing, and 30,000 in the university, white-collar town of East Lansing. The individuals were members of a panel initiated in 1958. They were interviewed five times in all, the first wave covering general background information, such as age, education, occupation, and religion, the second and third covering exposure and information about the 1958 campaign and voting intentions, and the fourth and fifth covering the same data for the first TV debate.

Lansing is Republican territory, with a fairly normal voting split of 60 per cent Republican and 40 per cent Democratic. In this respect, our sample was like the total population. We established party identification just before the debate. It showed that 49 per cent called themselves Republicans, 17 per cent Independents (or wouldn't indicate a choice), and 34 per cent Democrats. Of those who indicated a choice, 59 per cent were Republican and 41 per cent Democratic. These percentages are highly similar to those obtained in the 1958 data, indicating that our losses of subjects over the two-year period were approximately equal across groups.

While the 159 individuals who participated in waves four and five represented only about 40 per cent of the original panel, no overwhelming biases arose through the variety of attrition factors which operated over the two-year period. All were registered voters; 60 per cent were female; 15 per cent were Catholic; 35 per cent had had some college education, and 25 per cent less than a high school education. In general, they were at a fairly high socio-economic level, which would be expected after non-registered voters had been eliminated in a community where the average income is in excess of $6,500 per family.

Our previous work, which was carefully pretested, demonstrated that we could obtain a wide range of data in reliable fashion in telephone interviews. The refusal rate was consistently low, and repeated call-backs eliminated a large part of the "not-at-home" problem. Further, our earlier investigations had demonstrated that such a sample should provide a cross-section of communication patterns of the sort needed for our "field experiment."

COMMUNICATION ABOUT THE DEBATE

By one means or another, 91 per cent of our subjects received some communication about the first debate within forty-eight hours of the event. We inquired into three clases of exposure: (1) direct—watched the TV version or listened to the radio version; (2) supplementary mass media—viewed, listened, or read *about* the debates after the first broadcasts; (3) face-to-face—talked to other individuals about the debates.

DIRECT EXPOSURE

Seven out of ten of our subjects saw at least a part of the TV version and 44 per cent viewed the entire program. About one in eight listened to all or part of the radio version, which was available in the Lansing area an hour before the TV broadcast. The distributions of exposures to the debate are provided in Tables 1 and 2.

TABLE 13—1. TELEVISION AND RADIO EXPOSURE TO THE DEBATE
(*per cent of all respondents*)

Viewed or Listened	Television	Radio
To all..............	44	6
To most...........	9	2
To part...........	17	5
To none...........	30	87
(Number).........	(159)	(159)

TABLE 13—2. COMBINATION USE OF TELEVISION AND RADIO
(*per cent of all respondents*)

TV and radio......................	8
TV only..........................	63
Radio only.......................	7
Neither..........................	25
(Number)........................	(159)

We combined these data into an over-all index of direct exposure, setting up three classes: full or "high" exposure, 49 per cent; "partial," 26 per cent; "no exposure," 25 per cent.

FOLLOW-UP MEDIA MESSAGES

The mass media played the debate as a big story after the television broadcast, and exposure to these supplemental reports was high. Over all respondents, we found 77 per cent who saw or heard at least one such item on radio, television, or in newspapers; 25 per cent were exposed to three or more items. To a significant degree, these additional media reports reached individuals who had already been exposed; 87 per cent of debate viewers got more information in this fashion; only 50 per cent of non-viewers picked up the debate story in the media.

A careful checking of newspapers circulated in the community for the period just following the debate revealed virtually no items with overt answers to the predominant question of who won the debate.

The bulk of the items, including editorials and commentaries, said in effect, "It was a draw." We monitored radio and television coverage, again seeking indications of directionality in the comment, and found virtually none. This judgment of the researchers was supported substantially by the judgments of the respondents, 79 per cent of whom said they could see no indications in the mass media reports they were exposed to that either Nixon or Kennedy won. Those who saw a direction were almost equally divided, 12 per cent saying the reports indicated Kennedy won and 9 per cent that Nixon was the victor.

FACE-TO-FACE CONVERSATION

One might have expected that conversation about the debate would be especially frequent among our respondents, whom we have characterized as somewhat more politically active than the general population. However, this did not appear to be the case. Only 56 per cent got into conversations about the debate. In contrast, an investigation of reactions to a major news item indicated that 76 per cent talked to someone about President Eisenhower's light stroke in 1957.[2]

We asked respondents to characterize the talking situations in terms of their own political views. Just under half (47 per cent) talked to persons of the same views as themselves; 42 per cent talked in group situations in which political opinions were mixed; only 11 per cent talked in clear-cut "conflict" situations with a person (or persons) of views contrary to their own. These results are very similar to those obtained in the 1958 election, where "direct conflict" talk was at a minimum and talking to one's group was at the same or higher levels.[3]

Another line of inquiry paralleled that concerning directionality in mass media reports. We asked: Did people our subjects conversed with say anything about who won? The results suggest that the content of conversation was not much more "directional" than that of the mass media, for only 22 per cent of the individuals involved in conversations reported a direction. There was also a slightly larger departure from a fifty-fifty split on the matter, with 14 per cent reporting talkers saying Kennedy won while 8 per cent heard people saying Nixon won.

We noted above that getting information *about* the debate from mass media was related to direct viewing. So also was talking—at beyond the chance level. The results are in Table 3.

When we take both direct viewing and follow-up media reports into consideration, we can pinpoint the individuals who eschewed the full

TABLE 13—3. CONVERSATION AND DIRECT DEBATE EXPOSURE

(*per cent of all respondents*)

	Full Exposure	Partial	No Exposure	Total
Talked about debate.......	72	46	38	56
Did not talk..............	28	54	62	44
(Number)...............	(78)	(41)	(40)	(159)

range of mass media offerings. The results, in Table 4, indicate that only 26 per cent of this group got involved in conversations. Actually, only six persons heard about the debate solely by face-to-face conversation. They represent 4 per cent of the total sample. These are relatively "pure" cases of Katz and Lazarsfeld's "relay function." The very small number of them—which is consistent with our earlier studies—suggests that the function operates for most people as a means of supplementing information already obtained by the mass media, rather than as a person-to-person communication system without media involvement.

TABLE 13—4. CONVERSATION AND DIRECT AND INDIRECT DEBATE EXPOSURE

(*per cent of all respondents*)

	Both Direct and Indirect	Either Direct or Indirect	Neither
Talked about debate.........	64	52	26
Did not talk...............	36	48	74
(Number).................	(103)	(33)	(23)

COMBINED COMMUNICATION ACTIVITY

As has been noted, the several kinds of communication activity were strongly related. Accordingly, we combined communication activity into a simple index, with the highest score indicating direct exposure, supplementary, and talking, and the lowest, none of these. The results showed that 41 per cent of the sample had all three activities, 34 per cent two, 16 per cent one, and 9 per cent none.

As we developed this information on communication activity and the debate, we checked out a number of factors that might account for it. For example: Were people of a given party more likely to be exposed or to talk about the debates? Here the results were uniformly negative, showing no difference in the behavior of Republicans, Democrats, and Independents.

There was a slight suggestion that individuals who had a party choice—that is, identified themselves before the debate as Democrats or Republicans—were more likely to get exposed or to talk about the debate. The same weak tendency was observed for these respondents concerning two Republican messages in the 1958 election. The suggestion of both results is that self-styled Independents do not expose themselves to political messages quite as much as party-liners.[4]

On the other hand, education was very strongly related to each of the components of the communication index and to the total index. Table 5 gives the results, which are highly significant: (p < .001).

TABLE 13—5. DEBATE COMMUNICATION ACTIVITY AND EDUCATION
(per cent of all respondents)

Communication Activity	Some College	High School Graduate	Less than High School Graduate	(Total No.)
High	62	34	25	(66)
Medium high	31	37	36	(55)
Low	7	18	21	(24)
None	—	11	18	(14)
(Number)	(55)	(65)	(39)	(159)

The same relationship was observed for occupation, which was highly correlated with education in our sample, as is usually found.

This tendency of the more highly educated to hear and talk about the debate parallels very closely the results we have obtained in studies of general exposure to and subsequent talking about the big news of the day.[5] Actually, this pattern has also been found in our studies of simple "exposure yesterday" to the mass media, ignoring the nature of the item. Generally speaking, it can be said that the higher the education (or occupation), the more likely is an American to be exposed to the mass media on any given day.[6] Thus it may be that the tendency found here for the TV debate is mainly an accentuation of this general characteristic to use the mass media, to keep up on things, to be *"au courant."*

RELIGION AND EXPOSURE

Although there was no "selectivity" in debate exposure by political party, when religion was taken into consideration, an interesting selectivity was discovered. Catholics and individuals with no religious affiliation were more likely to have viewed the debate than Protestants.[7]

TABLE 13—6. RELIGION AND DIRECT DEBATE VIEWING

	Protestants	Catholics	None or Other
Viewed or heard at least part of debate.........	68	96	94
Viewed or heard none....	32	4	6
(Number)...............	(120)	(23)	(16)

Yates correction used; p <.05.

Thus there seemed to be an avoidance behavior on the part of some Protestants. The nature of this was suggested by an analysis of another item from the pre-debate wave. Individuals were asked to indicate the "most important issue of the campaign." Of those who mentioned religion, 40 per cent missed the debate, while among those not mentioning it, only 20 per cent were not in the audience.

Although our subgroups become very small, a breakdown by party and religion further illuminates this situation. It is presented in Table

TABLE 13—7. DIRECT DEBATE EXPOSURE BY PARTY AND RELIGION[a]

	REPUBLICAN		INDEPENDENT		DEMOCRAT	
	%	No.	%	No.	%	No.
Protestant	76	(63)	59	(22)	60	(35)
Catholic	86	(7)	100	(5)	100	(11)
None or other	88	(8)	[b]	(0)	100	(8)

a. Read table as follows: Of 63 Protestant Republicans, 76 per cent viewed or heard part of the debate broadcast, while of 22 Protestant Independents, only 59 per cent were exposed.
b. There were no cases in the Independent-None or Other cell.

7. Actually, only two non-Protestants in the group missed the debate.

If we assume that Protestant predispositions were anti-Kennedy and consider that the debate would provide a direct exposure to him, this result appears to be an almost classic case of "selecting out" a mass media message in line with one's attitudes. While it seems reasonable to assume that Protestant Democrats had more cross-pressures urging them to avoid the debate (and Kennedy) than did Protestant Republicans, a comparison of these two groups only reaches the $p < .10$ level.

GETTING PAST SELECTIVITY

While selectivity has often been cited as the explanation for the lack of media effects, this approach has sometimes neglected the intensity of modern mass communications and the interplay of mass and interpersonal communications. With sufficient intensity, it is almost always possible to overcome conscious selectivity of the sort we have just been considering. This is what seems to have happened to our respondents. Half of the debate-avoiders were reached by the follow-up mass media reports in the next day and a half. Face-to-face conversation also played its part, with this mode of communication reaching 38 per cent. The combination of these means of communication reached 65 per cent, accounting for 78 per cent of the Democrats (all were Protestants), 59 per cent of the Republicans, and 56 per cent of the Independents. Thus it appears that whatever selectivity existed was pretty well eliminated by the messages which followed. Indeed, the intensity of coverage which characterized the debate (and for that matter, any other big "news break") suggests that an American must drastically change his ordinary mass media consumption habits today if he hopes to keep himself screened from "unwanted" messages. (There remains, of course, the opportunity for him to screen out the effects of the messages through unconscious distortions or interpretations.)

At the end of this multiple-media and two-stage flow of communication, we have only 9 per cent of the subjects unexposed. Despite the avoidance efforts of Protestants, 94 per cent of the Democrats had been exposed, 91 per cent of the Republicans, and 85 per cent of the Independents. Again, these differences are not significant, but suggest that the apparent non-partisan is the hardest person to reach, more likely out of a lack of interest than any other factor.

VOTING INTENTIONS

As well as establishing political party preferences in the first wave of the study, we obtained information on voting intentions. A battery of questions was utilized to sort out these classes, which were assigned arbitrary weights as indicated:

Nixon, positive	1
Nixon, might change	2
Lean Republican	3
Undecided	4
Lean Democratic	5
Kennedy, might change	6
Kennedy, positive	7

The "might change" and "positive" categories were obtained by a probe question after a direct statement of choice. The "lean" responses were obtained by a probe after an initial "no choice" or "don't know" response. Exactly the same questions on the presidential race were asked after the debate, enabling us to characterize each individual along this arbitrary seven-point scale of voting intentions on a before-after basis, and to show how much he had changed and in what direction.

RELIABILITY OF THESE MEASURES

The question might well be asked: How reliable are these measures? For one thing, the correspondence within a wave between the two approaches—party identification and voting intention—was very high. For example, those individuals who said they were Republican party adherents showed a strong tendency to intend to vote for Nixon.

The mean scale positions for the three groups are presented in Table 8, and show that voting intentions are almost identical with party positions. Independents, interestingly, were somewhat "Republican," a result we obtained also in the 1958 study. Democrats were considerably less certain about their intentions than were Republicans.

We can also note that the same kinds of scores were obtained in 1958, and at that time also showed a close relationship to party identification (as well as to a number of other indices of political position). Furthermore, from the first wave to the second wave, the degree of correlation is very high, even though many changes occurred.

TABLE 13—8. MEAN VOTING INTENTIONS BY PARTY CHOICE

Party	Mean Scale Position
Republicans................	1.26
Independents................	3.59
Democrats..................	5.98

While this line of argument is designed to support the reliability of the voting intention measure itself, we have another problem, concerning the reliability of the voting intentions which indicate changes—and an even more difficult problem of their validity: Do they measure real changes or just random shifts? We can argue face validity: A man who says he will vote for Kennedy and then says after the debate he will vote for Nixon has manifestly indicated a change. Support will also come if we can show that voting intention changes are related to other measures in a logical way or according to theory. For if the changes are indeed random, they can hardly relate to other variables in a systematic way.

CHANGES IN VOTING INTENTION

Some 25 per cent of our respondents changed their voting intentions one or more points on the 7-point scale. Let us first analyze these changes, without attending to their direction.

An initial check upon their validity and, indirectly, upon their reliability can be made by determining whether there is a relationship between party identification and change. We would expect that most committed individuals would show little change and that leaners or Independents would show more change. The data clearly support this expectation. Only 6 per cent of the strong Republicans or Democrats changed, while 37 per cent of the Independents did so. Actually, the greatest rate of change occurs among the "leaners," more than half of whom shifted their voting intention. Average party members include 20 per cent who changed.

We have from this some encouragement that the changes are not just random variations. They relate to strength of party identification at a level which could occur by chance only one time in 100.

Another approach was taken to determine the nature of the changers. It seems reasonable to expect that individuals who said before the debates that they had decided upon a candidate and "wouldn't change their minds" would have less tendency to shift than those who indicated some possibility of change or that they merely "leaned" toward a candidate or a party. Accordingly, we sorted out all persons who took an "extreme" Democratic or Republican position, and compared their rate of change with that of individuals who had less assurance about their intentions.

The resulting difference was in line with expectation and dramatically large. Of those who showed some doubts about having fully made up their minds, 57 per cent changed their voting intentions; of those who said they had it settled, only 10 per cent changed.

We might also expect that there would be more change among those exposed to the debate than among those who missed it. However, this is not the case. The percentage shifting is almost exactly the same for both groups.

As we have noted, however, respondents got messages about the debate by other than direct means. If we compare those who reported *no* communication at all, we would expect them to show less change than those who received some. The result is in this direction, but the difference is very small; 21 per cent of the non-communicators changed, 25 per cent of those who received some kind of communication. Such a difference could easily occur by chance even though the two groups were really the same.

How about education? The results suggest that the college-educated change less (18 per cent) than those with less education (28 per cent), but, again the difference is not large enough to be convincing.

What about talking? We expected, since conversation is generally found to be more persuasive than mass communication—and since it has been suggested as the paramount force in changes of political attitudes—that those who talk would change more than those who do not.[8] The results, however, are just the opposite of this: only 19 per cent of the talkers shifted their voting intention, while 30 per cent of those who *did not* talk changed. This difference, incidentally, could arise by chance only 5 times in 100.

When we examine the data more carefully, we find increased evidence that talking about the debate did not operate to change voting intentions. The group with no exposure at all, it will be remembered, included 21 per cent changers. The group which heard about the debates *only through talk* had not a single change. Even though the group is small (only six persons), the result gives no support for the notion that talk is the potent force for change.

When we compare those who got debate exposure through the

media, direct or supplementary, without talk, with those who had conversations as well as media messages, the difference is sharpened and remains beyond chance levels; 34 per cent of the individuals who got media debate exposure without talk shifted as against 19 per cent for talkers and 21 per cent for persons with no exposure at all.

These data on patterns of communication and voting intention changes do not prove, but suggest, the possibility that (1) exposure to the debate or media reports about it shifted voting intentions; but (2) talk—mainly to like-minded persons—restored previous voting intentions.

This result may be a special product of the debate situation but we suspect not. It may reflect an underlying pattern of the process of changes in attitude in politics today, with mass media playing the role of changers rather than status quo maintainers and talk playing the role of maintenance rather than of change. This interpretation, incidentally, is diametrically opposed to current views of the role of conversation and mass media in politics.

Can we answer unequivocally, then, whether voting intentions in our sample changed or not? We can summarize as follows: (1) The responses have face validity. (2) They are related sensibly to strength of party identification. (3) They are related to the *kind* of exposure, and the results are consistent with the notion that the debates themselves or reports of them produced change, while conversation with persons of like attitudes—added to such exposure—canceled out change.

DIRECTION OF CHANGES IN VOTING INTENTION

It is useful at this point to recall the debate format. It was designed to give equal time to the two candidates—to provide a chance for assertion and rebuttal. From a communication point of view, we should say—in advance—that the debate should have been a balanced message, containing equal parts pro-Republican and pro-Democratic.

For this prearranged balance to be disrupted, it was necessary for Nixon or Kennedy to operate within that framework in a way which turned part of the opposite time—so to speak—into a message for himself; or else to use his own time so poorly as to turn it into a message against himself.

A careful content analysis could test these tendencies. It might note, as some media commentators did, that Nixon made a fluff about farmers ("When we get rid of the farmers . . . ," quickly corrected to "the farm problem"); or that Kennedy was wrong on a date which many viewers knew; or that Nixon "gave up" time on several rebuttal possibilities, saying, very briefly, that he agreed with Kennedy's position. But such an analysis is difficult and probably inconclusive in this close contest between two able candidates.

PERCEIVED DIRECTION OF CHANGES

We have already noted that the media reports gave little or no indication to our subjects that either man won the debate. Conversation, on the other hand, seemed to be weighted in the direction of a Kennedy victory, but not by any large margin. We asked several other questions of this sort. For example, we asked respondents whether they thought anyone won or lost votes. The results on "votes won" put Kennedy ahead by a margin large enough to dispel statistical doubts.

TABLE 13—9. "WHO DO YOU FEEL WON VOTES AS A RESULT OF THE DEBATE?"

(by strength of party designation; percentages)

	(No.)	Nixon	Both, Mixed, Can't Tell	Kennedy	Kennedy's Net Advantage[a]
Strong Rep.	(24)	12	63	25	13
Average Rep.	(36)	8	67	25	17
Lean Rep.	(18)	11	54	33	22
Independent	(27)	4	77	19	15
Lean Dem.	(11)	0	73	27	27
Average Dem.	(20)	0	75	25	25
Strong Dem.	(23)	9	54	35	26
Total	(159)	7	67	26	19

a. The fact that all seven groups produce a "net advantage" for Kennedy is a result which would occur by chance less than one time in a hundred if feelings were randomly distributed. A further test of these data was made by assigning arbitrary values of +1 to feeling that Kennedy won, 0 to mixed, and −1 to Nixon. (The mean of this distribution is .19.) We may test the obtained value against the hypothesis that the mean is zero—the result expected if there were no significant deviation in either direction. The obtained value is significant beyond the .001 level.

Tables 9 and 10 show the consistency in the "feeling that Kennedy won" which extends across all degrees of political party attachment. And the over-all result is a net "advantage" of 19 per cent for Kennedy, not a "sweeping victory," but enough to give him encouragement. The contrast between the individual's feelings about the outcome and

TABLE 13—10. "WHO DID THE PERSONS YOU TALKED TO SAY WON THE DEBATE?"

(by strength of party designation; percentages)

	(No.)	Nixon	Both, Mixed, Didn't Talk	Kennedy	Kennedy's Net Advantage[a]
Strong Rep.	(24)	17	75	8	−8
Average Rep.	(36)	6	80	14	8
Lean Rep.	(18)	11	89	0	−11
Independent	(27)	4	77	19	15
Lean Dem.	(11)	11	88	11	0
Average Dem.	(20)	5	75	20	15
Strong Dem.	(23)	4	70	26	22
Total	(159)	8	78	14	6

a. Minus indicates net advantage for Nixon.

his report of conversations with others is illuminating. In Table 10, we find much smaller differences, and a net advantage which is not significantly larger than zero. Further, several of the Republican groups show a "net" for Nixon.

Both sets of "net advantage" scores, incidentally, are significantly related to strength of party attachment. (Feelings, Rho = .78, Conversations, Rho = .72, both beyond .05.)

What we can say at this point is that the "perceived" effect of the debate—averaged over all persons—was a Kennedy victory, but by a small margin.

DIRECTION OF VOTING INTENTION

We have already indicated that the debate "message" was two-sided, a condition which might well be expected to produce balanced shifting. In addition, previous research gives us little reason to expect that any

TABLE 13—11. VOTING INTENTIONS BEFORE AND AFTER DEBATE

	AFTER DEBATE							
	Rep. or Leaning		Undecided		Dem. or Leaning		Totals	
BEFORE DEBATE	%	(N)	%	(N)	%	(N)	%	(N)
Rep. or Leaning	50.3	(80)	0.6	(1)	1.3	(2)	52.2	(83)
Undecided	3.2	(5)	10.0	(16)	4.4	(7)	17.6	(28)
Dem. or Leaning	0.6	(1)	0.6	(1)	29.0	(46)	30.2	(48)
Total	54.1	(86)	11.3	(18)	34.6	(55)	100	(159)

TABLE 13—12. SHIFTS OF "BACKSLIDERS" AND "SOLIDIFIERS"

	Shifted in Rep. Direction		Stable		Shifted in Dem. Direction		(Total No.)
	%	(No.)	%	(No.)	%	(No.)	
Republican V.I. before and after		(5)		(68)		(7)	(80)
Democratic V.I. before and after		(3)		(36)		(7)	(46)
Total	6.3	(8)	82.6	(104)	11.1	(14)	(126)

TABLE 13—13. SUMMARY OF VOTING INTENTIONS SHIFT

	(N)	Per Cent	
Shifted to Rep. from neutral or Dem.	(7)	4.4	⎫ 9.4
Became more Rep. or less Dem.	(8)	5.0	⎭
No change	(120)	75.5	
Became more Dem. or less Rep.	(14)	8.8	⎫ 15.1
Shifted to Dem. from neutral or Rep.	(10)	6.3	⎭
Total	(159)	100	

massive shift in voting intentions might be produced by an event of this type.

At the same time, a measure of shifting took place, and the net result of it was that Kennedy gained ground in this sample. However, his over-all gain (about 6 per cent) was such that it could have arisen by chance. An examination of shifts by groups shows that Democrats, however, moved toward Kennedy significantly. The results are in Table 14.

TABLE 13—14. MEAN SHIFTS BY POLITICAL GROUPS[a]

	(N)	Mean Shift	s	t	p
Republicans	(78)	+.013	.41	< 1.00	n.s.
Independents	(27)	−.074	.62	< 1.00	n.s.
Democrats	(54)	+.185	.52	2.64	.01

a. Any shift in a Democratic direction is scored as +1, no shift as zero, and any shift in a Republican direction as −1. The mean of these distributions is the net proportion shifting.

CHANGE "FORCES" AND DIRECTION OF CHANGE

We have obtained information about a number of forces which might impel individuals toward change in one direction or another. The first of these is what we have called "political predisposition"— the party preference which was expressed in the first place. Such a predisposition can be thought of as a force impelling an individual toward a decision to vote for one or another candidate. In a practical sense, if a man is a Republican or Democrat and undecided about an election, he may very well *move himself* in the direction of his previous party attachment, even if no one argues with him, or if he escapes political propaganda. He has a "readiness" to respond in a Democratic or Republican fashion.

Another force which might impel him to change in one direction or another is face-to-face conversation. Research has given some indication of conversation's potency. Here we might expect that a person who talks to an individual of a given political position might be moved in the direction of such talk. This kind of force could be in line with predispositions (as a matter of fact, most conversations in our study were between Republican and Republican or Democrat and Democrat), but they also could involve receiving some opposing "talk."

Another force is communication through the mass media. We have already reported on our content analytic work and on our respondents' perceptions of the mass "messages"—the debate and subsequent radio, television, and newspaper reports and editorials. The consensus is that these messages pushed about equally in Republican and Democratic directions. For the present, let us accept this position, but reserve the right to test the notion that the debate itself was possibly a Democratic or a Republican message (by some small margin).

PREDISPOSITION AS "PREDICTOR" OF CHANGE

We have suggested, then, three key forces operating upon voting intentions; these do not exhaust the possibilities, but they may help us account for the *direction* of change which we encountered.

We shall attempt to do this by means of a "prediction" game, in which we can check, from time to time, on how we are doing.

Let us attempt to predict the direction of changes on the basis of political predisposition, using reported party "affiliation" as our index. We have 39 cases of change to handle, 24 of which went in a Democratic direction and 15 in a Republican.

Our prediction is a simple one, with some support from past research: A Democrat will change in a Democratic direction and a Republican in a Republican direction. With this method, we can't say anything about the seven Independents who changed and gave us no indication of their political leanings, although we can work with three who gave us some clues.

The results of our "prediction" are: correct, 20; incorrect, 12.

If we were predicting on a chance basis, we should expect to be right half of the time, or for 16 cases. So we have done somewhat better than chance. But a statistical test (chi square with expected proportions of 50 per cent right and wrong) indicates that we are not doing so well. The number right could have occurred by chance more than 10 times out of 100, even if our prediction system were simply working randomly.

ADDING DIRECTIONAL FACE-TO-FACE CONVERSATION

We noted that face-to-face conversation was another potential push. Suppose we utilize the cases in which we have an unequivocal indication of the direction of talk which the "changer" received, in addition to the predisposition data. We find seven cases who changed and who reported getting either Republican or Democratic talk. We shall use this to predict their changes, and predisposition for the remainder of the cases.

When we get through checking our score on this altered procedure, we find that we now correctly predict 22 cases and are in error on 10.

This event, our test tells us, could occur by chance fewer than 5 times in 100 if our scheme were random.

ADDING DEBATE EXPOSURE WITH "SOME ASSUMPTIONS"

Finally, let us question the previous evidence and assumptions concerning the directionality of the debate. What would happen, for example, if we supposed, along with some of our respondents, that Kennedy did "win the debate"—that it was a Democratic message? (We can also consider the alternative that the debate was a Republican message and that Nixon won.)

Let us add these new assumptions to our previous approaches and see how well we can predict. The steps in our prediction scheme are now as follows:

1. Check to see if the individual talked in a situation in which a clear direction of conversation is given. If so, we predict he will change in the direction of that conversation.
2. Of the remainder, check on direct exposure to the debate. If an individual was not exposed, we predict that he will change in the direction of his predisposition.
3. Of the remaining individuals (those who were exposed to the debate and who were involved in mixed conversations), we will proceed on two different assumptions, trying first the one, and then the other:

   A. Debate was Republican message—then a person exposed should change in a Republican direction.
   B. Debate was a Democratic message—then a person exposed should change in a Democratic direction.

When we apply this three-part prediction scheme utilizing 3A (that the debate was a Republican message), our ability to predict correctly declines markedly. As a matter of fact, we now get only 21 right and 18 wrong, so close to chance that the result could occur 50 per cent or more of the time in a random situation.[9]

When we change the assumption to 3B (that the debate was a Democratic message), our ability to predict improves strikingly. We now have 27 right and 12 wrong. This could occur by chance fewer than 2 times in 100, if we were, for example, just flipping coins to decide whether a person would change in a Republican or Democratic direction.

EVALUATION OF RESULTS

The "prediction game" lends some support to the "average" contention of our respondents and to our own speculations that Kennedy might in fact have "won the first debate." Beyond this, it lends some support to the notion that some combination of predisposition, face-to-face conversation, and mass media exposure may be utilized to predict changes in such a measure of voting intention.

Indeed, we proceeded upon this entire enterprise with assumptions concerning just this set of variations in human behavior and communication. We focused upon these, as a matter of fact, because of the analysis and theory advanced by Katz and Lazarsfeld in their writings on the "two-stage flow of influence."

While we do not have strong evidence, the whole complex of the data seems to support the hypothesis that attitudes as expressed in voting intentions are changed by the combination of forces we have examined.

SUMMARY

Answering the "debate mystery" in this fashion so long after the fact is not a particularly spectacular achievement. We suspect that most Americans made up their minds some time ago that Kennedy won. Even though the question may already have been answered, it seems to the writer that this kind of approach yields information about the general process of attitude change. Today, in the United States, this process is indeed a complex of forces, stemming partly from the mass media and partly from face-to-face conversation which we become involved in at home, work, and play.

As Katz and Lazarsfeld have pointed out, it is necessary for us to look at the combination of these forces, set against the powerful backdrop of prior attitude or predisposition. It so happens that they have viewed the mass media and face-to-face conversation playing roles somewhat different from those suggested in this study.

We advance the hypothesis that mass media are more likely to be instigators of changes in political attitudes and that conversation is more likely to be the force maintaining the status quo. The evidence here is certainly not conclusive. It may be, of course, a special function of the "great debate" which, as never before in American mass communication history, brought both sides to the public in a forceful way.

In any event, we feel that this approach has much potential utility for the examination of communication situations which involve various combinations of mass and face-to-face, and that further research will test the findings advanced here.

As for who won the first debate—we'd say Kennedy did, by a margin not a lot greater than the election.

NOTES

1. Elihu Katz and Paul Lazarsfeld, *Personal Influence* (Glencoe, Ill.: Free Press, 1955).

2. See Paul J. Deutschmann and Wayne A. Danielson, "Diffusion of Knowledge of the Major News Story," *Journalism Quarterly* (Summer, 1960), 37-3, pp. 345-55. The items studied had more "news value" in the sense of novel information than did the debate; 68 per cent talked about the first U. S. satellite in January 1958, and 54 per cent about Alaskan statehood in June 1958.

3. This information was obtained from the first three waves of the study, and was reported in "A Field Investigation of the Two-Stage Flow of Communication," paper presented by Paul J. Deutschmann and Frank A. Pinner to the Association for Education in Journalism convention, Pennsylvania State University, August 30, 1960.

4. For example, a comparison of debate viewing of Independents and those choosing a party yields a p level smaller than .20. About the same level was obtained between the two groups in 1958 for knowledge of Nixon's visit to Michigan and of a *Time* "cover story" on a Michigan Republican congressional candidate.

5. Deutschmann and Danielson, "Diffusion of Knowledge," p. 347.

6. Data on occupation follow the same trends. They are reported in "The X, Y, Z Papers," An Inland Anniversary Study, Inland Midwest Universities Committee on Research, October 15, 1960, East Lansing, Michigan. (Mimeographed.)

7. I am indebted to Dr. Barrow for this analysis, which he developed during a special investigation of religion, debate exposure, and attitude change.

8. See Katz and Lazarsfeld, *Personal Influence*, pp. 45 ff.

9. As it happens, this approach makes possible predictions for our seven independents, since all of them were exposed to the debate.

14

Some Effects of the Debates

RICHARD F. CARTER

THE QUESTION to be asked about the "Great Debates" of 1960 is whether, in the public interest, they are worth doing again in 1964, in the same or a modified form. Are they a public service or merely a spectacle? This can be determined only by studying the effects of the debates. What was the audience reaction to their format? What was emphasized—issues or personalities? Did the audience change its opinion of either candidate as a result of the debates? Did the debate format succeed in cracking the resistance often found toward listening to an opposing candidate's views?

Seeking some answers to such questions, the Institute for Communication Research of Stanford University made repeated surveys of 60 Republicans and 60 Democrats in four neighboring California cities. The Institute conducted personal interviews before the first debate, after the first debate, and after the fourth debate.[1] This panel technique allowed sensitive measures of change in audience reactions to the debates. Not all the results were statistically significant, but a pattern was found that is suggestive for the conduct of future debates—that is, for future debates held in the public interest.

How many viewed or listened? Among both Republican and Democratic panel members, the audience for the debates declined steadily from the phenomenal attendance of the first debate, but a majority still saw or listened to the fourth debate. Panel viewership of the debates is shown in Figure 1. (Radio listenership is a consistently small fraction of the total, varying from 3 to 8 per cent, and the term *viewing* is used for convenience.)

The average number of persons viewing in Republican homes was

FIGURE 1.

PANEL VIEWING OF THE DEBATES

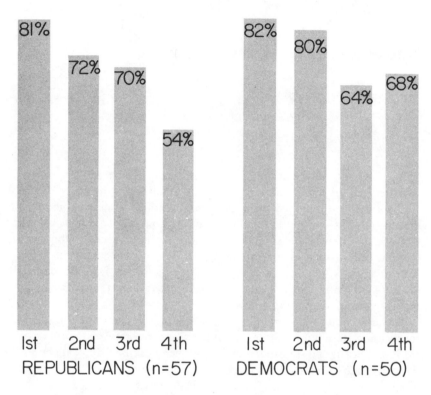

1.94; in Democratic homes, the average was 2.08. The spouse most often joined in viewing, with children, other family members, and occasionally friends and neighbors. Only one-fifth viewed alone.

Which debate was best liked? About one-fifth of the panel members had no preference among the four debates. Of those with an opinion, Republicans liked the later debates, Democrats preferred the second and fourth debates. The results are given in Figure 2.

The panelists liked a clash of personalities. Republicans, in explaining their choice of the later debates, used adjectives like "direct, lively, emotional, peppy, and spirited." Democrats referred to the emergence of "the true selves of the candidates under stress." The first debate, Republicans and Democrats said, lacked fire.

FIGURE 2.

PREFERENCE FOR DEBATES

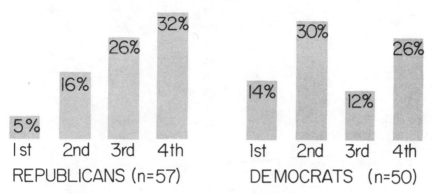

No preference: Republicans—23%; Democrats—22%.

What purposes were served? Panel members, in answer to an open question, credited the debates with helping them to learn about candidates and issues—in that order—and with increasing their interest and information. In addition, panel members said that television was a uniquely useful medium for learning during the campaign. Only 9 per cent saw no purpose served. Figure 3 gives the proportions for Republicans and Democrats combined.

In answer to a direct question as to which were better pictured, issues or candidates, 50 per cent said "both," 19 per cent said "candidates," and 7 per cent said "issues." The remaining 24 per cent said "neither" or did not say.

How could the debates be improved? Some 70 per cent of the panel members had suggestions on the future conduct of the debates, several with implications for the conduct of the campaign itself. Specific comments suggested that: (1) the audience should be able to question the candidates; (2) the atmosphere should be more relaxed (like a "fireside chat," said a Democrat); (3) the vice presidential candidates should be included; (4) the rules should be less strict; (5) the participants should be able to question each other; (6) they should allow more rebuttal; (7) the debates should be required by law (not "at the whim of the candidates," said a Republican); (8) the debates should be closer to the election and the whole campaign shortened; (9) listen-

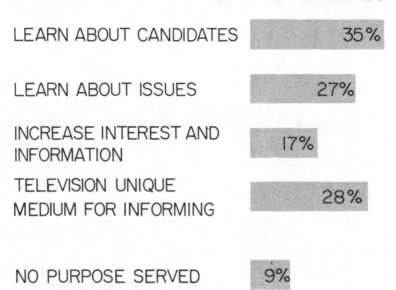

FIGURE 3.

PURPOSES SERVED BY THE DEBATES

LEARN ABOUT CANDIDATES   35%

LEARN ABOUT ISSUES   27%

INCREASE INTEREST AND
INFORMATION   17%

TELEVISION UNIQUE
MEDIUM FOR INFORMING   28%

NO PURPOSE SERVED   9%

N = 107. The entries do not add to 100 per cent because some respondents gave more than one answer.

ers should know more in advance so they can judge better; (10) a third party should be present with the Congressional Record to tell when one of them is lying.

In general, however, three suggestions dominated. They were, as shown in Figure 4: the debates should be longer; the interviewing newsmen should be eliminated; and there should be only one topic to each debate. The answers were volunteered and probably do not represent a full measure of the persons who would endorse these suggestions.

Who benefited? In estimating the effects of the debates, both Republicans and Democrats gave the decision to Kennedy. As Figure 5 shows, the Democrats were more certain of the decision. However, in estimating the impact of the debates on themselves, panel members did not see such striking effects. As Figures 6 and 7 show, the principal effect was that Kennedy impressed the Democrats more than Nixon impressed the Republicans. Approximately half of the panel said they had not changed their attitudes toward either candidate after viewing

FIGURE 4.
SUGGESTIONS FOR FUTURE DEBATES

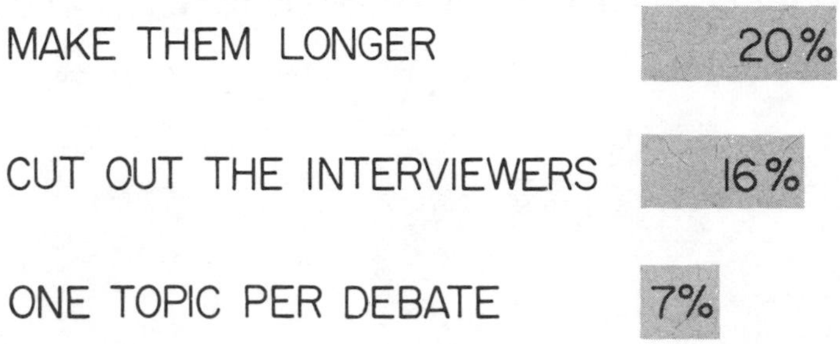

MAKE THEM LONGER   20%

CUT OUT THE INTERVIEWERS   16%

ONE TOPIC PER DEBATE   7%

N = 107.

the debates. On the basis of these self-estimates, the debates were not productive of any great shift in opinion. But more objective measures of attitudes brought out key changes favoring Kennedy.

How was Nixon seen? To get more objective estimates of possible effects from the debates, respondents were asked at three different times to indicate how they saw the presidential candidates—before the first debate, after the first debate, and after the fourth debate. Candidates were assessed on eight characteristics: *trustworthy, industrious, honest, experienced, sincere, intelligent, imaginative,* and *tough.* Scores ranged from 1 (very negative) to 12 (very positive).

As Table 1 shows, the pessimistic estimate of Republican panel members that Nixon did not fare too well was borne out. Neither Republicans nor Democrats accorded him an over-all increase in standing from before to after the debates. Both, however, did give him an increase in ratings on *tough.* Democrats gave Nixon slightly higher ratings after the first debate but, with the exception of *tough,* were less favorable after the last debate. Republicans, even on *tough,* did not see Nixon any more favorably after the first debate.

How was Kennedy seen? The objective measures confirmed subjective estimates that panel members were more favorably influenced by Kennedy's debate image. Table 2 shows a net gain for Kennedy among both Republicans and Democrats. They were most impressed with the characteristics of *industrious, experienced,* and *tough.* The gains were consistent, appearing after both the first and the fourth debate.

Some caution should be exercised in the interpretation of these re-

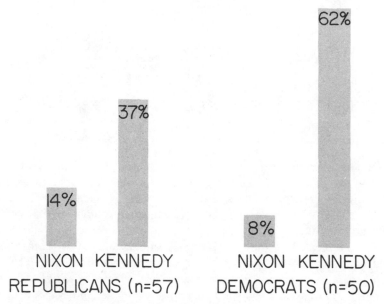

FIGURE 5.

WHO BENEFITED FROM THE DEBATES

sults. There was no control over events occurring simultaneously with the debates that might have produced the changes reported. However, the agreement of subjective and objective estimates is noteworthy.

What received emphasis? If indeed the debates brought about these changes in images, an important finding is the character of the changes. The only major changes were on characteristics of *industrious* and *experienced* (Kennedy) and *tough* (both candidates). The debates were not found to have produced substantial changes on such characteristics as *trustworthy, honest, sincere, intelligent,* and *imaginative.* It seems almost as if the audience searched for characteristics of strong leadership in the candidates or, perhaps, the candidates may have emphasized these characteristics as they sought to build acceptable images.

Were there other image changes? In addition to measuring changes in the favorability of images, an attempt was also made to ascertain any increased stereotyping of the images. Did panel members develop more tightly knit pictures of the candidates' characteristics? Did they,

FIGURE 6.

MORE FAVORABLE ATTITUDES TOWARD CANDIDATES AS A RESULT OF THE DEBATES

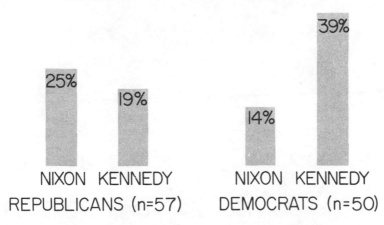

that is, tend to give each candidate much the same rating on every characteristic, thus forming a more cohesive image? Psychologically, it was to be expected that respondents would find it easier to hold a stereotype of the candidates.[2]

Figure 8 shows the relative increases in stereotyping as the debates progressed. The most important stereotyping would seem to have occurred as a consequence of the first debate. The panel member's own candidate was more stereotyped than the opposition candidate.

Did panel members see only what they wanted to see? All too frequently, to the detriment of public affairs discussions, people tend to hear and see only what they want to see.[3] The Republican hears only his own party's arguments and shuts out the opposition; the Democrat reciprocates. One of the potential assets of the debates was the possibility that this behavior could be minimized. If the debates could draw large audiences from both parties, as they did, then at least a chance existed that cognizance would be taken of opposing arguments. There might be at least exposure to both points of view, if not agreement with both.

Two questions were involved: first, whether party members tended

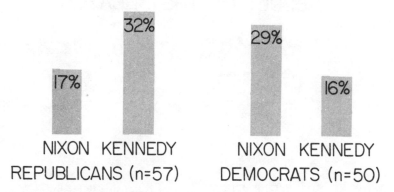

FIGURE 7.

MORE NEGATIVE ATTITUDES
TOWARD CANDIDATES AS A
RESULT OF THE DEBATES

to accept only their own candidate's arguments; second, whether they were, nevertheless, effectively exposed to the opposing arguments. As shown in Figure 9, panel members were more likely to say that the opposition candidate had made no effective arguments. This biased perception of effectiveness is more noticeable in reactions to the first debate than to the later debates.

Did the debates work? As might have been expected from previous research, panel members tended to say that the opposition candidate had not made any effective arguments. Yet the other question remains: Were the panel members, for all their denial of the opposition's arguments, effectively exposed to those arguments? If such were the case, an important potential had been shown in the debate format.

To measure relative exposure to arguments of the opposition, panel members were given a 16-item information test following the first debate.[4] Eight items were constructed for each candidate, based on statements made during the first debate. Scores were standardized, statistically, so that Republicans and Democrats could be grouped together for analysis. The question is whether panelists recalled more from the preferred candidate than from the opposition candidate. If the debate format had been effective, there would be little difference in arguments recalled—even among those panelists who denied the effectiveness of the opposition arguments.

TABLE 14—1. THE NIXON IMAGE

CHARACTERISTIC	DEMOCRATS			
	Before 1st Debate	After 1st Debate	After 4th Debate	Net Change[a]
Trustworthy	8.2	8.5	8.2	0.0
Industrious	9.8	9.9	9.7	−.1
Honest	8.9	8.7	8.4	−.5
Experienced	10.0	10.1	10.0	0.0
Sincere	8.5	8.6	8.3	−.2
Intelligent	10.2	10.2	9.9	−.3
Imaginative	8.5	8.7	8.3	−.2
Tough	8.8	9.2	9.4	+.6
Average	9.11	9.24	9.02	−.09
	(N=42)	(N=59)	(N=50)	

CHARACTERISTIC	REPUBLICANS			
Trustworthy	10.5	10.5	10.3	−.2
Industrious	10.9	10.9	11.0	+.1
Honest	10.7	10.6	10.5	−.2
Experienced	11.3	11.0	11.0	−.3
Sincere	10.6	10.6	10.3	−.3
Intelligent	11.0	11.0	11.0	0.0
Imaginative	10.0	10.0	10.0	0.0
Tough	10.2	10.2	10.7	+.5
Average	10.65	10.60	10.60	−.05
	(N=51)	(N=59)	(N=57)	

a. For *tough:* t (Rep) = 1.21, p is less than .30; t (Dem.) = .72, p is less than .50.

Figure 10 tells the story. There was little difference in recall of arguments by panel members who said both candidates made effective arguments. More important, there was little difference in recall of arguments by panel members who said only their own candidate made effective arguments. Perhaps most important, there *was* a considerable difference in arguments recalled in favor of the panelist's own candi-

TABLE 14—2. THE KENNEDY IMAGE

| | DEMOCRATS | | | |
CHARACTERISTIC	Before 1st Debate	After 1st Debate	After 4th Debate	Net Change[a]
Trustworthy	10.2	10.2	[10.4	+.2
Industrious	10.0	10.6	10.8	+.8
Honest	10.4	10.3	10.3	−.1
Experienced	8.6	9.5	9.9	+1.3
Sincere	10.4	10.4	10.5	+.1
Intelligent	11.0	10.8	11.0	0.0
Imaginative	9.6	9.7	10.0	+.4
Tough	9.2	9.9	10.0	+.8
Average	9.92	10.18	10.36	+.44
	(N=42)	(N=59)	(N=50)	
	REPUBLICANS			
Trustworthy	8.6	9.0	8.6	0.0
Industrious	9.4	9.9	10.1	+.7
Honest	9.1	9.4	9.1	0.0
Experienced	6.9	8.3	8.4	+1.5
Sincere	8.9	9.0	8.8	−.1
Intelligent	10.2	10.1	10.2	0.0
Imaginative	9.1	8.7	9.0	−.1
Tough	8.8	9.1	9.5	+.7
Average	8.88	9.19	9.21	+.33
	(N=51)	(N=59)	(N=57)	

a. For *industrious:* t (Rep.) = 3.28, p is less than .01; t (Dem.) = 2.55, p is less than .02. For *experienced:* t (Rep.) = 4.65, p is less than .01; t (Dem) = 5.15, p is less than .01. For *tough:* t (Rep.) = 2.86, p is less than .01; t (Dem.) = 1.55, p is less than .15.

date *only when neither candidate was seen to have made an effective argument.* In short, the panel member had to dismiss the whole presentation in order to preserve his bias.

Panel members were asked: "Did the program lack interest at some points so that you didn't feel you missed anything if you left the room

FIGURE 8.
STEREOTYPING OF IMAGES

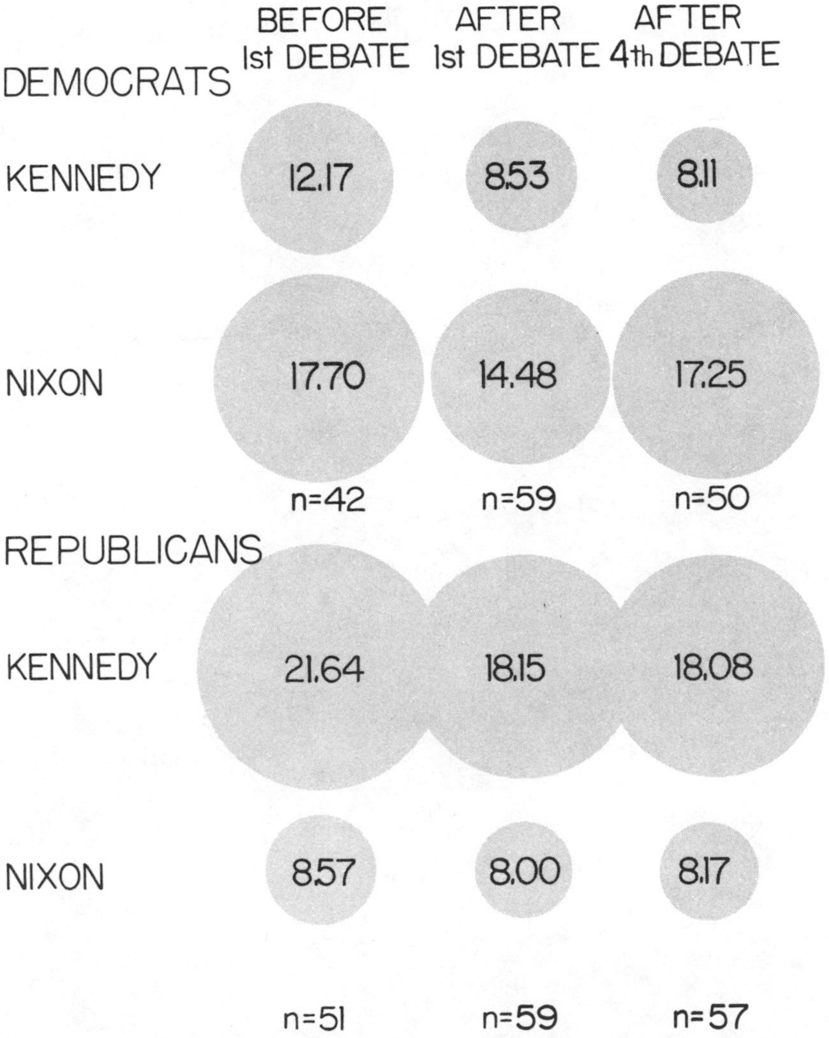

	BEFORE 1st DEBATE	AFTER 1st DEBATE	AFTER 4th DEBATE
DEMOCRATS			
KENNEDY	12.17	8.53	8.11
NIXON	17.70	14.48	17.25
	n=42	n=59	n=50
REPUBLICANS			
KENNEDY	21.64	18.15	18.08
NIXON	8.57	8.00	8.17
	n=51	n=59	n=57

Note: The smaller the score—and circle—the greater the stereotyping. Stereotyping is measured by the absolute differences in ratings on paired characteristics. For Kennedy: t (Rep.) = 1.94, p < .06; t (Dem.) = 2.76, p < .01.

FIGURE 9.
PERCEPTIONS OF NO EFFECTIVE ARGUMENTS

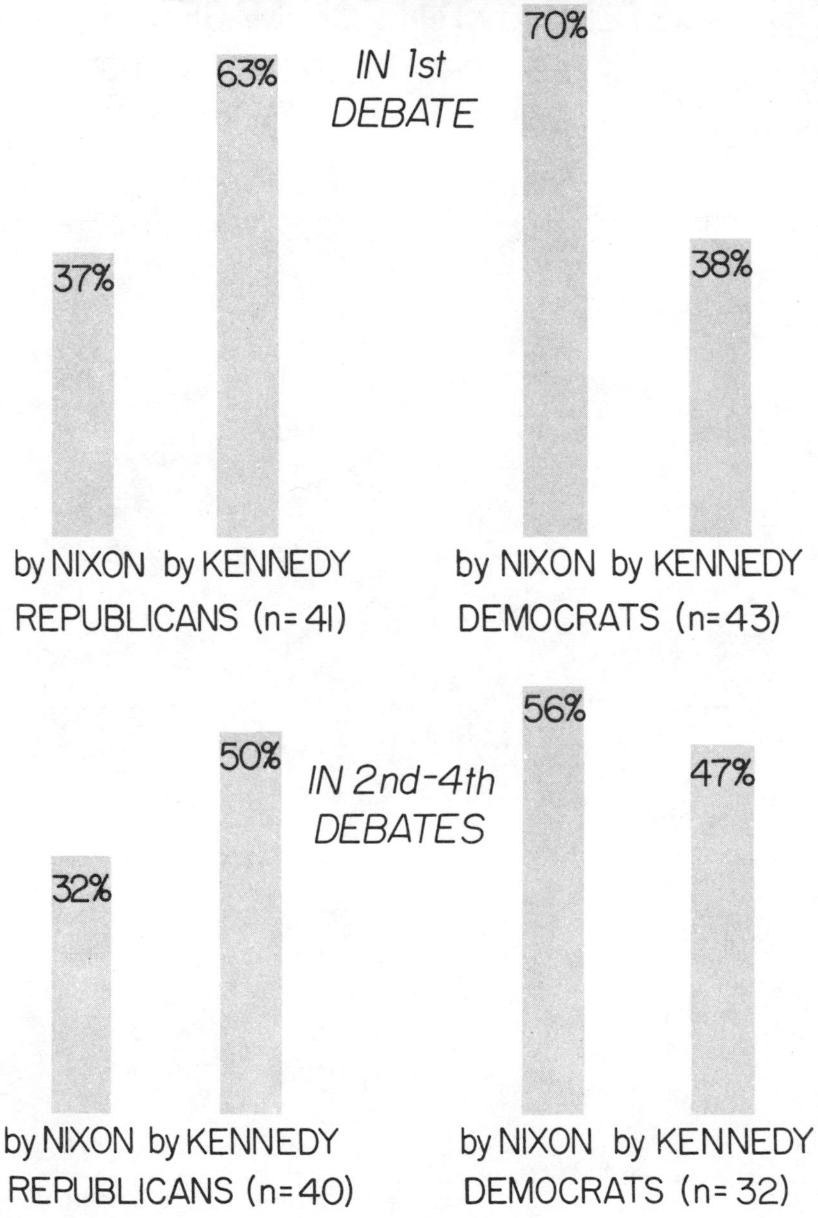

IN 1st DEBATE

IN 2nd-4th DEBATES

For first debate: chi square = 6.84, p is less than .01.

FIGURE 10.
RECALL OF CANDIDATE ARGUMENTS

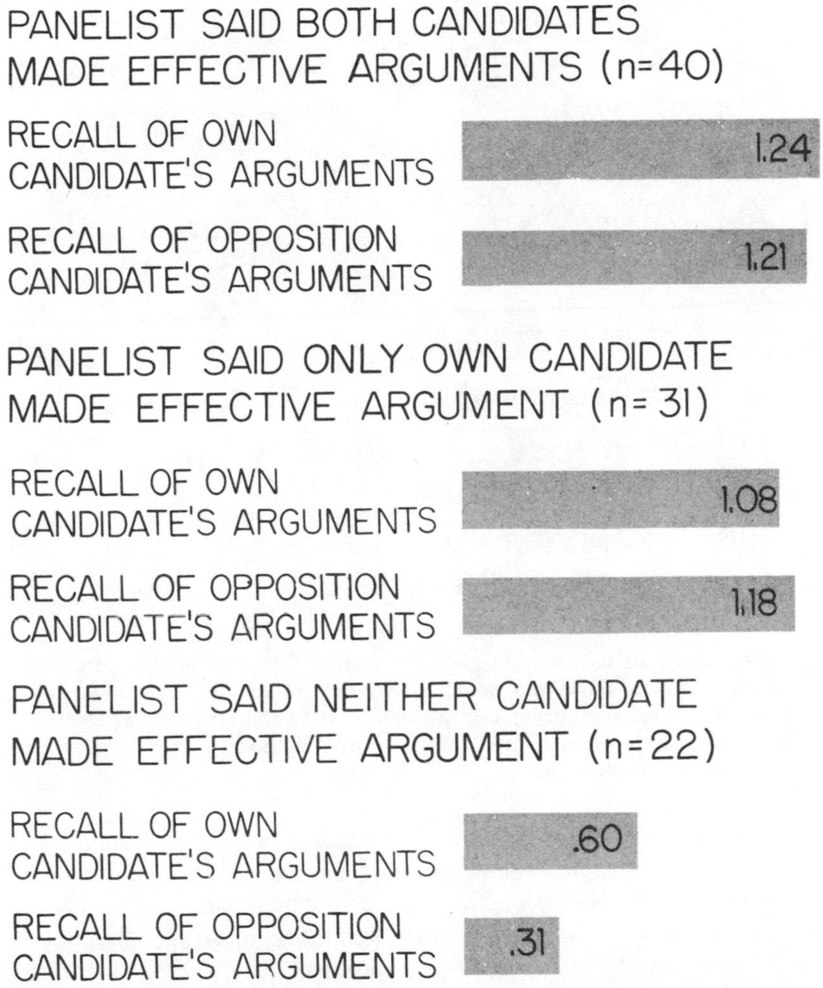

PANELIST SAID BOTH CANDIDATES
MADE EFFECTIVE ARGUMENTS (n=40)

RECALL OF OWN
CANDIDATE'S ARGUMENTS — 1.24

RECALL OF OPPOSITION
CANDIDATE'S ARGUMENTS — 1.21

PANELIST SAID ONLY OWN CANDIDATE
MADE EFFECTIVE ARGUMENT (n=31)

RECALL OF OWN
CANDIDATE'S ARGUMENTS — 1.08

RECALL OF OPPOSITION
CANDIDATE'S ARGUMENTS — 1.18

PANELIST SAID NEITHER CANDIDATE
MADE EFFECTIVE ARGUMENT (n=22)

RECALL OF OWN
CANDIDATE'S ARGUMENTS — .60

RECALL OF OPPOSITION
CANDIDATE'S ARGUMENTS — .31

A constant value of 1.00 has been added to all standard scores to avoid negative entries. The difference in arguments recalled for own and opposition candidate was not significant for those who thought neither made an effective argument. The difference in arguments recalled for either candidate between those who saw either candidate making an effective argument and those who saw neither making an effective argument was statistically significant (t = 2.53, with p less than .02).

FIGURE 11.

ATTENTION AND RECALL OF ARGUMENTS

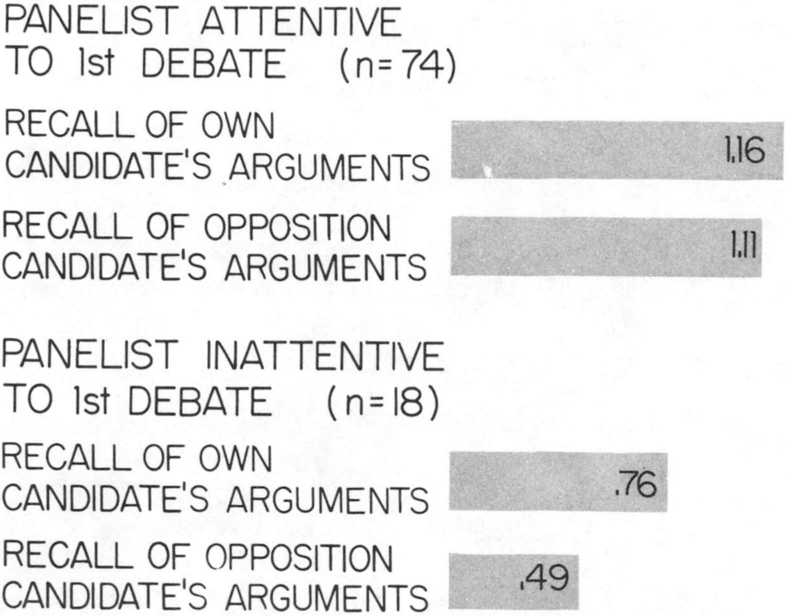

PANELIST ATTENTIVE
TO 1st DEBATE   (n=74)

RECALL OF OWN
CANDIDATE'S ARGUMENTS   1.16

RECALL OF OPPOSITION
CANDIDATE'S ARGUMENTS   1.11

PANELIST INATTENTIVE
TO 1st DEBATE   (n=18)

RECALL OF OWN
CANDIDATE'S ARGUMENTS   .76

RECALL OF OPPOSITION
CANDIDATE'S ARGUMENTS   .49

> The difference in arguments recalled for own and opposition candidate was not significant for those who were inattentive to the program. The difference in arguments recalled for either candidate between those who were attentive and those who were inattentive was not quite statistically significant (t = 1.96, with p less than .06).

or did something else while the program was on?" The inattentive, those who said "yes" in response to this question, were, like those who perceived no effective arguments by either candidate, less likely to recall arguments by either candidate—and, particularly, less likely to recall arguments by the opposition candidate. Figure 11 shows this tabulation.

The smaller recall of opposition arguments by inattentive panel members cannot be attributed to lesser interest. As Figure 12 shows, those with less interest recalled less over-all, but did not recall relatively less for the oppostion candidate.

Similarly, as Figure 13 shows, strength of party affiliation did not

FIGURE 12.

INTEREST AND RECALL OF ARGUMENTS

PANELIST INTERESTED
IN 1st DEBATE   (n=41)

RECALL OF OWN
CANDIDATE'S ARGUMENTS

1.21

RECALL OF OPPOSITION
CANDIDATE'S ARGUMENTS

1.20

PANELIST NOT INTERESTED
IN 1st DEBATE (n=52)

RECALL OF OWN
CANDIDATE'S ARGUMENTS
.88

RECALL OF OPPOSITION
CANDIDATE'S ARGUMENTS

.81

The difference in arguments recalled for either candidate between those who were more interested and those who were less interested was not statistically significant (t = 1.71, with p less than .10).

Interest measures were derived from responses to two questions: "What was your reaction to the program as a whole? Did you like it: very much, pretty much, somewhat, not very much, or not at all?" and, "How often did you discuss the television program with friends and neighbors after the broadcasts: not at all, not very often, sometimes, pretty often, or very often?" Responses to the questions were scored 4 . . . 0 and 0 . . . 4, respectively, then the scores were totaled for a composite score. The divisions in Figure 12 are: interested (6.8); not interested (0.5).

produce differences in arguments recalled from the opposition candidate. And only a small difference was found in recall between ardent and less fervent party members.

It should be remembered that the first debate was unlike the succeeding three in that it contained many specific arguments. Production figures, particular policies of both parties, and comparative estimates

FIGURE 13.

STRENGTH OF AFFILIATION
AND RECALL OF ARGUMENTS

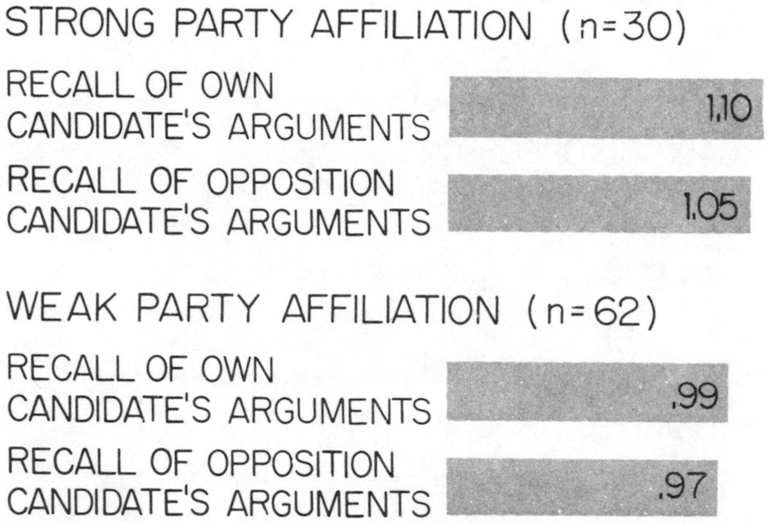

STRONG PARTY AFFILIATION (n=30)

RECALL OF OWN
CANDIDATE'S ARGUMENTS — 1.10

RECALL OF OPPOSITION
CANDIDATE'S ARGUMENTS — 1.05

WEAK PARTY AFFILIATION (n=62)

RECALL OF OWN
CANDIDATE'S ARGUMENTS — .99

RECALL OF OPPOSITION
CANDIDATE'S ARGUMENTS — .97

Strength of party affiliation was determined from responses to the question:
"As you remember your previous voting in national elections, would you say
your support of the party you favor has been: very strong, pretty strong,
fairly strong, or not very strong?" The divisions in Figure 13 are: strong
(very strong); weak (pretty strong, fairly strong, or not very strong).

abounded. It would have been much harder to formulate a test of arguments recalled in the later debates. It should also be noted that the seeming efficacy of the first debate may be quite irrelevant to the three which followed.

What can be concluded? This was a small panel study, conducted in four California cities. To generalize freely from it would be ridiculous. But to disregard it would be equally foolish. There were several consistent findings that suggest answers to the question of whether the debates should be repeated in 1964—and in what form.

There was a general feeling that the debates served a purpose, principally that the audience had a good look at the candidates. The unique opportunity that television provided for such a picture was cited. It was reported by Republicans and Democrats alike that Kennedy won this battle of images. Objective measures of panelists' attitudes toward the candidates substantiated this verdict. In this function, however, the debates were only an extension of routine campaign tactics—more spectacular at times, to be sure, but nothing new.

Yet, in the first debate, there was a promise of a new approach to responsible campaigning. The debate format appeared to have the potential to overcome a vexing problem, the biased rejection of an opposition candidate's views without hearing them. A test of arguments recalled from the first debate showed that the viewer had to "tune out" the program as a whole in order for the bias to operate. The opposition candidate was still unconvincing to most—but he was heard.

The audience, however, did not like the first debate. They enjoyed more the later, more heated clashes of personalities. The research on the first debate probably does not hold for the other debates, posing a dilemma to further use of the debate technique. Several avenues are open. If only a debate of specific, informative content is available, the absence of fiery controversy may not be regretted. And perhaps improvement of the programs would help. Panel members thought they should be longer and confined to one issue, and that the interviewers should be dropped. Under these suggested intimate conditions, there might still arise the warmth desired by the audience.

NOTES

1. The Institute also interviewed panel members after the election. A number of questions about the campaign itself were included. Quota samples, with controls for party affiliation and sex, were assigned to experienced interviewers. Selected findings are reported in a memorandum to panel members, "The 'Great Debates' and the 1960 Presidential Campaign," Institute for Communication Research, Stanford University, 1960.

2. This analysis is reported fully in "Stereotyping as a Process," a mimeographed report by Richard F. Carter, Institute for Communication Research, Stanford University, 1961. An important aspect of the development by panel members of more cohesive images is the different purposes served. Some used the image as a kind of temporary concept, to be dissolved if conditions warranted. These persons were more issue-oriented, more highly educated. Others

used it as a convenient bundling method, tying together all their opinions in a rigid, often extreme attitude. Whatever the use, however, it occurred more often among panelists who were highly interested in the campaign.

3. This biased response to, or even disregard, of the opposition is variously termed "perceptual defense," "selective perception," "selective exposure," and "selective retention." Klapper says: "By and large, people tend to expose themselves to those mass communications which are in accord with their existing attitudes and interests. . . . In the event of their being nevertheless exposed to unsympathetic material, they often seem not to perceive it, or to recast and interpret it to fit their existing views." Joseph T. Klapper, *The Effects of Mass Communication*. (Glencoe, Ill.: Free Press, 1960). Cf. pp. 19 ff.

4. The test of recall was based on two sets of eight true-false questions about specific points in the candidates' first debate presentations. In each set only two were true statements. The statements were:

Nixon said: More new schools were built under the Eisenhower administration than in the previous twenty years (T). Price increases in the Eisenhower administration were about the same as those in the Truman administration (F). None of Nixon's specific recommendations had been adopted by Eisenhower (F). Wages gained ten times as much in the Eisenhower administration as in the Truman administration (F). The new programs on domestic issues offered by the Republicans will cost about 4 or 5 billion dollars more per year (T). The Democratic farm policy will not mean higher consumer prices (F). Aid to education should go to teacher salaries and school buildings (F). Russia has about 75 per cent of our industrial capacity (F).

Kennedy said: About 60 per cent of our steel capacity is going unused at the present time (F). The United States has the lowest rate of economic growth of any major industrial nation (T). The Soviet Union will be producing more water power than we by 1965 (F). There are some 10,000,000 citizens over 65 living on social security payments (F). The farmer would find it easier to survive if there were a free market for his product (F). The tight money policy of the Eisenhower administration has succeeded only in preventing recessions (F). School aid should be given to the states for them to distribute as they see fit (T). More tax money could be raised from property owners (F).

Responses for both sets were normally distributed but, the Nixon test being easier, standard scores were used.

15

Candidate Images

PERCY H. TANNENBAUM, BRADLEY S. GREENBERG, & FRED
R. SILVERMAN

A MAJOR concern in any consideration of the impact of the debates is
the so-called *image* of the candidates as projected, and possibly altered,
during the course of the campaign. Before the debates began, one
political writer, who thought they would be "quite an ordeal" for the
candidates, asserted that "what counts is not the arguments they use
but the 'images' they convey."[1]

The question of images was the main focus of the present study.
Our concern was not so much with such matters as voting intentions,
changes in information and opinion, etc., as with changes in the judgments of the two contestants, first as presidential candidates, and
second as TV personalities. Of course, implicit in this approach is the
assumption that the voter's image of the candidates is intimately related
to his voting behavior.

Nor is this a study of trends in a sample of the general population.
Largely because of limitations of time and facilities, our investigation
was confined to a selected, rather homogeneous group of respondents.
Restricted as such evidence may be, we hope that our findings may
help to provide an empirical rather than a speculative basis for assessing the role of the TV debates in the 1960 election campaign.

This paper is based on research conducted as part of the general program
of research at the Mass Communications Research Center at the University of
Wisconsin. The authors wish to express their appreciation to the instructors and
students in several research methods courses in the School of Journalism at
Wisconsin for their aid in conducting the interviews.

271

METHOD AND PROCEDURE

The present paper is based on what were, in actuality, two separate studies. The first, developed within ten days of the opening debate, was designed to investigate the impact of this single event on viewers' perceptions of the two candidates. It was planned as a single study, with no intention of pursuing it further. With the approach of election day— and with the generation of increased interest in and discussion of the debates—it was decided to attempt a follow-up study shortly before the balloting.

The first study involved an assessment of respondents' images of the candidate immediately before and after the first debate. The follow-up survey also used the same group of respondents. Although there were some differences in the complete questionnaires used in the two studies, this paper will focus on image data which were common to both. Thus our project was essentially a panel study in which the respondents were "tested" at three distinct periods—just before the first debate (T_1), just after the first debate (T_2), and just before election day (T_3).

It is important to recognize that changes in images as detected in this general design may be attributed to factors other than the debates. In attempting to assess the effects of the TV debates, we obtained further information relating to the degree of exposure to the first debate and to all four debates. However, as we shall see, the exposure was generally very high for our sample, with very few respondents indicating no direct TV contact at all. Accordingly, our main data will be expressed in terms of the over-all sample, although we shall also briefly report our findings in terms of degree of exposure and party affiliations.

The Respondent Group

Our selection of a sample of respondents was based on the following criteria: (a) the subjects should be readily available for contact within a comparatively short time; (b) they should be relatively homogeneous in terms of such characteristics as age, sex, education, etc.; (c) they should possess enough political interest to expose themselves to the first debate at least, and (d) they should be willing to cooperate in a study of this type involving more than one interview.

The group consisted of persons living in the married students' housing development at the University of Wisconsin. The sample was drawn on a dwelling unit basis from a total of 600 apartments. The sample was predominantly and deliberately female (a handful of males was included only because their wives were not available). These were, then, mostly young married females, the majority with one child, of higher than average education, and having probably more interest in politics than the population as a whole. If anything, one might suspect that the images of candidates held by such persons would be less rather than more susceptible to change as a result of exposure to the video debates.

In terms of party affiliation the sample happened to split into 40 per cent Republican, 40 per cent Democratic, and 20 per cent who professed political independence. This was a completely fortuitous outcome, since no deliberate effort was made in drawing the sample to control for political party affiliation or candidate preference.

The original sample comprised 190 respondents in as many different households. With only three refusals on this initial contact, we had a total sample of 187 respondents. In the second wave, we obtained 165 completed and usable questionnaires. The third testing covered 165 respondents, of whom 145 were involved in the first two sessions.

Measuring Instrument

Although data on other variables were collected in the course of this project, our concern here will be mainly with the candidate images as dependent variables. These were measured through application of the *semantic differential* technique.[2] Since its development, the semantic differential has been applied to a wide variety of behavioral research problems, particularly in the field of communications, and has proved to be a reliable and sensitive instrument. It is also particularly well suited to the study of political images (cf., e.g., the semantic analysis of the 1952 presidential campaign by Osgood, Suci, and Tannenbaum).[3]

In applying the semantic differential, one or more concepts (objects of judgment) are rated against a set of seven-step, bi-polar scales. This allows for the determination of both the direction and the intensity of judgment of the concept on each scale.

In the present study, such ratings were obtained for each of five separate concepts. To begin with, there were the two candidates as presidential figures—NIXON AS PRESIDENT and KENNEDY AS PRESIDENT. In order to provide for a valid standard of measurement of the direction and magnitude of the changes on each of the above profiles, each respondent also rated the concept IDEAL PRESIDENT. In this manner, it was possible to obtain an assessment of the image of each candidate as president relative to the respondent's own image of what any candidate should ideally represent.

The final two concepts were KENNEDY AS TV PERFORMER and NIXON AS TV PERFORMER. These were included to obtain the images of both candidates as television personalities, and, perhaps more important, to assess any possible relationships between the presidential judgments and the respective TV judgments.

Each concept was rated in random order at each of the three test sessions. The only exception was that the ideal presidential ratings were not obtained at the second testing since it was assumed that this image would remain stable over the short time interval from the first testing.

The selection of scales—always a critical step in application of the semantic differential—was based on earlier uses of the technique in similar research undertakings. A basic set of twelve scales (wise-foolish, strong-weak, etc.) was used to assess the three presidential concepts— each candidate and the ideal. An additional six scales, deemed to be particularly appropriate, were included with the basic twelve in the measurement of the TV images. The actual scales for the presidential judgments are presented in Figures 1 and 2, those for the TV images in Figures 3 and 4. In both cases, however, the scale order received by the respondents was not as presented here, but in random fashion.

Testing Procedure

The first debate was televised in Madison at 8:30 P.M., Monday, September 26. The initial contact with the respondent was made on the preceding Friday and Saturday. On that occasion, the interviewer explained the purpose of the study and solicited the subject's cooperation. He also gave instructions for the use of the semantic differential and obtained the entire set of responses through personal interview.

At the termination of the interview (average time: 40 minutes), a sealed envelope containing the second test form was handed to the respondent with instructions to open it late Monday evening (i.e., immediately following the first debate, although no specific mention of the debate, as such, was made). These second wave forms were collected the morning after the debate.

When the decision was made to launch the third testing after the fourth debate, there was some doubt regarding a possible fifth debate. Inasmuch as this debate failed to materialize, the testing was conducted just before election day. Envelopes containing the third questionnaire were distributed along with a cover letter to all respondents on November 4, and the completed ones were collected two days later.

Generally, we found a high degree of cooperation from the respondents, with no evidence of inability or unwillingness to follow instructions. In cases where a return was not obtained, it was usually because of extenuating circumstances (illness, absence from home, etc.) rather than outright refusal.

RESULTS

Our analysis will focus on three major considerations: (a) changes in the images of the candidates as presidential figures, particularly as such changes are related to the judged image of an ideal president; (b) changes in the images of the two candidates as television performers, with an attempt to relate the TV images to their respective presidential images; (c) particularly for the first debate, and somewhat across all four debates, we have tried to assess such image changes as a function of degree of exposure to the debates and of political affiliation.

Such changes will be dealt with both in terms of comparisons of the mean profiles of the concepts on the semantic differential scales, and through the application of the multi-dimensional distance function, D^2.[4] This latter measure is an index of over-all similarity in profiles—either between different concepts at the same time, or the same concept at different times. The smaller the D^2, the more similar the over-all judgments of two concepts, or the less change for a single concept over time.

The Presidential Images

The basic data for assessment of the candidates' presidential images are contained in Figures 1 and 2. Each figure contains the same profile for the IDEAL PRESIDENT (I-P); Figure 1 also presents the mean ratings of KENNEDY AS PRESIDENT (K-P) for the three time periods— immediately before the first debate (T_1), immediately after the first debate (T_2), and near the end of the campaign (T_3). Similarly, Figure 2 presents, in addition to the same I-P profile, the corresponding rating on NIXON AS PRESIDENT—N-P at T_1, T_2, and T_3.

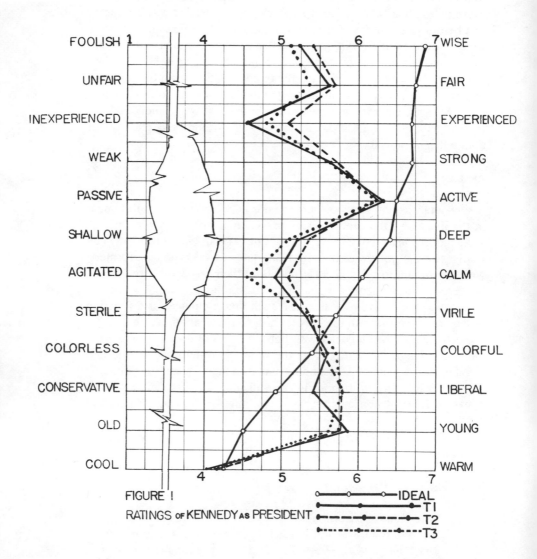

FIGURE I

RATINGS of KENNEDY as PRESIDENT

IDEAL
TI
T2
T3

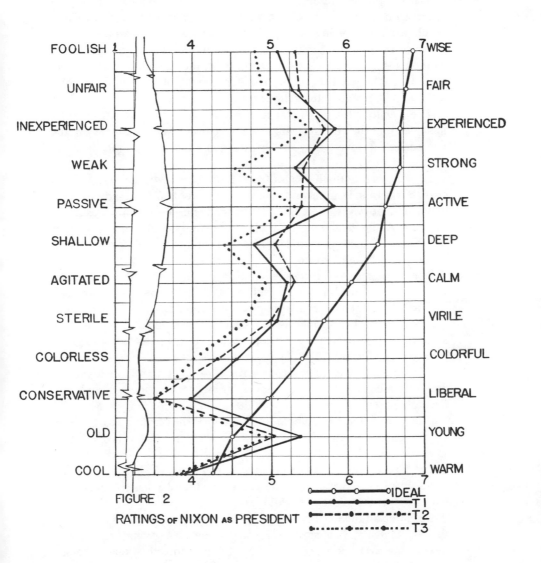

FIGURE 2

RATINGS of NIXON as PRESIDENT

IDEAL

T 1

T 2

T 3

The I-P profile presented here is actually that obtained at the first test session. This proved to be a highly homogeneous image, with very small variances obtained on most of the scales. When re-measured at the third session, this profile was essentially the same as at the outset, with only insignificant changes. In contrast, the candidate profiles were more varied largely because of the heterogeneity of the sample in political party and candidate preferences.

The Kennedy Image. A glance at the three K-P profiles in Figure 1 indicates that the changes which occurred were fairly minimal on any one scale. However, they are highly consistent across the array of scales.

Looking first at the K-P shift from T_1 to T_2, a statistically significant change was found on only one scale—Kennedy being judged more experienced. However, there is a pronounced shift across all scales in the direction of the ideal image. On all of the twelve scales, there is either no shift or a shift toward I-P—he was judged as somewhat wiser, deeper, calmer, and so on.

The third set of K-P ratings is strongly suggestive of a regression away from the ideal. Here we find the K-P image either shifting back toward what it was to start with, or even further away from I-P than it originally was. The change is not statistically significant on any one scale but is again highly consistent in direction across the scales. He is now judged as *less* wise, fair, calm, etc.

The Nixon Image. The profiles for Nixon, as shown in Figure 2, present a picture that is somewhat different from Kennedy's, and contains changes of a greater magnitude.

The main difference is apparent in the N-P shift from T_1 to T_2. Here we find a more erratic pattern—on some scales the N-P image changes toward the ideal, on others away. The one statistically significant shift is that Nixon becomes more conservative. He also is judged as somewhat older, less experienced, and less active than he was to begin with. On the other hand, he is slightly wiser and deeper.

But after all the debates and most of the campaign had spent itself, the N-P image at T_3 is most decidedly further away from the ideal—in most cases, even more removed than it was before the debates began. Here we found not only consistency in terms of the direction of change, but also in terms of the magnitude of change. At T_3, the N-P image is *less* wise, fair, strong, deep, and so on. Only on those attributes which are less salient (those at the bottom of Figure 2) are the changes minimal.

Kennedy vs. Nixon. Perhaps more important than the shifts within each candidate's image is the comparison between the candidates. Some of these differences are apparent from the foregoing: Whereas the K-P change, from T_1 to T_2, is dominantly in the direction of the ideal (on 10 of the 12 scales), this trend is much less so in the N-P shift from T_1 to T_2 (on only six scales does the N-P image at T_2 approach I-P). Furthermore, although both candidate images show a regression away from the ideal at the third testing, this trend is much more pronounced for the N-P image.

Perhaps a more rigorous demonstration of these differences is contained in Table 1, which presents the mean D^2 score at each time period between each candidate and the ideal, and between the two candidates. At T_1, the N-P and K-P profiles are almost equidistant from I-P—the slight preference for K-P being statistically insignificant. At T_2, the K-P image remains at about the same position, while the N-P image becomes more removed from I-P; the difference between the N-P/I-P and K-P/I-P distances at this point is significant beyond the .05 level. By T_3, these differences become even more vivid: While both candidate images become further removed from the ideal, the difference in their respective distances from the ideal is even more significant ($p < .01$).

TABLE 15—1. MEAN D^2 (DISTANCE) BETWEEN PRESIDENTIAL CANDIDATES

| | TESTING SESSIONS | | |
IMAGES	T_1	T_2	T_3
N-P/I-P	45.73	50.84	65.41
K-P/I-P	39.76	39.19	43.05
K-P/N-P	44.55	55.03	71.98

We can also look at these differences apart from their relation to the ideal image. One such procedure is indicated in the third line of Table 1, which demonstrates that the distance between the two candidates increased during the progress of the campaign, the total shift from start to finish being highly significant ($p < .001$). This trend can also be shown by computing the over-all change within each candidate image between time periods. When this is done, we find more over-all change in N-P than in K-P ($p < .05$) between the first two tests, and even more from T_1 to T_3.

These statistical findings may be summarized as follows:

(1) While there were few gross changes in judgments of either candidate on any single attribute, there were highly consistent shifts across the different attributes.

(2) Particularly with the first debate and as the campaign progressed, the differences in perception of the two candidates became more pronounced.

(3) While the images of both candidates changed somewhat during the campaign, the change for Nixon was significantly more pronounced than that for Kennedy.

(4) Toward the end of the campaign, both candidates had moved further away from the ideal image, but Nixon had moved much further away than had Kennedy.

The TV Performer Images

It will be recalled that we obtained judgments of Nixon and Kennedy as TV performers as well as their presidential images. These TV ratings were obtained at each test session on a set of eighteen semantic differential scales—the twelve used previously plus an additional six scales of a more denotative kind (boring-interesting, etc.), assumed to be appropriate to the TV judgments. It was thought that these TV ratings would be of interest in themselves, but even more so in relation to the presidential images.

The TV images for the two candidates—Figure 3 for the K-TV data, Figure 4 for the N-TV data—reveal a pattern that is highly consistent with that obtained for the presidential images. The Kennedy TV image again exhibits small but consistent changes on 17 of the 18 scales in a more favorable direction after the first debate. However, at the third testing there are signs of a less favorable judgment on most characteristics—less interesting, less handsome, less fair, etc.

The Nixon TV image shows a much stronger negative reaction—both after the first debate and at the last testing. On most attributes (15 of 18) he was judged as less favorable after the first debate than before it, and this trend continues throughout the campaign. On several of the characteristics, the final differences are highly significant—he emerges as less interesting, colorful, wise, calm, and so on. Moreover, these changes on Nixon are considerably larger generally than they are on Kennedy.

These differences between Nixon and Kennedy as TV personalities are further underlined in the D^2 data reported in Table 2, which also contains some interesting findings relating to the respective TV and presidential comparisons. Here we find that the distance between K-TV and N-TV increases with the subsequent testings and that these changes are statistically significant in all instances.

TABLE 15—2. MEAN D^2 (DISTANCE) BETWEEN TV IMAGES

| | TESTING SESSIONS | | |
IMAGES	T_1	T_2	T_3
K-TV/N-TV	47.80	78.08	96.50
N-P/N-TV	19.54	15.00	22.79
K-P/K-TV	18.19	11.70	16.44

Looking at the distances between a candidate's presidential profile and his TV profile, we find that with both candidates there is a significant ($p < .05$) *decrease* in these distances from T_1 to T_2—i.e., that the two images become more similar to one another. By T_3, however, these profiles become more disparate for both candidates—the change on Nixon being statistically significant ($p < .05$), but not quite so ($p = .13$) for Kennedy. To look at it another way, initially the distances between presidential and TV images are equal for Nixon and Kennedy, but at the end of the campaign, the distance for Nixon is significantly greater ($p < .01$) than for Kennedy. This finding of a generally greater shift in the Nixon image is also apparent when we look at the relative changes within the TV images for each candidate across the three time periods.

Generally, then, we can summarize these TV image data in the following manner:

(1) The impressions of Nixon and Kennedy as TV performers become more dissimilar after the first debate and throughout the campaign.

(2) The first debate appears to have set the pattern of change, with Kennedy's TV image becoming more favorable, while Nixon's becomes less favorable. By the final testing, the differences are even greater, again mainly because Nixon's TV image becomes even more negative.

(3) There is, after the first testing, a greater degree of similarity between Kennedy's presidential and his TV image than between Nixon's.

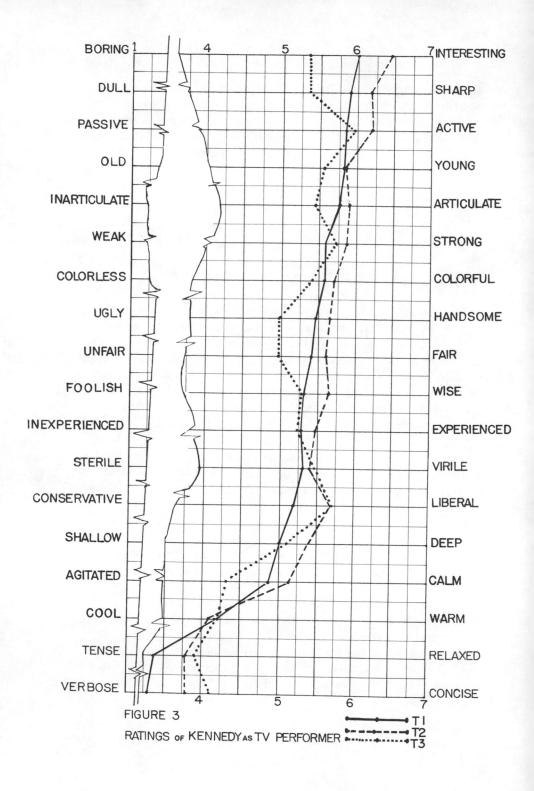

BORING	INTERESTING
DULL	SHARP
PASSIVE	ACTIVE
OLD	YOUNG
INARTICULATE	ARTICULATE
WEAK	STRONG
COLORLESS	COLORFUL
UGLY	HANDSOME
UNFAIR	FAIR
FOOLISH	WISE
INEXPERIENCED	EXPERIENCED
STERILE	VIRILE
CONSERVATIVE	LIBERAL
SHALLOW	DEEP
AGITATED	CALM
COOL	WARM
TENSE	RELAXED
VERBOSE	CONCISE

FIGURE 3

RATINGS OF KENNEDY AS TV PERFORMER

T 1
T 2
T 3

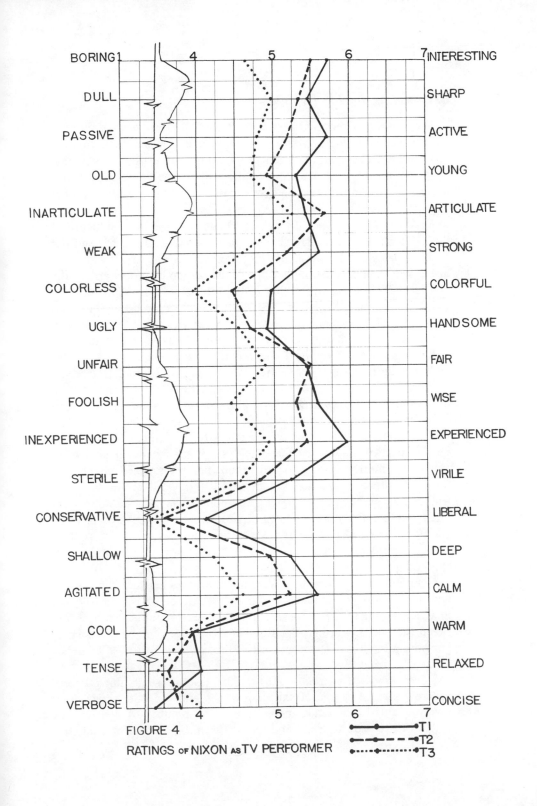

FIGURE 4

RATINGS of NIXON as TV PERFORMER

Exposure to the TV Debates

The main data reported above dealt with the responses of all subjects taken as a single group. And since events other than the TV debates were occurring between the various test sessions (including, of course, press reports and conversations about the debates), we cannot legitimately attribute whatever changes we have observed to the debates as such.

Effects of First Debate. In an effort better to assess the influence of the TV debates on candidate images, we obtained an index of exposure to the debates. At T_2, we ascertained exposure to the first debate with a simple question as to whether or not the respondents saw any of the debate on TV. It was found that of the total of 165 respondents, 128 (77 per cent) saw the debate, 15 (8.9 per cent) only listened to it on radio, and 22 (13.3 per cent) were not directly exposed to the debate.

We then were able to make some comparisons in the various image changes as between the TV-exposed and the non-exposed groups, omitting the radio-only group from this analysis. Although there are inherent limitations in this procedure due to the relatively small size of the non-exposed group, we were able to reach some general conclusions.

Space limitations prohibit citing each of the individual comparisons, but the over-all finding on these analyses is no significant change of any kind within the non-exposed group, but pronounced changes of the kind already indicated within the TV-exposed group. Further, where there were changes among the non-viewers, these shifts were often in a direction opposite to those observed among the debate viewers. For example, Kennedy and Nixon became *more alike* one another both as presidential candidates and as TV performers within the non-exposed group after the first debate.

Generally, then, while there were no differences between the viewing and non-viewing respondents on any concept comparison before the first debate, there were considerable and consistent differences between them after the first debate. Thus we have more confidence in attributing the T_1 to T_2 image shifts already observed to the influence of the TV debate *per se*.

Effects across All Debates. At the third testing, we obtained a more general index of degree of exposure to the entire debate series. This involved a 16-point scale, incorporating the number of debates, the extent of exposure to each, and the mode of exposure. For analytical purposes, the respondents were divided into four categories of exposure—"all or most" (50 per cent), some (25 per cent), little (17 per cent), and no exposure at all (8 per cent). Again with the usual limitations because of the small size of the cell in the lower categories, the various comparisons were conducted on the changes within each image from T_1 to T_3 and between candidates at T_3.

Ten such comparisons were made, and on none of them was there a significant difference among the four exposure levels. There was, however, a somewhat unexpected if not inconsistent finding across all ten comparisons taken together, in that the least exposed groups (little or no TV exposure) showed more (although not statistically significant) change from T_1 to T_3. These latter data may be something of an artifact in that our exposure groups were self-selected rather than manipulated, and hence any obtained differences may be as much a function of extraneous factors (e.g., party preference, degree of political interest, etc.) as of exposure to the debates proper.

We may summarize our findings on degree of exposure as follows.

(1) There were substantial and significant differences in the direction and magnitude of image change *as a result of the first debate* between those respondents who viewed it on TV and those who were not exposed at all. The non-viewers showed little or random change in the various images, while the viewers changed as indicated in the previous analyses.

(2) Across the four debates, relative degree of exposure appeared to make little difference in the image changes, with the possibility that factors other than the amount of exposure may have been responsible for those differences which did occur.

Party Affiliation

Of the many additional individual variables measured in the total survey, we selected the data on expressed party preference for further analysis. This was done mainly in the first phase of the study—that comparing the changes over the first debate—since this had proved to be a critical pivotal point in the previous analyses.

While there were few significant differences between party affiliations on any one comparison, there was some consistency across the various comparisons. Generally, we found that respondents who were originally Democratic changed the most as a result of the first debate—this change being clearly in favor of Kennedy and against Nixon both as presidential figures and as TV performers. The next largest shift was among the Independents, the changes here again being of the same pattern generally as for the Democrats. The Republicans changed the least, but although they stayed true to their party, they were not unaffected by the pro-Kennedy trend.

This pattern is perhaps best illustrated by a comparison of the Kennedy-as-president and Nixon-as-president images with the image of the ideal president immediately after the opening debate. As one might expect, the Nixon profile was closer to the ideal for the Republicans, the Kennedy profile for the Democrats. But there was a considerable disparity in the distances of the *opposing* party candidates: Kennedy was significantly closer to the ideal for Republicans than Nixon was for the Democrats, this disparity not having existed at the first testing. Thus, after the first debate, Republicans were apparently more favorably inclined toward Kennedy than Democrats were toward Nixon.

All this suggests that the first debate, at least, served to help consolidate the Kennedy image among the Democrats; helped somewhat in swinging the Independents to Kennedy's side; and apparently failed among the Republicans to consolidate the Nixon image.

One last word about party preference: It will be recalled that the original sample was 40 per cent Democratic, 40 per cent Republican, and 20 per cent Independent. The same proportions hold for the 145 respondents who were common to all three testing sessions. When the question of political affiliation was asked again at the last testing—a mere two to three days before the election—we obtained a split of 50 per cent Democratic, 39 per cent Republican, and 11 per cent Independent. This strongly suggests, though it does not prove, that the followers of each major party remained firm, but that the professed Independents switched for the most part toward the Democratic column.

CONCLUSIONS

We have already indicated the main limitations in the present study, and the tenuous nature of any broad generalizations that can be made from it. Within these limits, the data we have reported speak for themselves. If anything, they testify to a decided advantage for Kennedy as a result of the debates.

However, if we have to make a main conclusion it would be: *Kennedy did not necessarily win the debates, but Nixon lost them.* While we have referred to a "pro-Kennedy trend" in our data, it is quite apparent from the over-all image assessments that even the apparent victor did not emerge from the debate arena completely unscathed. Rather, it was the loser's image that suffered most.

This conclusion stems from the presidential image data—our main focus of inquiry since it is probably more intimately related to actual voting behavior. It is further underlined in the images of the candidates as TV performers. On both these sets of profiles and in the distance data, we see that the adversaries became more disparate from one another as the campaign progressed. Furthermore, it is apparent that this disparity is more a function of a pronounced negative trend in the Nixon profiles than of any major positive change in the Kennedy images.

We are also impressed with the consistency of the image data obtained. There were no real wholesale shifts in judgment from one test period to the next—nor did we expect any. But no matter how we chose to analyze the data—through profile comparisons, or D^2 measures across time periods, or D^2 measures across concepts within the same time period, or, for that matter, several additional analyses not reported here—the findings showed internal agreement. This uniformity extends to the scale data on the presidential analyses, where the use of the individual respondent's own meaning of an ideal president provides a valid standard for assessing relative changes in images.

Our data also point to the opening debate as a critical factor in setting the trend for the image changes noted. On both the presidential and the TV image, there is a noticeable shift toward Kennedy, while Nixon shows some signs of weakening. Indeed, the presidential images show a strikingly reciprocal change from T_1 to T_2; the small but consistent positive changes for Kennedy across the various scales are matched—in almost mirror-image fashion—by equally small but negative shifts for Nixon.

By the third testing, both candidates appear to be dragging somewhat—possibly a sign of public weariness with the debates and the total campaign. While this represents something of a shift for Kennedy from the T_2 period, it is again more obvious as a *continuing* negative trend in the Nixon images. The Republican standard-bearer started out almost equal with his opponent but slipped steadily.

These general trends are also apparent when we analyze the data in terms of party affiliation. There is some evidence to suggest that the debates helped Kennedy keep the normally Democratic followers and even attracted a portion of the "swing vote" of the Independents. They did not appear to cause Nixon to lose appreciably among the Republicans, but neither did they draw others to his side. In this connection, it is of some interest to note that the success of former President Eisenhower in the 1952 and more so in the 1956 campaign has been attributed to his ability to attract the politically unaffiliated and marginally Democratic voters.

Relative TV exposure *to the series* of debates did not appear to bear directly on image change—although for the first debate, the TV viewing was a precipitating factor in inducing image modifications. It can be argued that direct TV exposure was not necessary for an individual to be influenced by the debates. The video clashes were an integral and vital part of the 1960 campaign—not only as TV events, but also in terms of widespread reports in the press and radio, as topics of face-to-face discussion, and as the focal point for much commentary by political pundits and the like. This very pervasiveness of the debates throughout the contest implies that they may have exerted an impact quite independent of actual TV exposure. TV or not TV, the debates had their impact.

NOTES

1. "The Reporter's Notes," *The Reporter,* Sept. 15, 1960, p. 2.
2. Charles E. Osgood, George J. Suci, and Percy H. Tannenbaum, *The Measurement of Meaning* (Urbana, Ill.: University of Illinois Press, 1957).
3. *Ibid.,* pp. 104-24.
4. *Ibid.,* pp. 90-104.

16

Issues and Images

SIDNEY KRAUS & RAYMOND G. SMITH

DURING THE fourth and last debate, John Chancellor of NBC News asked Richard Nixon the following question about Quemoy and Matsu (italics ours):

. . . Both you and Senator Kennedy say you agree with the President on this subject and with our treaty obligations. *But the subject remains in the campaign as an issue.* . . . Is this because each of you feels obliged to respond to the other when he talks about Quemoy and Matsu, and if that's true, *do you think an end should be called to this discussion, or will it stay with us as a campaign issue?*

Mr. Nixon replied (italics ours):

I would say that *the issue will stay with us as a campaign issue just as long as Senator Kennedy persists in what I think is a fundamental error.*

In the above question and answer the meaning of the word *issue* is clear. Before something can become an issue there must be disagreement—people must feel differently about something.

In the same reply, Vice President Nixon stated that if Senator Kennedy retracted his previous views and admitted he was wrong on several positions *"then this will be right out of the campaign because there will be no issue between us"* (italics ours). It may with equal justification be said that when disagreement about something disappears, that something is no longer an issue.

A major part of this study* is concerned with *issues* before, during,

* Financial aid for this study was made possible by a grant from the Indiana University Faculty Research Division.

and after the televison debates. In addition to issues, this study investigated the images of the candidates as held by a sample of Democrats
and Republicans.

More specifically, our purpose was twofold: (1) To explore the
changes in candidate images and political issues against a background
of voter affiliation. (2) To determine the effect on political bias of
viewing the debates.

The first objective was pursued through use of the semantic differential technique, referred to throughout this report as the Semantic Differential Scale Study. To achieve the second, we employed a questionnaire, and the resulting analysis has been termed the Political Bias
Study. In addition to the primary measuring instruments, a Personal
Inventory Questionnaire which provided the usual demographic information was included.

THE SAMPLE

The Indianapolis City Telephone Directory was used as the sample
source. To get a total of 200 respondents every 1,119th name (plus
the name from the adjacent column on the same line, which provided
an alternate list of 200) was selected.

Each interviewer[1] was given a list of ten names and ten alternates
and was provided with a map which located his respondents. Interviewers were instructed to conduct their interviews in person at the respondent's residence. Each respondent was asked: (a) whether he was a
registered voter, (b) whether he owned a televison set. If either answer
was negative, the interview was terminated. Those answering affirm-
atively were persuaded, if possible, to participate in the research project. It was hoped that the two lists would provide a minimum of 200
respondents. The expectation was overly optimistic, however, since the
final sample consisted of 142 persons, only 49 of whom appeared on
the original list. When it became obvious that the sample was going
to be very small, 93 additional respondents were selected by returning
to the original addresses and interviewing the persons living next door.
It might be noted that there were but three and a half weeks from the
date the debates were set until the first debate, during which time testing materials were prepared and a sample selected.

It is interesting from the standpoint of sampling procedure to note
that of the 400 directory names, 140 could not be reached, 86 failed
to register, 14 did not own television sets, and 111 refused to participate. The 93 respondents selected from residences adjoining the orig-

inal sample were secured from a total of 176 additional attempts. Of this total, 37 could not be reached, 16 were not registered, and 30 refused to participate. It proved to be impossible to determine whether poor interviewing techniques were responsible for failure to secure the expected sample size. One reason for refusals to participate may have been the fact that the inhabitants of Indianapolis, the capital city of Indiana, have been frequently used as a research population and may well have been "over-researched." However, the small total of 177 successes (31 per cent) out of 576 attempted contacts is not readily explainable. An inspection of the social calendar for the period in question reveals nothing out of the ordinary, nor do other sources provide an explanation for these results.

Despite the sampling difficulties there is some evidence that the sample can be considered representative of the Indianapolis population. First, a geographical analysis of the Indianapolis population using a quadrant division—Northwest, Northeast, Southwest, and Southeast was made. The most heavily populated is the Northeast, followed by the Northwest, Southwest, and Southeast, respectively. The sample reflects this population distribution. Second, Indianapolis is predominantly a Republican community (the city voted for Nixon in the 1960 election). Again, the sample was representative. Third, the sample figures of both religious and income data were proportionately almost identical with those figures available for Indianapolis.[2]

Table 1 provides a breakdown of some of the characteristics of the respondents. Slightly more males than females appeared in the sample. Fifty-seven per cent of the respondents were under 41, and 40 per cent recorded their age as 41 or over (3 per cent failed to report their age). Of those reporting their income, more than 50 per cent earned $7,499 or less per year; a third may be classified in a "middle income" bracket. The respondents' religion was overwhelmingly Protestant, and as stated previously, their political preference was strongly Republican.

THE METHOD

The interviews (referred to as trials) were obtained during the following periods:

T_1—September 20-25
T_2—September 27-29
T_3—October 17-20
T_4—October 22-25

TABLE 16—1. CHARACTERISTICS OF RESPONDENTS

Characteristics	Number of Respondents[a]	Per Cent of Total N
Sex		
Male	60	42.86
Female	80	57.14
Age		
21-30	45	32.14
31-40	36	25.71
41-50	29	20.71
51-up	27	19.29
No response	3	2.14
Income (yearly)		
Under $5,000	18	12.86
$5,000-$7,499	51	36.43
$7,500-$10,000	19	13.57
Over $10,000	18	12.86
No response	13	9.29
Political preference		
Republican	87	62.14
Democratic	49	35.00
Independent	4	2.86
Religion		
Catholic	20	14.29
Protestant	119	85.00
Jewish	1	.71

a. Two respondents failed to complete any part of the personal inventory sheet and were subsequently eliminated from the sample.

This schedule provided before and after measures of the first and fourth debates—the two topic-structured debates: domestic and foreign policy, respectively.

Half of the respondents were instructed to view the first, and later the last, television debate. Most of the respondents were interviewed five times, four times to complete the measuring instruments, and once (by phone) to determine votes.

Interviewers were cautioned during the training session not to interfere with the respondent's procedure of filling in the response forms. Apparently the instructions on the measuring instruments were adequate since interviewers reported that few questions arose concerning procedure.

Six categories of information were collected from each respondent.

Five of these are recorded in Table 1; the sixth was Viewing (told to view and viewed, not told to view and did not view, not told to view and viewed, and told to view and did not view).

The semantic differential instrument which provided the scales used in this study was developed by one of the writers[3] specifically for use in speaking situations (public speaking, debates, etc.). It consists of ten bi-polar adjectival seven-step scales: optimistic-pessimistic, light-heavy, honest-dishonest, worthless-valuable, calm-excitable, negative-positive, serious-humorous, true-false, meaningless-meaningful, and cold-hot.

Three scales previously tested and used in a study[4] of the 1952 presidential campaign were added. These scales, which measured dimensions found by Osgood to be basic to most human judgments, were fair-unfair, active-passive, and strong-weak.

With the advice of colleagues from various disciplines, eight concepts were selected which would probably be issues in the campaign and around which the debates were expected to center. These concepts (including two image concepts) were: (1) Catholicism, (2) Federal Aid to Education, (3) Kennedy, (4) Our Military Preparedness, (5) The Taft-Hartley Labor Law, (6) Runaway Inflation, (7) Nixon, (8) Civil Rights for Negroes, (9) Social Security Medical Care, and (10) The United Nations.

All concepts were rated during each of the four trials and the political bias questionnaire was completed each time. (The method of analysis for the political bias questionnaire is discussed later in this report.) Fortunately, a political campaign provides a valid criterion of behavior against which opinion data can be measured, namely, the respondent's vote. There is, on the other hand, no comparable pre-test measure to use in validating initial attitude scores other than similarly derived expressions of opinion.

SEMANTIC DIFFERENTIAL SCALE STUDY

For each of the ten concepts (Catholicism, Federal Aid to Education, etc.) there were thirteen identical scales optimistic-pessimisitic, light-heavy, etc.). Respondents were instructed to rate each concept on each scale in terms of their own feelings; they were also instructed in terms of the values given between each side of the scale. For example, if a respondent felt that Kennedy was optimistic rather than pessimistic, he would place a mark on the optimistic side of the scale. If he placed his mark in the first division of the scale nearest the word "optimistic" he would thereby indicate a very favorable position. If he placed his mark in the last division (nearest "pessimistic") he would indicate a very unfavorable position with regard to Kennedy and that particular scale.

Quantitatively, divisions on the scales can be represented by a numerical value. Arbitrarily, the unfavorable end of the scale (pessimistic, excitable, etc.) was given the value "one" while the favorable extreme was given the value "seven." Divisions between the extreme values were consecutively numbered forming a scale range of one to seven. Hence, the greater the score of a given scale, the more favorable were the respondent's feelings with regard to a given concept.

For the analysis, the sample was separated into two groups—47 Democrats and 84 Republicans who had completed all four trials (T_1, T_2, T_3, T_4). Mean scale ratings of both groups during each trial for each concept were obtained, and *t* tests were used to test the significance of differences between the means.

Profiles of the mean scale ratings are presented in Figures 1 through 20. The concepts and scales were randomized for presentation to the respondents, but were ordered as presented here to facilitate the discussion which follows.

Inspection of the mean scale shifts from T_1 to T_2 and from T_3 to T_4 *within* each of the political parties reveals a high degree of homogeneity for each concept. With many of the profiles overlapping, none of the shifts appear to be significant. This suggests that respondents' attitudes toward these concepts were stable, having little or no convergence or divergence between trials from the beginning to the completion of the debates, and offers evidence of the difficulty encountered in changing political attitudes.

In the following analysis, therefore, comparisons are made *between* Democratic respondents' and Republican respondents' ratings of the two candidates and the eight issues. Operationally, we define opposing attitudes toward candidates and issues by locating for each trial the significant[5] mean scale difference between Republicans and Democrats.

Candidate Images

When comparing the Democratic profiles of T_1 through T_4 with the Republicans' for both Kennedy (Figures 1 and 2) and Nixon (Figures 3 and 4) we find most scale shifts significant.

KENNEDY

FIGURE 1. DEMOCRATS

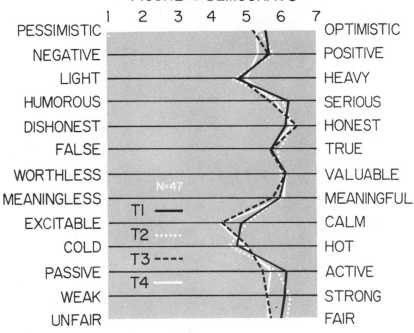

FIGURE 2. REPUBLICANS

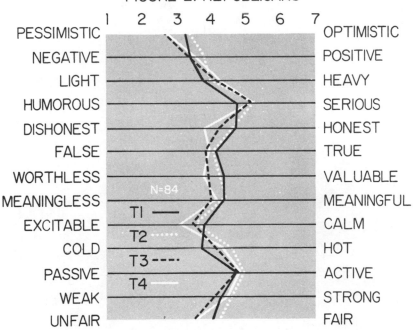

NIXON
FIGURE 3. DEMOCRATS

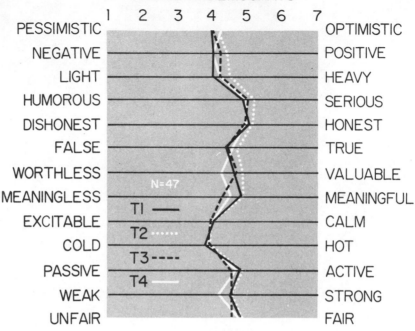

FIGURE 4. REPUBLICANS

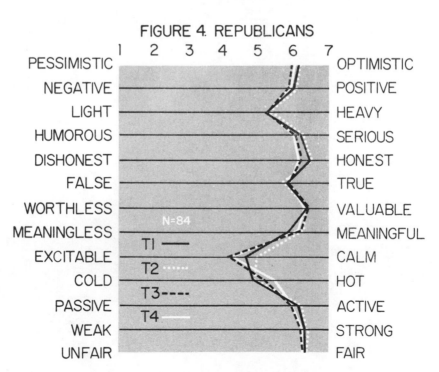

CATHOLICISM

FIGURE 5. DEMOCRATS

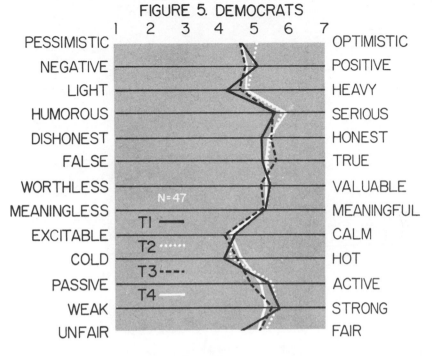

FIGURE 6. REPUBLICANS

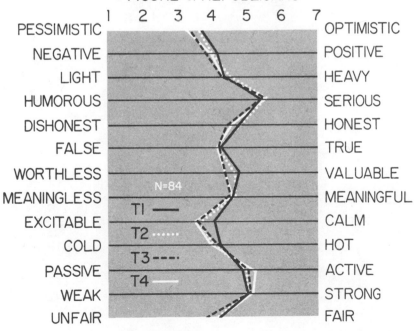

FEDERAL AID TO EDUCATION

FIGURE 7. DEMOCRATS

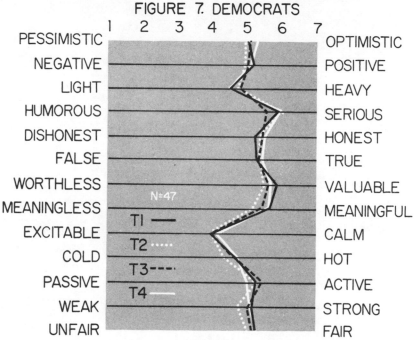

FIGURE 8. REPUBLICANS

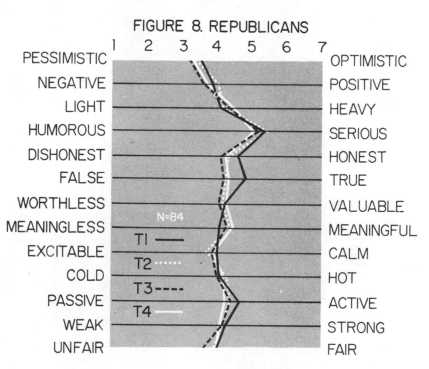

SOCIAL SECURITY MEDICAL CARE
FIGURE 9. DEMOCRATS

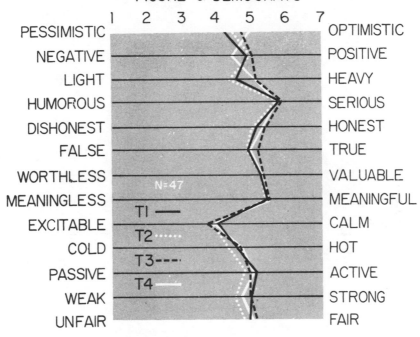

FIGURE 10. REPUBLICANS

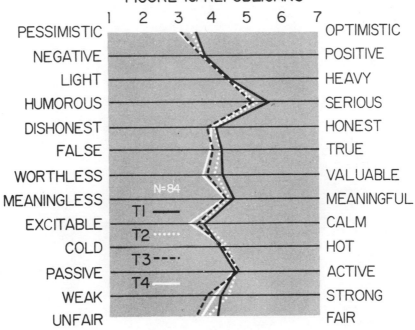

TAFT-HARTLEY LABOR LAW
FIGURE 11. DEMOCRATS

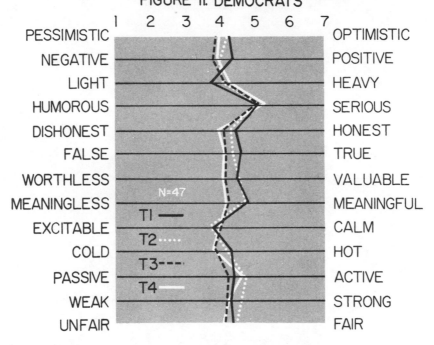

FIGURE 12. REPUBLICANS

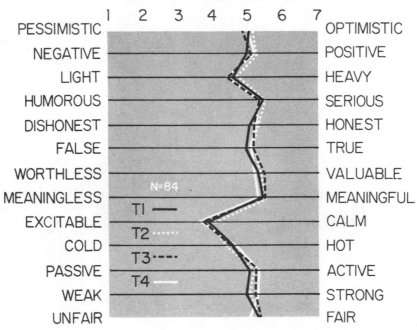

CIVIL RIGHTS FOR NEGROES

FIGURE 13. DEMOCRATS

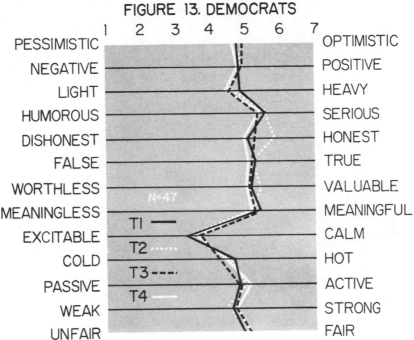

FIGURE 14. REPUBLICANS

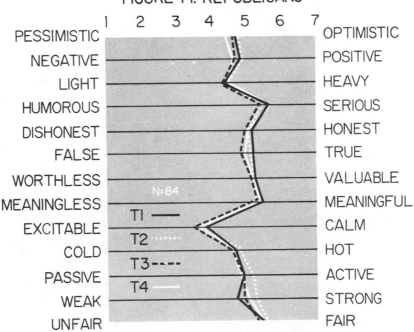

OUR MILITARY PREPAREDNESS

FIGURE 15. DEMOCRATS

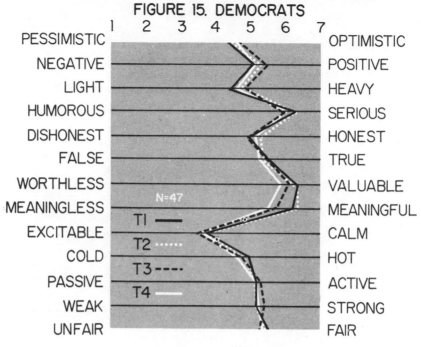

FIGURE 16. REPUBLICANS

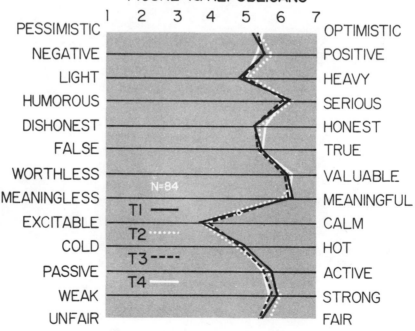

RUNAWAY INFLATION

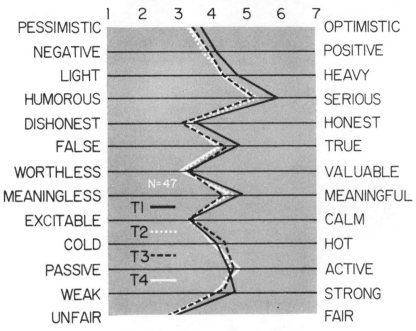

FIGURE 17. DEMOCRATS

	1	2	3	4	5	6	7	
PESSIMISTIC								OPTIMISTIC
NEGATIVE								POSITIVE
LIGHT								HEAVY
HUMOROUS								SERIOUS
DISHONEST								HONEST
FALSE								TRUE
WORTHLESS								VALUABLE
MEANINGLESS								MEANINGFUL
EXCITABLE								CALM
COLD								HOT
PASSIVE								ACTIVE
WEAK								STRONG
UNFAIR								FAIR

N=47
T1 ——
T2 ·······
T3 -----
T4 ——

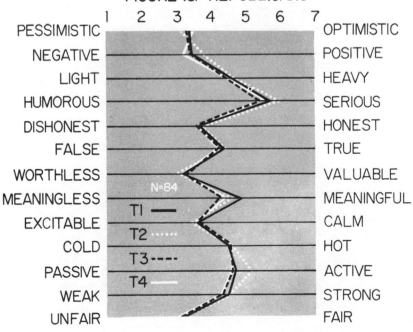

FIGURE 18. REPUBLICANS

	1	2	3	4	5	6	7	
PESSIMISTIC								OPTIMISTIC
NEGATIVE								POSITIVE
LIGHT								HEAVY
HUMOROUS								SERIOUS
DISHONEST								HONEST
FALSE								TRUE
WORTHLESS								VALUABLE
MEANINGLESS								MEANINGFUL
EXCITABLE								CALM
COLD								HOT
PASSIVE								ACTIVE
WEAK								STRONG
UNFAIR								FAIR

N=84
T1 ——
T2 ·······
T3 -----
T4 ——

THE UNITED NATIONS

FIGURE 19. DEMOCRATS

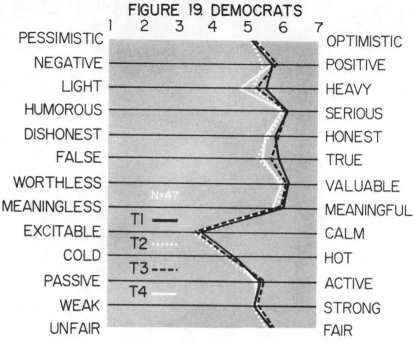

FIGURE 20. REPUBLICANS

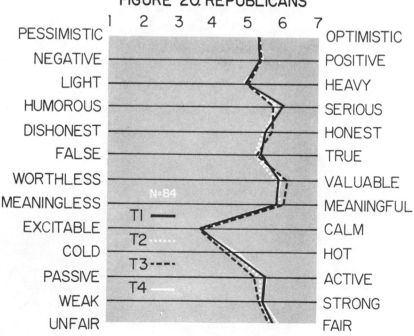

As might be expected, the Democrats' image of Kennedy is about as favorable as the Republicans' image of Nixon. The Republicans, however, display more extreme unfavorable attitudes toward Kennedy than do the Democrats toward Nixon. Republicans viewed Kennedy consistently as pessimistic, negative, excitable, and during the last debate their image of him was less favorable than before (though not significantly so) in terms of his being honest, true, valuable, and fair. Democrats, on the other hand, find Nixon a bit excitable and cold, but not enough so evidently to alter their relatively favorable image of him.

In locating those scale differences which are not significant (indicating relative agreement of candidate images) we find both parties in accord on their ratings of Nixon on the scale calm-excitable except after the first debate ($t = 2.89$). In only one instance does image agreement (no significance) appear between parties' ratings of Kennedy—cold-hot, T_2.

Issues

In considering the eight issues selected for analysis in this study, we find that four of these reveal sharp differences between Democrats and Republicans.

Profiles of Catholicism, Federal Aid to Education, Social Security Medical Care, and the Taft-Hartley Labor Law (Figures 5 through 12) exhibit statistically significant comparisons between the parties' mean ratings over the scales. Usually T_1 (before the first debate) records fewer significant differences between parties than do the other trials. With the exception of the Taft-Hartley Labor Law, where the means of most scales are higher for Republicans, these issues are more favorably rated by Democrats than by Republicans.

Since we would expect political differences toward these major issues during a presidential campaign, it may be fruitful to locate those issues where significant differences were not found. Profiles of Civil Rights for Negroes (Figures 13 and 14) reveal no significant differences between parties before the first debate (T_1) and after the fourth debate (T_4). At T_2 significant differences were found on the strong-weak and fair-unfair scales ($t = 3.36$ and 2.49, respectively). Only one significant difference was found at T_3—true-false ($t = 1.99$).

In terms of Our Military Preparedness (Figures 15 and 16), Democrats and Republicans were in agreement on all scales after the first debate (T_2), and differed in terms of their optimism on T_1, T_3, and

T_4. In each of these comparisons Republican means were significantly higher than Democratic, indicating that the Democrats were less optimistic about our military readiness than the Republicans.

According to the data, before and after the debates, Republicans had a more favorable impression of the strength of our military preparations than did Democrats. They further felt, by the end of the debates, that our preparedness was very meaningful (mean rating of 6.23 compared to the Democrats mean of 5.62 on the meaningless-meaningful scale, significant with a t of 2.72). Despite these differences, for the most part political parties were similar in their attitudes toward Our Military Preparedness.

Runaway Inflation profiles (Figures 17 and 18) show no significant differences at T_1 and T_3, and only one scale in T_2 and one in T_4 revealed significant differences—active-passive ($t = 2.78$) and negative-positive ($t = 2.34$), respectively. Not only is there general agreement on this issue, there is also pronounced agreement with regard to the polarity of the scales for this issue. The reader will note that the polarity (unfavorable, favorable) of some scales under this issue, unlike all other profiles, creates a "lightning-rod" profile. Runaway Inflation may have been a loaded issue causing the respondents to feel that it is *dishonest* but *true* and *worthless* but *meaningful* (these scales normally have similar polarity).

Further party agreement is found on the issue, The United Nations (Figures 19 and 20), where only one significant difference is noted—true-false, T_3 ($t = 2.04$).

The highlights of this discussion are simply presented in the following table, which lists those issues, foreign and domestic, on which political groups generally agreed and disagreed.

	Agreement	*Disagreement*
Domestic issues	Civil Rights for Negroes Runaway Inflation	Catholicism Federal Aid to Education Social Security Medical Care Taft-Hartley Labor Law
Foreign issues	Our Military Preparedness The United Nations	

It is obvious from the above table that the two political groups felt differently about our domestic affairs (excepting Civil Rights and Inflation) and were in accord in their feelings about the foreign issues. In the light of the Quemoy and Matsu discussions during the debate, one might suspect that sharp differences would exist between the parties on foreign issues; further, one could reasonably expect differences in this area based on the disagreement between the debating candidates about U. S. prestige. However, as this study reports, foreign issues failed to produce differences suggested by the debates.

Issues Linked to Images

To what extent are the issues linked to these political groups' images of their candidate? In other words, do respondents tend to rate any of the issues in the same way as they rate their candidate?

In order to answer this question we asked a panel of thirty adults (12 Democrats, 12 Republicans, and 6 Independents) to match image-profiles with issue-profiles. Each panel member was instructed to match, in terms of over-all similarity of the profiles, the Democrats' image of Kennedy (Figure 1) with the eight Democratic issue-profiles, and the Republicans' image of Nixon (Figure 4) with the eight Republican issue-profiles. All of the profile headings were masked so that it was impossible to identify parties, images, and issues.

A surprisingly high degree of agreement was obtained. Twenty-seven panel members agreed in the following matching (each listing only three issues for each image):

> Democratic image of Kennedy matched—
>> Catholicism
>> Federal Aid to Education
>> The United Nations
> Republican image of Nixon matched—
>> Taft-Hartley Labor Law
>> Our Military Preparedness
>> The United Nations

The three other panel members agreed to the above, but, in addition, listed Civil Rights for Negroes under *both* images; one of the three also listed Social Security Medical Care under the Kennedy image.

Excluding Civil Rights for Negroes and Social Security Medical Care, there exists 100 per cent agreement among the thirty panel members.

This analysis suggests that for respondents, the linked image-issues represent agreement between their attitude toward their candidate and their attitude toward the same issues. To put it differently, the Democrats, for example, may have felt that their feelings with regard to these issues were similar to those believed to be held by Kennedy.

Certain issues, however, were linked to a given candidate while others were not; also two issues were virtually unlinked with either image. Perhaps the debates, and the campaign in general, made certain issues salient, linking some of them to one or the other candidate. If we pursue this point, Our Military Preparedness, for example, might have been associated with the then present administration and therefore, the discussion about Quemoy and Matsu, during the debates, brought to mind Nixon's stand and not Kennedy's.

Although this analysis reveals a common connotative meaning between certain images and issues, it is recognized that a more rigorous research approach would be needed to determine linkage between images and issues.

POLITICAL BIAS STUDY

The political bias questionnaire was patterned after a similar test used in the Osgood study.[6] Eight questions were devised, four with Democratic bias and four with Republican bias.[7] A five-step scale ranging from "strongly agree" to "strongly disagree" was provided, which, coded positively with each question scaled from $+1$ to $+5$, gave a score range, Democratic to Republican, from $+8$ to $+40$ with a midpoint of 24.

Since our sample was predominantly Republican, we compared the degree of Republican bias before viewing with the degree of bias after viewing. Here the concern was with the effects of the debates (first and last) in terms of viewing and non-viewing. The Sign Test was used to evaluate the null hypothesis that the debates had no systematic effects.

In this test the *numbers* of respondents shifting from a previous score (before debate) on the questionnaire to another score (after debate) were grouped for analysis. If a respondent's post-debate score remained the same as his pre-debate score he was not included in the analysis. Only those respondents *shifting* from their initial scores were included. In other words, a comparison was made between the number of respondents changing from *more to less* Republican bias and from *less to more* Republican bias as a consequence of viewing the first and then the last debate. These debates (first and last), separately, produced a significant decrease in Republican bias; however, no significant decrease was found over the total period (Table 2). The Sign Test for small samples was used with the non-viewer data and revealed no significant differences for any of the testing periods. Thus, viewing

TABLE 16—2. SIGN TEST FOR POLITICAL BIAS QUESTIONNAIRE—FREQUENCY
OF REPUBLICAN BIAS BEFORE AND AFTER DEBATES FOR
VIEWERS

FREQUENCY OF REPUBLICAN BIAS		FREQUENCY OF REPUBLICAN BIAS After 1st debate		Z	Pa	
		Less	More			
Before 1st debate	More	25	20	2.36	.02	(S)
	Less	13	10			
		After 4th debate				
		Less	More			
Before 4th debate	More	26	19	2.14	.03	(S)
	Less	5	11			
		After 4th debate				
		Less	More			
Before 1st debate	More	22	31	1.03	.30	(NS)
	Less	12	12			

a. Two-tailed.

the debates did make a difference, but the over-all effect (debates plus concomitant influences) showed no permanent difference, indicating that separately the debates were influential in terms of viewing response, though when considered with other "contacts" these differences disappeared.

The entire area of basic differences in extent of knowledge, attitudes held, and personality differences between that great majority of persons who are interested in national affairs as evidenced by their viewing the debates, and the majority of persons who are not, should be explored. It is possible that these factors might account for differences in attitude irrespective of the television viewing factor.

VOTING BEHAVIOR

Table 3 shows that 47, or approximately 36 per cent of the sample, were registered as Democrats and 84, or 64 per cent, as Republicans. The actual vote of the total population (Marion County, Indiana) from which the sample was drawn was 42 per cent Democratic and 58 per cent Republican.

TABLE 16—3. REGISTRATION AND VOTING BEHAVIOR OF SAMPLE[a]

	N	Per Cent (approx.)	
Registered as Democrats	47	36	
Registered as Republicans	84	64	
	131	100	
			% of Democratic N
Democrats voting for Kennedy	31	25	66
Democrats voting for Nixon	6	5	13
Refused to disclose	10	8	21
	47	38	100
			% of Republican N
Republicans voting for Nixon	63	48	75
Republicans voting for Kennedy	3	2	4
Refused to disclose	18	14	21
	84	64	100

a. Based on same subjects used for semantic differential scale analysis.

The vote distribution generally follows party lines. We note, however, that the sample has 9 (7 per cent) cross-overs. Six Democrats and 3 Republicans crossed party lines to vote for the opposite candidate. Individual inspection of their records yields some rather interesting information. One of these, registered as a Democrat, was obviously a staunch Republican with a political bias in that direction of 39 out of a possible 40. It is therefore not at all surprising that he voted Republican. One, a registered Republican, also with an average bias of 39, voted Democratic. Excluding these two atypical cases, the average bias of the Republican cross-overs was 22 (24 is neutral), and they moved in a Democratic direction to 18 over the period of the debates. This may mean that, although registered as Republicans, they were Democratically biased at the beginning and even more so at the end of the debate period. Or, if the measuring instrument is inadequate,[8] it could mean that Nixon failed to reinforce their Republican bias during the debates.

The five registered Democrats, however, were initially almost neutral, and remained so over the period. Their initial mean rating was 23— with a final rating of 23+.

All three of the registered Republicans who voted Democratic were Protestant. Three of the registered Democrats who voted for Nixon were Catholic, three Protestant. This finding offers no support for the argument of voters voting "for" or "against" the candidate's religion.

CONCLUSIONS

With the usual reservations accompanying a study of this kind (small sample, etc.), the following conclusions are drawn:

1. Democrats and Republicans both held favorable opinions toward their respective candidates, and as also might be expected, held relatively unfavorable opinions toward the opposite candidate. In this respect, Republicans thought less of Kennedy than the Democrats thought of Nixon and the debates did not alter these relationships significantly.

2. Republicans and Democrats had similar attitudes toward Our Military Preparedness, the United Nations, Civil Rights for Negroes, and Runaway Inflation. They were in disagreement on Catholicism, Federal Aid to Education, Social Security Medical Care, and the Taft-Hartley Labor Law.

3. Unexpectedly, the debates and the campaign in general failed to bring disagreement between political groups' attitudes on foreign issues.

4. Catholicism, Federal Aid to Education, and The United Nations were issues associated with the Democrats' image of Kennedy. For Republicans, the Taft-Hartley Labor Law, Our Military Preparedness, and The United Nations were linked to the image of Nixon.

5. The first and fourth debates tended to decrease Republican bias. Over the total period, however, no decrease was found. Non-viewers virtually maintained their original biases. Though each debate tended to alter the bias of viewers, other factors seemed to counterbalance this effect.

6. Though parties disagreed on the issue of Catholocism, their voting behavior fails to support the contention that Catholicism was an issue at the polls; however, the voting behavior of the sample also fails to deny the contention.

It is difficult, if not impossible, to determine which candidate was helped or hindered by participating in the debates. Certainly, this study cannot award victory to either candidate.

If this study provides any insight for those who contemplate future

debates between presidential candidates (or for that matter any political debate), it is in the area of the correlation between images and
issues. More research is necessary to determine whether individuals
are persuaded by the position taken on a given issue by a candidate, by
the image projected by the candidate, or by a combination of both.

NOTES

1. Twenty students at the Indiana University Medical Center underwent a
four-hour training session to prepare for interviewing.

2. Religion and income figures for the Indianapolis population were obtained
from the *Catholic Directory* and *Standard Rate and Data* (figures for 1960),
respectively. In the former publication interpolation was necessary since figures
given were those of the archdiocese, which includes an area beyond the city
limits.

3. Raymond G. Smith, "The Development of a Semantic Differential for Use
with Speech Related Concepts," *Speech Monographs*, 26, pp. 263-72.

4. Charles E. Osgood, George J. Suci, and Percy H. Tannenbaum, *The
Measurement of Meaning* (Urbana, Ill.: University of Illinois Press, 1957), pp.
104-16.

5. The 5 per cent level of confidence was used to determine significance; a *t*
of 1.98 with 129 degrees of freedom equals .05 level.

6. See note 4.

7. The Political Bias Questionnaire included the following eight statements:
(1) The Republicans would hold down waste and bureaucracy in government.
(2) The Republicans have been too easy on Big Business. (3) Defense and war
problems can best be handled by the Republicans. (4) All in all the Republican
administration of the last eight years has been bad for the country. (5) The
Democrats would make more bad mistakes in foreign affairs than would the
Republicans. (6) A Democratic administration would help us catch up in the
space race. (7) There would be fewer international crises under the Democrats
than under the Republicans. (8) The right-to-work law *is* fair to working people.

8. By "inadequate" we mean that the "neutral point" of the measuring instrument set on some a priori basis may be off somewhat.

17

Reactions of Viewers

KURT LANG & GLADYS ENGEL LANG

IMMEDIATELY AFTER John F. Kennedy's narrow election victory in 1960, observers began to suggest that television had been the undoing of Richard M. Nixon. Since then, data accumulating from a number of studies of their joint appearances have indicated that the impression made by Kennedy was considerably the more favorable and that his advantage was especially great among the undecided and the independent voters. This article seeks neither to confirm nor to challenge the diagnosis that Kennedy could not have won had there been no televised debates. To disentangle the influence of any single campaign event or issue on the outcome of an election is always difficult. But in relation to the past campaign, it becomes a logical absurdity. The closeness of Kennedy's victory shows that to win he needed every single one of the breaks he got. His victory is attributable only to a concatenation of all the factors working in his favor. He needed the votes of Southern Negroes and obtained them apparently through his intervention for Martin Luther King. The support of New York's liberal Democrats—equally important—was obtained through the efforts of Eleanor Roosevelt, Herbert Lehman, and others in the party's reform wing. Labor's enthusiastic assist everywhere supplied a crucial balance, and the rise of unemployment in the fall undoubtedly helped. There is no way of showing that the TV debates rather than some other event supplied the decisive margin of victory.

A somewhat abridged version of this chapter appeared in the *Public Opinion Quarterly*, Summer 1961.

The issue of the impact of such televised debates can, however, be posed against a background of what has been fairly well established about the impact of mass communications during political campaigns and not just in the 1960 presidential election.[1] The mass political fare generally has two effects: (1) it increases the relevancy of political identifications in accordance with which people make up their minds, and (2) it promotes consistency between voting preferences and the images of candidates, opinions on issues, etc., through which individual voters support these preferences. Campaign events can have a clear influence on the outcome if they somehow crystallize the votes of one side more strongly than those of the other or if they bring about mass switches—the latter is much less likely an eventuality.

The potential for change during the span of a campaign is severely curtailed by the fact that a majority of voters have closed minds even before the campaign officially opens. Many persons simply direct their attention so as to bolster a preference already held. Generally speaking, there is little inclination to seek out deliberately and to weigh carefully and dispassionately the viewpoints and arguments presented by both sides. Hence the televised debates differed from the usual campaign communications in several respects. First, "double exposure" was inherent in their very format; there was no practical way for a viewer to expose himself to the personality of one candidate without the other or to listen to the arguments presented by him without surmising at the same time how well they stood up in the rebuttal. Second, it stands to reason that the debates, which emphasized the give-and-take between the two men, would have their main impact on the images of the candidates' personalities. Third, novelty, advance publicity, viewing habits, and perhaps the unique suitability of video for the debate format combined to attract audiences considerably larger than those usually exposed to campaign telecasts. The debates overshadowed most other campaign events.

This small-scale panel study of 95 New York viewers[2] enables us to detail how vivid new perceptions of the candidates arose in response to this double exposure and how these sometimes disturbing perceptions were handled by viewers and related to—or isolated from—their voting decisions. Each respondent was interviewed at some length three times: late in September just before the first debate, then immediately after that debate, and again after the fourth and last encounter. Although changes in voting intention unquestionably constitute the clearest measure of impact (and interview schedules did elicit data on these), the study *focused* on how the debates influenced the images and comparisons of the two candidates on the part of viewers.

On purely statistical grounds the observations reported warrant no inference about a larger population, national or local. Twenty-four of the interviews are self-interviews by college seniors in a mass communication course at Queens College, a non-resident campus. The other 71 were obtained by the same students from voters outside the college community. Selection procedures were designed to give us a fairly even distribution of potential Kennedy and Nixon supporters and as wide a range as possible on a number of other charactertistics.[3] The observations set forth illustrate processes underlying communication effects as they occur in individuals. While it is not known to what extent the specific factors shown to determine impact in this sample operated elsewhere, studies based on larger and more representative samples certainly indicate that some factors existing elsewhere worked to produce effects in the same direction as those observed here.

Among this panel there was an immediate and dramatic improvement in the Kennedy image right after the first debate, but it was not accompanied by shifts in voting intentions of anywhere near comparable proportions. Since the final decision did not depend on the outcome of the debates alone, this analysis will deal separately with changes in voting intentions, which reflect decisions made, and the manner in which new perceptions entered into candidate images and were then related to electoral choices.

CHANGES IN VOTING INTENTIONS

Among the shifts occurring in this sample one can distinguish three types. *Crystallization* represents a movement from "undecided" or deliberate abstention to a clear-cut preference for one of the two candidates. *Switching* is a movement from one candidate to the other. But a switch that is temporary or a weakening of commitment without any full switch to the other candidate constitutes *wavering*. No evidence was collected on how or whether respondents actually voted in November. Table 1 summarizes the aggregate change within the panel over the period in which the debates took place.

The largest gain for Kennedy came from crystallizers and illustrates his success in rallying behind himself a larger number of the uncommitted than Nixon. After the fourth debate the preferences of 23 per-

TABLE 17—1. VOTING INTENTIONS[a]

	Before Debates	After 1st Debate	After 4th Debate

Decided for Kennedy	37⎫
	  ⎬39
		47⎫
		  ⎬53
			52⎫
			  ⎬56

Leaning toward Kennedy	2⎭	6⎭	4⎭
Undecided	23	12	7

Leaning toward Nixon	2⎫
	  ⎬33
		2⎫
		  ⎬30
			1⎫
			  ⎬32

Decided for Nixon	31⎭	28⎭	31⎭
	95	95	95

a. Based on respondents for whom three interviews were completed.

sons initially uncommitted were thus distributed: 15 either for Kennedy or clearly leaning his way; 3 for Nixon; 5 still undecided or determined not to vote. The decisive shift to Kennedy came right after the first debate, when 8 decided for Kennedy and 4 more indicated a definite leaning toward him.

There were only four switchers. Three of them went from Nixon to Kennedy and one from Kennedy to Nixon. The Kennedy switchers defected (or at least began to lean) to Kennedy right after the first debate; all three said they had been impressed with the performance. The pro-Nixon switch recorded by the end of the debate series was not evident in any way after the initial television encounter.

Six persons initially for Nixon wavered. One of these moved into the undecided group after the first debate, and one after the series was over. The other four weakened in their preference but did not end up as undecided: they either continued to lean toward Nixon or had returned to Nixon after the last debate. Only one Kennedy supporter wavered in that he grew less certain of his preference after the first debate but continued to lean toward Kennedy.

All told, then, there were 22 changes within our panel—18 crystallizers plus 4 switchers. Over 80 per cent of these changes (18 out of 22 to be exact) benefited Kennedy. Apparently he was able to tap a traditionally Democratic potential of persons who, for a variety of reasons, had deferred their decision. His added strength came largely from weak Democratic party identifiers, that is, persons who considered themselves independent but acknowledged a general preference for Democrats. Among 11 weak Democratic identifiers who changed to Kennedy, 9 had been too young to vote in 1956 and 2 had defected to vote for Eisenhower in 1956. Five others who changed to Kennedy were self-styled Democrats; their switch in the course of the debate was a return to that allegiance. Only two of the votes gained by Kennedy can be said to have come from across party lines: one of these was a Republican, the other a self-styled Independent; both had voted for Eisenhower in 1956.

Nixon, on the other hand, won two votes from persons who favored Stevenson in 1956: one from a "Democrat" who had previously voted Republican and another from a new voter who thought of himself as Independent.

When viewed against the voter's party identification and voting history, very few of the intra-campaign switches contradict the voter's political past. The majority of them were merely responding to inclinations that had clearly been present earlier and might have been activated even without the debates.[4] Nixon failed to consolidate sufficiently the inroads Eisenhower had made into the large Democratic potential, heritage of the New Deal era—inroads that any Republican had to maintain or expand if he were to win. As the campaign progressed, among this panel of voters, Kennedy gained votes at a 4:1 ratio. The debates, being the major and perhaps the most dramatic campaign event, hastened the polarization of the electorate but not, as far as our evidence goes, along lines contrary to tradition.

PRE-DEBATE IMAGES

Voting preference is usually linked in various degrees with party identification, orientation to political issues, and images of the candidates.[5] The last two are clearly the more variable and volatile and usually account for cross-overs that contradict party identifications. But since one can reasonably assume that the debates would highlight competitive performance of the two candidates, one would expect any change in voting preferences resulting from the debates to be mediated primarily through the image of the candidates. Before the debate the image viewers had of Nixon was understandably much sharper than that of Kennedy, since Nixon had held national elective office and was far better known. Seventy per cent of the panel said they were "more familiar" with Nixon; 18 per cent said they were equally familiar (or unfamiliar) with both; only 12 per cent thought they knew Kennedy better. Yet certain well-defined images of each candidate were widely shared by the panel.

The image of Nixon. First, the impression that the vice presidency entailed more responsibility and afforded better preparation for the presidency than serving in the Senate was accepted, at least tacitly, even by most Democrats. Second, Nixon was remembered as a roving political ambassador who had dealt with angry mobs in South America and debated with Khrushchev in Russia, though viewers assessed these accomplishments differently. Third, Nixon's formidability as a TV personality and debater was acknowledged by both those for and against his candidacy. Finally, respondents saw in Nixon an experienced and skilled politician; even opponents who heartily disliked him doubted he would ever again resort in public to tactics which had been successful against past political opponents, tactics which they distrusted and which made them distrust Nixon.

The image of Kennedy. The Kennedy image was simpler but also somewhat more "personal;" it was less closely tied to his past political efforts and thus Kennedy, unlike Nixon, emerged more as a "man" than as a "political man." The dominant image of the Senator, even among many who intended to vote against him, was of a "fine young man" with some potential. He was most often viewed as competent and cool—an ambitious young fellow who knew how to build a political organization, as evidenced by his nomination. Both those for and against him widely referred to Kennedy as "vigorous" or "vital." Doubts were voiced, however, about his convictions; many considered him "snobbish" and were highly suspicious of the political influence of his family and of his Catholicism. As an aside it may be mentioned that the most unfriendly image of Kennedy was shared largely by the Catholic Republicans in the sample, of whom two were among the most outspoken in their opposition to a Catholic, especially a Catholic such as Kennedy, in the White House.

Expectations of the debate. Respondents looked forward to the debates as a match of the candidates' forensic skills: their ability, as it was so often expressed, to "put their views across." The partisan hoped to see his candidate perform effectively and thereby improve his chance of winning. Most of those interviewed thought the debates might affect the voting decisions of others but discounted in advance any effect on themselves.

There was, however, a significant difference between the expectations of Nixon partisans and Kennedy partisans (Table 2). Two-thirds of Nixon's partisans felt confident of their candidate's superior debating skills; only 3 out of 30 thought Kennedy would do better.

Even among Kennedy partisans, Nixon was considered a formidable opponent. A reading of the interviews reveals that only a few Kennedy supporters had real confidence that their man would be a match for Nixon. By their evasion of a flat prediction, many implied that they were worried by Nixon's reputation as a political infighter.

Respondents who thought they "might be influenced" by the debates put a special stress on the image the candidates would project. A number intended to look specifically for "the way a candidate answered" as apart from what he might say. "I want to see," said one, "whether they hem and haw before they answer, whether they mean what they say, and whether they are sincere." Others said they would look for signs of knowledgeability and an ability to stand up "courageously."

Finally, many who were undecided and a number of party faithfuls lukewarm to the candidate said they would seek information on how the candidates stood on important issues. They expected from the debate format, since it offered a unique opportunity for "instantaneous reply," that the candidates would force each other into clear-cut statements of policy and expose past records.

IMPACT OF THE FIRST DEBATE

Our detailed responses indicate that the impact of the first debate was fairly dramatic. Eighty-nine per cent of those who watched or heard the first debate thought Kennedy had bested Nixon in debate or at least had fought him to a draw (Table 2).[6] The single most important result of the debate lay in its destruction of the image, so widely held, of Richard Nixon as champion debater and television politician par excellence. This reevaluation of the comparative ability of the two men as performers is what helped crystallize the vote of undecideds and caused partisans to revise their images of the men as persons and as presidential timber.

Changes in the images of candidates as persons following the first encounter were generally in the direction of greater consonance between preference and image. But as Table 3 shows, Kennedy scored net gains, creating a more favorable personal image for himself. His unexpectedly able performance dissolved many doubts about his maturity and experience even among Nixon supporters. By contrast there was a dramatic deterioration of Nixon's personal image among Democrats and undecided; moreover, 5 out of 30 Nixon supporters had a less favorable view of Nixon, the person. Still, while some Kennedy sup-

TABLE 17—2. EXPECTATIONS AND ACTUAL PERFORMANCE IN FIRST DEBATE[a]

	EXPECTATIONS OF PERFORMANCE			
POLITICAL PREFERENCE BEFORE 1ST DEBATE	Nixon Better	About the Same	Kennedy Better	Don't Know, No Ans.
Nixon (30)	21	6	3	0
Undecided (22)	9	8	4	1
Kennedy (39)	11	12	13	3
Total	41	26	20	4
Per cent	45	29	22	4
	ACTUAL PERFORMANCE			
Nixon (30)	8	10	12	0
Undecided (22)	0	2	20	0
Kennedy (39)	2	9	28	0
Total	10	21	60	0
Per cent	11	23	66	—

a. Six of 97 respondents with whom pre-debate interviews were completed said they had not watched the first debate. The comparison remains essentially unaffected by whether or not the 6 non-viewers are included.

porters found Nixon less well informed than they had supposed, the Nixon supporters, who had thought their candidate very well informed before the debate, afterward found him even better informed. Thus, among the viewers as a whole (as shown in Table 3), the personal

TABLE 17—3. CHANGE IN CANDIDATES' IMAGE AFTER FIRST DEBATE[a]
(percentages)

	Better	Unchanged	Worse	No Ans.
Kennedy personal image	45	45	5	4
Nixon personal image	20	47	29	4
Kennedy informedness	41	53	3	3
Nixon informedness	14	67	11	8

a. Based on 91 respondents.

image of Nixon deteriorated but the judgment of Nixon's informedness remained pretty much as was.

A judgment of over-all attitude toward the two candidates was made

TABLE 17—4. CHANGES IN OVER-ALL VALUATION OF CANDIDATES AFTER
          DEBATE

POLITICAL PREFERENCE BEFORE 1ST DEBATE	Improvement	KENNEDY EVALUATIONS			
		Favorable Image Validated	No Change	Unfavorable Image Validated	Deterioration
Nixon (30)	10	1	7	12	0
Undecided (22)	11	0	9	2	0
Kennedy (39)	19	15	4	0	1
Total	40	16	20	14	1
Per cent	45	18	22	15	1
		NIXON EVALUATIONS			
Nixon (30)	1	16	7	0	6
Undecided (22)	2	0	9	3	8
Kennedy (39)	6	0	13	14	6
Total	9	16	29	17	20
Per cent	10	18	32	19	22

from answers to questions about what viewers had found out about
each man—how able he was, what he stood for, how he had voted,
how he performed, etc. Table 4 uses the categories "Improvement"
and "Deterioration" with regard to this *over-all* image. The categories
"Favorable (Unfavorable) Image Validated" were added to indicate
persons whose over-all judgment changed but only insofar as they become more certain in their judgment than they had been. The potential
for improvement was limited by the fact that each candidate entered
the debates with a fund of good will among his supporters; the potential for deterioration was limited by the hostility each already encountered among the opposition.

As expected, many respondents merely validated a favorable image
of their own candidate and an unfavorable image of his opponent.
What interests us is, first, that there was a general improvement of the
over-all impression of Kennedy, an improvement that was very marked
for those initially uncommitted, was only somewhat less marked among
Kennedy partisans, and extended even to supporters of Nixon.[7] Second, because the majority of Nixon supporters merely validated an
initially favorable image while five indicated less favorable impressions,
the image of Nixon held by the panel as a whole deteriorated. Third,

gains made by Nixon among Kennedy supporters are noteworthy even though they were not large enough to offset the trend, that is, they occurred among a group whose image to begin with had been strongly negative.

CUMULATIVE IMPACT

Reactions to the first encounter set the tone. The images of the candidates, once firmed up in response to that initial debate, changed very little thereafter, even though many of the perceptions of that initial debate were clearly incongruous with commitments. Both candidates had, for example, scored some gains among persons supporting their opponents. One would expect that exposure to information invalidating the grounds on which partisanship is based would force viewers to gear their subsequent communication behavior to the reestablishment of a consistent frame.[8] There are a number of ways besides change in preference in which it is possible to do this: by refusing to watch further debates, by turning to sources of information more favorable to one's candidate, and by continuing to look in subsequent debates for clues reaffirming one's original convictions.

Among our panel there is no evidence that dissonance introduced by the first debate led either to a general curtailment or to an increase in exposure. The number of debates watched was unrelated to (a) initial candidate preference, (b) judgment of who had won the first debate, (c) amount of change in image, or (d) education. The availability of alternative techniques for reducing dissonance, besides avoidance, militates against the emergence of a clear relationship to exposure.

Responses after the last debate showed rather clearly how much people had come to rely on interpretations they had read in newspapers and news magazines, usually publications reflecting their own views. Viewers' later observations exhibited considerable stereotypy and lacked the originality that had characterized responses after the first debate. From this it appears that journalistic interpretations and personal conversations supplied a frame of reference permitting the assimilation of information from subsequent debates without stirring new doubt or conflict.

The third way of reducing strain between image and voting preference involved a reassessment of the various component elements that make up a candidate's political personality and of their relevance to electoral choice. The televised debates dramatized competitive per-

formance. Because of this, it is assumed, any impact on voting intentions would be mediated through the image of the candidates.

To stress the importance of personality here is not to ignore the
stability introduced by party identification and by the network of associations that activate the electorate at election time. In the rhythmic
pattern of politics party images often become blurred between national
elections. The political personality chosen by each party to head the
ticket and to be the spokesman of party policy plays a crucial role in
the electoral campaign, which is aimed at moving party identifications
back into the foreground of attention and refurbishing the party image.
The party, temporarily united behind the candidate, appeals through
him to the electorate. But the "strain toward consistency" among images voters hold of personal self-interest, national interest, party policies, etc., includes the image of the party candidate.

The image of a political personality projected by television seems
to depend upon evaluations of three component elements: his television *performance,* here as a "debater;" his fitness for the *political role*
in which he is cast, here that of candidate aspiring to the presidency;
and his *personal image*—what kind of human being is he? what is he
like as a "real" person? In an earlier paper these writers showed these
three elements of the television personality to be clearly separable.[9]
The appeal of a political personality is a function of the way the man
on the screen projects along each of these dimensions and whether
they are related or isolated in the viewer's cognition. The relationship
among these elements as well as the relationship between these elements and political decisions is similar in certain respects to the relationship between information and attitudes on which the information
supposedly bears. New or negative information does not necessarily
mean a reassessment of pertinent attitudes. Neither does a changed
perception of performance necessarily carry over to perception of the
"man" performing, and so forth.[10] The rest of this paper takes up this
question of how new cognitive elements introduced so vividly in the
first debate were dealt with by viewers. The essential question is why
dramatic changes in evaluations were not followed by dramatic changes
in voting intentions.

PERFORMANCE, PERSONAL IMAGE, POLITICAL ROLE

Even though partisans wanted their man to "win" so that they could
reassure themselves and convince others, few viewers, whether partisan
or uncommitted, would have seriously proposed before the first debate

that a candidate's ability to score points under the rules agreed on for that debate was a test of fitness for office. Yet it was his unexpected performance that helped Kennedy project among his potential supporters a personal image congruent with the political role he was playing.

Kennedy supporters. The image of Kennedy was transformed from that of an eager, affable, young and ambitious political aspirant into one that emphasized the competent, dynamic, and quick-thinking candidate.

> "His debating techniques showed a quick mind."
> "He was alert and interested at all times."
> "He seemed to know all the time where to refute Nixon."
> "He never fumbled."
> "He presented himself as a doer, a leader, a positive thinker."

These are only illustrations of how Kennedy, by his performance, established among potential supporters his character as well as his "right" to the candidacy. Lukewarm supporters became enthusiastic because, as several put it, "people could *see* he was qualified." Said one: "I've switched from an anti-Nixon Democrat to a pro-Kennedy Democrat."

Most of these potential Democrats had expected Kennedy to be "beaten" and, because of this, were prepared to isolate competitive television performance from their consideration of the qualifications of the men to be president. At the same time, Nixon's much heralded competence as performer was a focus for many negative perceptions concerning his political role. But Nixon's failure to live up to expectations as a performer did not destroy this negative image. The focus on performance also meant that the personal image projected through TV was not likely to gain him trust or to inspire confidence in his qualifications among Democrats. On the contrary, some respondents who had explicitly discounted performance in this regard now went so far as to draw from his "poor" performance conclusions about his fitness. One interpreted "the way he fumbled, ingratiated himself, appeared nervous and not quite rational" to mean that Nixon was "psychologically too upset to be entrusted with the leadership of the country." Observed another, "The poor facial expressions and nervous tension leads me to go so far as to say he looked frightened." The relevance assigned to performance as a measure of the man and the candidate changed among many Democrats.

A poor performance, expected or not, need not result in deterioration of the personal image if it is not linked to political role. Thus six Kennedy supporters, though judging Nixon the poorer performer, emerged with a more positive over-all image of Nixon (Table 4). Reading what explanations they could be led to offer for their more charitable view, one discerns that a gnawing distrust of Kennedy led them to question the spontaneity of the latter's performance and to personalize the content. Sympathy was thus extended to the apparent victim; yet their electoral choice was not affected nor did they think less well of Kennedy. For example, one housewife (one of the few to anticipate Kennedy's superior performance) explained: "He is a magnetic person, with much polish and a great deal of sex appeal. He'll make a good appearance and will greatly appeal to the younger female voters." Her praise before the debates was thus given grudgingly. She emerged from the first debate unimpressed with "Kennedy's ability to quote figures . . . [since] Kennedy was paying others to get all facts" and went on to describe how pleased she was that "Nixon gave him a run for his money and didn't take a back seat." She was a regular Democrat, and her vote was not swayed by the increased attraction she felt for Nixon.

Again, one student (a new voter) found Nixon's performance "almost pathetic" and suffered for him. To him Nixon appeared "sometimes pleading, avoiding questions, shocked when attacked, nervous, and anxious, [and] at times I felt very sorry for him." For the first time, the young man said, he had recognized Nixon as a "human being, a complicated personality" rather than a political symbol. This student was one of the few who called the first debate "not quite fair" since newsmen had been "kinder" to Kennedy. But the pro-Republican press, he noted, must have helped "to heal Nixon's wounds" by calling the debate a draw—in the respondent's view Kennedy had clearly won. Performance ultimately moved him from undecided to Kennedy, but after the first debate he described himself as "less in favor of Kennedy than before" even though his over-all impression of Kennedy had clearly improved.

Nixon supporters. The Nixon political personality—as already pointed out—was dominated by the perceived political role. Statements by his supporters about the "kind of person Nixon was" were usually formulated in terms of qualifications for office and his ability to perform. An inventory of terms most frequently used before the first debate to describe the personal image includes: experienced, competent, better informed than Kennedy, a hard worker, a good American, forceful, honest, sincere, calm, strong, and such phrases as "he can face up to the Russians" and "he can handle Khrushchev." An occasional respondent noted that he was a good family man or had a pleasing personality and a few attributed the distrust he was known to evoke in others to his "reserve" or "efficiency."

Nixon's performance in the first debate undermined the image of a superior debater most of his supporters had held. The keen disappointment many of them felt was translated into votes for Kennedy only among those few whose electoral choice was founded on rather weak party identifications. The majority countered the strain that perceptions of Nixon's shaky performance introduced into their frame by one or more of three techniques: *isolation, selective perception,* and *personalization.*

Isolation (in the sense of denying the relevance of information to behavioral commitment) has already been noted in the pre-debate responses of Kennedy backers, who minimized debating skill as a test of political competence. But now it was the pro-Nixon group who, despite the fact that they had supported evaluations of their candidate by reference to the debating skills he had exhibited in the past, ceased to stress such skills when his performance proved disappointing.

Selective perception is illustrated by claims that both candidates had been "primed beforehand," an observation often documented by "Kennedy's ability to rattle off figures." Nixon's claim to the presidency was most often justified after the debate by his long advocacy of "sound policies." The candidate's performance was ignored while the policies he advocated came in for extra attention. By focusing on the political content of Nixon's statements his supporters, who, presumably, were in agreement with what he believed in, could still define him as the winner, and there was understandably a larger proportion who thought that he had done better or at least as well as Kennedy. Said one, "I think Nixon did better but of course I'm prejudiced." Others thought that reporters were favoring Kennedy, feeding him easier questions. Kennedy was also accused of having broken the rules by his note-taking and, in subsequent debates, by his reading from notes.[11] Different evaluations of performance thus are a function of the elements singled out for attention and of the context in which they are interpreted.

The technique of *personalization* is perhaps a special variant of selective perception in that it involves the reinterpretation of intrinsically ambiguous attributes into a personal image that imputes to persons with whom one is in disagreement unfavorable traits, and vice versa. For example, one of his supporters remarked on Nixon's "not smiling at all, being ill at ease, and on the defensive" but then went on to interpret this as being "more careful, more subtle, and thinking over a problem." Another woman admitted that "Kennedy came over nicely if you like his type. He was snide and impolite to make notes while Nixon was speaking." In her final interview the same woman explained at length that the better the Kennedy performance, the more she came personally to dislike him, while her confidence in Nixon increased; she felt, as she put it, "a real personal contact" with him. Nixon, it was said by another, though a target of Kennedy's "brashness," "never likes to offend anybody." His being "too polite" thus became an explanation of why he failed to live up to expectations.

Personal traits used to explain the performance were also related to political role. To many Nixon's hesitations indicated "thoughtfulness" and "cautious modesty," both congruent with the political role a president is expected to play, thus affording a favorable contrast with Kennedy's "boasting." As one Nixon supporter depicted it: "Kennedy always began his statements, 'I will do this' and 'I will do that.' Whenever Nixon started to say 'I,' he checked himself by saying 'the *Republican Party* will.' " In another reference Kennedy was seen as "quick-acting, but if he's to talk to Khrushchev, he'd say something he later would regret." Moreover Nixon, according to some, was not at his best in the first debate because he had recently been hospitalized for an infected knee. He had, however, shown great fortitude: "Nixon could stand up to Kennedy [said one person after the fourth debate]. That shows he could stand up to the Russians."

While Kennedy did improve his over-all image among one-third of the Nixon partisans with his performance, he improved it largely in terms of "informedness." Thirteen out of 30 Nixon supporters who saw the first debate came to consider Kennedy better informed than they had thought. But only 5 out of the same 30 got a more favorable personal image. Many Republicans could not but react with hostility on seeing that he was a formidable adversary. It is hardly surprising, therefore, especially in view of the short period covered in this study, that political preferences should on the whole have remained stable, even though the debates had a definite impact on imagery. Our data illustrate a variety of ways in which perceptions were brought into line with electoral choices.

SUMMARY AND IMPLICATIONS

1. Data from intensive interviews with a small panel of New York City viewers indicate that exposure to the televised debates resulted in some rather dramatic change in candidate image. Voting intentions changed much less. Some light was thrown on the process by which images were adjusted to preference.

2. In balance, the impact of these debates, as observed on this panel, appears to have favored Kennedy more than Nixon. But when viewed against the backgrounds of voters, the majority of whom had identified themselves with or voted for the Democratic party in the past, Kennedy's gain does not appear to have entailed a large-scale crossing of party lines. Most of the undecided were Democrats-in-conflict, who were won over because Kennedy succeeded in identifying himself with the tradition of the Democratic party.

3. Kennedy as the less well known of the candidates stood a greater chance of being helped by these joint appearances as well as by the campaign generally, an anticipation borne out by this and other research. We caution, however, against too much facile generalization, for some of the very elements in the Kennedy performance shown to have worked in his favor among this group of viewers might produce different responses in other surroundings. Attention is drawn to the personal hostility Kennedy's smooth performance aroused among some Nixon voters. Thus, in communities where attitudes prevail that were rarely encountered among this sample (such as anti-"big city" or fundamentalist sentiment) the distribution of responses might differ greatly.

4. Though evidence from this study does not suggest that dramatic and immediate changes in votes can be expected from such TV spectacles in the middle of a campaign, there may nevertheless be important "sleeper" effects that could not be observed by the methods employed. The reactions to the debates were influenced by what viewers remembered about the two performers from past telecasts or (especially in the case of Nixon) as they remembered it from what they read about those telecasts afterward. Images are thus created of which future actions must take account. Efforts to utilize the debates were revealed in interviews with campaign workers. Among Democrats the Kennedy

performance sparked the organization of viewing groups, generated enthusiasm, and perhaps led to greater campaign efforts, all of which together might have influenced the final vote gains as much as the debates as such.

NOTES

1. Among a number of good summaries of the impact are B. R. Berelson, P. F. Lazarsfeld, and W. N. McPhee, *Voting* (Chicago: University of Chicago Press, 1954), Appendix, and E. Burdick and A. J. Brodbeck, *American Voting Behavior* (Glencoe, Ill.: Free Press, 1959), chaps. 12 and 13.

2. Altogether 104 persons were interviewed before or after the debates. Ninety-seven were interviewed before the first debate, but two of them could not be reinterviewed. Seven others were interviewed only after the first debate. Statistics in this paper are based only on those 95 persons interviewed three times.

3. Of the 97 interviewed before the first debate, 13 were under 21 and too young to vote; 23 were between 21 and 24 and thus first voters; 19 were between 25 and 34; 33 were between 35 and 54; and 7 were 55 and over. The sample contained 50 persons of Jewish origin, 26 Protestant, 18 Catholic, and three who gave no answers; 7 persons added on the second wave were Catholic. The socio-economic level of the sample was somewhat above average and contained, as noted, a large number of students. Persons gainfully employed divided rather evenly among three groups: professional, managerial, and white-collar employees; sales personnel and small businessmen; and blue-collar workers. Our analysis fastens on political identification as the significant determinant of response to the telecasts (as we think it is *during a campaign*). Therefore the inclusion of a wide range offers some check on unwarranted generalizations. Of those who voted in 1956 and responded to a question about how they voted, 44 per cent had voted Republican and 56 per cent Democratic. Asked which party they belonged to or "identified" with, 59 per cent responded "Democratic," 21 per cent "Republican," with the others declaring themselves Independent or unaffiliated, or refusing to answer. In traditionally Democratic New York City most of the "Independents" revealed themselves to be, by voting record, attitudes, etc., inclined toward the Republicans. It must be added that a much condensed F-scale was used to try to get at personality and viewing reaction as a correlate of response, but this attempt was frankly a failure.

4. The small size of the sample prevents any meaningful statistical analysis of the many politically relevant background factors (like religion, occupation, etc.) that might shed further light on voting decisions.

5. See A. Campbell, G. Gurin, and W. E. Miller, *The Voter Decides* (Evanston, Ill.: Row, Peterson, 1954).

6. A national sample of approximately 1,000 viewers interviewed by the Gallup organization during the week September 24 to October 4, 1960 shows that about twice as many thought Kennedy did better than thought Nixon did better. Release of October 12, 1960.

7. Among a test audience recruited in the Trenton, New Jersey, area, the proportion who held a "very" favorable image of Kennedy increased 16 per cent following the debate compared with an increase of 4 per cent for Nixon. Gallup organization release, October 2, 1960. The Survey Research Center (University of Michigan) according to a press release found that among Independents favorable responses to Kennedy after the debates were twice as frequent as favorable responses to Nixon.

8. Cf. L. Festinger, *A Theory of Cognitive Dissonance* (Evanston, Ill.: Row, Peterson, 1957).

9. K. Lang and G. E. Lang, "The Television Personality in Politics," *Public Opinion Quarterly,* XX (Spring, 1956), 103-13.

10. See J. T. Klapper, *The Effects of Mass Communication* (Glencoe, Ill.: Free Press, 1960), pp. 84-90 on the relationship between information and attitude change and G. Lindzey, *Handbook of Social Psychology* (Cambridge, Mass.: Addison-Wesley, 1954), chap. 17 on person perception.

11. Accusations such as the one cited illustrate the interplay between press reports and political television. Nixon supporters maintained an image congruent with their preference because they had "seen" Kennedy "cheat" to best Nixon. The latter's official dissociation from the charge mattered little.

18

Effects and Implications

SAUL BEN-ZEEV & IRVING S. WHITE

BACKGROUND AND DESIGN OF THE STUDY

IN RETROSPECT it is now generally conceded that the debates were advantageous to Kennedy, and since the election was won by a hair's breadth, they may have made the difference between winning and losing. Yet the true meaning of the debates has not yet been fully assessed, and their implications for future elections and for mass communications have not been thoroughly drawn.

This report is a contribution to such an evaluation. It is based on surveys[1] carried out during the period of the debates by the psychological and market research firm of Creative Research Associates Incorporated of Chicago. These surveys were made in the Chicago area and some of the findings were published in the *Chicago Daily News*.

At the end of the first debate the press carried reports of some post-facto surveys and many interpretations were made on the basis of these. Most of the publicized surveys merely consisted of interviews with several hundred people who were asked, after the fact, whether they felt that the debates had influenced their opinions of the candidates and whether they had consequently changed their choice of candidate. Naturally such an approach is fraught with pitfalls and unreliabilities, and naturally few people were shown as admitting important changes.

It was therefore decided to apply a different technique to the problem. The technique used in the survey is conceptually simple. It involved double interviews of each voter in the sample. A modified area sampling procedure was used, selecting individuals old enough to vote. A typical respondent would be interviewed sometime during the day

331

preceding the debate and also sometime during the day following the debate.

At no time during the pre-debate interview was the respondent made aware of the survey's interest in the debates. The interview was introduced as part of a survey of political opinion. The post-debate interview was presented as a second part of the same survey. In actuality the second interview was almost a replica of the first, with variations in the order of presentation of some of the questions and with the addition of a set of questions at the end dealing with the respondent's viewing of the debate. It was possible, therefore, to compare pre-debate attitudes with post-debate attitudes, and to contrast the shifts that had occurred among viewers and non-viewers of each of the debates.

In each of the interviews the respondent was required to rate each candidate in terms of thirteen pairs of descriptive phrases, such as "modern" versus "old-fashioned," "experienced" versus "still-learning," "sincere" versus "slick," and so on. In addition, of course, the respondent was asked which candidate he favored at that point in the campaign.

Since the first debate was not investigated in this way, this study deals only with the second, third, and fourth. Each debate involved a double set of interviews with a sample of voters; thus the study in effect provides six check points in the campaign. A total of 996 respondents were given these double interviews during this period. The pattern developed through these three debates was very consistent, and we believe that even though the effect of the first debate may possibly have been greater in intensity, it was no different in direction and kind. Thus although the omission of the first debate from the study is regrettable, it is not felt that the information omitted is crucial.

THE FINDINGS

The response of the total sample in terms of over-all choice is presented in Table 1 as it occurred at our six check points. This table points to some striking tendencies: (1) Kennedy gained steadily and continuously from one check point to the next. (2) Nixon lost support initially and never recovered his loss. (3) "Within" debates there are generally increases for Kennedy, while Nixon merely tends to hold his own.

It turns out, too, that if after the fourth debate the "undecided" are apportioned in proportion to the decided voters, the percentages de-

TABLE 18—1. OVER-ALL CHOICE
        (*percentages*)

	2nd Debate (N=354)		3rd Debate (N=391)		4th Debate (N=251)	
	Pre-Debate	*Post-Debate*	*Pre-Debate*	*Post-Debate*	*Pre-Debate*	*Post-Debate*
Favored Kennedy	39	40	44	47	53	55
Favored Nixon	37	36	28	29	29	28
Undecided	24	24	28	24	18	17

rived are very close to the actual vote in the area investigated. The post-fourth-debate percentages are 64 to 36 for Kennedy and Nixon respectively and the official vote in Chicago was 66 per cent to 34 per cent. This provides us with at least some evidence of validation in terms of reality.

When viewers of each debate are compared with non-viewers it becomes apparent that most of the "within debate" changes in favor of Kennedy are due to the viewers (Table 2).

TABLE 18—2. WITHIN-DEBATE CHANGES
        (*percentages*)

VIEWERS

	2nd Debate (N=251)		3rd Debate (N=250)		4th Debate (N=166)	
	Pre-Debate	*Post-Debate*	*Pre-Debate*	*Post-Debate*	*Pre-Debate*	*Post-Debate*
Favored Kennedy	38	41	43	46	47	52
Favored Nixon	38	38	29	31	34	32
Undecided	24	21	28	23	19	16

NON-VIEWERS

	2nd Debate (N=103)		3rd Debate (N=141)		4th Debate (N=85)	
	Pre-Debate	*Post-Debate*	*Pre-Debate*	*Post-Debate*	*Pre-Debate*	*Post-Debate*
Favored Kennedy	42	38	46	50	62	62
Favored Nixon	38	33	26	25	21	21
Undecided	20	29	28	25	17	17

Among the viewers, it is apparent that within each debate Kennedy gained, while this was not true of non-viewers.

When all the "pre" scores are lumped together for each candidate and when the same is done for all the "post" scores, we get the result shown in Table 3.

TABLE 18—3. TOTAL "PRE" AND "POST" SCORES
        (*percentages*)

| | VIEWERS | |
	Total "Pre" Scores (N = 667)	Total "Post" Scores (N = 667)
Favored Kennedy	42	46
Favored Nixon	34	34
Undecided	24	20

| | NON-VIEWERS | |
	Total "Pre" Scores (N = 229)	Total "Post" Scores (N = 229)
Favored Kennedy	49	49
Favored Nixon	29	26
Undecided	22	25

The pre-post difference among the viewers is statistically significant (at the .05 level), while the equivalent difference for non-viewers is not.

Up to this point the data appear to show that: (1) Viewing the debates tended to shift opinion in favor of Kennedy. (2) The gain for Kennedy appeared to have come from the ranks of the undecided. (3) The average gain for Kennedy, in these data, was about 4 percentage points per debate. (4) On the whole, the debates did not cause Nixon to lose favor with those who favored him in the first place. Kennedy's advantage was his gain from the large reservoir of undecideds rather than a direct net gain from Nixon.

With these points established the next step is to investigate the underlying reasons for these patterns. The respondents rated each candidate on thirteen pairs of personality traits. It was therefore possible to assess the shifts in personal image resulting from the debates.

To begin with, the debates made Kennedy's image clearer as the debates proceeded, whereas the clarity of Nixon's image remained about the same. The following are per cent frequencies of viewers' ratings of both candidates on the item "You're not sure of where he stands":

	2ND DEBATE		3RD DEBATE		4TH DEBATE	
	Pre	Post	Pre	Post	Pre	Post
Pro-Kennedy	50	37	46	36	37	36
Pro-Nixon	46	41	45	42	52	41

The debates thus served to introduce the personality of the relatively unknown Kennedy to the American people.

At the same time they tended to decrease somewhat the perception of Kennedy as being inexperienced and to increase the component of inexperience on Nixon's side. The following are per cent frequencies of viewers' rating on the item "Still learning" (as opposed to "experienced"):

	2ND DEBATE		3RD DEBATE		4TH DEBATE	
	Pre	Post	Pre	Post	Pre	Post
Pro-Kennedy	63	64	56	52	55	50
Pro-Nixon	18	30	30	26	32	32

Nixon suffered most on this dimension during the second debate, and he never recovered his original level afterward.

Another pattern noted was a smooth development of perceptions for Kennedy, as contrasted with a "bounce-back" effect for Nixon. This is illustrated in Table 4, presenting changes among debate viewers.
In almost all of these traits, one observes a consistent weakening of Nixon during the period *between* two debates, and a consistent tendency to recover the previous position *after* each debate, while it is clear that Kennedy maintains a more even level of either gain or loss.

Kennedy's "image" appears to have developed through gradual but consistent changes. His progress chart, in terms of the public's perception of his personality, exhibited stable growth. The public did not appear to be continuously reformulating their impressions of him. On the other hand, it is evident that Nixon's difficulty, at least among voters in the area studied, lay in the fact that they could not maintain a constant image of him.

In short-range terms Nixon's gains after each debate appear to have

TABLE 18—4. PERCEPTIONS OF KENNEDY AND NIXON
(*percentages*)

	PRO-NIXON				
TRAIT	Post 2nd Debate	Pre 3rd Debate	Post 3rd Debate	Pre 4th Debate	Post 4th Debate
"Experienced	68	61	71	66	68
"Sincere"	81	74	78	75	80
"Thinks on his own feet"	71	50	53	51	68
"Thrifty"	77	70	73	72	79
"People like his looks"	80	70	73	72	80

	PRO-KENNEDY				
TRAIT	Post 2nd Debate	Pre 3rd Debate	Post 3rd Debate	Pre 4th Debate	Post 4th Debate
"Experienced"	35	45	40	43	45
"Sincere"	77	83	81	82	89
"Thinks on his own feet"	69	68	70	79	80
"Thrifty"	39	44	52	54	59
"People like his looks"	94	89	82	81	81

been more important for his cause than is the case for Kennedy. It seems that Nixon's physical presence *did* tend to produce a favorable effect. This effect, however, did not seem to be a lasting one, but appears to have dissipated quickly after its immediate impact. For Kennedy, on the other hand, the debates served the purpose of spurring on and reinforcing an image which was apparently building up in sources outside the TV debates.

There are some problems in generalizing these findings, for the study was carried out in only one metropolitan area, and comparable information on the first debate is not available. Yet if these data were to be used for the purpose of projection, as could reasonably be done at least for other metropolitan areas, the following conclusions would be drawn. (1) The over-all effect of the debates was certainly in Kennedy's favor. This favorable effect, however, was due not merely to the debates themselves as separate events, but to the fact that they fitted in with the emerging image of Kennedy as it was reflected in other events of the campaign. (2) Nixon might have benefited from the debates, had the image he emerged with after each debate been consistent with the image he was projecting outside the debate. It turns out, though, that the public was seeing two Nixons—the one in the newspapers between debates, and another on the TV screen during debates. There *is* evidence, however, that Nixon's "presence" did have a short-range favorable effect for him, and it might even be concluded, contrary to current belief, that Nixon might have really *benefited* from a fifth debate just before the election. (3) Although the over-all effect of the debates may have been decisive in an election as close as this one, there is no evidence here that this effect would have been as crucial in an election where the voters were less evenly divided.

IMPLICATIONS FOR TV'S FUTURE ROLE

The differing effects of the debates on the campaigns of the two candidates suggest two possible roles for television in the communication of material on public questions. (1) *A reinforcing role.* In this role television has shown itself to be effective. It makes tangible, puts flesh on, vaguely felt trends of public opinion. In serving this function it is capable of solidifying public opinion and organizing it for action. (2) *A molding role.* The results of this study of the debates leave the possibility of a "molding" role for television still debatable. It is not possible to say here that isolated television communications, taken separately from the influence of other media and other sources of public opinion, are capable of playing *the* crucial role in reversing, changing, or shifting, the prevailing atmosphere or mood.

19

The Problem of Textual Accuracy

THEODORE CLEVENGER, JR., DONALD W. PARSON, &
JEROME B. POLISKY

THE CONTENTS of this volume testify that the Kennedy-Nixon debates are destined to be among the most intensively studied events in the history of communication. Political scientists, linguists, historians, psychologists, anthropologists, and biographers, as well as students of speech and the mass media, will obtain data appropriate to their fields of study by applying to them the analytical techniques of their disciplines.

The intensive study of these debates demonstrates the often overlooked point that the text of a speech is a multi-dimensional document, limited only by the number and variety of points of view from which it is approached. To certain analysts it becomes a set of linguistic structures; to others a source of information about the values and issues of a period; to some investigators it is an index to the behavioral patterns of a society, to others a vehicle for evaluating the speaker, his ideas, his style.

In this sense, each analyst perceives a different speech, because each treats a different kind of data. Yet all are working with different aspects of the same concrete event, and the extent to which each analysis will be valid and meaningful depends upon the accuracy of the text.

There are many sources of textual inaccuracy, not all of which are equally important to every investigator. It may be sufficient for the purpose of one analyst to know that a speech was delivered; a second may require additional information about the subjects which the speaker discussed; a third might also need to know more about the arrangement and proportions of the divisions of the speech; in addition to this, a fourth might want to examine the wording of certain key concepts; a fifth might demand the exact language of the entire speech; and a sixth might require in addition to these details a record of certain aspects of delivery. The greater the number of details with respect to which a given text is accurate, the greater is the variety of analyses for which it provides a reliable basis.

In discussing the question of textual authenticity, it is important to preserve the distinctions among what a speaker intends to say, what he says, and what he later wishes others to believe that he said. Advance press releases, official versions, and revised editions of speeches are legitimate objects of study, as are preliminary drafts, speaking notes, and newspaper excerpts. However, since a speech is primarily an auditory event occurring at a particular time and place, we contend that the best text of a speech is that account which comes closest to what the audience heard. Only if the text is complete and accurate in this sense will it provide a sound basis for analyses of the speech.

Unhappily, the acquisition of authentic texts is a difficult and sometimes impossible task, as illustrated in the means by which existing texts of noted speeches have been produced. In our judgment, there are too few accurate accounts of speeches, and our experience in preparing the four Kennedy-Nixon debates for publication has persuaded us that the number may be considerably smaller than is generally supposed. The authenticity of these texts may be judged against seven levels of textual accuracy.

1. *Reconstruction from reports of observers.* After a speech has been delivered, its text may be reconstructed by observers either from notes taken at the time or entirely from memory. Most of us are familiar with Patrick Henry's phrase, "Give me liberty or give me death." The text of his speech before the Virginia Legislature in March, 1775, has become a classic of American oratory and literature. Yet the text which we possess was not written by Patrick Henry, but by William Wirt; not at the time of the speech, but half a century later, not from his own observations of the speech, but from reports he was able to gather. Louis Mallory contends that Wirt's text is neither a complete account of the speech, nor an accurate reflection of Henry's style of discourse, insofar as it is known.[1] Such texts provide shaky grounds for inferences concerning the speaker and his ideas, and no grounds at all for a stylistic analysis.

2. *Reconstruction by the speaker.* At times a speaker may reconstruct the text of a speech after its delivery, either from speaking notes

or entirely from memory. It has been contended that the earliest text of the Gettysburg Address was reconstructed by Lincoln several months after the speech was delivered.[2] President Kennedy's radio-television address before a joint session of Congress on May 24, 1961, illustrates another kind of reconstruction by the speaker. According to a contemporary columnist, as Kennedy spoke he either deleted or changed 1,500 words which appeared in the original manuscript. The White House later announced that the *Congressional Record* would publish a text of the speech including the sections which Kennedy eliminated as he spoke.[3] Loren Reid, who for twelve years worked in the Government Printing Office, observed the changes made in the speeches of the *Congressional Record* before publication, and commented that one of the major factors accounting for inaccuracy in speech texts is the lack of official insistence upon verbatim reports.[4]

3. *Revised editions published by the speaker.* When a speaker spends considerable time polishing his speech texts for publication, it is quite certain that the resulting texts depart in predictable ways from the original manuscripts. For example, a month elapsed between Webster's reply to Hayne and the publication of the speech, during which time Webster apparently altered the text considerably. A comparison of Webster's revised draft with a stenographic record of the speech showed that a collation was scarcely possible.[5] While revised editions provide a sounder basis for analyzing the speaker and his ideas than would a reconstruction by either the speaker or an auditor, the editing process seriously reduces their value for analysis as texts of speeches.

4. *Speaking manuscripts.* It is sometimes possible to obtain a text which the speaker prepared for the platform. However, a problem arises when speakers make errors in reading, change wordings to fit the audience mood or the demands of oral style, and incorporate new ideas and supporting materials when they finally confront the audience or microphone. Franklin D. Roosevelt's speeches, though composed with the greatest of care, nevertheless underwent many small changes in delivery.[6] Indeed, Roosevelt is said to have taken pleasure and pride in his ability to ad lib, and made frequent interpolations as he spoke.[7] Thus even these reading texts are not completely reliable reflections of the delivered speeches.

5. *Stenographic reports.* Within the last century, shorthand stenography has become so highly developed and widespread that a competent stenographer could record a version of the speech which rivaled—and in some cases exceeded—the accuracy of the reading text as a

report of what the speaker said. The speeches of Woodrow Wilson on his western tour in defense of the League of Nations were recorded in this manner.[8] Texts of this type provide good material for analysis of the man, his ideas, and his style; but the stenographer may not be able to hear well, he will be rushed by the speaker's rate, and he may be under pressure of a deadline in translating his shorthand notes into a written text.

6. *Written reproductions from sound recordings.* When a sound recording is available, it is possible to produce a text which corresponds very closely to the original speech. A major advantage of the recording is that the transcriber is not hurried; he may go back over an obscure passage as often as necessary to establish the exact wording, and he may check and recheck the completed transcript against the original to eliminate his own errors of hearing or transcribing. The accuracy of a text produced in this manner is limited only by the perception of the transcriber and the fidelity of his sound recording and reproducing equipment.

7. *Texts produced from audio-visual recordings.* There are limits to the fidelity of sound reproduction which lead to possible error. For example, in producing written records of the Kennedy-Nixon debate, one encounters instances where certain weak phonemes, demanded by the context, are not audible even on tapes of excellent quality. For instance, the expression ". . . these island . . ." occasionally appears. The context requires the z phoneme after "island," but no sound is audible. The transcriber working from sound recordings alone is obliged to record "island;" but he cannot be certain that the absence of the missing phoneme is not due merely to the limitations of his recording instrument. Working with kinescopes or videotapes, it might be possible to determine such instances with greater precision by careful observation of oral movements. Working from audio-visual recordings of the speech, it should be possible to produce essentially perfect texts.

An accurate stenographic account of a speech involves a considerable amount of work; and the amount of effort involved in producing additional fidelity to the original speech is probably related inversely to the amount of remaining error. That is, the last one per cent of error is probably more difficult to extract than the first 20 per cent; and thus the degree of textual accuracy in a given case is likely to be determined by the purposes of the transcriber.

For example, a phonetician who studied the Kennedy-Nixon debates might be interested in Vice President Nixon's use of the General American dialect, or Senator Kennedy's inconsistency in the use of the intrusive final "r." For his purposes, the only useful record of the debates would be a complete phonetic transcription, from which he could reduce the data appropriate to his study. At the other extreme, the newspaper editor, who must meet a deadline which will permit thousands of casual readers to digest the debates along with the morning coffee, will find a first-draft transcript from a stenorette tape more than adequate.

Between the two extremes, in the years ahead, research workers in politics, history, speech, mass communication, psychology, linguistics, and a variety of other fields will apply the analytical methods of their disciplines to these debates. If their analyses are to be meaningful, they should be made from accurate texts, and our purpose has been to supply them. Specifically, it has been our effort to produce texts in standard English orthography, which reflect accurately the verbal productions of the two speakers as these were preserved on magnetic sound tapes of professional broadcast quality.

Although we have used standard orthography, we have tried to avoid the "error of fluency" where false starts, vocalized pauses, and non-vocalized hesitations are omitted from the text of a speaker's remarks, where words or sounds not uttered by the speaker are added for the sake of grammatical form, and where unintelligible sounds are either rendered into proper words or omitted from the text. We have included transcriptions of all false starts and repetitions, all vocalized pauses (such as "uh," "eh," and "er"), and all unusually long vocalized hesitations (indicated by . . .). Occasionally, the speaker uttered clearly recognizable phonemes which constituted no recognizable word. These sounds are recorded as phonemic transcriptions and are set off from the remainder of the text by slash marks (/—/). The phonemic system is that in current use by most American linguists, not the "International Phonetic Alphabet."

Our punctuation of the texts, through the study of pause length, vocal inflection, and context, reflects our considered judgment of the punctuation necessary to reflect faithfully the meaning of what was said. Because paragraph indentations in the text of an extemporaneous speech represent certain judgments about the interrelationships among a speaker's ideas, we have not attempted to divide the speeches into paragraphs. While this procedure would undoubtedly have produced a more attractive page format, it would have introduced an unwarranted bias into possible future analyses by predisposing certain judgments concerning the relationships among ideas and sentences which are best left to the independent judgment of future analysts.

The reader may better judge the usefulness of the texts for various types of analysis if we describe briefly the techniques employed and the conventions which we followed in producing them.

Raw materials for each debate included a published newspaper transcript of the debates and a sound tape recording made by a local radio station from the live broadcast. Working from these two sources, a single auditor produced what appeared to be an accurate transcript of the debate. This was typed on a mimeograph stencil, proofread, and copies were run for further analysis. In all debates, our drafts differed in a substantial number of details from the texts published in the newspaper, and were considerably more accurate.

In the second stage of production, the three transcribers listened to the tape of the debate while reading from the mimeographed texts. When one of the three thought he detected a discrepancy between the text and the tape, the recorder was stopped and the passage was played back repeatedly until a consensus could be reached. Each auditor then recorded the correct version of the passage on his copy of the text. Because it was necessary to avoid auditory fatigue and lapse of attention, each session consumed several hours. When a debate had been proofread in this manner, one transcriber typed a ditto master of the revised draft, checking it against the three proofs.

In the third stage, a single auditor proofread the ditto master against the tape recording again. He noted typographical errors, suspected discrepancies between the tape and the text, and questionable punctuation. These passages were then checked by the three transcribers until a consensus could be reached. Indicated changes were made in the ditto masters and copies of a third draft were reproduced.

This third draft was then used as the basis for the fourth and last stage of production, in which the group proofread the third draft against the tape. When questions concerning this draft arose, the same procedure was employed for arriving at agreement as in previous sessions. Indicated corrections were made on the ditto masters and copies of the fourth and final draft were produced.

We believe the texts which follow represent highly accurate accounts of what was said in the Kennedy-Nixon debates. We hope the texts will be of value to those who are interested—for whatever reason—in accurate accounts of these notable speeches.

NOTES

1. Louis A. Mallory, "Patrick Henry," *A History and Criticism of American Public Address,* II, ed. W. Norwood Brigance (New York: Russell and Russell, 1960), pp. 591-94.

2. J. Jeffery Auer, *An Introduction to Research in Speech* (New York: Harper, 1959), p. 130.

3. David Lawrence, *The Wisconsin State Journal,* May 29, 1961, p. 8.

4. Loren D. Reid, "Factors Contributing to Inaccuracy in the Texts of Speeches," *Papers in Rhetoric,* ed. Donald C. Bryant (St. Louis: privately printed, 1940), pp. 39-40.

5. Elizabeth Gregory McPherson, "Reporting the Debates of Congress," *Quarterly Journal of Speech,* XXXVIII (April, 1942), p. 145.

6. Robert D. King, "Franklin D. Roosevelt's Second Inaugural Address: A Study in Text Authenticity," *Quarterly Journal of Speech,* XXVI (April, 1940), p. 441.

7. Auer, *Introduction to Research,* p. 129.

8. Dayton David McKean, "Woodrow Wilson," *A History and Criticism of American Public Address,* II, p. 982.

First Debate, September 26, 1960

HOWARD K. SMITH, moderator: Good evening. The television and radio stations of the United States and their affiliated stations are proud to provide facilities for a discussion of issues in the current political campaign by the two major candidates for the presidency. The candidates need no introduction. The Republican candidate, Vice President Richard M. Nixon, and the Democratic candidate, Senator John F. Kennedy. According to rules set by the candidates themselves, each man shall make an opening statement of approximately eight minutes' duration and a closing statement of approximately three minutes' duration. In between the candidates will answer, or comment upon answers to questions put by a panel of correspondents. In this, the first discussion in a series of four uh— joint appearances, the subject-matter has been agreed, will be restricted to internal or domestic American matters. And now for the first opening statement by Senator John F. Kennedy.

SENATOR KENNEDY: Mr. Smith, Mr. Nixon. In the election of 1860, Abraham Lincoln said the question was whether this nation could exist half-slave or half-free. In the election of 1960, and with the world around us, the question is whether the world will exist half-slave or half-free, whether it will move in the direction of freedom, in the direction of the road that we are taking, or whether it will move in the direction of slavery. I think it will depend in great measure upon what we do here in the United States, on the kind of society that we build, on the kind of strength that we maintain. We discuss tonight domestic issues, but I would not want that to be . . . any implication to be given that this does not involve directly our struggle with Mr. Khrushchev for survival. Mr. Khrushchev is in New York, and he maintains the Communist offensive throughout the world because of the productive power of the Soviet Union itself. The Chinese Communists have always had a large population. But they are important and dangerous now because they are mounting a major effort within their own country. The kind of country we have here, the kind of society we have, the kind of strength we build in the United States will be the defense of freedom. If we do well here, if we meet our obligations, if we're moving ahead, then I think freedom will be secure around the world. If we fail, then freedom fails. Therefore, I think the question before the American people is: Are we doing as much as we can do? Are we as strong as we should be? Are we as strong as we must be if we're going to maintain our independence, and if we're going to maintain and hold out the hand of friendship to those who look to us for assistance, to those who look to us for survival? I should make it very clear that I do not think we're doing enough, that I am not satisfied as an American with the progress that we're making. This is a great country, but I think it could be a greater country; and this is a powerful country, but I think it could be a more powerful country. I'm not satisfied to have fifty per cent of our steel-mill capacity unused. I'm not satisfied when the United States had last year the lowest rate of economic growth of any major industrialized society in the world. Because economic growth means strength and vitality; it means we're able to sustain our defenses; it means we're able to meet our commitments abroad. I'm not satisfied when we have over nine billion dollars worth of food—some of it rotting—even though there is a hungry world, and even though four million Americans wait every month for a food package from the government, which averages five cents a day per individual. I saw cases in West Virginia, here in the United States, where children took home part of their school lunch in order to feed their families because I don't think we're meeting our obligations toward these Americans. I'm not satisfied when the Soviet Union is turning out twice as many scientists and engineers as we are. I'm not satisfied when many of our teachers are inadequately paid, or when our children go to school part-time shifts. I think we should have an educational system second to none. I'm not satisfied when I see men like Jimmy Hoffa—in charge of the largest union in the United States—still free. I'm not satisfied when we are failing to develop the natural resources of the United States to the fullest. Here in the United States, which developed the Tennessee Valley and which built the Grand Coulee and the other dams in the Northwest United States . . . at the present rate of hydropower production—and that is the hallmark of an industrialized society—the Soviet Union by 1975 will be— d— be producing more power than we are. These are all the things, I think, in this country that can make our society strong, or can mean that it stands still. I'm not satisfied until every American enjoys his full constitutional rights. If a Negro baby is born—and this is true also of Puerto Ricans and Mexicans in some of our cities—he has about one-half as much chance to get through high school as a white baby. He has one-third as much chance to get through college as a white . . . student. He has about a third as much chance to be a professional man, about half as much chance to own a house. He has about uh— four times as much chance that he'll be out of work in his life as the white baby. I think we can do better. I don't want the talents of any American to go to waste. I know that there are those who say that we want to turn everything over to the government. I don't at all. I want the individuals to meet their responsibilities. And I want the states to meet their responsibilities. But I think there is also a national responsibility. The argument has been used against every piece of social legislation in the last twenty-five years. The people of the United States individually could not have developed the Tennessee Valley; collectively they could have. A cotton farmer in Georgia or a peanut farmer or a dairy farmer in Wisconsin and Minnesota, he cannot protect himself against the forces of supply and demand in the market place; but working together in effective governmental programs he can do so. Seventeen million Americans, who live over sixty-five on an average Social Security check of about seventy-eight dollars a month, they're not able to sustain themselves individually, but they can sustain themselves through the social security system. I don't believe in big government, but I believe in effective governmental action. And I think that's the only way that the United States is going to maintain its freedom. It's the only way that we're going to move ahead. I think we can do a better job. I think we're going to have to do a better job if we are going to meet the responsibilities which time and events have placed upon us. We cannot turn the job over to anyone else. If the United States fails, then the whole cause of freedom fails. And I think it depends in great measure on what we do here in this country. The reason Franklin Roosevelt was a good neighbor in Latin America was because he was a good neighbor in the United States. Because they felt that the American society was moving again. I want us to recapture that image. I want people in Latin America and Africa and Asia to start to look to America; to see how we're doing things; to wonder what the president of the United States is doing; and not to look at Khrushchev, or look at the Chinese Communists. That is the obligation upon our generation. In 1933, Franklin Roosevelt said in his inaugural that this generation of Americans has a rendezvous with destiny. I think our generation of Americans has the same rendezvous. The question now is: Can freedom be maintained under the most severe tack— attack it has ever known? I think it can be. And I think in the final analysis it depends upon what we do here. I think it's time America started moving again.

MR. SMITH: And now the opening statement by Vice President Richard M. Nixon.

MR. NIXON: Mr. Smith, Senator Kennedy. The things that Senator Kennedy has said many of us can agree with. There is no question but that we cannot discuss our internal affairs in the United States without recognizing that they have a tremendous bearing on our international position. There is no question but that this nation cannot stand still; because we are in a deadly competition, a competition not only with the men in the Kremlin, but the men in Peking. We're ahead in this competition, as Senator Kennedy, I think, has implied. But when you're in a race, the only way to stay ahead is to move ahead. And I subscribe completely to the spirit that Senator Kennedy has expressed tonight, the spirit that the United States should move ahead. Where, then, do we disagree? I think we disagree on the implication of his remarks tonight and on the statements that he has made on many occasions during his campaign to the effect that the United States has been standing still. We heard tonight, for example, the statement made that our growth in national product last year was the lowest of any industrial nation in the world. Now last year, of course, was 1958. That happened to be a recession year. But when we look at the growth of G.N.P. this year, a year of recovery, we find that it's six and nine-tenths per cent and one of the highest in the world today. More about that later. Looking then to this problem of how the United States should move ahead and where the United States is moving, I think it is well that we take the advice of a very famous campaigner: Let's look at the record. Is the United States standing still? Is it true that this Administration, as Senator Kennedy has charged, has been an Admin— ministration of retreat, of defeat, of stagnation? Is it true that, as far as this country is concerned, in the field of electric power, in all of the fields that he has mentioned, we have not been moving ahead? Well, we have a comparison that we can make. We have the record of the Truman Administration· of seven and a half years and the seven and a half years of the Eisenhower Administration. When we compare these two records in the areas that Senator Kennedy has— has discussed tonight, I think we find that America has been moving ahead. Let's take schools. We have built more schools in these last seven and a half years than we built in the previous seven and a half, for that matter in the previous twenty years. Let's take hydroelectric power. We have developed more hydroelectric power in these seven and a half years than was developed in any previous administration in history. Let us take hospitals. We find that more have been built in this Administration than in the previous Administration. The same is true of highways. Let's put it in terms that all of us can understand. We often hear gross national product discussed and in that respect may I say that when we compare the growth in this Administration with that of the previous Administration that then there was a total growth of eleven per cent over seven years; in this Administration there has been a total growth of nineteen per cent over seven years. That shows that there's been more growth in this Administration than in its predecessor. But let's not put it there; let's put it in terms of the average family. What has happened to you? We find that your wages have gone up five times as much in the Eisenhower Administration as they did in the Truman Administration. What about the prices you pay? We find that the prices you pay went up five times as much in the Truman Administration as they did in the Eisenhower Administration. What's the net result of this? This means that the average family income went up fifteen per cent in the Eisenhower years as against two per cent in the Truman years. Now, this is not standing still. But, good as this record is, may I emphasize it isn't enough. A record is never something to stand on. It's something to build on. And in building on this record, I believe that we have the secret for progress, we know the way to progress. And I think, first of all, our own record proves that we know the way. Senator Kennedy has suggested that he believes he knows the way. I respect the sincerity which he m— which he makes that suggestion. But on the other hand, when we look at the various programs that he offers, they do not seem to be new. They seem to be simply retreads of the programs of the Truman Administration which preceded it. And I would suggest that during the course of the evening he might indicate those areas in which his programs are new, where they will mean more progress than we had then. What kind of programs are we for? We are for programs that will expand educational opportunities, that will give to all Americans their equal chance for education, for all of the things which are necessary and dear to the hearts of our people. We are for programs, in addition, which will see that our medical care for the aged are— is— are much— is much better handled than it is at the present time. Here again, may I indicate that Senator Kennedy and I are not in disagreement as to the aims. We both want to help the old people. We want to see that they do have adequate medical care. The question is the means. I think that the means that I advocate will reach that goal better than the means that he advocates. I could give better examples, but for— for whatever it is, whether it's in the field of housing, or health, or medical care, or schools, or the eh— development of electric power, we have programs which we believe will move America, move her forward and build on the wonderful record that we have made over these past seven and a half years. Now, when we look at these programs, might I suggest that in evaluating them we often have a tendency to say that the test of a program is how much you're spending. I will concede that in all the areas to which I have referred Senator Kennedy would have the spe— federal government spend more than I would have it spend. I costed out the cost of the Democratic platform. It runs a minimum of thirteen and two-tenths billions dollars a year more than we are presently spending to a maximum of eighteen billion dollars a year more than we're presently spending. Now the Republican platform will cost more too. It will cost a minimum of four billion dollars a year more, a maximum of four and nine-tenths billion dollar a year more than we're presently spending. Now, does this mean that his program is better than ours? Not at all. Because it isn't a question of how much the federal government spends; it isn't a question of which government does the most. It's a question of which administration does the right thing. And in our case, I do believe that our programs will stimulate the creative energies of a hundred and eighty million free Americans. I believe the programs that Senator Kennedy advocates will have a tendency to stifle those creative energies. I believe, in other words, that his program would lead to the stagnation of the motive power that we need in this country to get progress. The final point that I would like to make is this: Senator Kennedy has suggested in his speeches that we lack compassion for the poor, for the old, and for others that are unfortunate. Let us understand throughout this campaign that his motives and mine are sincere. I know what it means to be poor. I know what it means to see people who are unemployed. I know Senator Kennedy feels as deeply about these problems as I do, but our disagreement is not about the goals for America but only about the means to reach those goals.

MR. SMITH: Thank you, Mr. Nixon. That completes the opening statements, and now the candidates will answer questions or comment upon one another's answers to questions, put by correspondents of the networks. The correspondents: [*introducing themselves:* "I'm Sander Vanocur, NBC News;" "I'm Charles Warren, Mutual News;" "I'm Stuart Novins, CBS News;" "Bob Fleming, ABC News."] The first question to Senator Kennedy from Mr. Fleming.

MR. FLEMING: Senator, the Vice President in his campaign has said that you were naive and at times immature. He has raised the question of leadership. On this issue, why do you think people should vote for you rather than the Vice President?

MR. KENNEDY: Well, the Vice President and I came to the Congress together . . . 1946; we both served in the Labor Committee. I've been there now for fourteen years, the same period of time that he has, so that our experience in uh— government is comparable. Secondly, I think the question is uh— what are the programs that we advocate, what is the party record that we lead? I come out of the Democratic party, which in this century has produced Woodrow Wilson and Franklin Roosevelt and Harry Truman, and which supported and sustained these programs which I've discussed tonight. Mr. Nixon comes out of the Republican party. He was nominated by it. And it is a fact that through most of these last twenty-five years the Republican leadership has opposed federal aid for education, medical care for the aged, development of the Tennessee Valley, development of our natural resources. I think Mr. Nixon is an effective leader of his party. I hope he would grant me the same. The question before us is: which point of view and which party do we want to lead the United States?

MR. SMITH: Mr. Nixon, would you like to comment on that statement?

MR. NIXON: I have no comment.

MR. SMITH: The next question: Mr. Novins.

MR. NOVINS: Mr. Vice President, your campaign stresses the value of your eight-year experience, and the question arises as to whether that experience was as an observer or as a participant or as an initiator of policy-making. Would you tell us please specifically what major proposals you have made in the last eight years that have been adopted by the Administration?

MR. NIXON: It would be rather difficult to cover them in eight and— in two and a half minutes. I would suggest that these proposals could be mentioned. First, after each of my foreign trips I have made recommendations that have been adopted. For example, after my first trip abroad— abroad, I strongly recommended that we increase our exchange programs particularly as they related to exchange of persons . . . of leaders in the labor field and in the information field. After my trip to South America, I made recommendations that a separate inter-American lending agency be set up which the South American nations would like much better than a lend—than to participate in the lending agencies which treated all the countries of the world the same. Uh— I have made other recommendations after each of the other trips; for example, after my trip abroad to Hungary I made some recommendations with regard to the Hungarian refugee situation which were adopted, not only by the President but some of them were enacted into law by the Congress. Within the Administration, as a chairman of the President's Committee on Price Stability and Economic Growth, I have had the opportunity to make recommendations which have been adopted within the Administration and which I think have been reasonably effective. I know Senator Kennedy suggested in his speech at Cleveland yesterday that that committee had not been particularly effective. I would only suggest that while we do not take the credit for it—I would not presume to—that since that committee has been formed the price line has been held very well within the United States.

MR. KENNEDY: Well, I would say in the latter that the—and that's what I found uh— somewhat unsatisfactory about the figures uh— Mr. Nixon, that you used in your previous speech, when you talked about the Truman Administration. You— Mr. Truman came to office in nineteen uh— forty-four and at the end of the war, and uh— difficulties that were facing the United States during that period of transition—1946 when price controls were lifted—so it's rather difficult to use an over-all figure taking those seven and a half years and comparing them to the last eight years. I prefer to take the over-all percentage record of the last twenty years of the Democrats and the eight years of the Republicans to show an over-all period of growth. In regard to uh— price stability uh— I'm not aware that that committee did produce recommendations that ever were certainly before the Congress from the point of view of legislation in regard to controlling prices. In regard to the exchange of students and labor unions, I am chairman of the subcommittee on Africa and I think that one of the most unfortunate phases of our policy towards that country was the very minute number of exchanges that we had. I think it's true of Latin America also. We did come forward with a program of students for the Congo of over three hundred which was more than the federal government had for all of Africa the previous year, so that I don't think that uh— we have moved at least in those two areas with sufficient vigor.

MR. SMITH: The next question to Senator Kennedy from Mr. Warren.

MR. WARREN: Uh— Senator Kennedy, during your brief speech a few minutes ago you mentioned farm surpluses.

MR. KENNEDY: That's correct.

MR. WARREN: I'd like to ask this: It's a fact, I think, that presidential candidates traditionally make promises to farmers. Lots of people, I think, don't understand why the government pays farmers for not producing certain crops . . . or paying farmers if they overproduce for that matter. Now, let me ask, sir, why can't the farmer operate like the business man who operates a factory? If an auto company overproduces a certain model car Uncle Sam doesn't step in and buy up the surplus. Why this constant courting of the farmer?

MR. KENNEDY: Well, because I think that if the federal government moved out of the program and withdrew its supports uh— then I think you would have complete uh— economic chaos. The farmer plants in the spring and harvests in the fall. There are hundreds of thousands of them. They really don't— they're not able to control their market very well. They bring their crops in or their livestock in, many of them about the same time. They have only a few purchasers . . . that buy their milk or their hogs—a few large companies in many cases—and therefore the farmer is not in a position to bargain very effectively in the market place. I think the experience of the twenties has shown what a free market could do to agriculture. And if the agricultural economy collapses, then the economy of the rest of the United States sooner or later will collapse. The farmers are the number one market for the automobile industry of the United States. The automobile industry is the number one market for steel. So if the farmers' economy continues to decline as sharply as it has in recent years, then I think you would have a recession in the rest of the country. So I think the case for the government intervention is a good one. Secondly, my objection to present farm policy is that there are no effective controls to bring supply and demand into better balance. The dropping of the support price in order to limit production does not work, and we now have the highest uh— surpluses—nine billion dollars worth. We've had a uh— higher tax load from the Treasury for the farmer in the last few years with the lowest farm income in many years. I think that this farm policy has failed. In my judgment the only policy that will work will be for effective supply and demand to be in balance. And that can only be done through governmental action. I therefore suggest that in those basic commodities which are supported, that the federal government, after endorsement by the farmers in that commodity, attempt to bring supply and demand into balance—attempt effective production controls—so that we won't have that five or six per cent surplus which breaks the price fif-

teen or twenty per cent. I think Mr. Benson's program has failed. And I
must say, after reading the Vice President's speech before the farmers, as
he read mine, I don't believe that it's very much different from Mr. Benson's. I don't think it provides effective governmental controls. I think the
support prices are tied to the average market price of the last three years,
which was Mr. Benson's theory. I therefore do not believe that this is a
sharp enough breach with the past to give us any hope of success for
the future.

MR. SMITH: Mr. Nixon, comment?

MR. NIXON: I of course disagree with Senator Kennedy insofar as his
suggestions as to what should be done uh— with re— on the farm program.
He has made the suggestion that what we need is to move in the direction
of more government controls, a suggestion that would also mean raising
prices uh— that the consumers pay for products and im— and imposing
upon the farmers uh— controls on acreage even far more than they have
today. I think this is the wrong direction. I don't think this has worked
in the past; I do not think it will work in the future. The program that I
have advocated is one which departs from the present program that we
have in this respect. It recognizes that the government has a responsibility
to get the farmer out of the trouble he presently is in because the government got him into it. And that's the fundamental reason why we can't let
the farmer go by himself at the present time. The farmer produced these
surpluses because the government asked him to through legislation during
the war. Now that we have these surpluses, it's our responsibility to indemnify the farmer during that period that we get rid of the farmer uh— the
surpluses. Until we get the surpluses off the farmer's back, however, we
should have a program such as I announced, which will see that farm
income holds up. But I would propose holding that income up not through
a type of program that Senator Kennedy has suggested that would raise
prices, but one that would indemnify the farmer, pay the farmer in kind
uh— from the products which are in surplus.

MR. SMITH: The next question to Vice President Nixon from Mr.
Vanocur.

MR. VANOCUR: Uh— Mr. Vice President, since the question of executive
leadership is a very important campaign issue, I'd like to follow Mr.
Novins' question. Now, Republican campaign slogans—you'll see them on
signs around the country as you did last week—say it's experience that
counts—that's over a picture of yourself; sir uh— implying that you've
had more governmental executive decision-making uh— experience than
uh— your opponent. Now, in his news conference on August twenty-
fourth, President Eisenhower was asked to give one example of a major
idea of yours that he adopted. His reply was, and I'm quoting: "If you
give me a week I might think of one. I don't remember." Now that was a
month ago, sir, and the President hasn't brought it up since, and I'm

wondering, sir, if you can clarify which version is correct—the one put out by Republican campaign leaders or the one put out by President Eisenhower?

MR. NIXON: Well, I would suggest, Mr. Vanocur, that uh— if you know the President, that was probably a facetious remark. Uh— I would also suggest that insofar as his statement is concerned, that I think it would be improper for the President of the United States to disclose uh— the instances in which members of his official family had made recommendations, as I have made them through the years to him, which he has accepted or rejected. The President has always maintained and very properly so that he is entitled to get what advice he wants from his cabinet and from his other advisers without disclosing that to anybody—including as a matter of fact the Congress. Now, I can only say this. Through the years I have sat in the National Security Council. I have been in the cabinet. I have met with the legislative leaders. I have met with the President when he made the great decisions with regard to Lebanon, Quemoy and Matsu, other matters. The President has asked for my advice. I have given it. Sometimes my advice has been taken. Sometimes it has not. I do not say that I have made the decisions. And I would say that no president should ever allow anybody else to make the major decisions. The president only makes the decisions. All that his advisers do is to give counsel when he asks for it. As far as what experience counts and whether that is experience that counts, that isn't for me to say. Uh— I can only say that my experience is there for the people to consider; Senator Kennedy's is there for the people to consider. As he pointed out, we came to the Congress in the same year. His experience has been different from mine. Mine has been in the executive branch. His has been in the legislative branch. I would say that the people now have the opportunity to evaluate his as against mine and I think both he and I are going to abide by whatever the people decide.

MR. SMITH: Senator Kennedy.

MR. KENNEDY: Well, I'll just say that the question is of experience . . . and the question also is uh— what our judgment is of the future, and what our goals are for the United States, and what ability we have to implement those goals. Abraham Lincoln came to the presidency in 1860 after a rather . . . little known uh— session in the House of Representatives and after being defeated for the Senate in fifty-eight and was a distinguished president. There's no certain road to the presidency. There are no guarantees that uh— if you take uh— one road or another that you will be a successful president. I have been in the Congress for fourteen years. I have voted in the last uh— eight years uh— and the Vice President was uh— presiding over the Senate and meeting his other responsibilities. I have met uh— decisions over eight hundred times on matters which affect not only the domestic security of the United States, but as a member of the

Senate Foreign Relations Committee. The question really is: which candidate and which party can meet the problems that the United States is going to face in the sixties?

MR. SMITH: The next question to Senator Kennedy from Mr. Novins.

MR. NOVINS: Senator Kennedy, in connection with these problems of the future that you speak of, and the program that you enunciated earlier in your direct talk, you call for expanding some˙of the welfare programs for schools, for teacher salaries, medical care, and so forth; but you also call for reducing the federal debt. And I'm wondering how you, if you're president in January, would go about paying the bill for all this. Does this mean that you—*

MR. KENNEDY: I didn't indicate* . . . I did not advocate reducing the federal debt because I don't believe that you're going to be able to reduce the federal debt very much in nineteen sixty-one, two, or three. I think you have heavy obligations which affect our security, which we're going to have to meet. And therefore I've never suggested we should uh— be able to retire the debt substantially, or even at all in nineteen sixty-one or two.

MR. NOVINS: Senator, I believe in— in one of your speeches—

MR. KENNEDY: No, never.

MR. NOVINS: —you suggested that reducing the interest rate would help toward—

MR. KENNEDY: No. No. Not reducing the interest—**

MR. NOVINS: —a reduction of the Federal debt.**

MR. KENNEDY: —reducing the interest rate. In my judgment, the hard money, tight money policy, fiscal policy of this Administration has contributed to the slow-down in our economy, which helped bring the recession of fifty-four; which made the recession of fifty-eight rather intense, and which has slowed, somewhat, our economic activity in 1960. What I have talked about, however, the kind of programs that I've talked about, in my judgment, are uh— fiscally sound. Medical care for the aged, I would put under social security. The Vice President and I disagree on this. The program—the Javits-Nixon or the Nixon-Javits program—would have cost, if fully used uh— six hundred million dollars by the government per year, and six hundred million dollars by the state. The program which I advocated, which failed by five votes in the United States Senate, would have put medical care for the aged in Social Security, and would have been paid for through the Social Security System and the Social Security tax. Secondly, I support federal aid to education and federal aid for teachers' salaries. I think that's a good investment. I think we're going to have to do it. And I think to heap the burden further on

* The opening words of Mr. Kennedy's reply overlapped the last few words of this portion of Mr. Novins' question, partially obscuring both.

** These two remarks overlapped and partially obscured each other.

the property tax, which is already strained in many of our communities, will provide, will make sh— insure, in my opinion, that many of our children will not be adequately educated, and many of our teachers not adequately compensated. There is no greater return to an economy or to a society than an educational system second to none. On the question of the development of natural resources, I would pay as you go in the sense that they would be balanced and the power revenues would bring back sufficient money to finance the projects, in the same way as the Tennessee Valley. I believe in the balanced budget. And the only conditions under which I would unbalance the budget would be if there was a grave national emergency or a serious recession. Otherwise, with a steady rate of economic growth—and Mr. Nixon and Mr. Rockefeller, in their meeting, said a five per cent economic growth would bring by 1962 ten billion dollars extra in tax revenues. Whatever is brought in, I think that we can finance essential programs within a balanced budget, if business remains orderly.

MR. SMITH: Mr. Nixon, your comment?

MR. NIXON: Yes. I think what Mr. Novins was referring to was not one of Senator Kennedy's speeches, but the Democratic platform, which did mention cutting the national debt. I think, too, that it should be pointed out that . . . of course it is not possible, particularly under the proposals that Senator Kennedy has advocated, either to cut the national debt or to reduce taxes. As a matter of fact it will be necessary to raise taxes. As Senator Kennedy points out that as far as his one proposal is concerned— the one for medical care for the aged—that that would be financed out of Social Security. That, however, is raising taxes for those who pay Social Security. He points out that he would make pay-as-you-go be the basis for our natural resources development. Where our natural resources development—which I also support, incidentally, however—whenever you uh— uh— in— in— uh— appropriates money for one of these projects, you have to pay now and appropriate the money and the eh— while they eventually do pay out, it doesn't mean that you— the government doesn't have to put out the money this year. And so I would say that in all of these proposals Senator Kennedy has made, they will result in one of two things: either he has to raise taxes or he has to unbalance the budget. If he unbalances the budget, that means you have inflation, and that will be, of course, a very cruel blow to the very people—the older people—that we've been talking about. As far as aid for school construction is concerned, I favor that, as Senator Kennedy did, in January of this year, when he said he favored that rather than aid to s— teacher salaries. I favor that because I believe that's the best way to aid our schools without running any risk whatever of the federal government telling our teachers what to teach.

MR. SMITH: The next question to Vice President Nixon from Mr. Warren.

MR. WARREN: Mr. Vice President you mentioned schools and it was just

yesterday I think you asked for a crash program to raise education standards, and this evening you talked about advances in education. Mr. Vice
President, you said—it was back in 1957—that salaries paid to school
teachers were nothing short of a national disgrace. Higher salaries for
teachers, you added, were important and if the situation wasn't corrected
it could lead to a national disaster. And yet, you refused to vote in the
Senate in order to break a tie vote when that single vote, if it had been yes,
would have granted salary increases to teachers. I wonder if you could
explain that, sir.

MR. NIXON: I'm awfully glad you ge— got that question because as you
know I got into it at the last of my other question and wasn't able to complete the argument. Uh— I think that the reason that I voted against having the federal government uh— pay teachers' salaries was probably the
very reason that concerned Senator Kennedy when in January of this
year, in his kick-off press conference, he said that he favored aid for
school construction, but at that time did not feel that there should be aid
for teachers' salaries—at least that's the way I read his remarks. Now, why
should there be any question about the federal government aiding s—
teachers' salaries? Why did Senator Kennedy take that position then? Why
do I take it now? We both took it then, and I take it now, for this reason:
we want higher teachers' salaries. We need higher teachers' salaries. But
we also want our education to be free of federal control. When the federal
government gets the power to pay teachers, inevitably in my opinion, it
will acquire the power to set standards and to tell the teachers what to
teach. I think this would be bad for the country; I think it would be bad
for the teaching profession. There is another point that should be made.
I favor higher salaries for teachers. But, as Senator Kennedy said in January of this year in this same press conference, the way that you get higher
salaries for teachers is to support school construction, which means that
all of the local school districts in the various states then have money which
is freed to raise the standards for teachers' salaries. I should also point out
this: once you put the responsibility on the federal government for paying
a portion of teachers' salaries, your local communities and your states are
not going to meet the responsibility as much as they should. I believe, in
other words, that we have seen the local communities and the state assuming more of that responsibility. Teachers' salaries very fortunately have
gone up fifty per cent in the last eight years as against only a thirty-four
per cent rise for other salaries. This is not enough; it should be more. But
I do not believe that the way to get more salaries for teachers is to have
the federal government get in with a massive program. My objection here
is not the cost in dollars. My objection here is the potential cost in controls and eventual . . . freedom for the American people by giving the
federal government power over education, and that is the greatest power
a government can have.

MR. SMITH: Senator Kennedy's comment?

MR. KENNEDY: When uh— the Vice President quotes me in January, sixty, I do not believe the federal government should pay directly teachers' salaries, but that was not the issue before the Senate in February. The issue before the Senate was that the money would be given to the state. The state then could determine whether the money would be spent for school construction or teacher salaries. On that question the Vice President and I disagreed. I voted in favor of that proposal and supported it strongly, because I think that that provided assistance to our teachers for their salaries without any chance of federal control and it is on that vote that th— Mr. Nixon and I disagreed, and his tie vote uh— defeated . . . his breaking the tie defeated the proposal. I don't want the federal government paying teachers' salaries directly. But if the money will go to the states and the states can then determine whether it shall go for school construction or for teachers' salaries, in my opinion you protect the local authority over the school board and the school committee. And therefore I think that was a sound proposal and that is why I supported it and I regret that it did not pass. Secondly, there have been statements made that uh— the Democratic platform would cost a good deal of money and that I am in favor of unbalancing the budget. That is wholly wrong, wholly in error, and it is a fact that in the last eight years the Democratic Congress has reduced the appropri— the requests for the appropriations by over ten billion dollars. That is not my view and I think it ought to be stated very clearly on the record. My view is that you can do these programs—and they should be carefully drawn—within a balanced budget if our economy is moving ahead.

MR. SMITH: The next question to Senator Kennedy from Mr. Vanocur.

MR. VANOCUR: Senator, you've been promising the voters that if you are elected president you'll try and push through Congress bills on medical aid to the aged, a comprehensive minimum hourly wage bill, federal aid to education. Now, in the August post-convention session of the Congress, when you at least held up the possibility you could one day be president and when you had overwhelming majorities, especially in the Senate, you could not get action on these bills. Now how do you feel that you'll be able to get them in January—

MR. KENNEDY: Well as you take the bills—*

MR. VANOCUR: —if you weren't able to get them in August?*

MR. KENNEDY: If I may take the bills, we did pass in the Senate a bill uh— to provide a dollar twenty-five cent minimum wage. It failed because the House did not pass it and the House failed by eleven votes. And I might say that two-thirds of the Republicans in the House voted against a dollar twenty-five cent minimum wage and a majority of the Democrats sustained it—nearly two-thirds of them voted for the dollar twenty-five.

* The opening words of Mr. Kennedy's reply overlapped the last few words of Mr. Vanocur's question, partially obscuring both.

We were threatened by a veto if we passed a dollar and a quarter—it's extremely difficult with the great power that the president does to pass any bill when the president is opposed to it. All the president needs to sustain his veto of any bill is one-third plus one in either the House or the Senate. Secondly, we passed a federal aid to education bill in the Senate. It failed to come to the floor of the House of Representatives. It was killed in the Rules Committee. And it is a fact in the August session that the four members of the Rules Committee who were Republicans joining with two Democrats voted against sending the aid to education bill to the floor of the House. Four Democrats voted for it. Every Republican on the Rules Committee voted against sending that bill to be considered by the members of the House of Representatives. Thirdly, on medical care for the aged, this is the same fight that's been going on for twenty-five years in Social Security. We wanted to tie it to Social Security. We offered an amendment to do so. Forty-four Democrats voted for it, one Republican voted for it. And we were informed at the time it came to a vote that if it was adopted the President of the United States would veto it. In my judgment, a vigorous Democratic president supported by a Democratic majority in the House and Senate can win the support for these programs. But if you send a Republican president and a Democratic majority and the threat of a veto hangs over the Congress, in my judgment you will continue what happened in the August session, which is a clash of parties and inaction.

MR. SMITH: Mr. Nixon, comment?

MR. NIXON: Well obviously my views are a little different. First of all, I don't see how it's possible for a one-third of a body, such as the Republicans have in the House and the Senate to stop two-thirds, if the two-thirds are adequately led. I would say, too, that when Senator Kennedy refers to the action of the House Rules Committee, there are eight Democrats on that committee and four Republicans. It would seem to me again that it is very difficult to blame the four Republicans for the eight Democrats' not getting a something through that particular committee. I would say further that to blame the President in his veto power for the inability of the Senator and his colleagues to get action in this special session uh—misses the mark. When the president exercises his veto power, he has to have the people upo— behind him, not just a third of the Congress. Because let's consider it. If the majority of the members of the Congress felt that these particular proposals were good issues—the majority of those who were Democrats—why didn't they pass them and send to the President and get a veto and have an issue? The reason why these particular bills in these various fields that have been mentioned were not passed was not because the President was against them; it was because the people were against them. It was because they were too extreme. And I am convinced that the alternate proposals that I have, that the Republicans have in the field of health, in the field of education, in the field of welfare, because they are not extreme, because they will accomplish the end uh— without too great cost in dollars or in freedom, that they could get through the next Congress.

MR. SMITH: The next question to Vice President Nixon fa— from Mr. Fleming.

MR. FLEMING: Mr. Vice President, do I take it then you believe that you can work better with Democratic majorities in the House and Senate than Senator Kennedy could work with Democratic majorities in the House and Senate?

MR. NIXON: I would say this: that we, of course, expect to pick up some seats in both in the House and the Senate. Uh— We would hope to control the House, to get a majority in the House uh— in this election. We cannot, of course, control the Senate. I would say that a president will be able to lead—a president will be able to get his program through—to the effect that he has the support of the country, the support of the people. Sometimes we—we get the opinion that in getting programs through the House or the Senate it's purely a question of legislative finagling and all that sort of thing. It isn't really that. Whenever a majority of the people are for a program, the House and the Senate responds to it. And whether this House and Senate, in the next session is Democratic or Republican, if the country will have voted for the candidate for the presidency and for the proposals that he has made, I believe that you will find that the president, if it were a Republican, as it would be in my case, would be able to get his program through that Congress. Now, I also say that as far as Senator Kennedy's proposals are concerned, that, again, the question is not simply one of uh— a presidential veto stopping programs. You must always remember that a president can't stop anything unless he has the people behind him. And the reason President Eisenhower's vetoes have been sustained—the reason the Congress does not send up bills to him which they think will be vetoed—is because the people and the Congress, the majority of them, know the country is behind the President.

MR. SMITH: Senator Kennedy.

MR. KENNEDY: Well, now let's look at these bills that the Vice President suggests were too extreme. One was a bill for a dollar twenty-five cents an hour for anyone who works in a store or company that has a million dollars a year business. I don't think that's extreme at all; and yet nearly two-thirds to three-fourths of the Republicans in the House of Representatives voted against that proposal. Secondly was the federal aid to education bill. It— it was a very uh— because of the defeat of teacher salaries, it was not a bill that uh— met in my opinion the need. The fact of the matter is it was a bill that less than you recommended, Mr. Nixon, this morning in your proposal. It was not an extreme bill and yet we could not get one Republican to join, at least I think four of the eight Democrats voted to send it to the floor of the House—not one Republican—and they joined with those Democrats who were opposed to it. I don't say the Democrats are united in their support of the program. But I do say a majority are. And I say a majority of the Republicans are opposed to it. The third is medical care for the aged which is tied to Social Security, which is financed out of Social Security funds. It does not put a deficit on the Treasury. The proposal advanced by you and by Mr. Javits would have cost six hundred millions of dollars—Mr. Rockefeller rejected it in New York, said he didn't agree with the financing at all, said it ought to be on Social Security. So these are three programs which are quite moderate. I think it shows the difference between the two parties. One party is ready to move in these programs. The other party gives them lip service.

MR. SMITH: Mr. Warren's question for Senator Kennedy.

MR. WARREN: Senator Kennedy, on another subject, Communism is so often described as an ideology or a belief that exists somewhere other than in the United States. Let me ask you, sir: just how serious a threat to our national security are these Communist subversive activities in the United States today?

MR. KENNEDY: Well, I think they're serious. I think it's a matter that we should continue to uh— give uh— great care and attention to. We should support uh— the laws which the United States has passed in order to protect us from uh— those who would destroy us from within. We should sustain uh— the Department of Justice in its efforts and the F.B.I., and we should be continually alert. I think if the United States is maintaining a strong society here in the United States, I think that we can meet any internal threat. The major threat is external and will continue.

MR. SMITH: Mr. Nixon, comment?

MR. NIXON: I agree with Senator Kennedy's appraisal generally in this respect. The question of Communism within the United States has been one that has worried us in the past. It is one that will continue to be a problem for years to come. We have to remember that the cold war that Mr. Khrushchev is waging and his colleagues are waging, is waged all over the world and it's waged right here in the United States. That's why we have to continue to be alert. It is also essential in being alert that we be fair; fair because by being fair we uphold the very freedoms that the Communists would destroy. We uphold the standards of conduct which they would never follow. And, in this connection, I think that uh—we . . . must look to the future having in mind the fact that we fight Communism at home not only by our laws to deal with Communists uh— the few who do become Communists and the few who do become tra— fellow travelers, but we also fight Communism /ən/ . . . at home by moving against those various injustices which exist in our society which the Communists feed upon. And in that connection I again would say that while Senator Kennedy says we are for the status quo, I . . . do . . . believe that he uh— would agree that I am just as sincere in believing that my proposals for federal aid to education, my proposals for health care are just as sincerely held as his. The question again is not one of goals—we're for those goals— it's one of means.

MR. SMITH: Mr. Vanocur's question for Vice President Nixon.

MR. VANOCUR: Mr. Vice President uh— in one of your earlier statements you said we've moved ahead, we've built more schools, we've built more hospitals. Now, sir, isn't it true that the building of more schools is a . . . local matter for financing? Uh— Were you claiming that the Eisenhower Administration was responsible for the building of these schools, or is it the local school districts that provide for it?

MR. NIXON: Not at all. As a matter of fact your question brings out a point that I very glad to make. Too often in appraising whether we are moving ahead or not we think only of what the federal government is doing. Now that isn't the test of whether America moves. The test of whether America moves is whether the federal government, plus the state government, plus the local government, plus the biggest segment of all— individual enterprise—moves. We have for example a gross national product of approximately five hundred billion dollars. Roughly a hundred billion to a hundred and a quarter billion of that is the result of government activity. Four hundred billion, approximately, is a result of what individuals do. Now, the reason the Eisenhower Administration has moved, the reason that we've had the funds, for example, locally to build the schools, and the hospitals, and the highways, to make the progress that we have, is because this Administration has encouraged individual enterprise; and it has resulted in the greatest expansion of the private sector of the economy that has ever been witnessed in an eight-year period. And that is growth. That is the growth that we are looking for; it is the growth that this Administration has supported and that its policies have stimulated.

MR. SMITH: Senator Kennedy.

MR. KENNEDY: Well, I must say that the reason that the schools have been constructed is because the local school districts were willing to increase the property taxes to a tremendously high figure—in my opinion, almost to the point of diminishing returns in order to sustain these schools. Secondly, I think we have a rich uh— country. And I think we have a powerful country. I think what we have to do, however, is have the president and the leadership set before our country exactly what we must do in the next decade, if we're going to maintain our security in education, in economic growth, in development of natural resources. The Soviet Union is making great gains. It isn't enough to compare what might have been done eight years ago, or ten years ago, or fifteen years ago, or twenty years ago. I want to compare what we're doing with what our adversaries are doing, so that by the year 1970 the United States is ahead in education, in health, in building, in homes, in economic strength. I think that's the big assignment, the big task, the big function of the federal government.

MR. SMITH: Can I have the summation time please? We've completed our questions and our comments, and in just a moment, we'll have the summation time.

VOICE: This will allow three minutes and twenty seconds for the summation by each candidate.

MR. SMITH: Three minutes and twenty seconds for each candidate. Vice President Nixon, will you make the first summation?

MR. NIXON: Thank you, Mr. Smith. Senator Kennedy. First of all, I think it is well to put in perspective where we really do stand with regard to the Soviet Union in this whole matter of growth. The Soviet Union has been moving faster than we have. But the reason for that is obvious. They start from a much lower base. Although they have been moving faster in growth than we have, we find, for example, today that their total gross national product is only forty-four per cent of our total gross national product. That's the same percentage that it was twenty years ago. And as far as the absolute gap is concerned, we find that the United States is even further ahead than it was twenty years ago. Is this any reason for complacency? Not at all. Because these are determined men. They are fanatical men. And we have to get the very most of uh— out uh— out of our economy. I agree with Senator Kennedy completely on that score. Where we disagree is in the means that we would use to get the most out of our economy. I respectfully submit that Senator Kennedy too often would rely too much on the federal government, on what it would do to solve our problems, to stimulate growth. I believe that when we examine the Democratic platform, when we examine the proposals that he has discussed tonight, when we compare them with the proposals that I have made, that these proposals that he makes would not result in greater growth for this country than would be the case if we followed the programs that I have advocated. There are many of the points that he has made that I would like to comment upon. The one in the field of health is worth mentioning. Our health program—the one that Senator Javits and other Republican Senators, as well as I supported—is one that provides for all people over sixty-five who want health insurance, the opportunity to have it if they want it. It provides a choice of having either government insurance or private insurance. But it compels nobody to have insurance who does not want it. His program under Social Security, would require everybody who had Social Security to take government health insurance whether he wanted it or not. And it would not cover several million people who are not covered by Social Security at all. Here is one place where I think that our program does a better job than his. The other point that I would make is this: this downgrading of how much things cost I think many of our people will understand better when they look at what happened when— during the Truman Administration when the government was spending more than it took in—we found savings over a lifetime eaten up by inflation. We found the people who could least afford it—people on retired incomes uh—people on fixed incomes—we found them unable to meet their bills at the end of the month. It is essential that a man who's president of this country certainly stand for every program that will mean for growth. And I stand for programs that will mean growth and progress. But it is also essential that he not allow a dollar spent that could be better spent by the people themselves.

MR. SMITH: Senator Kennedy, your conclusion.

MR. KENNEDY: The point was made by Mr. Nixon that the Soviet production is only forty-four per cent of ours. I must say that forty-four per cent and that Soviet country is causing us a good deal of trouble tonight. I want to make sure that it stays in that relationship. I don't want to see the day when it's sixty per cent of ours, and seventy and seventy-five and eighty and ninety per cent of ours, with all the force and power that it could bring to bear in order to cause our destruction. Secondly, the Vice President mentioned medical care for the aged. Our program was an amendment to the Kerr bill. The Kerr bill provided assistance to all those who were not on Social Security. I think it's a very clear contrast. In 1935, when the Social Security Act was written, ninety-four out of ninety-five Republicans voted against it. Mr. Landon ran in 1936 to repeal it. In August of 1960, when we tried to get it again, but this time for medical care, we received the support of one Republican in the Senate on this occasion. Thirdly, I think the question before the American people is: as they look at this country and as they look the world around them, the goals are the same for all Americans. The means are at question. The means are at issue. If you feel that everything that is being done now is satisfactory, that the relative power and prestige and strength of the United States is increasing in relation to that of the Communists; that we've b— gaining more security, that we are achieving everything as a nation that we should achieve, that we are achieving a better life for our citizens and greater strength, then I agree. I think you should vote for Mr. Nixon. But if you feel that we have to move again in the sixties, that the function of the president is to set before the people the unfinished business of our society as Franklin Roosevelt did in the thirties, the agenda for our people— what we must do as a society to meet our needs in this country and protect our security and help the cause of freedom. As I said at the beginning, the question before us all, that faces all Republicans and all Democrats, is: can freedom in the next generation . . . conquer, or are the Communists going to be successful? That's the great issue. And if we meet our responsibilities I think freedom will conquer. If we fail, if we fail to move ahead, if we fail to develop sufficient military and economic and social strength here in this country, then I think that uh— the tide could begin to run against us. And I don't want historians, ten years from now, to say, these were the years when the tide ran out for the United States. I want them to say these were the years when the tide came in; these were the years when the United States started to move again. That's the question before the American people, and only you can decide what you want, what you want this country to be, what you want to do with the future. I think we're ready to move. And it is to that great task, if we're successful, that we will address ourselves.

MR. SMITH: Thank you very much, gentlemen. This hour has gone by all too quickly. Thank you very much for permitting us to present the next president of the United States on this unique program. I've been asked by the candidates to thank the American networks and the affiliated stations for providing time and facilities for this joint appearance. Other debates in this series will be announced later and will be on different subjects. This is Howard K. Smith. Good night from Chicago.

Second Debate, October 7, 1960

FRANK MC GEE, moderator: Good evening. This is Frank McGee, NBC News in Washington. This is the second in a series of programs unmatched in history. Never have so many people seen the major candidates for president of the United States at the same time; and never until this series have Americans seen the candidates in face-to-face exchange. Tonight the candidates have agreed to devote the full hour to answering questions on any issue of the campaign. And here tonight are: the Republican candidate, Vice President Richard M. Nixon; and the Democratic candidate, Senator John F. Kennedy. Now representatives of the candidates and of all the radio and television networks have agreed on these rules: neither candidate will make an opening statement or a closing summation; each will be questioned in turn; each will have an opportunity to comment upon the answer of the other; each reporter will ask only one question in turn. He is free to ask any question he chooses. Neither candidate knows what questions will be asked and only the clock will determine who will be asked the last question. These programs represent an unprecedented opportunity for the candidates to present their philosophies and programs directly to the people and for the people to compare these and the candidates. The four reporters on tonight's panel include a newspaperman and a wire service representative. These two were selected by lot by the press secretaries of the candidates from among the reporters traveling with the candidates. The broadcasting representatives were selected by their respective companies. The reporters are: Paul Niven of CBS, Edward P. Morgan of ABC, Alvin Spivak of United Press Interational, and Harold R. Levy of Newsday. Now the first question is from Mr. Niven and is for Vice President Nixon.

MR. NIVEN: Mr. Vice President, Senator Kennedy said last night that the Administration must take responsibility for the loss of Cuba. Would you compare the validity of that statement with the validity of your own statements in previous campaigns that the Truman Administration was responsible for the loss of China to the Communists?

369

MR. NIXON: Well first of all, I don't agree with Senator Kennedy that Cuba is lost and certainly China was lost when this Administration came into power in 1953. As I look at Cuba today, I believe that we are following the right course, a course which is difficult but a course which under the circumstance is the only proper one which will see that the Cuban people get a chance to realize their aspirations of progress through freedom and that they get that with our cooperation with the other organi— of the states in the Organization of American States. Now Senator Kennedy has made some very strong criticisms of my part—or alleged part—in what has happened in Cuba. He points to the fact that I visited Cuba while Mr. Batista was in power there. I can only point out that if we are going to judge the Administrations in terms of our attitude toward dictators, we're glad to have a comparison with the previous administration. There were eleven dictators in South America and in Central America when we came in, in 1953. Today there are only three left including the one in Cuba. We think that's pretty good progress. Senator Kennedy also indicated with regard to Cuba that he thought that I had made a mistake when I was in Cuba in not calling for free elections in that country. Now I'm very surprised that Senator Kennedy, who is on the Foreign Relations Committee, would have made such a statement as this kind. As a matter of fact in his book, *The Strategy for Peace,* he took the right position. And that position is that the United States has a treaty—a treaty with all of the Organization of American States—which prohibits us from interfering in the internal affairs of any other state and prohibits them as well. For me to have made such a statement would been in direct uh— opposition to that treaty. Now with regard to Cuba, let me make one thing clear. There isn't any question but that we will defend our rights there. There isn't any question but that we will defend Guantanamo if it's attacked. There also isn't any question but that the free people of Cuba—the people who want to be free—are going to be supported and that they will attain their freedom. No, Cuba is not lost, and I don't think this kind of defeatist talk by Senator Kennedy helps the situation one bit.

MR. MCGEE: Senator Kennedy, would you care to comment?

MR. KENNEDY: In the first place I've never suggested that Cuba was lost except for the present. In my speech last night I indicated that I thought that Cuba one day again would be free. Where I've been critical of the Administration's policy, and where I criticized Mr. Nixon, was because in his press conference in Havana in 1955, he praised the competence and stability of the bicta— bict— Batista dictatorship—that dictatorship had killed over twenty thousand Cubans in seven years. Secondly, I did not criticize him for not calling for free elections. What I criticized was the failure of the Administration to use its great influence to persuade the Cuban government to hold free elections, particularly in 1957 and 1958. Thirdly, Arthur Gardner, a Republican Ambassador, Earl Smith, a Republican Ambassador, in succession—both have indicated in the past six weeks that they reported to Washington that Castro was a Marxist, that Raul Castro was a Communist, and that they got no effective results. Instead our aid continued to Batista, which was ineffective; we never were on the side of freedom; we never used our influence when we could have used it most effectively—and today Cuba is lost for freedom. I hope some day it will rise; but I don't think it will rise if we continue the same policies toward Cuba that we did in recent years, and in fact towards all of Latin America—when we've almost ignored the needs of Latin America; we've beamed not a single Voice of America program in Spanish to all of Latin America in the last eight years, except for the three months of the Hungarian uh— revolution.

MR. MC GEE: Mr. Morgan, with a question for Senator Kennedy.

MR. MORGAN: Senator, last May, in Oregon, you discussed the possibilities of sending apologies or regrets to Khrushchev over the U-2 incident. Do you think now that that would have done any good? Did you think so then?

MR. KENNEDY: Mr. Morgan, I suggested that if the United States felt that it could save the summit conference that it would have been proper for us to have expressed regrets. In my judgment that statement has been distorted uh— by Mr. Nixon and others in their debates around the country and in their discussions. Mr. Lodge, on "Meet the Press" a month ago, said if there was ever a case when we did not have law on our side it was in the U-2 incident. The U-2 flights were proper from the point of view of protecting our security. But they were not in accordance with international law. And I said that I felt that rather than tell the lie which we told, rather than indicate that the flights would continue—in fact, I believe Mr. Nixon himself said on May fifteenth that the flights would continue even though Mr. Herter testified before the Senate Foreign Relations Committee that they had been canceled as of May twelfth—that it would have been far better that if we had expressed regrets, if that would have saved the summit, and if the summit is useful—and I believe it is. The point that is always left out is the fact that we expressed regrets to Castro this winter; that we expressed regrets—the Eisenhower Administration expressed regrets—for a flight over Southern Russia in 1958. We expressed regrets for a flight over Eastern Germany under this Administration. The Soviet Union in 1955 expressed regrets to us over the Bering Sea incident. The Chinese Communists expressed regrets to us over a plane incident in 1956. That is the accepted procedure between nations; and my judgment is that we should follow the advice of Theodore Roosevelt: Be strong; maintain a strong position; but also speak softly. I believe that in those cases where international custom calls for the expression of a regret, if that would have kept the summit going, in my judgment it was a proper action. It's not appeasement. It's not soft. I believe we should be stronger than we now are. I believe we should have a stronger military force. I believe we should increase our strength all over the world. But I don't confuse words with strength; and in my judgment if the summit was useful, if it would have brought us closer to peace, that rather than the lie that we told— which has been criticized by all responsible people afterwards—it would have been far better for us to follow the common diplomatic procedure of expressing regrets and then try to move on.

MR. MCGEE: Mr. Vice President.

MR. NIXON: I think kenne— Senator Kennedy is wrong on three counts. First of all, he's wrong in thinking th— er— even suggesting that Mr. Khrushchev might have continued the conference if we had expressed regrets. He knew these flights were going on long before and that wasn't the reason that he broke up the conference. Second, he's wrong in the analogies that he makes. The United States is a strong country. Whenever we do anything that's wrong, we can express regrets. But when the president of the United States is doing something that's right, something that is for the purpose of defending the security of this country against surprise attack, he can never express regrets or apologize to anybody, including Mr. Khrushchev. Now in that connection Senator Kennedy has criticized the President on the ground not only of not expressing regrets, but because he allowed this flight to take place while the summit conference—or immediately before the summit conference occurred. This seems to me is criticism that again is wrong on his part. We all remember Pearl Harbor. We lost three thousand American lives. We cannot afford an intelligence gap. And I just want to make my position absolutely clear with regard to getting intelligence information. I don't intend to see to it that the United States is ever in a position where, while we're negotiating with the Soviet Union, that we discontinue our intelligence effort. And I don't intend ever to express regrets to Mr. Khrushchev or anybody else if I'm doing something that has the support of the Congress and that is right for the purpose of protecting the security of the United States.

MR. MCGEE: Mr. Spivak with a question for Vice President Nixon.

MR. SPIVAK: Mr. Vice President, you have accused Senator Kennedy of avoiding the civil rights issue when he has been in the South and he has accused you of the same thing. With both North and South listening and watching, would you sum up uh— your own intentions in the field of civil rights if you become president.

MR. NIXON: My intentions in the field of civil rights have been spelled out in the Republican platform. I think we have to make progress first in the field of employment. And there we would give statutory authority to the Committee on Government Contracts, which is an effective way of getting real progress made in this area, since about one out of every four jobs is held by and is allotted by people who have government contracts. Certainly I think all of us agree that when anybody has a government contract, certainly the money that is spent under that contract ought to be disbursed equally without regard to the race or creed or color of the individual who is to be employed. Second, in the field of schools, we believe that there should be provisions whereby the federal government would give assistance to those districts who do want to integrate their schools. That of course was rejected as was the government contracts provision by the special session of the Congress to— in which Mr. Kennedy was quite active. And then as far as other areas are concerned, I think that we have to look to presidential leadership. And when I speak of presidential leadership, I refer for example to our attitude on the sit-in strikes. Here we have a situation which causes all of us concern—causes us concern because of the denial of the rights of people to the equality which we think belongs to everybody. I have talked to Negro mothers. I've heard them explain— try to explain—how they tell their children how they can go into a store and buy a loaf of bread but then can't go into that store and sit at the counter and get a Coca Cola. This is wrong, and we have to do something about it. So, under the circumstances, what do we do? Well what we do is what the Attorney-General of the United States did under the direction of the President: call in the owners of chain stores and get them to take action. Now there are other places where the executive can lead, but let me just sum up by saying this: why do I talk every time I'm in the South on civil rights? Not because I am preaching to the people of the South because this isn't just a Southern problem; it's a Northern problem and a Western problem; it's a problem for all of us. I do it because it's the responsibility of leadership. I do it because we have to solve this problem together. I do it right at this time particularly because when we have Khrushchev in this country—a man who has enslaved millions, a man who has slaughtered thousands—we cannot continue to have a situation where he can point the finger at the United States of America and say that we are denying rights to our citizens. And so I say both the candidates and both the vice presidential candidates, I would hope as well—including Senator Johnson—should talk on this issue at every opportunity.

MR. MCGEE: Senator Kennedy.

MR. KENNEDY: Well, Mr. Nixon hasn't discussed the two basic questions: what is going to be done and what will be his policy on implementing the Supreme Court decision of 1954? Giving aid to schools technically that are trying to carry out the decision is not the great question. Secondly, what's he going to do to provide fair employment? He's been the head of the Committee on Government Contracts that's carried out two cases, both in the District of Columbia. He has not indicated his support of an attempt to provide fair employment practices around the country, so that everyone can get a job regardless of their race or color. Nor has he indicated that he will support Title Three, which would give the Attorney General additional powers to protect Constitutional rights. These are the great questions: equality of education in school. About two per cent of our population of white people are—is illiterate, ten per cent of our colored population. Sixty to seventy per cent of our colored children do not finish high school. These are the questions in these areas that the North and South, East and West are entitled to know. What will be the leadership of the president in these areas to provide equality of opportunity for employment? Equality of opportunity in the field of housing, which could be done on all federal supported housing by a stroke of the president's pen. What will be done to provide equality of education in all sections of the United States? Those are the questions to which the president must establish a moral tone and moral leadership. And I can assure you that if I'm elected president we will do so.

MR. MC GEE: Mr. Levy with a question for Senator Kennedy.

MR. LEVY: Senator, on the same subject, in the past you have emphasized the president's responsibility as a moral leader as well as an executive on civil rights questions. What specifically might the next president do uh— in the event of an uh— an occurrence such as Little Rock or the lunch-counter sit-ins? From the standpoint of —*

MR. KENNEDY: Well let me say that I think that the president operates in a number of different areas. First, as a legislative leader. And as I just said that I believe that the passage of the so-called Title Three, which gives the Attorney General the power to protect Constitutional rights in those cases where it's not possible for the person involved to bring the suit. Secondly, as an executive leader. There have been only six cases brought by this Attorney General under the voting bill passed in 1957 and the voting bill passed in 1960. The right to vote is basic. I do not believe that this Administration has implemented those bills which represent the will of the majority of the Congress on two occasions with vigor. Thirdly, I don't believe that the government contracts division is operated with vigor. Everyone who does business with the government should have the opportunity to make sure that they do not practice discrimination in their hiring. And that's in all sections of the United States. And then fourthly, as a moral leader. There is a very strong moral basis for this concept of equality of opportunity. We are in a very difficult time. We need all the talent we can get. We sit on a conspicuous stage. We are a goldfish bowl before the world. We have to practice what we preach. We set a very high standard for ourselves. The Communists do not. They set a low standard of materialism. We preach in the Declaration of Independence and in the Constitution, in the statement of our greatest leaders, we preach very high standards; and if we're not going to be s— charged before the world with hypocrisy we have to meet those standards. I believe the president of the United States should indicate it. Now lastly, I believe in the case of Little

* The last portion of Mr. Levy's question overlapped with the first few words of Mr. Kennedy's reply, partially obscuring both.

Rock. I would have hoped that the president of the United States would have been possible for him to indicate it clearly that uh— the Supreme Court decision was going to be carried out. I would have hoped that it would have been possible to use marshals to do so. But it wou— uh— evidently uh— under the handling of the case it was not. I would hope an incident like that would not happen. I think if the president is responsible, if he consults with those involved, if he makes it clear that the Supreme Court decision is going to be carried out in a way that the Supreme Court planned—with deliberate speed—then in my judgment, providing he's behind action, I believe we can make uh— progress. Now the present Administration—the President—has said—never indicated what he thought of the 1954 decision. Unless the president speaks, then of course uh— the country doesn't speak, and Franklin Roosevelt said: "The pre— uh— the presidency of the United States is above all a place of moral leadership." And I believe on this great moral issue he should speak out and give his views clearly.

MR. MCGEE: Mr. Vice President.

MR. NIXON: Senator Kennedy has expressed some high hopes in this field, hopes which I think all Americans would share who want some problem—some progress in this area. But let's look at the performance. When he selected his vice presidential running mate, he selected a man who had voted against most of these proposals and a man who opposes them at the present time. Let me s— look also at what I did. I selected a man who stands with me in this field and who will talk with me and work with me on it. Now the Senator referred to the Committee on Government Contracts. And yet that very committee of which I am chairman has been handicapped by the fact that we have not had adequate funds; we have not had adequate powers; we haven't had an adequate staff. Now in the special session of Congress and also in the session that preceded it, the Democratic Congress—in which there's a two-to-one Democratic majority—was asked by the President to give us the funds and give us the power to do a job and they did nothing at all. And in the special session in which Senator Kennedy was calling the signals, along with Senator Johnson, they turned it down and he himself voted against giving us the powers despite the fact that the bill had already been considered before, that it already had hearings on, and the Congress already knew what it had before it. All that I can say is this: what we need here are not just high hopes. What we need is action. And in the field of executive leadership, I can say that I believe it's essential that the president of the United States not only set the tone but he also must lead; he must act as he talks.

MR. MCGEE: Mr. Morgan with a question for Vice President Nixon.

MR. MORGAN: Mr. Vice President, in your speeches you emphasize that the United States is doing basically well in the cold war. Can you square that statement with a considerable mass of bipartisan reports and studies, including one prominently participated in by Governor Rockefeller, which almost unanimously conclude that we are not doing nearly so well as we should?

MR. NIXON: Mr. Morgan, no matter how well we're doing in the cold war, we're not doing as well as we should. And that will always be the case as long as the Communists are on the international scene, in the aggressive tac— uh— tendencies that they presently are following. Now as far as the present situation is concerned, I think it's time that we nail a few of these distortions about the United States that have been put out. First of all, we hear that our prestige is at an all-time low. Senator Kennedy has been hitting that point over and over again. I would suggest that after Premier kush— Khrushchev's uh— performance in the United Nations, compared with President Eisenhower's eloquent speech, that at the present time Communist prestige in the world is at an all-time low and American prestige is at an all-time high. Now that, of course, is just one factor, but it's a significant one. When we look, for example, at the vote on the Congo. We were on one side; they were on the other side. What happened? There were seventy votes for our position and none for theirs. Look at the votes in the United Nations over the past seven and a half years. That's a test of prestige. Every time the United States has been on one side and they've been on the other side, our position has been sustained. Now looking to what we ought to do in the future. In this cold war we have to recognize where it is being fought and then we have to develop programs to deal with it. It's being fought primarily in Asia, in Africa, and in Latin America. What do we need? What tools do we need to fight us? Well we need, for example, economic assistance; we need technical assistance; we need exchange; we need programs of diplomatic and other character which will be effective in that area. Now Senator Kennedy a moment ago referred to the fact that there was not an adequate Voice of America program for Latin America. I'd like to point out that in the last six years, the Democratic Congresses, of which he'd been a member, have cut twenty million dollars off of the Voice of America programs. They also have cut four billion dollars off of mutual security in these last six years. They also have cut two billion dollars off of defense. Now when they talk about our record here, it is well that they recognize that they have to stand up for their record as well. So let me summarize by saying this: I'm not satisfied with what we're doing in the cold war because I believe we have to step up our activities and launch an offensive for the minds and hearts and souls of men. It must be economic; it must be technological; above all it must be ideological. But we've got to get help from the Congress in order to do this.

MR. MCGEE: Senator Kennedy.

MR. KENNEDY: Of course Mr. Nixon is wholly inaccurate when he says that the Congress has not provided more funds in fact than the President recommended for national defense. Nineteen fifty-three we tried to put an appropriation of five billion dollars for our defenses. I was responsible for the amendment with Senator Monroney in 1954 to strengthen our ground forces. The Congress of the United States appropriated six hundred and seventy-seven million dollars more than the President was willing to use up till a week ago. Secondly, on the question of our position in the United Nations. We all know about the vote held this week—of the five neutralists—and it was generally regarded as a defeat for the United States. Thirdly, in 1952, there were only seven votes in favor of the admission of Red China into the United Nations. Last year there were twenty-nine and tomorrow when the preliminary vote is held you will see a strengthening of that position or very closely to it. We have not maintained our position and our prestige. A Gallup Poll taken in February of this year asking the—in eight out of nine countries—they asked the people, who do they think would be ahead by 1970 militarily and scientifically, and a majority in eight of the nine countries said the Soviet Union would be by 1970. Governor Rockefeller has been far more critical in June of our position in the world than I have been. The Rockefeller Brothers report, General Ridgway, General Gavin, the Gaither Report, various reports of Congressional committees all indicate that the relative strength of the p— United States both militarily, politically, psychologically, and scientifically and industrially—the relative strength of the so—of United States compared to that of the Soviet Union and the Chinese Communists together—has deteriorated in the last eight years and we should know it, and the American people should be told the facts.

MR. MCGEE: Mr. Spivak with a question for Senator Kennedy.

MR. SPIVAK: Senator, uh— following this up, how would you go about increasing the prestige you say we're losing, and could the programs you've devised to do so be accomplished without absolutely wrecking our economy?

MR. KENNEDY: Yes. We have been wholly indifferent to Latin America until the last few months. The program that was put forward this summer, after we broke off the sugar quota with Cuba, really was done because we wanted to get through the O.A.S. meeting a condemnation of Russian infiltration of Cuba. And therefore we passed an authorization—not an aid bill—which was the first time, really, since the Inter-American Bank which was founded a year ago was developed, that we really have looked at the needs of Latin America; that we have associated ourselves with those people. Secondly, I believe that in the ca— that it's far better for the United States, instead of concentrating our aid, particularly in the underdeveloped world, on surplus military equipment—we poured three hundred million dollars of surplus military equipment into Laos. We paid more military aid, more aid into Laos po— per— per person than in

any country in the world and we ought to know now that Laos is moving
from neutralism in the direction of the Communists. I believe instead of
doing that, we should concentrate our aid in long-term loans which these
people can pay back either in hard money or in local currency. This permits them to maintain their self-respect. It permits us to make sure that
the projects which are invested in are going to produce greater wealth.
And I believe that in cases of India and Africa and Latin America that
this is where our emphasis should be. I would strengthen the Development
Loan Fund. And Senator Fulbright, Senator Humphrey and I tried to do
that. We tried to provide an appropriation of a billion and a half for five
years, on a long-term loan basis, which this Administration opposed. And
unless we're ready to carry out programs like that in the sixties, this battle
for economic survival which these people are waging are going to be lost.
And if India should lose her battle, with thirty-five per cent of the people
of the underdeveloped world within her borders, then I believe that the
balance of power could move against us. I think the United States can
afford to do these things. I think that we could not afford not to do these
things. This goes to our survival. And here in a country which if it is
moving ahead, if it's developing its economy to the fullest—which we are
not now—in my judgment, we'll have the resources to meet our military
commitments and also our commitments overseas. I believe it's essential
that we do it because in the next ten years the balance of power is going
to begin to move in the world from one direction or another—towards us
or towards the Communists—and unless we begin to identify ourselves
not only with the anti-Communist fight, but also with the fight against
poverty and hunger, these people are going to begin to turn to the Communists as an example. I believe we can do it. If we build our economy
the way we should, we can afford to do these things and we must do it.

MR. MCGEE: Mr. Vice President.

MR. NIXON: Senator Kennedy has put a great deal of stress on the necessity for economic assistance. This is important. But it's also tremendously
important to bear in mind that when you pour in money without pouring
in technical assistance at w— as well, that you have a disastrous situation.
We need to step up exchange; we need to step up technical assistance so
that trained people in these newly developing countries can operate the
economies. We also have to have in mind something else with regard to
this whole situation in the world, and that is: that as America moves
forward, we not only must think in terms of fighting Communism, but we
must also think primarily in terms of the interests of these countries. We
must associate ourselves with their aspirations. We must let them know
that the great American ideals—of independence, of the right of people
to be free, and of the right to progress—that these are ideals that belong
not to ourselves alone, but they belong to everybody. This we must get
across to the world. And we can't do it unless we do have adequate funds

for, for example, information which has been cut by the Congress, adequate funds for technical assistance. The other point that I would make with regard to economic assistance and technical assistance is that the United States must not rest its case here alone. This is primarily an ideological battle—a battle for the minds and the hearts and the souls of men. We must not meet the Communists purely in the field of gross atheistic materialism. We must stand for our ideals.

MR. MCGEE: Mr. Levy with a question for Vice President Nixon.

MR. LEVY: Mr. Vice President, the Labor Department today added five more major industrial centers to the list of areas with substantial unemployment. You said in New York this week that as president you would use the full powers of the government, if necessary, to combat unemployment. Specifically what measures would you advocate and at what point?

MR. NIXON: To combat unemployment we first must concentrate on the very areas to which you refer—the so-called depressed areas. Now in the last Congress—the special session of the Congress—there was a bill: one by the President, one by Senator Kennedy and members of his party. Now the bill that the President had submitted would have provided more aid for those areas that really need it—areas like Scranton and Wilkes-Barre and the areas of West Virginia—than the ones that Senator Kennedy was supporting. On the other hand we found that the bill got into the legislative difficulties and consequently no action was taken. So point one, at the highest priority we must get a bill for depressed areas through the next Congress. I have made recommendations on that and I have discussed them previously and I will spell them out further in the campaign. Second, as we consider this problem of unemployment, we have to realize where it is. In analyzing the figures we will find that our unemployment exists among the older citizens; it exists also among those who are inadequately trained; that is, those who do not have an adequate opportunity for education. It also exists among minority groups. If we're going to combat unemployment, then, we have to do a better job in these areas. That's why I have a program for education, a program in the case of equal job opportunities, and one that would also deal with our older citizens. Now finally, with regard to the whole problem of combating recession, as you call it, we must use the full resources of the government in these respects: one, we must see to it that credit is expanded as we go into any recessionary period—and understand, I do not believe we're going into a recession. I believe this economy is sound and that we're going to move up. But second, in addition to that, if we do get into a recessionary period we should move . . . on that part of the economy which is represented by the private sector, and I mean stimulate that part of the economy that can create jobs —the private sector of the economy. This means through tax reform and if necessary tax cuts that will stimulate more jobs. I favor that rather than massive federal spending programs which will come into effect usually long after you've passed through the recessionary period. So we must use all of these weapons for the purpose of combating recession if it should come. But I do not expect it to come.

MR. MCGEE: Senator Kennedy.

MR. KENNEDY: Well Mr. Nixon has stated the record inaccurately in regard to the depressed area bill. I'm very familiar with it. It came out of the committee of which I was the chairman—the labor subcommittee— in fifty-five. I was the floor manager. We passed an area redevelopment bill far more effective than the bill the Administration suggested, on two occasions, and the President vetoed it both times. We passed a bill again this year in the cong— in the Senate and it died in the Rules Committee of the House of Representatives. Let me make it very clear that the bill that Mr. Nixon talked about did not mention Wilkes-Barre or Scranton; it did not mention West Virginia. Our bill was far more effective. The bill introduced and erd— sponsored by Senator Douglas was far more effective in trying to stimulate the economy of those areas. Secondly, he has mentioned the problem of our older citizens. I cannot still understand why this Administration and Mr. Nixon oppose putting medical care for the aged under Social Security to give them some security. Third, I believe we should step up the use of our surplus foods in these areas until we're able to get the people back to work. Five cents a day—that's what the food package averages per person. Fourthly, I believe we should not carry out a hard money, high interest rate policy which helped intensify certainly the recession of 1958, and I think helped bring /ta/ slow-down of 1960. If we move into a recession in sixty-one, then I would agree that we have to put more money into the economy, and it can be done by either one of the two methods discussed. One is by ex— the programs such as aid to education. The other would be to make a judgment on what's the most effective tax program to stimulate our economy.

MR. MCGEE: Mr. Niven with a question for Senator Kennedy.

MR. NIVEN: Senator, while the main theme of your campaign has been this decline of American power and prestige in the last eight years, you've hardly criticized President Eisenhower at all. And in a speech last weekend you said you had no quarrel with the President. Now isn't Mr. Eisenhower and not Mr. Nixon responsible for any such decline?

MR. KENNEDY: Well I understood that this was the Eisenhower-Nixon Administration according to all the Republican uh— propaganda that I've read. The question is what we're going to do in the future. I've been critical of this Administration and I've been critical of the President. In fact uh— Mr. Nixon uh— discussed that a week ago in a speech. I believe that our power and prestige in the last eight years has declined. Now what is the issue is what we're going to do in the future. Now that's an issue between Mr. Nixon and myself. He feels that we're moving ahead uh— in a— we're not going into a recession in this country, economically; he feels that our power and prestige is stronger than it ever was relative to that of the Communists, that we're moving ahead. I disagree. And I believe the American people have to make the choice on November eighth between the view of whether we have to move ahead faster, whether what we're doing now is not satisfactory, whether we have to build greater strength at home and abroad and Mr. Nixon's view. That's the great issue. President Eisenhower moves from the scene on January twentieth and the next four years are the critical years. And that's the debate. That's the argument between Mr. Nixon and myself and on that issue the American people have to make their judgment and I think it's a important judgment. I think in many ways this election is more important than any since 1932, or certainly almost any in this century. Because we disagree very fundamentally on the position of the United States, and if his view prevails then I think that's going to bring an important result to this country in the sixties. If our view prevails that we have to do more, that we have to make a greater national and international effort, that we have lost prestige in Latin America—the President of Brazil—the new incumbent running for office called on Castro during his campaign because he thought it was important to get the vote of those who were supporting Castro in Latin America. In Africa, the United States has ignored Latin uh— Africa. We gave more scholarships to the Congo—this summer we offered them—than we've given to all of Africa the year before. Less than two hundred for all the countries of Africa and they need trained leadership more than anything. We've been uh— having a very clear decision in the last eight years. Mr. Nixon has been part of that Administration. He's had experience in it. And I believe this Administration has not met its responsibilities in the last eight year, that our power relative to that of the Communists is declining, that we're facing a very hazardous time in the sixties, and unless the United States begin to move here—unless we start to go ahead—I don't believe that we're going to meet our responsibility to our own people or to the cause of freedom. I think the choice is clear and it involves the future.

MR. MCGEE: Mr. Vice President.

MR. NIXON: Well first of all, I think Senator Kennedy should make up his mind with regard to my responsibility. In our first debate he indicated that I had not had experience or at least uh— had not participated significantly in the making of the decisions. I'm glad to hear tonight that he does suggest that I have had some experience. Let me make my position clear. I have participated in the discussions leading to the decisions in this Administration. I'm proud of the record of this Administration. I don't stand on it because it isn't something to stand on but something to build on. Now looking at Senator Kennedy's credentials: he is suggesting that he will move America faster and further than I will. But what does he offer? He offers retreads of programs that failed. I submit to you that as you look at his programs, his program for example with regard to the Federal Reserve and uh— free money or loose money uh— high— low interest rates, his program in the economic field generally are the programs that were adopted and tried during the Truman Administration. And when we compare the economic progress of this country in the Truman Administration with that of the Eisenhower Administration, we find that in every index there has been a tr— great deal more performance and more progress in this Administration than in that one. I say the programs and the leadership that failed then is not the program and the leadership that America needs now. I say that the American people don't want to go back to those policies. And incidentally if Senator Kennedy disagrees, he should indicate where he believes those policies are different from those he's advocating today.

MR. MCGEE: Mr. Spivak with a question for Vice President Nixon.

MR. SPIVAK: Mr. Vice President, according to news dispatches Soviet Premier Khrushchev said today that Prime Minister Macmillan had assured him that there would be a summit conference next year after the presidential elections. Have you given any cause for such assurance, and do you consider it desirable or even possible that there would be a summit conference next year if Mr. Khrushchev persists in the conditions he's laid down?

MR. NIXON: No, of course I haven't talked to Prime Minister Macmillan. It would not be appropriate for me to do so. The President is still going to be president for the next four months and he, of course, is the only one who could commit this country in this period. As far as a summit conference is concerned, I want to make my position absolutely clear. I would be willing as president to meet with Mr. Khrushchev or any other world leader if it would serve the cause of peace. I would not be able wou— would be willing to meet with him however, unless there were preparations for that conference which would give us some reasonable certainty—some reasonable certainty—that you were going to have some success. We must not build up the hopes of the world and then dash them as was the case in Paris. There, Mr. Khrushchev came to that conference determined to break it up. He was going to break it up because he would—knew that he wasn't going to get his way on Berlin and on the other key matters with which he was concerned at the Paris Conference. Now, if we're going to have another summit conference, there must be negotiations at the diplomatic level—the ambassadors, the Secretaries of State, and others at that level—prior to that time, which will delineate the issues and which will prepare the way for the heads of state to meet and make some progress. Otherwise, if we find the heads of state meeting and not making progress, we will find that the cause of peace will have been hurt rather than helped. So under these circumstances, I, therefore, strongly urge and I will strongly hold, if I have the opportunity to urge or to hold—this position:

that any summit conference would be gone into only after the most careful preparation and only after Mr. Khrushchev—after his disgraceful conduct at Paris, after his disgraceful conduct at the United Nations—gave some assurance that he really wanted to sit down and talk and to accomplish something and not just to make propaganda.

MR. MCGEE: Senator Kennedy.

MR. KENNEDY: I have no disagreement with the Vice President's position on that. It—my view is the same as his. Let me say there is only one uh— point I would add. That before we go into the summit, before we ever meet again, I think it's important that the United States build its strength; that it build its military strength as well as its own economic strength. If we negotiate from a position where the power balance or wave is moving away from us, it's extremely difficult to reach a successful decision on Berlin as well as the other questions. Now the next president of the United States in his first year is going to be confronted with a very serious question on our defense of Berlin, our commitment to Berlin. It's going to be a test of our nerve and will. It's going to be a test of our strength. And because we're going to move in sixty-one and two, partly because we have not maintained our strength with sufficient vigor in the last years, I believe that before we meet that crisis, that the next president of the United States should send a message to Congress asking for a revitalization of our military strength, because come spring or late in the winter we're going to be face to face with the most serious Berlin crisis since 1949 or fifty. On the question of the summit, I agree with the position of Mr. Nixon. I would not meet Mr. Khrushchev unless there were some agreements at the secondary level—foreign ministers or ambassadors— which would indicate that the meeting would have some hope of success, or a useful exchange of ideas.

MR. MCGEE: Mr. Levy with a question for Senator Kennedy.

MR. LEVY: Senator, in your acceptance speech at Los Angeles, you said that your campaign would be based not on what you intend to offer the American people, but what you intend to ask of them. Since that time you have spelled out many of the things that you intend to do but you have made only vague reference to sacrifice and self-denial. A year or so ago, I believe, you said that you would not hesitate to recommend a tax increase if you considered it necessary.

MR. KENNEDY: That's right.

MR. LEVY: Is this what you have in mind?

MR. KENNEDY: Well I don't think that in the winter of sixty-one under present economic conditions, it uh— a— uh— tax uh— increase would be desirable. In fact, it would be deflationary; it would cause great unemployment; it would cause a real slowdown in our economy. If it ever becomes necessary, and is wise economically and essential to our security, I would have no hesitancy in suggesting a tax increase or any other policy which would defend the United States. I have talked in every speech about the fact that these are going to be very difficult times in the nineteen-sixties and that we're going to have to meet our responsibilities as citizens. I'm talking about a national mood. I'm talking about our willingness to bear any burdens in order to maintain our own freedom and in order to meet our freedom around the globe. We don't know what the future's going to bring. But I would not want anyone to elect me uh— president of the United States—or vote for me—under the expectation that life would be easier if I were elected. Now, many of the programs that I'm talking about —economic growth, care for the aged, development of our natural re-sources—build the strength of the United States. That's how the United States began to prepare for its great . . . actions in World War II and in the post-war period. If we're moving ahead, if we're providing a viable economy, if our people have sufficient resources so that they can consume what we produce; then this country's on the move, then we're stronger, then we set a better example to the world. So we have the problem of not only building our own uh— military strength and extending uh— our policies abroad, we have to do a job here at home. So I believe that the policies that I recommend come under the general heading of strengthen-ing the United States. We're using our steel capacity fifty-five per cent today. We're not able to consume what we're able to produce at a time when the Soviet Union is making great economic gains. And all I say is, I don't know what the sixties will bring—except I think they will bring hard times in the uh— international sphere; I hope we can move ahead here at home in the United States; I'm confident we can do a far better job of mobilizing our economy and resources in the United States. And I merely say that they—if they elect me president, I will do my best to carry the United States through a difficult period; but I would not want people to elect me because I promised them the easy, soft life. I think it's going to be difficult; but I'm confident that this country can meet its responsibil-ities.

MR. MCGEE: Mr. Vice President.

MR. NIXON: Well I think we should be no— under no illusions whatever about what the responsibilities of the American people will be in the sixties. Our expenditures for defense, our expenditures for mutual security, our expenditures for economic assistance and technical assistance are not going to get less. In my opinion they're going to be de— be greater. I think it may be necessary that we have more taxes. I hope not. I hope we can economize elsewhere so that we don't have to. But I would have no hesita-tion to ask the American people to pay the taxes even in 1961—if necessary—to maintain a sound economy and also to maintain a sound dollar. Because when you do not tax, and tax enough to pay for your outgo, you pay it many times over in higher prices and inflation; and I simply will not do that. I think I should also add that as far as Senator Kennedy's proposals are concerned, if he intends to carry out his platform—the one adopted in Los Angeles—it is just impossible for him to make good on those promises without raising taxes or without having a rise in t— prices or both. The platform suggests that it can be done through economic growth; that it can be done, in effect, with mirrors. But it isn't going to be working that way. You can't add billions of dollars to our expenditures and not pay for it. After all, it isn't paid for by my money, it isn't paid for by his, but by the people's money.

MR. MCGEE: Mr. Niven with a question for Vice President Nixon.

MR. NIVEN: Mr. Vice President, you said that while Mr. Khrushchev is here, Senator Kennedy should talk about what's right with this country as well as what's wrong with the country. In the 1952 campaign when you were Republican candidate for Vice President, and we were eh— at war with the Communists, did you feel a similar responsibility to t— talk about what was right with the country?

MR. NIXON: I did. And as I pointed out in 1952, I made it very clear that as far as the Korean War was concerned, that I felt that the decision to go into the war in Korea was right and necessary. What I criticized were the policies that made it necessary to go to Korea. Now incidentally, I should point out here that Senator Kennedy has attacked our foreign policy. He's said that it's been a policy that has led to defeat and retreat. And I'd like to know where have we been defeated and where have we retreated? In the Truman Administration, six hundred million people went behind the Iron Curtain including the satellite countries of Eastern Europe and Communist China. In this Administration we've stopped them at Quemoy and Matsu; we've stopped them in Indochina; we've stopped them in Lebanon; we've stopped them in other parts of the world. I would also like to point out that as far as Senator Kennedy's comments are concerned, I think he has a perfect right and a responsibility to criticize this Administration whenever he thinks we're wrong. But he has a responsibility to be accurate, and not to misstate the case. I don't think he should say that our prestige is at an all-time low. I think this is very harmful at a time Mr. Khrushchev is here—harmful because it's wrong. I don't think it was helpful when he suggested—and I'm glad he's corrected this to an extent—that seventeen million people go to bed hungry every night in the United States. Now this just wasn't true. Now, there are people who go to bed hungry in the United States—far less, incidentally, than used to go to bed hungry when we came into power at the end of the Truman Administration. But the thing that is right about the United States, it should be emphasized, is that less people go to bed hungry in the United States than in any major country in the world. We're the best fed; we're the best clothed, with a better distribution of this world's goods to all of our people than any people in history. Now, in pointing out the things that are wrong, I think we ought to emphasize America's strengths. It isn't necessary to— to run America down in order to build her up. Now, /sis/ so that we get it absolutely clear: Senator Kennedy must as a candidate—as I as a candidate in fifty-two—criticize us when we're wrong. And he's doing a very effective job of that, in his way. But on the other hand, he has a responsibility to be accurate. And I have a responsibility to correct him every time he misstates the case; and I intend to continue to do so.

MR. MCGEE: Senator Kennedy.

MR. KENNEDY: Well, Mr. Nixon uh-– I'll just give you the testimony of Mr. George Aiken—Senator George Aiken, the ranking minority member—Republican member—and former chairman of the Senate Agricultural Committee testifying in 1959—said there were twenty-six million Americans who did not have the income to afford a decent diet. Mr. Benson, testifying on the food stamp plan in 1957, said there were twenty-five million Americans who could not afford a elementary low-cost diet. And he defined that as someone who uses beans in place of meat. Now I've seen a good many hundreds of thousands of people who are uh— not adequately fed. You can't tell me that a surplus food distribution of five cents po— per person—and that n— nearly six million Americans receiving that—is adequate. You can't tell me that any one who uses beans instead of meat in the United States—and there are twenty-five million of them according to Mr. Benson—is well fed or adequately fed. I believe that we should not compare what our figures may be to India or some other country that has serious problems but to remember that we are the most prosperous country in the world and that these people are not getting adequate food. And they're not getting in many cases adequate shelter. And we ought to try to meet the problem. Secondly, Mr. Nixon has continued to state—and he stated it last week—these fantastic figures of what the Democratic budget would c— uh— platform would cost. They're wholly inaccurate. I said last week I believed in a balanced budget. Unless there was a severe recession—and after all the worst unbalanced budget in history was in 1958, twelve billion dollars—larger than in any Administration in the history of the United States. So that I believe that on this subject we can balance the budget unless we have a national emergency or unless we have a severe recession.

MR. MCGEE: Mr. Morgan with a question for Senator Kennedy.

MR. MORGAN: Senator, Saturday on television you said that you had always thought that Quemoy and Matsu were unwise places to draw our defense line in the Far East. Would you comment further on that and also address to this question: couldn't a pullback from those islands be interpreted as appeasement?

MR. KENNEDY: Well, the United States uh— has on occasion attempted uh— mostly in the middle fifties, to persuade Chiang Kai-shek to pull his troops back to Formosa. I believe strongly in the defense of Formosa.

These islands are a few miles—five or six miles—off the coast of Red China, within a general harbor area and more than a hundred miles from Formosa. We have never said flatly that we will defend Quemoy and Matsu if it's attacked. We say we will defend it if it's part of a general attack on Formosa. But it's extremely difficult to make that judgment. Now, Mr. Herter in 1958, when he was Under Secretary of State, said they were strategically undefensible. Admirals Spruance and Collins in 1955 said that we should not attempt to defend these islands, in their conference in the Far East. General Ridgway has said the same thing. I believe that when you get into a w— if you're going to get into war for the defense of Formosa, it ought to be on a clearly defined line. One of the problems, I think, at the time of South Korea was the question of whether the United States would defend it if it were attacked. I believe that we should defend Formosa. We should come to its defense. To leave this rather in the air, that we will defend it under some conditions but not under other, I think is a mistake. Secondly, I would not suggest the withdrawal at the point of the Communist gun. It is a decision finally that the Nationalists should make and I believe that we should consult with them and attempt to work out a plan by which the line is drawn at the island of Formosa. It leaves a hundred miles between the sea. But with General Ridgway, Mr. Herter, General Collins, Admiral Spruance and many others, I think it's unwise to take the chance of being dragged into a war which may lead to a world war over two islands which are not strategically defensible, which are not, according to their testimony, essential to the defense of Formosa. I think that uh— we should protect our commitments. I believe strongly we should do so in Berlin. I believe strongly we should d— do so in Formosa and I believe we should meet our commitments to every country whose security we've guaranteed. But I do not believe that that line in case of war should be drawn on those islands but instead on the island of Formosa. And as long as they are not essential to the defense of Formosa, it's been my judgment ever since 1954, at the time of the Eisenhower Doctrine for the Far East, that our line should be drawn in the sea around the island itself.

MR. MCGEE: Mr. Vice President.

MR. NIXON: I disagree completely with Senator Kennedy on this point. I remember in the period immediately before the Korean War, South Korea was supposed to be indefensible as well. Generals testified to that. And Secretary Acheson made a very famous speech at the Press Club, early in the year that k— Korean War started, indicating in effect that South Korea was beyond the defense zone of the United States. I suppose it was hoped when he made that speech that we wouldn't get into a war. But it didn't mean that. We had to go in when they came in. Now I think as far as Quemoy and Matsu are concerned, that the question is not these two little pieces of real estate—they are unimportant. It isn't the few people who live on them—they are not too important. It's the principle involved. These two islands are in the area of freedom. The Nationalists have these two islands. We should not uh— force our Nationalist */aylay/* allies to get off of them and give them to the Communists. If we do that we start a chain reaction; because the Communists aren't after Quemoy and Matsu, they're a— they're after Formosa. In my opinion this is the same kind of woolly thinking that led to disaster for America in Korea. I am against it. I would never tolerate it as president of the United States, and I will hope that Senator Kennedy will change his mind if he should be elected.

MR. MCGEE: Gentlemen, we have approximately four minutes remaining. May I ask you to make your questions and answers as brief as possible consistent with clarity. And Mr. Levy has a question for Vice President Nixon.

MR. LEVY: Mr. Vice President, you are urging voters to forget party labels and vote for the man. Senator Kennedy says that in doing this you are trying to run away from your party on such issues as housing and aid to education by advocating what he calls a me-too program. Why do you say that party labels are not important?

MR. NIXON: Because that's the way we elect a president in this country, and it's the way we should. I'm a student of history as is Senator Kennedy, incidentally; and I have found that in the history of this country we've had many great presidents. Some of them have been Democrats and some of them have been Republicans. The people, some way, have always understood that at a particular time a certain man was the one the country needed. Now, I believe that in an election when we are trying to determine who should lead the free world—not just America—perhaps, as Senator Kennedy has already indicated, the most important election in our history —it isn't the label that he wears or that I wear that counts. It's what we are. It's our whole lives. It's what we stand for. It's what we believe. And consequently, I don't think it's enough to go before Republican audiences —and I never do—and say, "Look, vote for me because I'm a Republican." I don't think it's enough for Senator Kennedy to go before the audiences on the Democratic side and say, "Vote for me because I'm a Democrat." That isn't enough. What's involved here is the question of leadership for the whole free world. Now that means the best leadership. It may be Republican, it may be Democratic. But the people are the ones that determine it. The people have to make up their minds. And I believe the people, therefore, should be asked to make up their minds not simply on the basis of, "Vote the way your grandfather did; vote the way your mother did." I think the people should put America first, rather than party first. Now, as far as running away from my party is concerned, Senator Kennedy has said that we have no compassion for the poor, that we are against progress—the enemies of progress, is the term that he's used, and the like. All that I can say is this: we do have programs in all of these fields—education, housing, defense—that will move America forward. They will move her forward faster, and they will move her more surely than in his program. This is what I deeply believe. I'm sure he believes just as deeply that his will move that way. I suggest, however, that in the interest of fairness that he could give me the benefit of also believing as he believes.

MR. MC GEE: Senator Kennedy.

MR. KENNEDY: Well, let me say I do think that parties are important in that they tell something about the program and something about the man. Abraham Lincoln was a great president of all the people; but he was selected by his party at a key time in history because his party stood for something. The Democratic party in this century has stood for something. It has stood for progress; it has stood for concern for the people's welfare. It has stood for a strong foreign policy and a strong national defense; and as a result, produced Wilson, President Roosevelt, and President Truman. The Republican party has produced McKinley and Harding, Coolidge, Dewey, and Landon. They do stand for something. They stand for a whole different approach to the problems facing this country at home and abroad. That's the importance of party; only if it tells something about the record. And the Republicans in recent years—not only in the last twenty-five years, but in the last eight years—have opposed housing, opposed care for the aged, opposed federal aid to education, opposed minimum wage and I think that record tells something.

MR. MC GEE: Thank you gentlemen. Neither the questions from the reporters nor the answers you heard from Senator John Kennedy or Vice President Richard Nixon were rehearsed. By agreement neither candidate made an opening statement or a closing summation. They further agreed that the clock alone would decide who would speak last and each has asked me to express his thanks to the networks and their affiliated stations. Another program similar to this one will be presented Thursday, October thirteenth, and the final program will be presented Friday, October twenty-first. We hope this series of radio and television programs will help you toward a fuller understanding of the issues facing our country today and that on election day, November eighth, you will vote for the candidate of your choice. This is Frank McGee. Good night from Washington.

Third Debate, October 13, 1960

BILL SHADEL, moderator: Good evening. I'm Bill Shadel of ABC News. It's my privilege this evening to preside at this the third in the series of meetings on radio and television of the two major presidential candidates. Now like the last meeting the subjects to be discussed will be suggested by questions from a panel of correspondents. Unlike the first two programs, however, the two candidates will not be sharing the same platform. In New York the Democratic presidential nominee, Senator John F. Kennedy; separated by three thousand miles in a Los Angeles studio, the Republican presidential nominee, Vice President Richard M. Nixon; now joined for tonight's discussion by a network of electronic facilities which permits each candidate to /sitriy/ see and hear the other. Good evening, Senator Kennedy.

MR. KENNEDY: Good evening, Mr. Shadel.

MR. SHADEL: And good evening to you, Vice President Nixon.

MR. NIXON: Good evening, Mr. Shadel.

MR. SHADEL: And now to meet the panel of correspondents. Frank McGee, NBC News; Charles Von Fremd, CBS News; Douglass Cater, *Reporter* magazine; Roscoe Drummond, *New York Herald Tribune*. Now, as you've probably noted, the four reporters include a newspaper man and a magazine reporter; these two selected by lot by the press secretaries of the candidates from among the reporters traveling with the candidates. The broadcasting representatives were chosen by their companies. The rules for this evening have been agreed upon by the representatives of both candidates and the radio and television networks and I should like to read them. There will be no opening statements by the candidates nor any closing summation. The entire hour will be devoted to answering questions from the reporters. Each candidate to be questioned in turn with opportunity for comment by the other. Each answer will be limited to two and one-half minutes, each comment to one and a half minutes. The reporters are free to ask any question they choose on any subject. Neither candidate knows what questions will be asked. Time alone will dete— determine who will be asked the final question. Now the first question is from Mr. McGee and is for Senator Kennedy.

MR. MCGEE: Senator Kennedy, yesterday you used the words "trigger-happy" in referring to Vice President Richard Nixon's stand on defending the islands of Quemoy and Matsu. Last week on a program like this one, you said the next president would come face to face with a serious crisis in Berlin. So the question is: would you take military action to defend Berlin?

MR. KENNEDY: Mr. McGee, we have a contractual right to be in Berlin coming out of the conversations at Potsdam and of World War II. That has been reinforced by direct commitments of the president of the United States; it's been reinforced by a number of other nations under NATO. I've stated on many occasions that the United States must meet its commitment on Berlin. It is a commitment that we have to meet if we're going to protect the security of Western Europe. And therefore on this question I don't think that there is any doubt in the mind of any American; I hope there is not any doubt in the mind of any member of the community of West Berlin; I'm sure there isn't any doubt in the mind of the Russians. We will meet our commitments to maintain the freedom and independence of West Berlin.

MR. SHADEL: Mr. Vice President, do you wish to comment?

MR. NIXON: Yes. As a matter of fact, the statement that Senator Kennedy made was that— to the effect that there were trigger-happy Republicans, that my stand on Quemoy and Matsu was an indication of trigger-happy Republicans. I resent that comment. I resent it because th— it's an implication that Republicans have been trigger-happy and, therefore, would lead this nation into war. I would remind Senator Kennedy of the past fifty years. I would ask him to name one Republican president who led this nation into war. There were three Democratic presidents who led us into war. I do not mean by that that one party is a war party and the other party is a peace party. But I do say that any statement to the effect that the Republican party is trigger-happy is belied by the record. We had a war when we came into power in 1953. We got rid of that; we've kept out of other wars; and certainly that doesn't indicate that we're trigger-happy. We've been strong, but we haven't been trigger-happy. As far as Berlin is concerned, there isn't any question about the necessity of defending Berlin; the rights of people there to be free; and there isn't any question about what the united American people—Republicans and Democrats alike—would do in the event there were an attempt by the Communists to take over Berlin.

MR. SHADEL: The next question is by Mr. Von Fremd for Vice President Nixon.

MR. VON FREMD: Mr. Vice President, a two-part question concerning the offshore islands in the Formosa Straits. If you were president and the

Chinese Communists tomorrow began an invasion of Quemoy and Matsu, would you launch the uh— United States into a war by sending the Seventh Fleet and other military forces to resist this aggression; and secondly, if the uh— regular conventional forces failed to halt such uh— such an invasion, would you authorize the use of nuclear weapons?

MR. NIXON: Mr. Von Fremd, it would be completely irresponsible for a candidate for the presidency, or for a president himself, to indicate the course of action and the weapons he would use in the event of such an attack. I will say this: in the event that such an attack occurred and in the event the attack was a prelude to an attack on Formosa—which would be the indication today because the Chinese Communists say over and over again that their objective is not the offshore islands, that they consider them only steppingstones to taking Formosa—in the event that their attack then were a prelude to an attack on Formosa, there isn't any question but that the United States would then again, as in the case of Berlin, honor our treaty obligations and stand by our ally of Formosa. But to indicate in advance how we would respond, to indicate the nature of this response would be incorrect; it would certainly be inappropriate; it would not be in the best interests of the United States. I will only say this, however, in addition: to do what Senator Kennedy has suggested—to suggest that we will surrender these islands or force our Chinese Nationalist allies to surrender them in advance—is not something that would lead to peace; it is something that would lead, in my opinion, to war. This is the history of dealing with dictators. This is something that Senator Kennedy and all Americans must know. We tried this with Hitler. It didn't work. He wanted first uh— we know, Austria, and then he went on to the Sudetenland and then Danzig, and each time it was thought this is all that he wanted. Now what do the Chinese Communists want? They don't want just Quemoy and Matsu; they don't want just Formosa; they want the world. And the question is if you surrender or indicate in advance that you're not going to defend any part of the free world, and you figure that's going to satisfy them, it doesn't satisfy them. It only whets their appetite; and then the question comes, when do you stop them? I've often heard President Eisenhower in discussing this question, make the statement that if we once start the process of indicating that this point or that point is not the place to stop those who threaten the peace and freedom of the world, where do we stop them? And I say that those of us who stand against surrender of territory—this or any others—in the face of blackmail, in the s— face of force by the Communists are standing for the course that will lead to peace.

MR. SHADEL: Senator Kennedy, do you wish to comment?

MR. KENNEDY: Yes. The whole th— the United States now has a treaty —which I voted for in the United States Senate in 1955—to defend Formosa and the Pescadores Island. The islands which Mr. Nixon is discussing are five or four miles, respectively, off the coast of China. Now when Senator Green, the chairman of the Senate Foreign Relations Committee, wrote to the President, he received back on the second of October, 1958—"neither you nor any other American need feel the U.S. will be involved in military hostilities merely in the defense of Quemoy and Matsu." Now, that is the issue. I believe we must meet our commitment to uh—Formosa. I support it and the Pescadores Island. That is the present American position. The treaty does not include these two islands. Mr. Nixon suggests uh— that the United States should go to war if these two islands are attacked. I suggest that if Formosa is attacked or the Pescadores, or if there's any military action in any area which indicates an attack on Formosa and the Pescadores, then of course the United States is at war to defend its treaty. Now, I must say what Mr. Nixon wants to do is commit us—as I understand him, so that we can be clear if there's a disagreement—he wants us to be committed to the defense of these islands merely as the defense of these islands as free territory, not as part of the defense of Formosa. Admiral Yarnell, the commander of the Asiatic fleet, has said that these islands are not worth the bones of a single American. The President of the United States has indicated they are not within the treaty area. They were not within the treaty area when the treaty was passed in fifty-five. We have attempted to persuade Chiang Kai-shek as late as January of 1959 to reduce the number of troops he has on them. This is a serious issue, and I think we ought to understand completely if we disagree, and if so, where.

MR. SHADEL: Mr. Cater has the next question for Senator Kennedy.

MR. CATER: Senator Kennedy, last week you said that before we should hold another summit conference, that it was important that the United States build its strength. Modern weapons take quite a long time to build. What sort of prolonged period do you envisage before there can be a summit conference? And do you think that there can be any new initiatives on the grounds of nuclear disarmament uh— nuclear control or weapons control d— uh— during this period?

MR. KENNEDY: Well I think we should st— strengthen our conventional forces, and we should attempt in January, February, and March of next year to increase the airlift capacity of our conventional forces. Then I believe that we should move full time on our missile production, particularly on Minuteman and on Polaris. It may be a long period, but we must— we must get started immediately. Now on the question of disarmament, particularly nuclear disarmament, I must say that I feel that another effort should be made by a new Administration in January of 1961, to renew negotiations with the Soviet Union and see whether it's possible to come to some conclusion which will lessen the chances of contamination of the atmosphere, and also lessen the chances that other powers will begin to possess a nuclear capacity. There are indications, because of new inventions, that ten, fifteen, or twenty nations will have a nuclear capacity—including Red China—by the end of the presidential office in 1964. This is extremely serious. There have been many wars in the history of mankind. And to take a chance uh— now be— and not make every effort that we could make to provide for some control over these weapons, I think would be a great mistake. One of my disagreements with the present Administration has been that I don't feel a real effort has been made on this very sensitive subject, not only of nuclear controls, but also of general disarmament. Less than a hundred people have been working throughout the entire federal government on this subject, and I believe it's been reflected in our success and failures at Geneva. Now, we may not succeed. The Soviet Union may not agree to an inspection system. We may /miyat/ be able to get satisfactory assurances. It may be necessary for us to begin testing again. But I hope the next Administration—and if I have anything to do with it, the next Administration will—make one last great effort to provide for control of nuclear testing, control of nuclear weapons, if possible, control of outer space, free from weapons, and also to begin again the subject of general disarmament levels. These must be done. If we cannot succeed, then we must strengthen ourselves. But I would make the effort because I think the fate not only of our own civilization, but I think the fate of world and the future of the human race is involved in preventing a nuclear war.

MR. SHADEL: Mr. Vice President, your comment?

MR. NIXON: Yes. I am going to make a major speech on this whole subject next week before the next debate, and I will have an opportunity then to answer any other questions that may arise with regard to my position on it. There isn't any question but that we must move forward in every possible way to reduce the danger of war; to move toward controlled disarmament; to control tests; but also let's have in mind this: when Senator Kennedy suggests that we haven't been making an effort, he simply doesn't know what he's talking about. It isn't a question of the number of people who are working in an Administration. It's a question of who they are. This has been one of the highest level operations in the whole State Department right under the President himself. We have gone certainly the extra mile and then some in making offers to the Soviet Union on control of tests, on disarmament, and in every other way. And I just want to make one thing very clear. Yes, we should make a great effort. But under no circumstances must the United States ever make an agreement based on trust. There must be an absolute guarantee. Now, just a comment on Senator Kennedy's last answer. He forgets that in this same debate on the Formosa resolution, which he said he voted for—which he did—that he voted against an amendment, or was recorded against an amendment—and on this particular—or for an amendment, I should say—which passed the Senate overwhelmingly, seventy to twelve. And that amendment put the Senate of the United States on record with a majority of the Senator's own party voting for it, as well as the majority of Republicans—put them on record—against the very position that the Senator takes now of surrendering, of indicating in advance, that the United States will not defend the offshore islands.

MR. SHADEL: The next question is by Mr. Drummond for Vice President Nixon.

MR. DRUMMOND: Mr. Nixon, I would like to ask eh— one more aspect or raise another aspect of this same question. Uh— it is my understanding that President Eisenhower never advocated that Quemoy and Matsu should be defended under all circumstances as a matter of principle. I heard Secretary Dulles at a press conference in fifty-eight say that he thought that it was a mistake for Chiang Kai-shek to deploy troops to these islands. I would like to ask what has led you to take what appears to be a different position on this subject.

MR. NIXON: Well Mr. Drummond, first of all, referring to Secretary Dulles' press conference, I think if you read it all—and I know that you have—you will find that Secretary Dulles also indicated in that press conference that when the troops were withdrawn from Quemoy, that the implication was certainly of everything that he said, that Quemoy could better be defended. There were too many infantrymen there, not enough heavy artillery; and certainly I don't think there was any implication in Secretary Dulles' statement that Quemoy and Matsu should not be defended in the event that they were attacked, and that attack was a preliminary to an attack on Formosa. Now as far as President Eisenhower is concerned, I have often heard him discuss this question. As I uh— related a moment ago, the President has always indicated that we must not make the mistake in dealing with the dictator of indicating that we are going to make a concession at the point of a gun. Whenever you do that, inevitably the dictator is encouraged to try it again. So first it will be Quemoy and Matsu, next it may be Formosa. What do we do then? My point is this: that once you do this—follow this course of action—of indicating that you are not going to defend a particular area, the inevitable result is that it encourages a man who is determined to conquer the world to press you to the point of no return. And that means war. We went through this tragic experience leading to World War II. We learned our lesson again in Korea. We must not learn it again. That is why I think the Senate was right, including a majority of the Democrats, a majority of the Republicans, when they rejected Senator Kennedy's position in 1955. And incidentally, Senator Johnson was among those who rejected that position—voted with the seventy against the twelve. The Senate was right because they knew the lesson of history. And may I say, too, that I would trust that Senator Kennedy would change his position on this—change it; because as long as he as a major presidential candidate continues to suggest that we are going to turn over these islands, he is only encouraging the aggressors—the Chinese Communist and the Soviet aggressors—to press the United States, to press us to the point where war would be inevitable. The road to war is always paved with good intentions. And in this instance the good intentions, of course, are a desire for peace. But certainly we're not going to have peace by giving in and indicating in advance that we are not going to defend what has become a symbol of freedom.

MR. SHADEL: Senator Kennedy.

MR. KENNEDY: I don't think it's possible for Mr. Nixon to state the record in distortion of the facts with more precision than he just did. In 1955, Mr. Dulles at a press conference said: "The treaty that we have with the Republic of China excludes Quemoy and Matsu from the treaty area." That was done with much thought and deliberation. Therefore that treaty does not commit the United States to defend anything except Formosa and the Pescadores, and to deal with acts against that treaty area. I completely sustained the treaty. I voted for it. I would take any action necessary to defend the treaty, Formosa, and the Pescadores Island. What we're now talking about is the Vice President's determination to guarantee Quemoy and Matsu, which are four and five miles off the coast of Red China, which are not within the treaty area. I do not suggest that Chiang Kai-shek— and this Administration has been attempting since 1955 to persuade Chiang Kai-shek to lessen his troop commitments. Uh— He sent a mission—the President—in 1955 of Mr. uh— Robertson and Admiral Radford. General Twining said they were still doing it in 1959. General Ridgway said—who was Chief of Staff: "To go to war for Quemoy and Matsu to me would seem an unwarranted and tragic course to take. To me that concept is completely repugnant." So I stand with them. I stand with the Secretary of State, Mr. Herter, who said these islands were indefensible. I believe that we should meet our commitments, and if the Chinese Communists attack the Pescadores and Formosa, they know that it will mean a war. I would not ho— hand over these islands under any point of gun. But I merely say that the treaty is quite precise and I sustain the treaty. Mr. Nixon would add a guarantee to islands five miles off the coast of the re— Republic of China when he's never really protested the Communists seizing Cuba, ninety miles off the coast of the United States.

MR. SHADEL: Mr. Von Fremd has a question for Senator Kennery.

MR. VON FREMD: Senator Kennedy, I'd like to uh— shift the conversation, if I may, to a domestic uh— political argument. The chairman of the Republican National Committee, Senator Thruston Morton, declared earlier this week that you owed Vice President Nixon and the Republican party a public apology for some strong charges made by former President Harry Truman, who bluntly suggested where the Vice President and the

Republican party could go. Do you feel that you owe the Vice President an apology?

MR. KENNEDY: Well, I must say that uh— Mr. Truman has uh— his methods of expressing things; he's been in politics for fifty years; he's been president of the United States. They may— are not my style. But I really don't think there's anything that I could say to President Truman that's going to cause him, at the age of seventy-six, to change his particular speaking manner. Perhaps Mrs. Truman can, but I don't think I can. I'll just have to tell Mr. Morton that. If you'd pass that message on to him.

MR. SHADEL: Any comment, Mr. Vice President?

MR. NIXON: Yes, I think so. Of course, both er— Senator Kennedy and I have felt Mr. Truman's ire; and uh— consequently, I think he can speak with some feeling on this subject. I just do want to say one thing, however. We all have tempers; I have one; I'm sure Senator Kennedy has one. But when a man's president of the United States, or a former president, he has an obligation not to lose his temper in public. One thing I've noted as I've traveled around the country are the tremendous number of children who come out to see the presidential candidates. I see mothers holding their babies up, so that they can see a man who might be president of the United States. I know Senator Kennedy sees them, too. It makes you realize that whoever is president is going to be a man that all the children of America will either look up to, or will look down to. And I can only say that I'm very proud that President Eisenhower restored dignity and decency and, frankly, good language to the conduct of the presidency of the United States. And I only hope that, should I win this election, that I could approach President Eisenhower in maintaining the dignity of the office; in seeing to it that whenever any mother or father talks to his child, he can look at the man in the White House and, whatever he may think of his policies, he will say: "Well, there is a man who maintains the kind of standards personally that I would want my child to follow."

MR. SHADEL: Mr. Cater's question is for Vice President Nixon.

MR. CATER: Mr. Vice President, I'd like to return just once more, if I may, to this area of dealing with the Communists. Critics have claimed that on at least three occasions in recent years—on the sending of American troops to Indochina in 1954, on the matter of continuing the U-2 flights uh— in May, and then on this definition of the—of our commitment to the offshore island—that you have overstated the Administration position, that you have taken a more bellicose position than President Eisenhower. Just two days ago you said that you called on uh— Senator Kennedy to serve notice to Communist aggressors around the world that we're not going to retreat one inch more any place, where as we did retreat from the Tachen Islands, or at least Chiang Kai-shek did. Would you say this was a valid criticism of your statement of foreign policy?

MR. NIXON: Well, Mr. Cater, of course it's a criticism that uh— is being made. Uh— I obviously don't think it's valid. I have supported the Administration's position and I think that that position has been correct; I think my position has been correct. As far as Indochina was concerned, I stated over and over again that it was essential during that period that the United States make it clear that we would not tolerate Indochina falling under Communist domination. Now, as a result of our taking the strong stand that we did, the civil war there was ended; and today, at least in the south of Indochina, the Communists have moved out and we do have a strong, free bastion there. Now, looking to the U-2 flights, I would like to point out that I have been supporting the President's position throughout. I think the President was correct in ordering these flights. I think the President was correct, certainly, in his decision to continue the flights while the conference was going on. I noted, for example, in reading a— uh— a— a particular discussion that Senator Kennedy had with Dave Garroway shortly after the uh— his statement about regrets, that uh— he made the statement that he felt that these particular flights uh— were ones that shouldn't have occurred right at that time, and the indication was how would Mr. Khrushchev had felt if we had uh— had a flight over the uni— how would we have felt if Mr. Khrushchev ha— uh— had a flight over the United States while uh— he was visiting here. And the answer, of course, is that Communist espionage goes on all the time. The answer is that the United States can't afford to have a ts —an es— a espionage lack or should we s— uh— lag—or should I say uh— an intelligence lag—any more than we can afford to have a missile lag. Now, referring to your question with regard to Quemoy and Matsu. What I object to here is the constant reference to surrendering these islands. Senator Kennedy quotes the record, which he read from a moment ago, but what he forgets to point out is that the key vote—a uh— vote which I've referred to several times—where he was in the minority was one which rejected his position. Now, why did they reject it? For the very reason that those Senators knew, as the President of the United States knew, that you should not indicate to the Communists in advance that you're going to surrender an area that's free. Why? Because they know as Senator Kennedy will have to know that if you do that you encourage them to more aggression.

MR. SHADEL: Senator Kennedy?

MR. KENNEDY: Well number one on Indochina, Mr. Nixon talked in— before the newspaper editors in the spring of 1954 about putting, and I quote him, "American boys into Indochina." The reason Indochina was preserved was the result of the Geneva Conference which /pətifənd/ Indochina. Number two, on the question of the U-2 flights. I thought the U-2 flight in May just before the conference was a mistake in timing because of the hazards involved, if the summit conference had any hope for success. I never criticized the U-2 flights in general, however. I never suggested espionage should stop. It still goes on, I would assume, on both sides. Number three, the Vice President—on May fifteenth after the U-2 flight—indicated that the flights were going on, even though the Administration and the President had canceled the flights on May twelfth. Number three, the pre— Vice President suggests that we should keep the Communists in doubt about whether we would fight on Quemoy and Matsu. That's not the position he's taking. He's indicating that we should fight for these islands come what may because they are, in his words, in the area of freedom. He didn't take that position on Tibet. He didn't take that position on Budapest. He doesn't take that position that I've seen so far in Laos. Guinea and Ghana have both moved within the Soviet sphere of influence in foreign policy; so has Cuba. I merely say that the United States should meet its commitments to Que— to uh— Formosa and the Pescadores. But as Admiral Yarnell has said, and he's been supported by most military authority, these islands that we're now talking about are not worth the bones of a single American soldier; and I know how difficult it is to sustain troops close to the shore under artillery bombardment. And therefore, I think, we should make it very clear the disagreement between Mr. Nixon and myself. He's extending the Administration's commitment.

MR. SHADEL: Mr. Drummond's question is for Senator Kennedy.

MR. DRUMMOND: Uh— Mr. Kennedy, Representative Adam Clayton Powell, in the course of his speaking tour in your behalf, is saying, and I quote: "The Ku Klux Klan is riding again in this campaign. If it doesn't stop, all bigots will vote for Nixon and all right-thinking Christians and Jews will vote for Kennedy rather than be found in the ranks of the Klan-minded." End quotation. Governor Michael DiSalle is saying much the same thing. What I would like to ask, Senator Kennedy, is what is the purpose of this sort of thing and how do you feel about it?

MR. KENNEDY: Well the que— the— Mr. Griffin, I believe, who is the head of the Klan, who lives in Tampa, Florida, indicated a— in a statement, I think, two or three weeks ago that he was not going to vote for me, and that he was going to vote for Mr. Nixon. I do not suggest in any way, nor have I ever, that that indicates that Mr. Nixon has the slightest sympathy, involvement, or in any way imply any inferences in regard to the Ku Klux Klan. That's absurd. I don't suggest that, I don't support it. I would disagree with it. Mr. Nixon knows very well that in this— in this whole matter that's been involved with the so-called religious discussion in this campaign, I've never suggested, even by the vaguest implication, that he did anything but disapprove it. And that's my view now. I disapprove of the issue. I do not suggest that Mr. Nixon does in any way.

MR. SHADEL: Mr. Vice President.

MR. NIXON: Well I welcome this opportunity to join Senator Kennedy completely on that statement and to say before this largest television audience in history something that I have been saying in the past and want to— will always say in the future. On our last television debate, I pointed out that it was my position that Americans must choose the best man that either party could produce. We can't settle for anything but the best. And that means, of course, the best man that this nation can produce. And that means that we can't have any test of religion. We can't have any test of race. It must be a test of a man. Also as far as religion is concerned. I have seen Communism abroad. I see what it does. Communism is the enemy of all religions; and we who do believe in God must join together. We must not be divided on this issue. The worst thing that I can think can happen in this campaign would be for it to be decided on religious issues. I obviously repudiate the Klan; I repudiate anybody who uses the religious issue; I will not tolerate it. I have ordered all of my people to have nothing to do with it and I say— say to this great audience, whoever may be listening, remember, if you believe in America, if you want America to set the right example to the world, that we cannot have religious or racial prejudice. We cannot have it in our hearts. But we certainly cannot have it in a presidential campaign.

MR. SHADEL: Mr. McGee has a question for Vice President Nixon.

MR. MCGEE: Mr. Vice President, some of your early campaign literature said you were making a study to see if new laws were needed to protect the public against excessive use of power by labor unions. Have you decided whether such new laws are needed, and, if so, what would they do?

MR. NIXON: Mr. McGee, I am planning a speech on that subject next week. Uh— Also, so that we can get the uh— opportunity for the questioners to question me, it will be before the next television debate. Uh— I will say simply, in advance of it, that I believe that in this area, the laws which should be passed uh— as far as the big national emergency strikes are concerned, are ones that will give the president more weapons with which to deal with those strikes. Now, I have a basic disagreement with Senator Kennedy, though, on this point. He has taken the position, when he first indicated in October of last year, that he would even favor compulsory arbitration as one of the weapons the president might have to stop a national emergency strike. I understand in his last speech before the Steelworkers Union, that he changed that position and indicated that he felt that government seizure might be the best way to stop a strike which could not be settled by collective bargaining. I do not believe we should have either compulsory arbitration or seizure. I think the moment that you give to the union, on the one side, and to management, on the other side, the escape hatch of eventually going to government to get it settled, that most of these great strikes will end up being settled by government, and that will be a— be in the end, in my opinion, wage control; it would mean price control—all the things that we do not want. I do believe, however, that we can give to the president of the United States powers, in addition to what he presently has in the fact-finding area, which would enable him to be more effective than we have been in handling these strikes. One last point I should make. The record in handling them has been very good during this Administration. We have had less man-hours lost by strikes in these last seven years than we had in the previous seven years, by a great deal. And I only want to say that however good the record is, it's got to be better. Because in this critical year—period of the sixties we've got to move forward, all Americans must move forward together, and we have to get the greatest cooperation possible between labor and management. We cannot afford stoppages of massive effect on the economy when we're in the terrible competition we're in with the Soviets.

MR. SHADEL: Senator, your comment.

MR. KENNEDY: Well, I always have difficulty recognizing my positions when they're stated by the Vice President. I never suggested that compulsory arbitration was the solution for national emergency disputes. I'm opposed to that, was opposed to it in October, 1958. I have suggested that the president should be given other weapons to protect the national interest in case of national emergency strikes beyond the injunction provision of the Taft-Hartley Act. I don't know what other weapons the Vice President is talking about. I'm talking about giving him four or five tools—not only the fact-finding committee that he now has under the injunction provision, not only the injunction, but also the power of the fact-finding commission to make recommendations—recommendations which would not be binding, but nevertheless would have great force of public opinion behind them. One of the additional powers that I would suggest would be seizure. There might be others. By the president having five powers—four or five powers—and he only has very limited powers today, neither the company nor the union would be sure which power would be used; and therefore, there would be a greater incentive on both sides to reach an agreement themselves without taking it to the government. The difficulty now is the president's course is quite limited. He can set up a fact-finding committee. The fact-finding committee's powers are limited. He can provide an injunction if there's a national emergency for eighty days, then the strike can go on; and there are no other powers or actions that the president could take unless he went to the Congress. This is a difficult and sensitive matter. But to state my view precisely, the president should have a variety of things he could do. He could leave the parties in doubt as to which one he would use; and therefore there would be incentive, instead of as now—the steel companies were ready to take the strike because they felt the injunction of eighty days would break the union, which didn't happen.

MR. SHADEL: The next question is by Mr. Cater for Senator Kennedy.

MR. CATER: Uh— Mr. Kennedy, uh— Senator—uh— Vice President Nixon says that he has costed the two party platforms and that yours would run at least ten billion dollars a year more than his. You have denied his figures. He has called on you to supply your figures. Would you do that?

MR. KENNEDY: Yes, I have stated in both uh— debates and state again that I believe in a balanced budget and have supported that concept during my fourteen years in the Congress. The only two times when an unbalanced budget is warranted would be during a serious recession—and we had that in fifty-eight in an unbalanced budget of twelve billion dollars— or a national emergency where there should be large expenditures for national defense, which we had in World War II and uh— during part of the Korean War. On the question of the cost of our budget, I have stated that it's my best judgment that our agricultural program will cost a billion and a half, possibly two billion dollars less than the present agricultural program. My judgment is that the program the Vice President put forward, which is an extension of Mr. Benson's program, will cost a billion dollars more than the present program, which costs about six billion dollars a year, the most expensive in history. We've spent more money on agriculture in the last eight years than the hundred years of the Agricultural Department before that. Secondly, I believe that the high interest-rate policy that this Administration has followed has added about three billion dollars a year to interest on the debt—merely funding the debt—which is a burden on the taxpayers. I would hope, under a different monetary policy, that it would be possible to reduce that interest-rate burden, at least a billion dollars. Third, I think it's possible to . . . gain a seven hundred million to a billion dollars through tax changes which I believe would close up loof— loopholes on dividend withholding, on expense accounts. Fourthly, I have suggested that the medical care for the aged—and the bill which the Congress now has passed and the President signed if fully implemented would cost a billion dollars on the Treasury—out of Treasury funds and a billion dollars by the states—the proposal that I have put forward and which many of the members of my party support is for medical care financed under Social Security; which would be financed under the Social Security taxes; which is less than three cents a day per person for medical care, doctors' bills, nurses, hospitals, when they retire. It is actuarially sound. So in my judgment we would spend more money in this Administration on aid to education, we'd spend more money on housing, we'd spend more money and I hope more wisely on defense than this Administration has. But I believe that the next Administration should work for a balanced budget, and that would be my intention. Mr. Nixon misstates my figures constantly, which uh— is of course his right, but the fact of the matter is: here is where I stand and I just want to have it on the public record.

MR. SHADEL: Mr. Vice President?

MR. NIXON: Senator Kennedy has indicated on several occasions in this program tonight that I have been misstating his record and his figures. I will issue a white paper after this broadcast, quoting exactly what he said on compulsory arbitration, for example, and the record will show that I have been correct. Now as far as his figures are concerned here tonight, he again is engaging in this, what I would call, mirror game of "here-it-is-and-here-it-isn't." Uh— On the one hand, for example, he suggests that as far as his medical care program is concerned that that really isn't a problem because it's from Social Security. But Social Security is a tax. The people pay it. It comes right out of your paycheck. This doesn't mean that the people aren't going to be paying the bill. He also indicates as far as his agricultural program is concerned that he feels it will cost less than ours. Well, all that I can suggest is that all the experts who have studied the program indicate that it is the most fantastic program, the worst program, insofar as its effect on the farmers, that the— America has ever had foisted upon it in an election year or any other time. And I would also point out that Senator Kennedy left out a part of the cost of that program —a twenty-five per cent rise in food prices that the people would have to pay. Now are we going to have that when it isn't going to help the farmers? I don't think we should have that kind of a program. Then he goes on to say that he's going to change the interest-rate situation and we're going to get some more money that way. Well, what he is saying there in effect, we're going to have inflation. We're going to go right back to what we had under Mr. Truman when he had political control of the Federal Reserve Board. I don't believe we ought to pay our bills through inflation, through a phony interest rate.

MR. SHADEL: Next, Mr. Drummond's question for Vice President Nixon.

MR. DRUMMOND: Uh— Mr. Nixon uh— before the convention you and Governor Rockefeller said jointly that the nation's economic growth ought to be accelerated; and the Republican platform states that uh— the nation needs to quicken the pace of economic growth. Uh— Is it fair, therefore, Mr. Vice President, to conclude that you feel that there has been insufficient economic growth during the past eight years; and if so, what would you do beyond uh— present Administration policies uh— to step it up?

MR. NIXON: Mr. Drummond, I am never satisfied with the economic growth of this country. I'm not satisfied with it even if there were no Communism in the world, but particularly when we're in the kind of a race we're in, we have got to see that America grows just as fast as we can, provided we grow soundly. Because even though we have maintained, as I pointed out in our first debate, the absolute gap over the Soviet Union; even though the growth in this Administration has been twice as much as it was in the Truman Administration; that isn't good enough. Because America must be able to grow enough not only to take care of our needs at home for better education and housing and health—all these things we want. We've got to grow enough to maintain the forces that we have abroad and to wage the non-military battle for the war— uh— for the world in Asia, in Africa and Latin America. It's going to cost more money, and growth will help us to win that battle. Now, what do we do about it? And here I believe basically that what we have to do is to stimulate that sector of America, the private enterprise sector of the economy, in which there is the greatest possibility for expansion. So that is why I advocate a program of tax reform which will stimulate more investment in our economy. In addition to that, we have to move on other areas that are holding back growth. I refer, for example, to distressed areas. We have to move into those areas with programs so that we make adequate use of the resources of those areas. We also have to see that all of the people of the United States—the tremendous talents that our people have —are used adequately. That's why in this whole area of civil rights, the equality of opportunity for employment and education is not just for the benefit of the minority groups, it's for the benefit of the nation so that we can get the scientists and the engineers and all the rest that we need. And in addition to that, we need programs, particularly in higher education, which will stimulate scientific breakthroughs which will bring more growth. Now what all this, of course, adds up to is this: America has not been standing still. Let's get that straight. Anybody who says America's been standing still for the last seven and a half years hasn't been traveling around America. He's been traveling in some other country. We have been moving. We have been moving much faster than we did in the Truman years. But we can and must move faster, and that's why I stand so strongly for programs that will move America forward in the sixties, move her forward so that we can stay ahead of the Soviet Union and win the battle for freedom and peace.

MR. SHADEL: Senator Kennedy.

MR. KENNEDY: Well first may I correct a statement which was made before, that under my agricultural program food prices would go up twenty-five per cent. That's untrue. The fa— the farmer who grows wheat gets about two and a half cents out of a twenty-five-cent loaf of bread. Even if you put his income up ten per cent, that would be two and three-quarters per cent three pers— or three cents out of that twenty-five cents. The t— man who grows tomatoes—it costs less for those tomatoes than it does for the label on the can. And I believe when the average hour for many farmers' wage is about fifty cents an hour, he should do better. But anybody who suggests that that program would c— come to any figure indicated by the Vice President is in error. The Vice President suggested a number of things. He suggested that we aid distressed areas. The Administration has vetoed that bill passed by the Congress twice. He suggested we pass an aid to education bill. But the Administration and the Republican majority in the Congress has opposed any realistic aid to education. And the Vice President cast the deciding vote against federal aid for teachers' salaries in the Senate, which prevented that being added. This

Administration and this country last year had the lowest rate of economic growth—which means jobs—of any major industrialized society in the world in 1959. And when we have to find twenty-five thousand new jobs a week for the next ten years, we're going to have to grow more. Governor Rockefeller says five per cent. The Democratic platform and others say five per cent. Many say four and a half per cent. The last eight years the average growth has been about two and a half per cent. That's why we don't have full employment today.

MR. SHADEL: Mr. McGee has the next question for Senator Kennedy.

MR. MCGEE: Uh— Senator Kennedy, a moment ago you mentioned tax loopholes. Now your running mate, Senator Lyndon Johnson, is from Texas, an oil-producing state and one that many political leaders feel is in doubt in this election year. And reports from there say that oil men in Texas are seeking assurance from Senator Johnson that the oil depletion allowance will not be cut. The Democratic platform pledges to plug loopholes in the tax laws and refers to inequitable depletion allowance as being conspicuous loopholes. My question is, do you consider the twenty-seven and a half per cent depletion allowance inequitable, and would you ask that it be cut?

MR. KENNEDY: Uh— Mr. McGee, there are about a hundred and four commodities that have some kind of depletion allowance—different kind of minerals, including oil. I believe all of those should be gone over in detail to make sure that no one is getting a tax break; to make sure that no one is getting away from paying the taxes he ought to pay. That includes oil; it includes all kinds of minerals; it includes everything within the range of taxation. We want to be sure it's fair and equitable. It includes oil abroad. Perhaps that oil abroad should be treated differently than the oil /ir/ here at home. Now the oil industry recently has had hard times. Particularly some of the smaller producers. They're moving about eight or nine days in Texas. But I can assure you that if I'm elected president, the whole spectrum of taxes will be gone through carefully. And if there is any inequities in oil or any other commodity, then I would vote to close that loophole. I have voted in the past to reduce the depletion allowance for the largest producers; for those from five million dollars down, to maintain it at twenty-seven and a half per cent. I believe we should study this and other allowances; tax expense, dividend expenses and all the rest, and make a determination of how we can stimulate growth; how we can provide the revenues needed to move our country forward.

MR. SHADEL: Mr. Vice President.

MR. NIXON: Senator Kennedy's position and mine are completely different on this. I favor the present depletion allowance. I favor it not because I want to make a lot of oil men rich, but because I want to make America rich. Why do we have a depletion allowance? Because this is the stimulation, the incentive for companies to go out and explore for oil, to develop it. If we didn't have a depletion allowance of certainly, I believe, the present amount, we would have our oil exploration cut substantially in this country. Now, as far as my position then is concerned, it is exactly opposite to the Senator's. And it's because of my belief that if America is going to have the growth that he talks about and that I talk about and that we want, the thing to do is not to discourage individual enterprise, not to discourage people to go out and discover more oil and minerals, but to encourage them. And so he would be doing exactly the wrong thing. One other thing. He suggests that there are a number of other items in this whole depletion field that could be taken into account. He also said a moment ago that we would get more money to finance his programs by revising the tax laws, including depletion. I should point out that as far as depletion allowances are concerned, the oil depletion allowance is one that provides eighty per cent of all of those involved in depletion, so you're not going to get much from revenue insofar as depletion allowances are concerned, unless you move in the area that he indicated. But I oppose it. I oppose it for the reasons that I mentioned. I oppose it because I want us to have more oil exploration and not less.

MR. SHADEL: Gentlemen, if I may remind you, time is growing short, so please keep your questions and answers as brief as possible consistent with clarity. Mr. Von Fremd for Vice President Nixon.

MR. VON FREMD: Mr. Vice President, in the past three years, there has been an exodus of more than four billion dollars of gold from the United States, apparently for two reasons: because exports have slumped and haven't covered imports, and because of increased American investments abroad. If you were president, how would you go about stopping this departure of gold from our shores?

MR. NIXON: Well, Mr. Von Fremd, the first thing we have to do is to continue to keep confidence abroad in the American dollar. That means that we must continue to have a balanced budget here at home in every possible circumstance that we can; because the moment that we have loss of confidence in our own fiscal policies at home, it results in gold flowing out. Secondly, we have to increase our exports, as compared with our imports. And here we have a very strong program going forward in the Department of Commerce. This one must be stepped up. Beyond that, as far as the gold supply is concerned, and as far as the movement of gold is concerned, uh— we have to bear in mind that we must get more help from our allies abroad in this great venture in which all free men are involved of winning the battle for freedom. Now America has been carrying a tremendous load in this respect. I think we have been right in carrying it. I have favored our programs abroad for economic assistance and for military assistance. But now we find that the countries of Europe for example, that we have aided, and Japan, that we've aided in the Far East;

these countries—some our former enemies, some our friends—have now recovered completely. They have got to bear a greater share of this load of economic assistance abroad. That's why I am advocating, and will develop during the course of the next Administration—if, of course, I get the opportunity—a program in which we enlist more aid from these other countries on a concerted basis in the programs of economic development for Africa, Asia and Latin America. The United States cannot continue to carry the major share of this burden by itself. We can /kehr/ a big share of it, but we've got to have more help from our friends abroad; and these three factors, I think, will be very helpful in reversing the gold flow which you spoke about.

MR. SHADEL: Senator Kennedy.

MR. KENNEDY: Just to uh— correct the record, Mr. Nixon said on de-pletion that his record was the opposite of mine. What I said was that this matter should be thoroughly gone into to make sure that there aren't loop-holes. If his record is the opposite of that, that means that he doesn't want to go into it. Now on the question of gold. The difficulty, of course, is that we do have heavy obligations abroad, that we therefore have to main-tain not only a favorable balance of trade but also send a good deal of our dollars overseas to pay our troops, maintain our bases, and sustain other economies. In other words, if we're going to continue to maintain our position in the sixties, we have to maintain a sound monetary and fiscal policy. We have to have control over inflation, and we also have to have a favorable balance of trade. We have to be able to compete in the world market. We have to be able to sell abroad more than we consume uh— from abroad if we're going to be able to meet our obligations. In addition, many of the countries around the world still keep restrictions against our goods, going all the way back to the days when there was a dollar shortage. Now there isn't a dollar shortage, and yet many of these countries continue to move against our goods. I believe that we must be able to compete in the market—steel and in all the basic commodities abroad—we must be able to compete against them because we always did because of our technological lead. We have to be sure to maintain that. We have to persuade these other countries not to restrict our goods coming in, not to act as if there was a dollar gap; and third, we have to persuade them to assume some of the responsibilities that up till now we've main-tained, to assist underdeveloped countries in Africa, Latin America and Asia make an economic breakthrough on their own.

MR. SHADEL: Mr. Drummond's question now for Senator Kennedy.

MR. DRUMMOND: Senator Kennedy, a question on American prestige. In light of the fact that the Soviet Ambassador was recently expelled from the Congo, and that Mr. Khrushchev has this week canceled his trip to Cuba for fear of stirring resentment throughout all Latin America, I would like to ask you to spell out somewhat more fully how you think we should measure American prestige, to determine whether it is rising or whether it is falling.

MR. KENNEDY: Well, I think there are many uh— tests, Mr. Drummond, of prestige. And the significance of prestige, really, is because we're so identified with the cause of freedom. Therefore, if we are on the mount, if we are rising, if our influence is spreading, if our prestige is spreading, then those uh— who stand now on the razor edge of decision between us or between the Communist system, wondering whether they should use the system of freedom to develop their countries or the system of Communism, they'll be persuaded to follow our example. There have been several indications that our prestige is not as high as it once was. Mr. George Allen, the head of our information service, said that a result of our being second in space, in the sputnik in 1957, and I quote him, I believe I paraphrase him accurately. He said that many of these countries equate space . . . developments with scientific productivity and scientific advancement. And therefore, he said, many of these countries now feel that the Soviet Union, which was once so backward, is now on a par with the United States. Secondly, the economic growth of the Soviet Union is greater than ours. Mr. Dulles has suggested it's from two to three times as great as ours. This has a great effect on the s— underdeveloped world, which faces problems of low income and high population density and inadequate resources. Three, a Gallup Poll taken in February asked people in ten countries which country they thought would be first in 1970, both scientifically and militarily. And a majority in every country except Greece, felt that it would be the Soviet Union by 1970. Four, in the votes at the U.N., particularly the vote dealing with Red China last Saturday, we received the support on the position that we had taken of only two African countries—one, Liberia, which had been tied to us for more than a century, and the other, Union of South Africa, which is not a popular country in Africa. Every other ca— African country either abstained or voted against us. A— More countries voted against us in Asia on this issue than voted with us. On the neutralists' resolution, which we were so much opposed to, the same thing happened. The candidate who was a candidate for the president of Brazil, took a trip to Cuba to call on Mr. Castro during the election in order to get the benefit of the Castro supporters uh— within Brazil. There are many indications. Guinea and Ghana, two independent countries within the last three years—Guinea in fifty-seven, Ghana within the last eighteen months—both now are supporting the Soviet foreign policy at the U.N. Mr. Herter said so himself. Laos is moving in that direction. So I would say our prestige is not so high. No longer do we give the image of being on the rise. No longer do we give an image of vitality.

MR. SHADEL: Mr. Vice President.

MR. NIXON: Well, I would say first of all that Senator's— Kennedy's statement that he's just made is not going to help our Gallup Polls abroad and it isn't going to help our prestige either. Let's look at the other side of the coin. Let's look at the vote on the Congo, the vote was seventy to nothing against the Soviet Union. Let's look at the situation with regard to economic growth as it really is. We find that the Soviet Union is a very primitive economy. Its growth rate is not what counts; it's whether it is catching up with us and it is not catching up with us. We're well ahead and we can stay ahead, provided we have confidence in America and don't run her down in order to build her up. We could look also at other items which Senator Kennedy has named, but I will only conclude by saying this: in this whole matter of prestige, in the final analysis, its whether you stand for what's right. And getting back to this matter that we discussed at the outset, the matter of Quemoy and Masu. I can think of nothing that will be a greater blow to the prestige of the United States among the free nations in Asia than for us to take Senator Kennedy's advan— advice to go— go against what a majority of the members of the Senate, both Democrat and Republican, did— said in 1955, and to say in advance we will surrender an area to the Communists. In other words, if the United States is going to maintain its strength and its prestige, we must not only be strong militarily and economically, we must be firm diplomatically. Thi— Certainly we have been speaking, I know, of whether we should have retreat or defeat. Let's remember the way to win is not to retreat and not to surrender.

MR. SHADEL: Thank you gentlemen. As we mentioned at the opening of this program, the candidates agreed that the clock alone would determine who had the last word. The two candidates wish to thank the networks for the opportunity to appear for this discussion. I would repeat the ground rules likewise agreed upon by representatives of the two candidates and the radio and television networks. The entire hour was devoted to answering questions from the reporters. Each candidate was questioned in turn and each had the opportunity to comment on the answer of his opponent. The reporters were free to ask any question on any subject. Neither candidate was given any advance information on any question that would be asked. Those were the conditions agreed upon for this third meeting of the candidates tonight. Now I might add that also agreed upon was the fact that when the hour got down to the last few minutes, if there was not sufficient time left for another question and suitable time for answers and comment, the questioning would end at that point. That is the situation at this moment. And after reviewing the rules for this evening I might use the remaining moments of the hour to tell you something about the other arrangements for this debate with the participants a continent apart. I would emphasize first that each candidate was in a studio alone except for three photographers and three reporters of the press and the television technicians. Those studios identical in every detail of lighting, background, physical equipment, even to the paint used in decorating. We newsmen in a third studio have also experienced a somewhat similar isolation. Now, I would remind you the fourth in the series of these historic joint appearances, scheduled for Friday, October twenty-first. At that time the candidates will again share the same platform to discuss foreign policy. This is Bill Shadel. Goodnight.

Fourth Debate, October 21, 1960

QUINCY HOWE, moderator: I am Quincy Howe of CB— of ABC News saying good evening from New York where the two major candidates for president of the United States are about to engage in their fourth radio-television discussion of the present campaign. Tonight these men will confine that discussion to foreign policy. Good evening, Vice President Nixon.

MR. NIXON: Good evening, Mr. Howe.

MR. HOWE: And good evening, Senator Kennedy.

MR. KENNEDY: Good evening, Mr. Howe.

MR. HOWE: Now let me read the rules and conditions under which the candidates themselves have agreed to proceed. As they did in their first meeting, both men will make opening statements of about eight minutes each and closing statements of equal time running three to five minutes each. During the half hour between the opening and closing statements, the candidates will answer and comment upon questions from a panel of four correspondents chosen by the nationwide networks that carry the program. Each candidate will be questioned in turn with opportunity for comment by the other. Each answer will be limited to two and one-half minutes, each comment to one and one-half minutes. The correspondents are free to ask any questions they choose in the field of foreign affairs. Neither candidate knows what questions will be asked. Time alone will determine the final question. Reversing the order in their first meeting, Senator Kennedy will make the second opening statement and the first closing statement. For the first opening statement, here is Vice President Nixon.

MR. NIXON: Mr. Howe, Senator Kennedy, my fellow Americans. Since this campaign began I have had a very rare privilege. I have traveled to forty-eight of the fifty states and in my travels I have learned what the people of the United States are thinking about. There is one issue that stands out above all the rest, one in which every American is concerned, regardless of what group he may be a member and regardless of where he may live. And that issue, very simply stated, is this: how can we keep the

411

peace—keep it without surrender? How can we extend freedom—extend it without war? Now in determining how we deal with this issue, we must find the answer to a very important but simple question: who threatens the peace? Who threatens freedom in the world? There is only one threat to peace and one threat to freedom—that that is presented by the international Communist movement. And therefore if we are to have peace, if we are to keep our own freedom and extend it to others without war, we must know how to deal with the Communists and their leaders. I know Mr. Khrushchev. I also have had the opportunity of knowing and meeting other Communist leaders in the world. I believe there are certain principles we must find in dealing with him and his colleagues—principles, if followed, that will keep the peace and that also can extend freedom. First, we have to learn from the past, because we cannot afford to make the mistakes of the past. In the seven years before this Administration came into power in Washington. we found that six hundred million people went behind the Iron Curtain. And at the end of that seven years we were engaged in a war in Korea which cost over thirty thousand American lives. In the past seven years, in President Eisenhower's Administration, this situation has been reversed. We ended the Korean War; by strong, firm leadership we have kept out of other wars; and we have avoided surrender of principle or territory at the conference table. Now why were we successful, as our predecessors were not successful? I think there're several reasons. In the first place, they made a fatal error in misjudging the Communists; in trying to apply to them the same rules of conduct that you would apply to the leaders of the free world. One of the major errors they made was the one that led to the Korean War. In ruling out the defense of Korea, they invited aggression in that area. They thought they were going to have peace—it brought war. We learned from their mistakes. And so, in our seven years, we find that we have been firm in our diplomacy; we have never made concessions without getting concessions in return. We have always been willing to go the extra mile to negotiate for disarmament or in any other area. But we have never been willing to do anything that, in effect, surrendered freedom any place in the world. That is why President Eisenhower was correct in not apologizing or expressing regrets to Mr. Khrushchev at the Paris Conference, as Senator Kennedy suggested he could have done. That is why Senator wh— President Eisenhower was also correct in his policy in the Formosa Straits, where he declined, and refused to follow the recommendations—recommendations which Senator Kennedy voted for in 1955; again made in 1959; again repeated in his debates that you have heard—recommendations with regard to—again—slicing off a piece of free territory, and abandoning it, if— in effect, to the Communists. Why did the President feel this was wrong and why was the President right and his critics wrong? Because again this showed a lack of understanding of dictators, a lack of understanding particularly of Communists, because every time you make such a concession it does not lead to peace; it only encourages them to blackmail you. It encourages them to begin a war. And so I say that the record shows that we know how to keep the peace, to keep it without surrender. Let us move now to the future. It is not enough to stand on this record because we are dealing with the most ruthless, fanatical . . . leaders that the world has ever seen. That is why I say that in this period of the sixties, America must move forward in every area. First of all, although we are today, as Senator Kennedy has admitted, the strongest nation in the world militarily, we must increase our strength, increase it so that we will always have enough strength that regardless of what our potential opponents have—if they should launch a surprise attack—we will be able to destroy their war-making capability. They must know, in other words, that it is national suicide if they begin anything. We need this kind of strength because we're the guardians of the peace. In addition to military strength, we need to see that the economy of this country continues to grow. It has grown in the past seven years. It can and will grow even more in the next four. And the reason that it must grow even more is because we have things to do at home and also because we're in a race for survival—a race in which it isn't enough to be ahead; it isn't enough simply to be complacent. We have to move ahead in order to stay ahead. And that is why, in this field, I have made recommendations which I am confident will move the American economy ahead —move it firmly and soundly so that there will never be a time when the Soviet Union will be able to challenge our superiority in this field. And so we need military strength, we need economic strength, we also need the right diplomatic policies. What are they? Again we turn to the past. Firmness but no belligerence, and by no belligerence I mean that we do not answer insult by insult. When you are proud and confident of your strength, you do not get down to the level of Mr. Khrushchev and his colleagues. And that example that President Eisenhower has set we will continue to follow. But all this by itself is not enough. It is not enough for us simply to be the strongest nation militarily, the strongest economically, and also to have firm diplomacy. We must have a great goal. And that is: not just to keep freedom for ourselves but to extend it to all the world, to extend it to all the world because that is America's destiny. To extend it to all the world because the Communist aim is not to hold their own but to extend Communism. And you cannot fight a victory for Communism or a strategy of victory for Communism with the strategy simply of holding the line. And so I say that we believe that our policies of military strength, of economic strength, of diplomatic firmness first will keep the peace and keep it without surrender. We also believe that in the great field of ideals that we can lead America to the victory for freedom— victory in the newly developing countries, victory also in the captive countries—provided we have faith in ourselves and faith in our principles.

friends, that we want them to be free again? Africa is now the emerging area of the world. It contains twenty-five per cent of all the members of the General Assembly. We didn't even have a Bureau of African Affairs until 1957. In the Africa south of the Sahara, which is the major new section, we have less students from all of Africa in that area studying under government auspices today than from the country of Thailand. If there's one thing Africa needs it's technical assistance. And yet last year we gave them less than five per cent of all the technical assistance funds that we distributed around the world. We relied in the Middle East on the Bagdad Pact, and yet when the Iraqi Government was changed, the Bagdad Pact broke down. We relied on the Eisenhower Doctrine for the Middle East, which passed the Senate. There isn't one country in the Middle East that now endorses the Eisenhower Doctrine. We look to Europe uh— to Asia because the struggle is in the underdeveloped world. Which system, Communism or freedom, will triumph in the next five or ten years? That's what should concern us, not the history of ten, or fifteen, or twenty years ago. But are we doing enough in these areas? What are freedom's chances in those areas? By 1965 or 1970, will there be other Cubas in Latin America? Will Guinea and Ghana, which have now voted with the Communists frequently as newly independent countries of Africa—will there be others? Will the Congo go Communist? Will other countries? Are we doing enough in that area? And what about Asia? Is India going to win the economic struggle or is China going to win it? Who will dominate Asia in the next five or ten years? Communism? The Chinese? Or will freedom? The question which we have to decide as Americans—are we doing enough today? Is our strength and prestige rising? Do people want to be identified with us? Do they want to follow United States leadership? I don't think they do, enough. And that's what concerns me. In Africa—these countries that have newly joined the United Nations. On the question of admission of Red China, only two countries in all of Africa voted with us—Liberia and the Union of South Africa. The rest either abstained or voted against us. More countries in Asia voted against us on that question than voted with us. I believe that this struggle is going to go on, and it may be well decided in the next decade. I have seen Cuba go to the Communists. I have seen Communist influence and Castro influence rise in Latin America. I have seen us ignore Africa. There are six countries in Africa that are members of the United Nations. There isn't a single American diplomatic representative in any of those six. When Guinea became independent, the Soviet Ambassador showed up that very day. We didn't recognize them for two months; the American Ambassador didn't show up for nearly eight months. I believe that the world is changing fast. And I don't think this Administration has shown the foresight, has shown the knowledge, has been identified with the great fight which these people are waging to be free, to get a better standard of living, to live better. The average income in some of those countries is twenty-five dollars a year. The Communists say, "Come with us; look what we've done." And we've been in— on the whole, uninterested. I think we're going to have to do better. Mr. Nixon talks about our being the strongest country in the world. I think we are today. But we were far stronger relative to the Communists five years ago, and what is of great concern is that the balance of power is in danger of moving with them. They made a breakthrough in missiles, and by nineteen sixty-one, two, and three, they will be outnumbering us in missiles. I'm not as confident as he is that we will be the strongest military power by 1963. He talks about economic growth as a great indicator of freedom. I agree with him. What we do in this country, the kind of society that we build, that will tell whether freedom will be sustained around the world. And yet, in the last nine months of this year, we've had a drop in our economic growth rather than a gain. We've had the lowest rate of increase of economic growth in the last nine months of any major industrialized society in the world. I look up and see the Soviet flag on the moon. The fact is that the State Department polls on our prestige and influence around the world have shown such a sharp drop that up till now the State Department has been unwilling to release them. And yet they were polled by the U.S.I.A. The point of all this is, this is a struggle in which we're engaged. We want peace. We want freedom. We want security. We want to be stronger. We want freedom to gain. But I don't believe in these changing and revolutionary times this Administration has known that the world is changing—has identified itself with that change. I think the Communists have been moving with vigor—Laos, Africa, Cuba—all around the world today they're on the move. I think we have to revitalize our society. I think we have to demonstrate to the people of the world that we're determined in this free country of ours to be first—not first if, and not first but, and not first when—but first. And when we are strong and when we are first, then freedom gains; then the prospects for peace increase; then the prospects for our society . . . gain.

MR. HOWE: That completes the opening statements. Now the candidates will answer and comment upon questions put by these four correspondents: Frank Singiser of Mutual News, John Edwards of ABC News, Walter Cronkite of CBS News, John Chancellor of NBC News. Frank Singiser has the first question for Vice President Nixon.

MR. SINGISER: Mr. Vice President, I'd like to pin down the difference between the way you would handle Castro's regime and prevent the establishment of Communist governments in the Western Hemisphere and the way that Senator Kennedy would proceed. Uh— Vice President Nixon, in what important respects do you feel there are differences between you, and why do you believe your policy is better for the peace and security of the United States in the Western Hemisphere?

MR. NIXON: Our policies are very different. I think that Senator Kennedy's policies and recommendations for the handling of the Castro regime are probably the most dangers— dangerously irresponsible recommendations that he's made during the course of this campaign. In effect, what Senator Kennedy recommends is that the United States government should give help to the exiles and to those within Cuba who oppose the Castro regime—provided they are anti-Batista. Now let's just see what this means. We have five treaties with Latin America, including the one setting up the Organization of American States in Bogota in 1948, in which we have agreed not to intervene in the internal affairs of any other American country—and they as well have agreed to do likewise. The charter of the United Nations—its Preamble, Article I and Article II—also provide that there shall be no intervention by one nation in the internal affairs of another. Now I don't know what Senator Kennedy suggests when he says that we should help those who oppose the Castro regime, both in Cuba and without. But I do know this: that if we were to follow that recommendation, that we would lose all of our friends in Latin America, we would probably be condemned in the United Nations, and we would not accomplish our objective. I know something else. It would be an open invitation for Mr. Khrushchev to come in, to come into Latin America and to engage us in what would be a civil war, and possibly even worse than that. This is the major recommendation that he's made. Now, what can we do? Well, we can do what we did with Guatemala. There was a Communist dictator that we inherited from the previous Administration. We quarantined Mr. Arbenz. The result was that the Guatemalan people themselves eventually rose up and they threw him out. We are quarantining Mr. Castro today. We're quarantining him diplomatically by bringing back our Ambassador; economically by cutting off trade, and Senator Kennedy's suggestion that the trade that we cut off is not significant is just one hundred per cent wrong. We are cutting off the significant items that the Cuban regime needs in order to survive. By cutting off trade, by cutting off our diplomatic relations as we have, we will quarantine this regime so that the people of Cuba themselves will take care of Mr. Castro. But for us to do what Senator Kennedy has suggested would bring results which I know he would not want, and certainly which the American people would not want.

MR. KENNEDY: Mr. Nixon uh— shows himself i— misinformed. He surely must be aware that most of the equipment and arms and resources for Castro came from the United States, flowed out of Florida and other parts of the United States to Castro in the mountains. There isn't any doubt about that, number one. Number two, I believe that if any economic sanctions against Latin America are going to be successful they have to be multilateral. They have to include the other countries of Latin America. The very minute effect of the action which has been taken this week on Cuba's economy—I believe Castro can replace those markets very easily through Latin America, through Europe, and through Eastern Europe. If the United States had stronger prestige and influence in Latin America it could persuade—as Franklin Roosevelt did in 1940—the countries of Latin America to join in an economic quarantine of Castro. That's the only way you can bring real economic pressure on the Castro regime—and also the countries of Western Europe, Canada, Japan and the others. Number three, Castro is only the beginning of our difficulties throughout Latin America. The big struggle will be to prevent the influence of Castro spreading to other countries—Mexico, Panama, Bolivia, Colombia. We're going to have to try to provide closer ties, to associate ourselves with the great desire of these people for a better life if we're going to prevent Castro's influence from spreading throughout all of Latin America. His influence is strong enough today to prevent us from joi— getting the other countries of Latin America to join with us in economic quarantine. His influence is growing—mostly because this Administration has ignored Latin America. You yourself said, Mr. Vice President, a month ago, that if we had provided the kind of economic aid five years ago that we are now providing we might never have had Castro. Why didn't we?

MR. HOWE: John Edwards has his first question for Senator Kennedy.

MR. EDWARDS: Senator Kennedy, one test of a new president's leadership will be the caliber of his appointments. It's a matter of interest here and overseas as to who will be the new secretary of state. Now, under our rules, I must ask this question of you, but I would hope that the Vice President also would answer it. Will you give us the names of three or four Americans, each of whom, if appointed, would serve with distinction in your judgment as secretary of state?

MR. KENNEDY: Mr. Edwards, I don't think it's a wise idea for presidential candidates to appoint the members of his cabinet prospectively, or to suggest four people—indicate that one of them surely will be appointed. This is a decision that the president of the United States must make. The last candidate who indicated that he knew who his cabinet was going to be was Mr. Dewey in 1948. This is a race between the Vice President and myself for the presidency of the United States. There are a good many able men who could be secretary of state. I've made no judgment about who should be secretary of state. I think that judgment could be made after election, if I'm successful. The people have to make a choice between Mr. Nixon and myself, between the Republican party and the Democratic party, between our approach to the problems which now disturb us as a nation and disturb us as a world power. The president bears the constitutional responsibility, not the secretary of state, for the conduct of foreign affairs. Some presidents have been strong in foreign policy; others have relied heavily on the secretary of state. I've been a member of the Senate Foreign Relations Committee; I run for the presidency with full knowledge that his great responsibility, really, given to him by the Constitution and by the force of events, is in the field of foreign affairs. I'm asking the people's support as president. We will select the best man we can get. But I've not made a judgment, and I have not narrowed down a list of three or four people, among whom would be the candidate.

MR. HOWE: Mr. Vice President, do you have a comment?

MR. NIXON: Well Mr. Edwards, as you probably know, I have consistently answered all questions with regard to who will be in the next cabinet by saying that that is the responsibility of the next president, and it would be inappropriate to make any decisions on that or to announce any prior to the time that I had the right to do so. So that is my answer to this question. If you don't mind, I'd like to use the balance of the time to respond to one of the comments that Senator Kennedy made on the previous question. Eh— He was talking about the Castro regime and what we had been eh— doing in Latin America. I would like to point out that when we look at our programs in Latin America, we find that we have appropriated five times as much for Latin America as was appropriated by the previous Administration; we find that we have two billion dollars more for the Export-Import Bank; we have a new bank for Latin America alone of a billion dollars; we have the new program which was submitted at the Bogota Conference—this new program that President Eisenhower submitted, approved by the last Congress—for five hundred million dollars. We have moved in Latin America very effectively, and I'd also like to point this out: Senator Kennedy complains very appropriately about our inadequate ra— radio broadcasts for Latin America. Let me point out again that his Congress—the Democratic Congress—has cut eighty million dollars off of the Voice of America appropriations. Now, he has to get a better job out of his Congress if he's going to get us the money that we need to conduct the foreign affairs of this country in Latin America or any place else.

MR. HOWE: Walter Cronkite, you have your first question for Vice President Nixon.

MR. CRONKITE: Thank you Quincy. Mr. Vice President, Senator Fulbright and now tonight, Senator Kennedy, maintain that the Administration is suppressing a report by the United States Information Agency that shows a decline in United States prestige overseas. Are you aware of such a report, and if you are aware of the existence of such a report, should not that report, because of the great importance this issue has been given in this campaign, be released to the public?

MR. NIXON: Mr. Cronkite, I naturally am aware of it, because I, of course, pay attention to everything Senator Kennedy says, as well as Senator Fulbright. Now, in this connection I want to point out that the facts simply aren't as stated. First of all, the report to which Senator Kennedy refers is one that was made many, many months ago and related particularly to the uh— period immediately after Sputnik. Second, as far as this report is concerned, I would have no objection to having it made public. Third, I would say this with regard to this report, with regard to Gallup Polls of prestige abroad and everything else that we've been hearing about "what about American prestige abroad": America's prestige abroad will be just as high as the spokesmen for America allow it to be. Now, when we have a presidential candidate, for example—Senator Kennedy—stating over and over again that the United States is second in space and the fact of the matter is that the space score today is twenty-eight to eight—we've had twenty-eight successful shots, they've had eight; when he states that we're second in education, and I have seen Soviet education and I've seen ours, and we're not; that we're second in science because they may be ahead in one area or another, when over-all we're way ahead of the Soviet Union and all other countries in science; when he says as he did in January of this years that we have the worst slums, that we have the most crowded schools; when he says that seventeen million people go to bed hungry every night; when he makes statements like this, what does this do to American prestige? Well, it can only have the effect certainly of reducing it. Well let me make one thing clear. Senator Kennedy has a responsibility to criticize those things that are wrong, but he has also a responsibility to be right in his criticism. Every one of these items that I have mentoned he's been wrong—dead wrong. And for that reason he has contributed to any lack of prestige. Finally, let me say this: as far as prestige is concerned, the first place it would show up would be in the United Nations. Now Senator Kennedy has referred to the vote on Communist China. Let's look at the vote on Hungary. There we got more votes for condemning Hungary and looking into that situation than we got the last year. Let's look at the reaction eh— reaction to Khrushchev and Eisenhower at the last U.N. session. Did Khrushchev gain because he took his shoe off and pounded the table and shouted and insulted? Not at all. The President gained. America gained by continuing the dignity, the decency that has characterized us and it's that that keeps the prestige of America up, not running down America the way Senator Kennedy has been running her down.

MR. HOWE: Comment, Senator Kennedy?

MR. KENNEDY: I really don't need uh— Mr. Nixon to tell me about what my responsibilities are as a citizen. I've served this country for fourteen years in the Congress and before that in the service. I've just as high a devotion, just as high an opinion. What I downgrade, Mr. Nixon, is the leadership the country is getting, not the country. Now I didn't make most of the statements that you said I made. The s— I believe the Soviet Union is first in outer space. We have— may have made more shots but the size of their rocket thrust and all the rest—you yourself said to Khrushchev, "You may be ahead of us in rocket thrust but we're ahead of you in color television" in your famous discussion in the kitchen. I think that color television is not as important as rocket thrust. Secondly, I didn't say we had the worst slums in the world. I said we had too many slums. And that they are bad, and we ought to do something about them, and we ought to support housing legislation which this Administration has opposed. I didn't say we had the worst education in the world. What I said was that ten years ago, we were producing twice as many scientists and engineers as the Soviet Union and today they're producing twice as many as we are, and that this affects our security around the world. And fourth, I believe that the polls and other studies and votes in the United Nations and anyone reading the paper and any citizen of the United States must come to the conclusion that the United States no longer carries the same image of a vital society on the move with its brightest days ahead as it carried a decade or two decades ago. Part of that is because we've stood still here at home, because we haven't met our problems in the United States, because we haven't had a moving economy. Part of that, as the Gallup Polls show, is because the Soviet Union made a breakthrough in outer space. Mr. George Allen, head of your Information Service, has said that that made the people of the world begin to wonder whether we were first in science. We're first in other areas of science but in space, which is the new science, we're not first.

MR. HOWE: John Chancellor, your first question for Senator Kennedy.

MR. CHANCELLOR: Senator, another question uh— in connection with our relations with the Russians. There have been stories from Washington from the Atomic Energy Commission hinting that the Russians may have resumed the testing of nuclear devices. Now if—sir, if this is true, should the United States resume nuclear testing, and if the Rusisans do not start testing, can you foresee any circumstances in 1961 in which the United States might resume its own series of tests?

MR. KENNEDY: Yes, I think the next president of the United States should make one last effort to secure an agremeent on the cessation of tests, number one. I think we should go back to Geneva, who's ever elected president, Mr. Nixon or myself, and try once again. If we fail then, if we're unable to come to an agreement—and I hope we can come to an agreement because it does not merely involve now the United States, Britain, France, and the Soviet Union as atomic powers. Because new breakthroughs in atomic energy technology there's some indications that by the time the next president's term of office has come to an end, there may be ten, fifteen, or twenty countries with an atomic capacity; perhaps that many testing bombs with all the effect that it could have on the atmosphere and with all the chances that more and more countries will have an atomic capacity, with more and more chance of war. So one more effort should be made. I don't think that even if that effort fails that it will be necessary to carry on tests in the atmosphere which pollute the atmosphere. They can be carried out underground, they c— could be carried on in outer space. But I believe the effort should be made once more by who's ever elected president of the United States. If we fail, it's been a great serious failure for everyone—for the human race. I hope we can succeed. But then if we fail responsibility will be clearly on the Russians and then we'll have to meet our responsibilities to the security of the United States, and there may have to be testing underground. I think the Atomic Energy Committee is prepared for it. There may be testing in outer space. I hope it will not be necessary for any power to resume uh— testing in the atmosphere. It's possible to detect those kind of tests. The kind of tests which you can't detect are underground or in— in uh— perhaps in outer space. So that I'm hopeful we can try once more. If we fail then we must meet our responsibilities to ourselves. But I'm most concerned about the whole problem of the spread of atomic weapons. China may have it by 1963, Egypt. War has been the constant companion of mankind, so to have these weapons disseminated around the world, I believe means that we're going to move through a period of hazard in the next few years. We ought to make one last effort.

MR. HOWE: Any comment, Mr. Vice President?

MR. NIXON: Yes. I would say first of all that we . . . must have in mind the fact that we have been negotiating to get tests inspected and uh— to get an agreement for many, many months. As a matter of fact, there's been a moratorium on testing as a result of the fact that we have been negotiating. I've reached the conclusion that the Soviet Union is actually filibustering. I've reached the conclusion, too, based on the reports that have been made, that they may be cheating. I don't think we can wait until the next president is inaugurated and then uh— select a new team and then all the months of negotiating that will take place before we reach a decision. I think that immediately after this election we should set a time-table—the next president, working with the present President, President Eisenhower—a timetable to break the Soviet filibuster. There should be no tests in the atmosphere; that rules out any fall-out. But as far as underground tests for developing peaceful uses of atomic energy, we should not allow this Soviet filibuster to continue. I think it's time for them to fish or cut bait. I think that the next president immediately after his election should sit down with the President, work out a timetable, and get a decision on this before January of next year.

MR. HOWE: Our second round of questions begins with one from Mr. Edwards for the Vice President.

MR. EDWARDS: Mr. Nixon, carrying forward this business about a time-table; as you know, the pressures are increasing for a summit conference. Now, both you and Senator Kennedy have said that there are certain conditions which must be met before you would meet with Khrushchev. Will you be more specific about these conditions?

MR. NIXON: Well the conditions I laid out in one of our previous television debates, and it's rather difficult to be much more specific than that. Uh— First of all, we have to have adequate preparation for a summit conference. This means at the secretary of state level and at the ambassadorial level. By adequate preparation I mean that at that level we must prepare an agenda, an agenda agreed upon with the approval of the heads of state involved. Now this agenda should delineate those issues on which there is a possibility of some agreement or negotiation. I don't believe we should go to a summit conference unless we have such an agenda, unless we have some reasonable insur— assurance from Mr. Khrushchev that he intends seriously to negotiate on those points. Now this may seem like a rigid, inflexible position. But let's look at the other side of the coin. If we build up the hopes of the world by having a summit conference that is not adequately prepared, and then, if Mr. Khrushchev finds some excuse for breaking it up—as he did this one—because he isn't going to get his way—we'd set back the cause of peace. We do not help it. We can, in other words, negotiate many of these items of difference between us without going to the summit. I think we have to make a greater effort than we have been making at the secretary of state level, at the ambassadorial level, to work out the differences that we have. And so far as the summit conference is concerned, it should only be entered in upon, it should only be agreed upon, if the negotiations have reached the point that we have some reasonable assurance that something is going to come out of it, other than some phony spirit—a spirit of Geneva, or Camp David, or whatever it is. When I say "phony spirit," I mean phony, not because the spirit is not good on our side, but because the Soviet Union simply doesn't intend to carry out what they say. Now, these are the conditions that I can lay out. I cannot be more precise than that, because until we see what Mr. Khrushchev does and what he says uh— we cannot indicate what our plans will be.

MR. HOWE: Any comments, Senator Kennedy?

MR. KENNEDY: Well, I think the president of the United States last winter indicated that before he'd go to the summit in May /sən/ he did last fall, he indicated that there should be some agenda, that there should be some prior agreement. He hoped that there would be uh— b— be an agreement in part in disarmament. He also expressed the hope that there should be some understanding of the general situation in Berlin. The Soviet Union refused to agree to that, and we went to the summit and it was disastrous. I believe we should not go to the summit until there is some reason to believe that a meeting of minds can be obtained on either Berlin, outer space, or general disarmament—including nuclear testing. In addition, I believe the next president in January and February should go to work in building the strength of the United States. The Soviet Union does understand strength. We arm to parley, Winston Churchill said ten years ago. If we are strong, particularly as we face a crisis over Berlin—

which we may in the spring, or in the winter—it's important that we maintain our determination here; that we indicate that we're building our strength; that we are determined to protect our position; that we're determined to protect our commitment. And then I believe we should indicate our desire to live at peace with the world. But until we're strong here, until we're moving here, I believe a summit could not be successful. I hope that before we do meet, there will be preliminary agreements on those four questions, or at least two of them, or even one of them, which would warrant such a meeting. I think if we had stuck by that position last winter, we would have been in a better position in May.

MR. HOWE: We have time for only one or two more questions before the closing statements. Now Walter Cronkite's question for Senator Kennedy.

MR. CRONKITE: Senator, the charge has been made frequently that the United States for many years has been on the defensive around the world, that our policy has been uh— one of reaction to the Soviet Union rather than positive action on our own. What areas do you see where the United States might take the offensive in a challenge to Communism over the next four to eight years?

MR. KENNEDY: One of the areas, and of course the most vulnerable area is— I have felt, has been Eastern Europe. I've been critical of the Administration's failure to suggest policies which would make it possible for us to establish, for example, closer relations with Poland, particularly after the fifty-five-fifty-six period and the Hungarian revolution. We indicated at that time that we were not going to intervene militarily. But there was a period there when Poland demonstrated a national independence and even the Polish government moved some differn— di— distance away from the Soviet Union. I suggested that we amend our legislation so that we could enjoy closer economic ties. We received the support first of the Administration and then not, and we were defeated by one vote in the Senate. We passed the bill in the Senate this year but it didn't pass the House. I would say Eastern Europe is the area of vulnerability of the uh— s— of the Soviet Union. Secondly, the relations between Russia and China. They are now engaged in a . . . debate over whether war is the means of Communizing the world or whether they should use subversion, infiltration, economic struggles and all the rest. No one can say what that course of action will be, but I think the next president of the United States should watch it carefully. If those two powers should split, it could have great effects throughout the entire world. Thirdly, I believe that India represents a great area for affirmative action by the free world. India started from about the same place that China did. Chinese Communists have been moving ahead the last ten years. India under a free society has been making some progress. But if India does not succeed—with her four hundred and fifty million people, if she can't make freedom work—then people around the world are going to determine—particularly in the underdeveloped world—that the only way that they can develop their resources is through the Communist system. Fourth, let me say that in Africa, Asia, Latin America, Eastern Europe, the great force on our side is the desire of people to be free. This has expressed itself in the revolts in Eastern Europe. It's expressed itself in the desire of the people of Africa to be independent of Western Europe. They want to be free. And my judgment is that they don't want to give their freedom up to become Communists. They want to stay free, independent perhaps of us, but certainly independent of the Communists. And I believe if we identify ourselves with that force, if we identify ourselves with it as Lincoln, as Wilson did, as Franklin Roosevelt did, if we become known as the friend of freedom, sustaining freedom, helping freedom, helping these people in the fight against poverty and ignorance and disease, helping them build their lives, I believe in Latin America, Africa, and Asia, eventually in the . . . Eastern Europe and the Middle East, certainly in Western Europe, we can strengthen freedom. We can make it move. We can put the Communists on the defensive.

MR. HOWE: Your comment, Mr. Vice President?

MR. NIXON: First, with regard to Poland, when I talked to Mr. Gomulka, the present leader of Poland, for six hours in Warsaw last year, I learned something about their problems and particularly his. Right under the Soviet gun, with Soviet troops there, he is in a very difficult position in taking anything independent, a position which would be independent of the Soviet Union. And yet let's just see what we've done for Poland. A half a billion dollars worth of aid has gone to Poland, primarily economic, primarily to go to the people of Poland. This should continue and it can be stepped up to give them hope and to keep alive the hope for freedom that I can testify they have so deeply within them. In addition we can have more exchange with Poland or with any other of the Iron Curtain countries which show some desire to take a different path than the path that has been taken by the ones that are complete satellites of the Soviet Union. Now as far as the balance of the world is concerned, I of course don't have as much time as Senator Kennedy had. I would just like to s— add this one point. If we are going to have the initiative in the world, we must remember that the people of Africa and Asia and Latin America don't want to be pawns simply in a struggle between two great powers—the Soviet Union and the United States. We have to let them know that we want to help them, not because we're simply trying to save our own skins, not because we're simply trying to fight Communism; but because we care for them, because we stand for freedom, because if there were no Communism in the world, we would still fight poverty and misery and disease and tyranny. If we can get that across to the people of these countries, in this decade of the sixties, the struggle for freedom will be won.

MR. HOWE: John Chancellor's question for Vice President Nixon.

MR. CHANCELLOR: Sir, I'd like to ask you an— another question about Quemoy and Matsu. Both you and Senator Kennedy say you agree with the President on this subject and with our treaty obligations. But the subject remains in the campaign as an issue. Now is— sir, is this because each of you feels obliged to respond to the other when he talks about Quemoy and Matsu, and if that's true, do you think an end should be called to this discussion, or will it stay with us as a campaign issue?

MR. NIXON: I would say that the issue will stay with us as a campaign issue just as long as Senator Kennedy persists in what I think is a fundamental error. He says he supports the President's position. He says that he voted for the resolution. Well just let me point this out: he voted for the resolution in 1955 which gave the president the power to use the forces of the United States to defend Formosa and the offshore islands. But he also voted then for an amendment—which was lost, fortunately—an amendment which would have drawn a line and left out those islands and denied the p— right to the president to defend those islands if he thought that it was an attack on Formosa. He repeated that error in 1959, in the speech that he made. He repeated it again in a television debate that we had. Now, my point is this: Senator Kennedy has got to be consistent here. Either he's for the President and he's against the position that those who opposed the President in fifty-five and fifty-nine—and the Senator's position itself, stated the other day in our debate—either he is for the President and against that position or we simply have a disagreement here that must continue to be debated. Now if the Senator in his answer to this question will say "I now will depart, or retract my previous views; I think I was wrong in 1955; I think I was wrong in 1959; and I think I was wrong in our television debate to say that we should draw a line leaving out Quemoy and Matsu—draw a line in effect abandoning these islands to the Communists;" then this will be right out of the campaign because there will be no issue between us. I support the President's position. I have always opposed drawing a line. I have opposed drawing a line because I know that the moment you draw a line, that is an encouragement for the Communists to attack—to step up their blackmail and to force you into the war that none of us want. And so I would hope that Senator Kennedy in his answer today would clear it up. It isn't enough for him to say "I support the President's position, that I voted for the resolution." Of course, he voted for the resolution—it was virtually unanimous. But the point is, what about his error in voting for the amendment, which was not adopted, and then persisting in it in fifty-nine, persisting in it in the debate. It's very simple for him to clear it up. He can say now that he no longer believes that a line should be drawn leaving these islands out of the perimeter of defense. If he says that, this issue will not be discussed in the campaign.

MR. HOWE: Senator Kennedy, your comment.

MR. KENNEDY: Well, Mr. Nixon, to go back to 1955. The resolution commits the president in the United States, which I supported, to defend uh— Formosa, the Pescadores, and if it was his military judgment, these islands. Then the President sent a mission, composed of Admiral Radford and Mr. Robertson, to persuade Chiang Kai-shek in the spring of fifty-five to withdraw from the two islands, because they were exposed. The President was unsuccessful; Chiang Kai-shek would not withdraw. I refer to the fact that in 1958, as a member of the Senate Foreign Relations Committee, I'm very familiar with the position that the United States took in negotiating with the Chinese Communists on these two islands. General Twining, in January, fifty-nine, described the position of the United States. The position of the United States has been that this build-up, in the words of the president, has been foolish. Mr. Herter has said these islands are indefensible. Chiang Kai-shek will not withdraw. Because he will not withdraw, because he's committed to these islands, because we've been unable to persuade him to withdraw, we are in a very difficult position. And therefore, the President's judgment has been that we should defend the islands if, in his military judgment and the judgment of the commander in the field, the attack on these islands should be part of an over-all attack on Formosa. I support that. In view of the difficulties we've had with the islands, in view of the difficulties and disputes we've had with Chiang Kai-shek, that's the only position we can take. That's not the position you took, however. The first position you took, when this matter first came up, was that we should draw the line and commit ourselves, as a matter of principle, to defend these islands. Not as part of the defense of Formosa and the Pescadores. You showed no recognition of the . . . Administration program to try to persuade Chiang Kai-shek for the last five years to withdraw from the islands. And I challenge you tonight to deny that the Administration has sent at least several missions to persuade Chiang Kai-shek's withdrawal from these islands.

MR. HOWE: Under the agreed—*

MR. KENNEDY: And that's the testimony of uh— General Twining and the Assistant Secretary of State in fifty-eight.*

MR. HOWE: Under the agreed rules, gentlemen, we've exhausted the time for questions. Each candidate will now have four minutes and thirty seconds for his closing statement. Senator Kennedy will make the first final closing statement.

MR. KENNEDY: I uh— said that I've served this country for fourteen years. I served it uh— in the war. I'm devoted to it. If I lose this election, I will continue in the Senate to try to build a stronger country. But I run

* The opening portion of Mr. Howe's statement overlapped the final portion of Mr. Kennedy's answer, partially obscuring both.

because I believe this year the United States has a great opportunity to make a move forward, to make a determination here at home and around the world, that it's going to reestablish itself as a vigorous society. My judgment is that the Republican party has stood still here in the United States, and it's also stood still around the world. Uh— We're using about fifty per cent of our steel capacity today. We had a recession in fifty-eight. We had a recession in fifty-four. We're not moving ahead in education the way we should. We didn't make a judgment in fifty-seven and fifty-six and fifty-five and fifty-four that outer space would be important. If we stand still here, if we appoint people to ambassadorships and positions in Washington who have a status quo outlook, who don't recognize that this is a revolutionary time, then the United States does not maintain its influence. And if we fail, the cause of freedom fails. I believe it incumbent upon the next president of the United States to get this country moving again, to get our economy moving ahead, to set before the American people its goals, its unfinished business. And then throughout the world appoint the best people we can get, ambassadors who can speak the language—not merely people who made a political contribution but who can speak the language. Bring students here; let them see what kind of a country we have. Mr. Nixon said that we should not regard them as pawns in the cold war; we should identify ourselves with them. If that were true, why didn't we identify ourselves with the people of Africa? Why didn't we bring students over here? Why did we suddenly offer Congo three hundred students last June when they had the tremendous revolt? That was more than we had offered to all of Africa before from the federal government. I believe that this party—Republican party—has stood still really for twenty-five years—its leadership has. It opposed all of the programs of President Roosevelt and others—the minimum wage and for housing and economic growth and development of our natural resources, the Tennessee Valley and all the rest. And I believe that if we can get a party which believes in movement, which believes in going ahead, then we can reestablish our position in the world—strong defense, strong in economic growth, justice for our people, co— guarantee of constitutional rights, so that people will believe that we practice what we preach, and then around the world, particularly to try to reestablish the atmosphere which existed in Latin America at the time of Franklin Roosevelt. He was a good neighbor in Latin America because he was a good neighbor in the United States; because they saw us as a society that was compassionate, that cared about people, that was moving this country ahead. I believe it my responsibility as the leader of the Democratic party in 1960 to try to warn the American people that in this crucial time we can no longer afford to stand still. We can no longer afford to be second best. I want people all over the world to look to the United States again, to feel that we're on the move, to feel that our high noon is in the future. I want Mr. Khrushchev to know that a new generation of Americans who fought in Europe and Italy and the Pacific for freedom in World War II have now taken over in the United States, and that they're going to put this country back to work again. I don't believe that there is anything this country cannot do. I don't believe there's any burden, or any responsibility, that any American would not assume to protect his country, to protect our security, to advance the cause of freedom. And I believe it incumbent upon us now to do that. Franklin Roosevelt said in 1936 that that generation of Americans had a rendezvous with destiny. I believe in 1960 and sixty-one and two and three we have a rendezvous with destiny. And I believe it incumbent upon us to be the defenders of the United States and the defenders of freedom; and to do that, we must give this country leadership and we must get America moving again.

MR. HOWE: Now, Vice President Nixon, your closing statement.

MR. NIXON: Senator Kennedy has said tonight again what he has said several times in the course of this— these debates and in the campaign, that American is standing still. America is not standing still. It has not been standing still. And let's set the record straight right now by looking at the record, as Al Smith used to say. He talks about housing. We built more houses in the last seven years than in any Administration and thirty per cent more than in the previous Administration. We talk about schools— three times as many classrooms built in the past Administration—and Eisenhower—than under the Truman Administration. Let's talk about civil rights. More progress in the past eight years than in the whole eighty years before. He talks about the progress in the field of slum clearance and the like. We find four times as many projects undertaken and completed in this Administration than in the previous one. Anybody that says America has been standing still for the last seven and a half years hasn't been traveling in America. He's been in some other country. Let's get that straight right away. Now the second point we have to understand is this, however. America has not been standing still. But America cannot stand pat. We can't stand pat for the reason that we're in a race, as I've indicated. We can't stand pat because it is essential with the conflict that we have around the world that we not just hold our own, that we not keep just freedom for ourselves. It is essential that we extend freedom, extend it to all the world. And this means more than what we've been doing. It means keeping America even stronger militarily than she is. It means seeing that our economy moves forward even faster than it has. It means making more progress in civil rights than we have so that we can be a splendid example for all the world to see—a democracy in action at its best. Now, looking at the other parts of the world—South America—talking about our record and the previous one. We had a good neighbor policy, yes. It sounded fine. But let's look at it. There were eleven dictators when we came into power in 1953 in Latin America. There are only three left. Let's look at Africa. Twenty new countries in Africa during the course of this Administration. Not one of them selected a Communist government. All of them voted for freedom—a free type of government. Does this show that Communism has the bigger pull, or freedom has the bigger pull? Am I trying to indicate that we have no problems in Africa or Latin America or Asia? Of course not. What I am trying to indicate is that the tide of history's on our side, and that we can keep it on our side, because we're on the right side. We're on the side of freedom. We're on the side of justice against the forces of slavery, against the forces of injustice. But we aren't going to move America forward and we aren't going to be able to lead the world to win this struggle for freedom if we have a permanent inferiority complex about American achievements. Because we are first in the world in space, as I've indicated; we are first in science; we are first in education, and we're going to move even further ahead with the kind of leadership that we can provide in these years ahead. One other point I would make: what could you do? Senator Kennedy and I are candidates for the presidency of the United States. And in the years to come it will be written that one or the other of us was elected and that he was or was not a great president. What will determine whether Senator Kennedy or I, if I am elected, was a great president? It will not be our ambition that will determine it, because greatness is not something that is written on a campaign poster. It will be determined to the extent that we represent the deepest ideals, the highest feelings and faith of the American people. In other words, the next president, as he leads America and the free world, can be only as great as the American people are great. And so I say in conclusion, keep America's faith strong. See that the young people of America, particularly, have faith in the ideals of freedom and faith in God, which distinguishes us from the atheistic materialists who oppose us.

MR. HOWE: Thank you gentlemen. Both candidates have asked me to express their thanks to the networks for this opportunity to appear on this discussion. May I repeat that all those concerned in tonight's discussion have, sometimes reluctantly, followed the rules and conditions read at the outset and agreed to in advance by the candidates and the networks. The opening statements ran eight minutes each. The closing statements ran four minutes, thirty seconds. The order of speaking was reversed from their first joint appearance, when they followed the same procedure. A panel of newsmen questioned each candidate alternately. Each had two and a half minutes to reply. The other had a minute and a half to comment. But the first discussion dealt only with domestic policy. This one dealt only with foreign policy. One last word. As members of a new political generation, Vice President Nixon and Senator Kennedy have used new means of communication to pioneer a new type of political debate. The character and courage with which these two men have spoken sets a high standard for generations to come. Surely, they have set a new precedent. Perhaps they have established a new tradition. This is Quincy Howe. Good night from New York.

Index

Note: This index does not include the debate texts.

debate *(cont.)*

Dewey-Stassen, 39; direct, 20; fifth, 117-20, 125, 129, 337; first proposal to televise, 57; format, 23, 39, 60, 70, 74, 77-80, 97, 106, 108, 114, 116, 119, 121, 122, 128-29, 136-37, 147-49, 165-66, 168, 219, 260-63, 314; future of, 122, 131, 135, 149, 152, 154, 163-69, 195, 213, 218, 255-56, 337; genuine, 21, 22, 60, 128, 219; ground rules, 90, 105, 112-13, 122, 123, 125, 129-30, 138, 167-69, 219; influence on voting intentions, 132, 133, 135-36, 160-61, 173ff, 184, 205-13, 241-49, 309-11, 315-17, 318, 323, 328; invitations, 59; issues, *see* issues; learning from, 200-205; "Lincoln-Cherney," 111; Lincoln-Douglas, 56-57, 63, 123, 147; Lindsay-Heuvel, 63; Oregon Style, 39, 77, 78, 119, 123, 146; president's participation in, 71, 131, 163-69; proposals, 74; pseudo, 35; sponsorship of, 61, 168; text of, 341ff; use of notes, 112-13, 129-30; "who won?," 134, 157, 158, 184, 195-200, 201, 204, 205, 208, 215, 219, 235-36, 245-46, 250-52, 269, 286-87, 311, 313, 322; *see also* advertising

"Debate of Tweedledum and Tweedledee," 40

debaters' sincerity, 130

Debating Society of Hingham, 144

decision-making, 25, 186, 211-12

Declaration of Independence, 31

De Forest, Lee, 25

Democratic National Committee, 33, 34, 36, 37, 38, 40

Denny, George V., Jr., 145

Department of Commerce, 26

Detroit News, 57

Deutschmann, Paul J., 173, 184, 194, 208, 209, 217, 221, 252

Dewey, Thomas E., 36, 37, 39, 53, 54, 63, 146

Diskin, Marshall, 107, 111, 112, 113, 115, 125

Doerfer, John, 49

Donnelly, Thomas C., 52, 53

Dorfsman, Lou, 79, 80, 83, 123

Douglas, Stephen A., 56-57, 63, 123, 145, 147

Drake, Daniel, 144, 149

Drake, Galen, 38

Drucker, Ralph, 125

Drummond, Roscoe, 107

Dulles, John Foster, 113

DuMont, 45

Dunlap, Orrin E., Jr., 53

Edelstein, Alex S., 173, 221, 222

editorial freedom, 51

Edwards, India, 38

Edwards, John, 114

Eisenhower, Dwight D., 21, 41, 44, 45, 47, 58, 113, 155, 156, 161, 163, 167, 194, 236, 270, 288, 317

Electoral College, 70

"equal time," *see* Federal Communications Act (Section 315)

Ernst, Morris, 144

Eubank, Henry Lee, 149, 150

Evening Star (Washington, D.C.), 54

"Face the Nation," 145

Factor, Max, 85

Farley, James A., 34, 54

Farrell, Fran, 173

Federal Communications Act, 58, 66, 72; Section 315, 23, 29, 33, 40, 42, 44, 47, 48, 49, 58-59, 62-63, 64, 66, 72, 74, 138-41, 155; Section 315 suspended, 62, 117, 128, 132

Federal Communications Commission, 33, 42, 47, 48, 49, 58, 60, 62

Federal Radio Act, 33; Section 18, 33, 48

Federal Radio Commission, 33

Feldman, Jacob J., 15

Festinger, Leon, 222, 231, 330

Field, Mervin D., 173

Field Research Company, 173

Fiorentino, Imero, 102, 111

"fire-house research," 186

First Amendment, 128